The Urbanism Reader

The Urbanism Reader

Design, Technology, Culture, and the Future of Cities

STEFAN AL AND TOM VEREBES

BLOOMSBURY VISUAL ARTS
LONDON · NEW YORK · OXFORD · NEW DELHI · SYDNEY

BLOOMSBURY VISUAL ARTS
Bloomsbury Publishing Plc
50 Bedford Square, London, WC1B 3DP, UK
1385 Broadway, New York, NY 10018, USA
29 Earlsfort Terrace, Dublin 2, Ireland

BLOOMSBURY, BLOOMSBURY VISUAL ARTS and the Diana logo are trademarks of
Bloomsbury Publishing Plc

First published in Great Britain 2025

Copyright © Stefan Al and Tom Verebes, 2025

Stefan Al and Tom Verebes have asserted their right under the Copyright, Designs and Patents Act, 1988, to be identified as Editors of this work.

For legal purposes the Disclaimer on p. ix constitutes an extension of this copyright page.

Cover design by Eleanor Rose
Cover image: Copenhagen cityscape: Nørreport station. © jonathanfilskov-photography / E+ / Getty Images

All rights reserved. No part of this publication may be reproduced or transmitted in any form or by any means, electronic or mechanical, including photocopying, recording, or any information storage or retrieval system, without prior permission in writing from the publishers.

Bloomsbury Publishing Plc does not have any control over, or responsibility for, any third-party websites referred to or in this book. All internet addresses given in this book were correct at the time of going to press. The author and publisher regret any inconvenience caused if addresses have changed or sites have ceased to exist, but can accept no responsibility for any such changes.

A catalogue record for this book is available from the British Library.

A catalog record for this book is available from the Library of Congress.

ISBN: HB: 978-1-3503-7791-2
PB: 978-1-3503-7790-5
ePDF: 978-1-3503-7793-6
eBook: 978-1-3503-7794-3

Typeset by RefineCatch Limited, Bungay, Suffolk
Printed and bound in Great Britain by Bell & Bain Ltd, Glasgow

To find out more about our authors and books visit www.bloomsbury.com
and sign up for our newsletters.

Contents

List of Figures vi
List of Credits vii

Introduction 1

1 Spatial Heterogeneity, Diversity, and Difference after Modernist Planning 9
2 Urbanism and Models of Design Complexity 33
3 Intensities, Flows, Connectivity, and Network Urbanism 57
4 Density, the Compact City, and Metropolitan Culture 81
5 Ecology, Resilience, and Green Infrastructure 99
6 Health, Equity, and Livable Cities 120
7 Emergent, Tactical, and Informal Urbanism 141
8 Evolutionary, Computational, and Parametric Urbanism 163
9 Virtuality, Extended Realities, and the Metaverse 189
10 Artificial Intelligence, the Internet of Things, and Technological Determinism 213

Notes 238
Bibliography 250
Index 262

Figures

1.1	Las Vegas Strip in the 1960s	12
1.2	Parc de la Villette, Paris, Bernard Tschumi Architects	27
2.1	Federation Square, Melbourne, Lab Architecture Studio	42
2.2	Field organization diagrams, Stan Allen	44
2.3	Shibuya Crossing, Tokyo	56
3.1	Cities Without Ground, Admiralty diagram, Adam Frampton, Jonathan Solomon, Clara Wong	71
3.2	Yokohama International Ferry Terminal, Foreign Office Architects	76
3.3	Arnhem Central Station, The Netherlands, UNStudio,	79
4.1	Fok Cheong Building, Quarry Bay, Hong Kong	82
4.2	Les Halles, Paris, Office for Metropolitan Architecture	93
4.3	Markthal, Rotterdam, MDRDV	95
5.1	The High Line, New York, Diller, Scofidio + Renfro, James Corner Field Operations	105
5.2	Emergent Development Diagrams, Downsview Park, Toronto, James Corner Field Operations	109
5.3	Xi'an Horticultural Expo, Xi'an, China, Plasma Studio	111
6.1	Outdoor dining on streets and parking spaces during Covid-19 on Main Street, San Francisco	120
6.2	"Superilla" (superblock), Barcelona	124
6.3	A three-block-long "Black Lives Matter" mural, Fulton Street, San Francisco,	135
7.1	Barrio, Caracas, Venezuela	142
7.2	Xiasha Village, Shenzhen, China	143
7.3	Quinta Monroy housing, Iquique, Chile, Elemental	154
8.1	Umekita Second Development Area Masterplan, Osaka, Japan, OCEAN CN and Arup Transportation	172
8.2	Munich Olympiapark, Munich, Germany, Günther Behnisch and Frei Otto	176
8.3	Soho Galaxy, Beijing, Zaha Hadid Architects	180
9.1	Shinjuku, Tokyo	190
9.2	A man interacting with virtual computer graphics	192
9.3	The CityScope Project, MIT Media Lab's City Science Group	200
10.1	Datacenters at Agriport, The Netherlands	220
10.2	Generative AI image of a green public space, created in Midjourney	226
10.3	Arrays of urban plan diagrams using MidJourney generative AI	236

Credits

Alexander, Christopher. "The City Is Not a Tree, Part 1." *Architectural Forum* 122, no. 1 (April 1965): 58–62; and Part 2. *Architectural Forum* 122, no. 2 (May 1965): 58–61.

Allen, Stan. "From Object to Field." In Greg Lynn (ed.), *Folding in Architecture, AD (Architectural Design)* 67, no. 5–6 (May–June, 1997): 24–31.

Aravena, Alejandro. "Elemental: A Do Tank." In Greg Lynn (ed.), *Architectural Design* 81, no. 3 (2011): 32–37.

Batty, Michael. "Introduction: Understanding Cities." In *Cities and Complexity: Understanding Cities with Cellular Automata, Agent-based Models, and Fractals*. Cambridge, MA: MIT Press, 2005, pp. 1–16.

Brillembourg, Alfredo and Hubert Klumpner. "Rules of Engagement: Caracas and the Informal City." In *Rethinking the Informal City: Critical Perspectives from Latin America* 11. Oxford: Berghahn Books, 2011.

Crawford, Kate. *Atlas of AI. Power, Politics and the Planetary Costs of Artificial Intelligence*. London: Yale University Press, 2021.

De Landa, Manuel. "Introduction," "Conclusion." In *A Thousand Years of Nonlinear History*. New York: Zone Books, 1997, pp. 11–13, 257–60, 271–74.

del Campo, Matias. "Chapter VI – How Machines Learn to Plan: A Critical Interrogation of Machine Vision Techniques in Architecture." In *Neural Architecture: Design and Artificial Intelligence*. Shenzhen: ORO, 2022. © Matias del Campo, 2022.

Easterling, Keller. "The Action Is the Form." In Mark Shepard, (ed.), *Sentient City: Ubiquitous Computing, Architecture and The Future of Urban Space*. New York and Cambridge, MA: Architectural League and MIT Press, 2011, pp. 154–58. Courtesy of Keller Easterling and The Architectural League.

Eisenman, Peter. "Diagrams of Exteriority." In Diagram Diaries. London: Thames and Hudson, 1999, pp. 164–209.

Frampton, Kenneth. "Towards a Critical Regionalism: Modern Architecture and Cultural Identity." In *Modern Architecture* © 1980, 1985, 1992, 2007 and 2020. London: Thames & Hudson Ltd, 1983 (5th Edition). Reprinted by kind permission of Thames & Hudson.

Frazer, John. *An Evolutionary Architecture*. London: AA Publications, 1995. © John Frazer and the Architectural Association.

Gehl, Jan. *Life Between Buildings*. Washington, DC: Island Press, 2011. Copyright © 2011 Jan Gehl. Reproduced by permission of Island Press, Washington, DC.

Hood, Walter and Grace Mitchell Tada (eds.). *Black Landscapes Matter*. Charlottesville, VA: University of Virginia Press, 2020, pp. 1–5, 7, 8. © 2020 by the Rector and Visitors of the University of Virginia. Reprinted by permission of the University of Virginia Press.

Kalms, Nicole. *She City: Designing Out Women's Inequity in Cities*. London: Bloomsbury, 2024.

Koolhaas, Rem. "The Future's Past." *The Wilson Quarterly* 3, no. 1 (Winter, 1979): 135–40.

Kubo, Michael, Farshid Moussavi and Alejandro Zaera Polo. *The Yokohama Project*. Barcelona: Actar, 2002. © Actar Publishers, Michael Kubo, Farshid Moussavi, and Alejandro Zaera Polo.

Kwinter, Sanford. "Wildness: Prolegomena to a New Urbanism." In *Far from Equilibrium: Essays on Technology and Design Culture*. Barcelona: Actar, 2007, pp. 186–91. © Actar Publishers, Sanford Kwinter.

Leach, Neil. *Architecture in the Age of Artificial Intelligence: An Introduction to AI for Architects*. London: Bloomsbury, 2022.

Lydon, Mike and Anthony Garcia. *Tactical Urbanism*. Washington, DC: Island Press, 2015. Copyright © 2015 The Streets Plans Collaborative, Inc. Reproduced by permission of Island Press, Washington, DC.

Maas, Winy. *Datascape: The Final Extravaganza. Daidalos* 69, no. 70 (1998): 48–54.

Markopoulou, Areti. *Learning Cities: Collective Intelligence in Urban Design*. Barcelona: Actar, 2023. © Actar Publishers, Areti Markopoulou.

McHarg, Ian. "Introduction" and "Nature in the Metropolis." In *Design with Nature*. New York: American Museum of Natural History, 1969.

Mitchell, William J. "Boundaries/Networks." In *Me++: The Cyborg Self and the Networked City*. Cambridge, MA: MIT Press, 2003. pp. 7–18.

Moneta, Andrea. "Architecture, Heritage, and the Metaverse." *Traditional Dwellings and Settlements Review* 32, no. 1 (Fall 2020): 37–49. This material first appeared in *Traditional Dwellings and Settlements Review* 32, no. 1 (Fall 2020). Reprinted by permission.

Otto, Frei. In Berthold Burkhardt (ed.), *Occupying and Connecting: Thoughts on Territories and Spheres of Influence with Particular Reference to Human Settlement*. Fellbach: Edition Axel Menges, 2009.

Pask, Gordon. "The Architectural Relevance of Cybernetics." *Architectural Design* September, no. 7/6 (1969): 494–96. ©John Wiley & Sons Ltd. With the permission of Amanda Heitler and Hermione Pask.

Ratti, Carlo and Matthew Claudel. *The City of Tomorrow: Sensors, Networks, Hackers, and the Future of Urban Life*. London: Yale University Press, 2016.

Rogers, Richard. *Cities for a Small Planet*. New York: Basic Books, 2008. Reprinted by permission of Peter Frasers + Dunlop on behalf of the Estate of Richard Rogers.

Rowe, Colin and Fred Koetter. "Collision City and the Politics of Bricolage." In *Collage City*. Cambridge, MA: MIT Press, 1978, pp. 86–117.

Roy, Ananya. "Urban Informality: Toward an Epistemology of Planning." *Journal of the American Planning Association* 71, no. 2 (2005): 147–58.

Schumacher, Patrik. "Parametricist vs. Modernist Urbanism." In *The Autopoiesis of Architecture: A New Agenda for Architecture,* Volume II. London: John Wiley and Sons, 2012, pp. 680–99.

Solomon, Jonathan D. "Hong Kong – Aformal Urbanism." In Rodolphe El-Khoury, Edwards Robbins, (eds.), *Shaping the City: Studies in History, Theory and Urban Design*. New York: Routledge, 2013, pp. 109–31.

Spirn, Anne Whiston. *The Granite Garden*. New York: Basic Books, 1984. Copyright © 1984. Reprinted by permission of Basic Books, an imprint of Hachette Book Group, Inc.

Tschumi, Bernard. "De-, Dis-, Ex-." In *Architecture and Disjunction*. Cambridge, MA: MIT Press, 1987, pp. 214–26.

Venturi, Robert, Denise Scott Brown, and Steven Izenour. "Preface" and "Part 1: A Significance for A&P Parking Lots, or Learning from Las Vegas." In *Learning from Las Vegas: The Forgotten Symbolism of Architectural Form*. Cambridge, MA: MIT Press, 1972, pp. xi, 3, 6, 8, 13, 18, 19, 52, 74, 75, 76, and 83. © 1972 Massachusetts Institute of Technology, by permission of The MIT Press.

Verebes, Tom. "The Death of Masterplanning in the Age of Indeterminacy." In *Masterplanning the Adaptive City: Computational Urbanism in the Twenty-first Century*. New York: Routledge, 2013, pp. 87–117.

Waldheim, Charles. "Landscape as Urbanism." In *The Landscape Urbanism Reader*. Princeton, NJ: Princeton Architectural Press, 2006, pp. 35–53.

Watson, Julia et al. "Designing by Radical Indigenism" in *Landscape Architecture Frontiers* 8, no. 3 (2020): 148–55.

Weinstock, Michael. "Chapter 7 – City Forms." In *The Architecture of Emergence: The Evolution of Form in Nature and Civilisation*. London: John Wiley and Sons Inc., 2010, pp. 176–209.

Disclaimer

Every effort has been made to trace copyright holders and to obtain their permission for the use of copyright material. The publisher apologizes for any errors or omissions and would be grateful if notified of any corrections that should be incorporated in future reprints or editions of this book.

Introduction

After Modernity

In the 1920s in Frankfurt, architect Ernst May was one of the first to apply modernist principles to city design. He created an entire suburb, Westhausen, in such a way that each apartment would be positioned to receive ample sunlight. The architect prioritized heliotropic design principles, advocating for "*Licht, Luft und Sonnenschein*" (light, air, and sunshine) — and probably to a fault, often to the detriment of other aspects, such as site design and public space. The arrayed buildings, following the Zeilenbau concept, translated to "row building," were oriented toward the south. They were spaced far enough from one another so that even when the sun was at its lowest point in winter, during winter solstice, the lower apartments would not be cast in shadow by the adjacent buildings.

Ernst May's project had become paradigmatic for modernist urbanism and has had an enduring influence into the twenty-first century. Together with its higher density twin, the "towers in the park" proposed by architect Le Corbusier in his 1924 urban prototype *Ville Radieuse* (The Radiant City), and published in a book bearing this title (1933), they profoundly influenced the design of new urban development and urban renewal. Both designs drew inspiration from Fordist principles of standardization. The models of repetitive, shallow rows of residential slabs, as well as uniform, discrete towers separated by large open spaces, proliferated. However, from an urban design perspective, these modernist urban tropes often lacked human scale, spatial diversity, sociability, and contextual sensitivity, leading to a sense of monotony. Nevertheless, the modernist paradigm of city design spread widely, becoming mainstream, and has largely prevailed. In the aftermath of World War II, modernist urbanism and International Style Modernism in architecture were exported globally, as nations sought to rebuild in Europe, and to roll out the world's social housing. While modernist housing has often fallen short of expectations in Europe and North America, it nevertheless has had greater success in East and Southeast Asia and in Latin America.

From the second half of the twentieth century, architects and urban designers began to formulate and deliver various responses against modernist urbanism. They did so in part because of their frustration with the monotony of modernist urban design and the lack of human scale. At the same time, their world was fundamentally different from the time when modernists Le Corbusier and Ernst May first developed their theories and prototypes. Despite the utopian ambitions of Modernism, disappointment took root in younger generations. Architecture and urban planning, both as disciplines and professions, grew estranged in the post-war era, leading to a disciplinary divergence. These contextual changes in the aftermath of Modernism strengthened the call for new paradigms to come to terms with the increasingly complex landscape of contemporary urbanism and to develop new methods to design cities.

As a distinct profession and academic discipline, urban planning emerged in the late nineteenth century. The first use of the disciplinary term, urban design, was by Josep Lluís Sert, then Dean at Harvard University Graduate School of Design (GSD), for the title of a conference, the *Harvard Urban Design Conference*, held at the GSD in 1956. The first academic curricula in urban design began to appear from 1960 onwards, alongside already established urban planning and architecture programs. Differing in emphasis from the more sociological and policy-based methods of urban planning, urban design has rapidly evolved as a design discipline in recent decades, often aligning itself more with architecture than with urban planning. Moreover, landscape architecture, environmental design, and the more recent development of Landscape Urbanism as a new discipline in the 1990s, have all sought to expand their conceptual field to encompass broader issues related to the design of cities.

The 1960s was a time of great social upheaval. Amidst significant social changes, architects began to scrutinize the modernist legacy of their discipline, questioning its relevance in capturing contemporary interests and desires. As interest in the city was rekindled, architecture began to emerge as a critical and speculative practice, coinciding with the rise of political turmoil in the West. Creative and cultural disciplines were imbued with new orientations in the arts and philosophy, whilst the sciences, mathematics, and computer science advanced in understanding and managing complexity. This reader commences its chronology during and shortly after the 1960s, focusing on agendas formulated during the heterogeneous culture of postmodernity, while omitting the radical projects and platforms of the 1960s.

The Urban Century and Its Challenges

Nearly a quarter through the twenty-first century, designers have increasingly accepted the onus to respond to the complex and challenging realities of the twenty-first century, the first Urban Century. Never before has more than half of the world's population lived in cities, attracted by the many and diverse opportunities of urban life. This trend shows no signs of slowing down. The world's urban population is expected to grow from 56 percent today to 68 percent in 2050, particularly due to the growth of cities in developing nations.[1] To accommodate the planet's increasing human population, the world's building stock will have to double by then. In addition to new housing, this urban drive will require a massive increase in city infrastructure. The scale of growth is staggering, equivalent to building a new New York City every single month for the next thirty years, presenting architects and planners with an immense challenge.

In addition, much of the world's urbanization occurs informally, outside of institutional structures such as building regulations, zoning laws, or land tenure. According to the United Nations, over one billion people around the world are excluded from formal housing, explaining the existence of the favelas in Rio de Janeiro, the barrios in Mexico City, and the shantytowns of Mumbai and Lagos. These complex and adaptive forms of urbanization cannot be adequately understood or addressed using modernist theories that advocate for a *tabula rasa* mode, which aims to create a clean slate and impose a fixed, predetermined vision of the future.

Urbanization has come with a significant environmental toll. The built environment is responsible for approximately 40 percent of the world's carbon emissions. Urbanization has led to the

INTRODUCTION

destruction of natural habitats, to the alterations of topography through the excavation of hillsides, and to the paving over of green spaces and culverts with asphalt and concrete. By the late twentieth century, with climate change and global warming increasing the intensity and frequency of storms, as well as sea level rise, undeniable problems had arisen. About 40 percent of the world's population lives within 100 km of a coastline or riverfront, and urbanization continues to densify coastal urban territories, putting more people in harm's way. Flooding, wildfires in forests, and extreme weather events are becoming more frequent and are affecting larger populations with more severity. Rising temperatures, compounded by the urban heat island effect, are increasing heat stress and heat-related illnesses. Architects and urban designers must urgently address these environmental challenges and develop strategies for climate resilience and adaptation in cities.

Urbanization has also had a profound impact on human health. Many of our cities are designed to be reliant on private car transportation, an urban model spread by modernist architect Le Corbusier. However, each year, road traffic claims the lives of 1.25 million people. The public health of car-dependent societies has been compromised in other ways as well, with increased rates of obesity and sedentary lifestyles. Vehicular-centric urbanism has contributed to the atomization and dispersion of society, fostering a more individualistic way of life.

At the same time, urbanization may also increase societal risk, as it became apparent during the Covid-19 pandemic. The "culture of congestion" of dense cities, once revered by architect Rem Koolhaas, became a culture of contagion. Sociologist Ulrich Beck claimed modernization has created a "risk society," and now requires systematic efforts to handle uncertainty. Architects and urban planners can no longer design cities for a certain future, but will have to design with risk, probability and resilience in mind. Increasingly, the future has become a moving target.

At the onset of the pandemic, many predicted the demise of cities. Yet, despite the shift towards remote work reshaping urban landscapes, city populations globally continue to grow. Consequently, there has been a prevailing optimism in the 2020s that the pandemic might galvanize citizens, politicians, architects, and urban planners to reimagine and transform cities into healthier and more livable spaces.

Meanwhile, in an increasingly networked society interconnected through social media, existing inequities have become all the more visible. In 2020, the brutal police killing of George Floyd triggered protests worldwide in support of the Black Lives Matter (BLM) movement. The protests and social movement highlighted the systemic inequalities deeply rooted in contemporary society. This watershed moment echoed historical urban planning practices that perpetuated segregation and exclusion, such as "red lining," which had rendered minorities unable to buy homes through mortgage discrimination. The protests underscored how past injustices continue to shape present-day societal structures, serving as a wake-up call for greater racial, economic, and social justice in the built environment.

In light of these intertwined environmental, public health, social and economic crises, it is evident that cities can no longer be understood nor designed solely following the theories, methods and tools of modernist urbanism. To effectively address the complex urban challenges of the twenty-first century, architects and urban designers must develop innovative approaches that are better equipped to respond to the multifaceted issues we face today. As we stand at this critical juncture in the third decade of the twenty-first century, it is imperative we re-evaluate the long-standing theories and approaches in urbanism, many of which have their roots in the early 1900s. As we shift towards contemporary paradigms that encapsulate the intricate facets of urban living, we must also embrace cutting-edge methods and tools to support this shift. These advancements are essential for shaping a more sustainable, equitable, and resilient future for cities.

Technological Acceleration and Urbanity

As urbanization accelerates globally at an unprecedented rate, a transformative industrial paradigm emerges alongside. This shift, known as post-Fordism, evolves from the twentieth-century Fordist model, which prioritized standardized mass production and resulted in cities characterized by uniform spatial structures. Post-Fordism, in contrast, emphasizes flexibility, decentralization, and the harnessing of vast amounts of information. This change is reshaping how designers envision and interact with urban landscapes, leveraging data, computational design, and smart technologies to better inform their projects. The recent revolution in intelligence is marked by a deluge of data, enhanced computational design techniques in urbanism, and the integration of smart sensing and actuation mechanisms within cities' core structures. The rapid advancements in information technology have given rise to innovative tools dedicated to urban design, monitoring, and governance, initiating extensive automation within urban areas. This technological surge is propelling urban intelligence to new heights, seemingly heralding an era of "smarter" cities. Yet, while advocates of the smart city paradigm celebrate its promises of increased comfort, security, and efficiency, critics caution against potential threats to democratic principles and the risks of heightened citizen surveillance. At one extreme, there is a tendency towards neo-cybernetics, and at the other, there is a desire for greater democratization, openness, equity and justice.

There is a significant risk of positivism and technological determinism in lauding the current industrial and technological advances. Nevertheless, today's access to city data, insights into citizen behaviors, and metrics on urban infrastructures and environmental impacts is unparalleled. Yet, the full spectrum of implications stemming from our recent technological strides remains only partly understood. Ultimately, it is humans who invent, design, and train technologies, and more accountability should be demanded to address the ethical and environmental concerns surrounding Artificial Intelligence (AI) and technology in general. This reader is situated within the historical background of the contemporary condition in which new media, tools, and techniques have invigorated the design disciplines. It focuses on the potential cultural implications and applications of technological advances for cities in the twenty-first century.

A Roadmap to Urban Complexity

In the twenty-first century, cities stand as vivid exemplars of the intricate complexity intrinsic to life on Earth, rather than as rationalist "machines" as modernist Le Corbusier imagined them to be. In fact, some critics point to our current "post-natural" era, where the lines between the organic and the mechanistic blur, giving rise to urban hybrids that intertwine the biological with the mechanical. Urbanism, whether viewed as a design practice, a research discipline, or an academic curriculum, is a fundamental reflection of the societal fabric.

INTRODUCTION

The paradigms guiding city design have already shifted. Navigating the diverse interdisciplinary field which has arisen since the waning of Modernism requires a new kind of roadmap or guidebook, one which enables greater comprehension of the intricate forces shaping cities. Over the past decades, writers, filmmakers, designers, and technologists have attempted to characterize the behavior and experience of the contemporary city. Recent urban discourse has conceived of the city as the host of various complex adaptive systems. Having moved away from the mechanical paradigm of modernists, contemporary urbanists embrace the life-like qualities of cities and reject stasis and permanence. They value the emergent properties of real-time urban fluxes and the transformation of cities over longer durations. They reconsider the conception, design, and behavior of cities as increasingly intelligent. In this reader, the city is understood paradigmatically more as an organism than as a machine.

Reading Urbanism

Urbanism refers to the study and design of cities, including the ways people interact with and shape the urban environment. Given the new perspectives on the contemporary city and its possible futures, this reader offers a disciplinary overview of seminal texts related to the disciplines of architecture, urban design, environmental design, landscape architecture, and landscape urbanism. Rather than reinforcing disciplinary boundaries, it aims to bring together diverse perspectives into an unprecedented interdisciplinary compilation. The aim is not to amplify, nor to simplify, the historical debates between design and planning, nor to see urban design as a mediator between architecture and urban planning, as we believe today's disciplinary field is far richer in diversity than a debate with just two polar disciplines.

As an interdisciplinary anthology, the readings selected for this reader have overlaps with computer science, biology, climate science, data science, philosophy, feminism, and critical theory, among others, while also resonating with diverse creative practices. The selected readings trace a historical trajectory through design theory and the built environment, presenting a wide range of perspectives. Central to this compilation is an exploration of urban complexity and the significant cultural transformations instigated by technological advances, which are reshaping the fabric and dynamics of city life.

The compilation of texts in *The Urbanism Reader* aims to encapsulate the manifold agendas of contemporary design culture. It is organized as a series of thematic chapters, which describe the diverse qualities of cities through taxonomies, or prefixes, of urbanism, such as, heterogeneous, diverse, inclusive, dense, intense, fluid, connected, networked, ecological, resilient, sustainable, green, healthy, equitable, emergent, evolutionary, informal, computational, parametric, algorithmic, systemic, responsive, augmented, virtual, automated, and intelligent, among others.

There remains an absence of a collection of seminal texts on urbanism from a design perspective, which brings together the authoritative voices on urban complexity in the twenty-first century. *The Urbanism Reader* fills this gap in the literature for the design-oriented global community of students, researchers, scholars, and professionals in urbanism. This compilation distinguishes itself from the histories and theories of urban planning, which typically focus on social science methods and policy. Instead, it gathers seminal texts that concentrate on design theory, design technologies, and other design-centric approaches to urbanism, offering a unique perspective on the study and conceptualization of cities.

This anthology on urbanism offers both a forward-looking projection on the design implications of technological breakthroughs and a reflection on design strategies that have evolved since the era of Modernism. While the so-called digital revolution has transformed architecture and other smaller scale design disciplines, the larger-scale urban consequences of computational modeling, simulation, and analysis, are rapidly gaining traction.

Embracing circular design and adaptive environmental strategies in city design is now seen as both imperative and inescapable. Innovative methods of designing and analysing urban spaces, aided by computational design, sensors, and robotics are now making their mark on urbanism. Extended realities, supported by augmented and virtual technologies, are redefining both how designers envision and articulate their ideas, and how urban dwellers perceive and experience their environments. The impact of the information revolution is also evident in the application of data analytics, artificial intelligence, and automation now playing a role to address urban design challenges. Debates on the "smartness" of cities are raising as much enthusiasm about their design potentials as they are raising alarm over mass surveillance.

The early 2020s has been transformative for the design disciplines, with a wide variety of Generative AI tools poised to impact cities. This compilation not only delves into the technological advancements but also explores crucial concerns related to economic, environmental, social, racial, and digital inequities within urban contexts. By weaving together both cultural and technological themes, *The Urbanism Reader* offers a curated exploration of urban narratives spanning from the recent past to future projections.

Who Is this Reader for?

This reader is meant for students, researchers, scholars, and professionals interested in contemporary urbanism. These include architects, urban designers, landscape architects, and urban planners. Unlike other readers on urbanism, this book focuses on both the study and design of cities. It offers students, academics, and professionals, a primer with seminal texts as important sources and references that help them make sense of the contemporary city, while also providing actionable design strategies and comprehensive methodologies for urban interventions.

Thematic and Textual Content

In charting the many possible futures for urbanism, this reader addresses questions about how cities are understood, the methods by which cities are designed, and the processes by which they evolve.

The first chapter, "Spatial Heterogeneity, Diversity, and Difference after Modernist Planning," highlights several efforts to dismantle the hegemony and ubiquity of modernist city design. It emphasizes a transition in values from singularity to plurality, and from uniformity to radical difference. Postmodern fragmentation emerged from the disillusionment with utopian visions of Modernism. This marked a shift toward urban complexity being generated and communicated through the dominance of collage as a design methodology, which was later questioned in the 1990s.

INTRODUCTION

Building upon this foundation, Chapter 2, titled, "Urbanism and Models of Design Complexity," introduces the paradigms that had aimed to capture the urban complexity inherent to contemporary cities. Critics understood urbanism as the outcome of the interaction of multiple forces, systems, and agencies. Surveying diverse world views after Modernism, this chapter focuses specifically on the significance of the early digital revolution of the 1990s. Designers proposed a new field based organizational model for urbanism, and saw potential in computation to harness the multifaceted nature of the city. In addition, text excerpts explore the design consequences of animated, forces-based, computational models, organization, and information structures, leading to a new interest in fluidity and dynamics.

The fundamental link between urbanism, infrastructure, and networks is addressed in Chapter 3, "Intensities, Flows, Connectivity, and Network Urbanism." Rather than being defined solely by their static spatial configurations, cities can also be perceived as shaped by the flows and intensities within networks. By examining the evolutionary patterns and dynamics of cities—from ancient to modern times—we gain insights into the flow of resources that lead to various types of urban places. The chapter further delves into concepts of single and continuous surfaces, used by designers as an organizing principle for complex projects, as well as innovative form-finding through the simulation of flows.

Another aspect of contemporary urbanism is density. Compact and dense urban development helps preserve land for environmental or agricultural benefits, and allows for more possible social connections between people in urban areas, which can stimulate innovation and economic productivity. But what are the design qualities of high-density urbanism? How can architects and urban designers exploit density and create new metropolitan cultures? In which ways can high-density urbanism catalyze social activities and foster interaction? In Chapter 4, "Density, the Compact City, and Metropolitan Culture," we reflect on the values of compact and high-density urbanism, and the ways in which packing and juxtaposing contrasting uses on a site can lead to urban vibrancy and vitality.

Shifting the focus to the natural environment, Chapter 5, titled, "Ecology, Resilience, and Green Infrastructure," focuses on a biological and environmental conception of urbanity having greater synergies with the natural environment, in response to the previous mechanical world view during industrialization. In a fight against climate change, designers are reintroducing nature into cities as a structuring force for urban development. They also value the practical aspect of nature, for instance in "green infrastructure," where absorptive green spaces manage stormwater. They argue for a synthesis of environmental planning and design, landscape architecture, architecture, and various environmental engineering fields. Finally, Landscape Urbanists find inspiration in the indeterminacy and lack of formal unity that nature brings.

Health and equity considerations are also vital in urban design. As early as the nineteenth century, cholera epidemics prompted the integration of sewer and drinking water systems in cities. Today, concerns about health and inequity continue to preoccupy architects and urban designers, having been exacerbated and elevated as a result of the impact of the Covid-19 pandemic. Chapter 6, titled, "Health, Equity, and Livable Cities," focuses on architects and urban designers who are conscious of the various ways in which the built environment can fuel inequality and encourage behavior with detrimental impacts on our mental and physical health. At the intersection of design and health, they propose more livable, sociable and equitable cities and landscapes.

In contrast to formal planning, informal settlements are a result of the collective of individual actions without an overall design framework, leading to incremental growth. Notwithstanding the crisis of socioeconomic inequity inherent to informal urbanization, there is an opportunity for designers to learn from emergent and unintended urbanism. This seventh chapter, titled, "Emergent, Tactical, and Informal Urbanism," focuses on the ways in which designers have tried to harvest some of the self-organizing processes in cities. Eschewing traditional top-down urban design, these innovative approaches seek to integrate the organic, adaptive qualities found in informal settlements, championing flexibility, spontaneity, and a built-in potential for evolutionary transformation.

The eighth chapter, "Evolutionary, Computational, and Parametric Urbanism," highlights the transformation of urban design in the past two decades as a result of architecture's experimentation with an expanded computational toolbox, leading to the development of digital design approaches that cater to the complex and varied aspects of city design. At the nexus of computer science and urbanism, designers are gaining access to greater capacities to interact with the emergent properties of cities, and to capture the inherent complexities of vast urban systems. This chapter explores a range of paradigms and perspectives from various design disciplines and scales, focusing on the emergent properties of urban systems over time. Readings hash out the debates surrounding Parametricism and Parametric Urbanism.

The digital realm is blending with the physical in cities. Architecture and the visual arts have long histories with creating illusory spatial, visual and cognitive effects. But today, social media platforms, digital communication, and extended realities summon a plethora of often- competing images of cities. This ninth chapter, titled, "Virtuality, Extended Realities, and the Metaverse," highlights the recent use of extended realities of cities. It features theorists describing the impact of "media buildings" and "hyperreality." They call for designers to bridge the physical and digital world, from the use of "digital twins" that simulate and evaluate many scenarios in the cloud to create a more sustainable world, to the creation of artistic augmented realities that enhance our experience of urban life.

The tenth chapter, "Artificial Intelligence, the Internet of Things, and Technological Determinism," explores recent technological and cultural shifts at the convergence of artificial intelligence, architecture, and urban design, concluding with speculations on the future of urbanism. Authors explain this accelerating technological realm, in which computational systems are automating the design of urban spaces. Non-human agency and the ubiquity of sensing and actuating systems in cities and our personal devices, have raised a debate about smart cities. On one hand they promise greater comfort, security, and efficiency, while on the other they raise alarm over diminishing democracy and empowerment, through increased surveillance and control of citizens. This final chapter also highlights the emerging ethical issues arising as a repercussion of the proliferation of AI systems.

Within the turbulent context of a vastly expanding global urban population, the project of the city has never been more relevant. Today, the design disciplines and professions need to come to terms with new global challenges and their impact on urbanism. New design paradigms, methods, and tools have emerged and are rapidly taking root as alternatives to those of the twentieth century. This anthology of seminal readings at the intersection of design, technology, and culture, aims to provide a comprehensive survey of the critical issues, cutting-edge technologies, and important voices shaping urbanism. Looking back at the past half century may provide urbanists today with a foundation from which to spring into the future.

1

Spatial Heterogeneity, Diversity, and Difference after Modernist Planning

Post-Second World War urbanism remained deeply rooted in Modernist principles. However, by the middle of the twentieth century, the positivist idealism which had characterized modernist architecture and urban planning was increasingly reaching a state of exhaustion. Architects, urbanists, writers, and critics grew disillusioned with the utopian visions of early twentieth-century models. The urbanist and activist Jane Jacobs, for instance, in her book The *Death and Life of Great American Cities* (1961), frequently attacked the theories of Le Corbusier and Ebenezer Howard. "There is no logic that can be superimposed on the city," she wrote. "People make it, and it is to them, not buildings, that we must fit our plans."[1]

While architects reassessed the International Style in architecture and rejected modernist principles of city design in favor of new spatial and social agendas, urban planners turned to social science methods. Unfortunately, the disciplines of architecture and urban planning became increasingly estranged. How, and when, do we mark the demise of Modernist architecture and planning? The disbanding of CIAM (Congrès Internationaux d'Architecture Moderne) in 1956 was an early indication of disunity. One year later, in 1957, Josep Lluís Sert, the final president of CIAM, formulated and announced the new discipline of urban design. The 1960s saw radical architectural experiments, as well as grass roots resistance to modernist urban planning, exemplified by Jane Jacob's resistance to modernist planner Robert Moses.[2] 1960s groups such as Archigram, Archizoom, and Superstudio, among others, charted new approaches to conceiving and communicating the qualities of the contemporary city. Charles Jencks had declared the death of Modernism, and the arrival of Postmodernism, with the televised implosion of the Pruitt-Igoe housing complex in St. Louis in 1972. He saw it as a failure of modernist architectural design principles—although others have since attributed the failure of this social housing project to institutional and socioeconomic factors rather than flaws in its design.[3]

The readings selected in this chapter highlight the multifaceted efforts to challenge the dominance of modernist city design. They represent a shift from singularity to plurality, and from uniformity to a celebration of difference. These changes included Postmodernism's emphasis on regional and local specificities, which emerged as a response to the growing influence of globalization. A wide range of architectural and urban design approaches developed to counter the prevailing modernist design ethos, featuring various dissenting voices such as Populism, Postmodern Eclecticism, Deconstructivism, Neoclassicism, and New Urbanism, each offering a unique perspective on the future of urban design.

The chapters in this reader generally focus on only three to five authors and their texts. Although this chapter sets out to summarize the plurality of the early post-modern era through four texts, many other protagonists can be credited with deepening and diversifying the design discourses in urbanism in the 1960s and 1970s. In the last CIAM meetings held in the 1950s, Team X, founded by Alison and Peter Smithson, John Voelcker, and William and Jill Howell (England), Aldo van Eyck, Jaap Bakema (Netherlands), Georges Candilis and Shadrach Woods (France), was instrumental in challenging the orthodoxy of modernist planning, contributing to a new understanding of the contemporary city, as perceived by their generation in post-Second World War Europe. Manfredo Tafuri, in his book, *Architecture and Utopia* (1973),[4] highlighted the ways in which modern architecture had been subsumed by capitalist interests, undermining its utopian ambition.

Aldo Rossi's work has also contributed to this deepening with his seminal book, *Architecture and the City*, published in 1966 and later republished in 1984 with an introduction by Peter Eisenman. Rossi argued for a retreat from orthodox modernist principles and a rediscovery of the formal and epistemological qualities of the traditional, historic, European city.[5] Beyond the scope of this book are some of the tendencies expressing more conservative reactions to Modernism, for example in the writing and projects of the Luxembourger brothers, Léon and Rob Krier, who were commissioned by Prince Charles to design and build a model village, Poundbury in southwest England, based on medieval civic principles. Neoclassicism is perhaps the most extreme abandonment of Modernism within post-modernity. Finally, the New Urbanism movement made a compelling case for historical continuity, drawing upon the historical principles of human-centered, walkable towns and small city centers. Urban designers Andres Duany and Elizabeth Plater-Zyberk, the foremost champions of New Urbanism, have designed and built several town centers from the 1980s onwards, resisting and rethinking suburban sprawl. They have published widely on New Urbanist principles, notably in their manifesto, *Charter of the New Urbanism* (2000).[6]

In the wake of Modernism's decline, this chapter's first reading from the seminal book, *Learning from Las Vegas* (1972), explores the initially significance of history and popular forms of urbanity.[7] Subsequently, we delve into the heightened historical consciousness in Colin Rowe and Fred Koetter's influential book, *Collage City* (1978).[8] The chapter then examines Kenneth Frampton's essay and book chapter, "Critical Regionalism," which emphasizes the resistance to universality and the the primacy of regional and local traditions and historical vernacular, and identity.[9]

The decline of Modernism brought a new acceptance of vernacular architecture and popular culture. Bernard Rudofsky's groundbreaking exhibition and book, titled, *Architecture without Architects* (1965), advocated for a "non-pedigreed" vernacular architecture. Where Rudofsky only acknowledged pre-industrial vernacular environments,[10] *Learning from Las Vegas*, by Robert Venturi, Denise Scott Brown, and Steven Izenour, extended the interest in the vernacular to contemporary commercial environments.[11]

Venturi had already gained notoriety as one of Modernism's most vocal critics, having published *Complexity and Contradiction in Architecture* (1966), an attack on the purism and simplicity of modernist architecture, in which he irreverently adapted Mies van der Rohe's maxim, one of Modernism's founding fathers, "Less is more" to "Less is a bore." Scott Brown had previously visited Las Vegas, following her interest in pop culture. She had studied under the British Independent Group which had laid the groundwork for Pop Art, such as member Richard Hamilton who challenged fine art traditions with his art collage assembled from *Ladies Home Journal* advertisements.

Controversially, Venturi and Scott Brown accepted the status quo of the commercial strip, which found its epitome in the Las Vegas Boulevard of the 1960s. Learning from Las Vegas declared its interest in this "new type of urban form." They likened the importance of the "careful documentation and analysis" of the physical form of the strip to "the study of mediaeval Europe and ancient Rome and Greece to earlier generations."[12] This was urbanism's Pop Art moment.[13]

Scott Brown and Venturi were going to take a Pop artist approach to Las Vegas commercial architecture. "We can learn . . . from Las Vegas as have other artists from their own profane and stylistic sources," they wrote.[14] Scott Brown and Venturi would draw from Las Vegas casinos like Roy Lichtenstein migrated cartoon bubbles from comics and Andy Warhol painted Campbell's soup cans.

The authors and their Yale students, on a study trip to Las Vegas, employed new media and mapping techniques to record spatial and temporal dynamics in the city. For ten days, they meticulously diagrammed and documented commercial billboards, neon signs, replica statues, and even parking lots. They argued that mapping urban behaviors and traditionally neglected phenomena such as outdoor lightning required mixed media methods, such as photography, film, graphic design, collage and montage. "How can the traditional city planning methods for depicting activity patterns (land-use and transportation maps) be adapted to a city such as Las Vegas . . . How does one describe new form and space using techniques derived from the old? . . . What techniques can represent the 60mph form and space of the strip? . . . . We need new concepts and theories to handle it."[15]

A city like Las Vegas, Venturi and Scott Brown argued, managed to communicate messages faster and further than for instance in Rome. The Strip, with its large billboards and signs, was designed to be experienced from the car. The car had made signage the new arches, and neon light the new mosaics. Their text theorized speed and mobility in which vast urban space was perceived and recorded at high speed. In their analysis, the city and its buildings acted as communication interfaces, in today's parlance. They identified two primary architectural models on the Strip: the "Duck," where the building's form itself conveys meaning, and the "Decorated Shed," where generic structures are adorned with signage and ornamentation to communicate identity.

In addition to Las Vegas representing a new semiotic type for urbanism, it was also better understood by more people than Modernism, they argued. Whereas only the elite, who had a learned appreciation for it, would understand the abstract meaning of modernist buildings, everyone could understand Las Vegas' references to "our great commonplaces or old clichés." The uncomplicated references made the Strip into an immersive environment for everybody. Scott Brown and Venturi lauded Las Vegas' "inclusion and allusion" aspects: "the ability to engulf the visitor in a new role: for three days one may imagine oneself a centurion at Caesar's Palace, a ranger at the Frontier, or a jetsetter at the Riviera rather than a salesperson from Des Moines, Iowa . . ." The architecture of Las Vegas, Scott Brown and Venturi concluded, was "socially less coercive and aesthetically more vital."

Ironically, modernist architects also included symbolic aspects, but these architects never explicitly claimed to use these references. Scott Brown and Venturi show how modernists relied on a nostalgia for the industrial vernacular, exemplified by Corbusier's focus on grain elevators, and Mies' turn to industrial steel detailing.

Venturi and Scott-Brown sought an alternative to modernist planning and architecture. They were looking for "a new way out of the CIAM grid." Where Le Corbusier proposed to tear down a large swathe of Paris to realize his vision of Plan Voisin, Scott Brown and Venturi proposed "learning from the existing landscape as a way of being revolutionary for an architect."[16] Venturi and Scott-Brown refer to Frank Lloyd Wright, and what they call the anti-urbanist tendency throughout American history, vindicating the "travesty of Broadacre City." In their view, the order of the strip "includes," with incongruous mixtures of land uses and media.

Provocatively, this text requests that we suspend morality and accept the world as is.[17] Scott Brown and Venturi had never bothered with judging the morals of the Strip. "Las Vegas's values are not questioned here. The morality of commercial advertising, gambling interests, and the competitive instinct is not at issue," they wrote. For them, the Las Vegas Strip was merely a "phenomenon of architectural communication." They were after the medium, not the message.

In Chapter 7 in this book, "Emergent, Tactical, and Informal Urbanism," the notion of everyday urbanism is explored further. Ultimately, Las Vegas has been studied again and again, as it has evolved. Stefan Al's book *The Strip: Las Vegas and the Architecture of the American Dream* (2017), positioned Scott Brown's and Venturi's work within one of the Strip's many metamorphoses.[18] A decade after *Learning from Las Vegas*, most of the neon signage celebrated by Venturi and Scott Brown had been dismantled. Today, the Strip is one of the most dense and pedestrian streets of the American West, a major change from its previous character as a sprawling car-based commercial corridor in the 1960s, highlighting the dynamic nature of cities and the ongoing need to reassess our understanding of urbanism.

FIGURE 1.1 Neon roadside signs flicker vibrantly in front of the hotels, casting an electrifying glow along the Las Vegas Strip in the 1960s. Courtesy Getty Images.

ROBERT VENTURI, DENISE SCOTT BROWN, AND STEVEN IZENOUR
"Preface" and
"Part 1: A Significance for A&P Parking Lots, or Learning from Las Vegas"
Learning from Las Vegas: The Forgotten Symbolism of Architectural Form

Because we have criticized Modern architecture, it is proper here to state our intense admiration of its early period when its founders, sensitive to their own times, proclaimed the right revolution. Our argument lies mainly with the irrelevant and distorted prolongation of that old revolution today.

Learning from the existing landscape is a way of being revolutionary for an architect. Not the obvious way, which is to tear down Paris and begin again, as Le Corbusier suggested in the 1920s, but another, more tolerant way; that is, to question how we look at things.

The commercial strip, the Las Vegas Strip in particular – the example par excellence – challenges the architect to take a positive, non-chip-on-the-shoulder view. Architects are out of the habit of looking nonjudgmentally at the environment, because orthodox Modern architecture is progressive, if not revolutionary, utopian, and puristic; it is dissatisfied with existing conditions. Modern architecture has been anything but permissive: Architects have preferred to change the existing environment rather than enhance what is there. . . .

. . . There is a perversity in the learning process: We look backward at history and tradition to go forward; we can also look downward to go upward. And withholding judgment may be used as a tool to make later judgment more sensitive. This is a way of learning from everything.

COMMERCIAL VALUES AND COMMERCIAL METHODS

. . . Analysis of existing American urbanism is a socially desirable activity to the extent that it teaches us architects to be more understanding and less authoritarian in the plans we make for both inner-city renewal and new development.

ARCHITECTURE AS SPACE

. . . Architects have been bewitched by a single element of the Italian landscape: the piazza. Its traditional, pedestrian-scaled, and intricately enclosed space is easier to like than the spatial sprawl of Route 66 and Los Angeles.

SYMBOL IN SPACE BEFORE FORM IN SPACE: LAS VEGAS AS A COMMUNICATION SYSTEM

. . . This architecture of styles and signs is antispatial; it is an architecture of communication over space; communication dominates space as an element in the architecture and in the landscape. But it is for a new scale of landscape . . . The commercial persuasion of roadside eclecticism provokes bold impact in the vast and complex setting of a new landscape of big spaces, high speeds, and complex programs.

VAST SPACE IN THE HISTORICAL TRADITION AND AT THE A&P

The A&P parking lot is a current phase in the evolution of vast space since Versailles. The space that divides high-speed highway and low, sparse buildings produces no enclosure and little direction. To move through a piazza is to move between high enclosing forms. To move through this landscape is to move over vast expansive texture: the megatexture of the commercial landscape. The parking lot is the *parterre* of the asphalt landscape. . . But it is the highway signs, through their sculptural forms or pictorial silhouettes, their particular positions in space, their inflected shapes, and their graphic meanings, that identify and unify the megatexture. They make verbal and symbolic connections through space, communicating a complexity of meanings through hundreds of associations in few seconds from far away. . . . The big sign and the little building is the rule of Route 66.

FROM ROME TO LAS VEGAS

. . .Las Vegas is the apotheosis of the desert town. Visiting Las Vegas in the mid-1960s was like visiting Rome in the late 1940s. For young Americans in the 1940s, familiar only with the auto-scaled, gridiron city and the antiurban theories of the previous architectural generation, the traditional urban spaces, the pedestrian scale, and the mixtures, yet continuities, of styles of the Italian piazzas were a significant revelation.

They rediscovered the piazza. Two decades later architects are perhaps ready for similar lessons about large open space, big scale, and high speed. Las Vegas is to the Strip what Rome is to the Piazza.

. . .Nolli's map of the mid-eighteenth century reveals the sensitive and complex connections between public and private space in Rome (p. 18) A "Nolli" map of the Las Vegas Strip reveals and clarifies what is public and what is private, but here the scale is enlarged by the inclusion of the parking lot, and the solid-to-void ratio is reversed by the open spaces of the desert.

THE ARCHITECTURE OF PERSUASION

In *The View From the Road*, Appleyard, Lynch, and Myer describe the driving experience as 'a sequence played to the eyes of a captive, somewhat fearful, but partially inattentive audience, whose vision is filtered and directed forward.'[1] Movement perception along a road is within a structural order of constant elements – the road, sky, lamppost spacing, and yellow stripes.

VAST SPACE IN THE HISTORICAL TRADITION AND AT THE A&P

The Las Vegas Strip eludes our concepts of urban form and space, ancient or modern. It has as little to do with Haussmann as with Ville Radieuse, with Ebenezer Howard as with the Metabolists, with Lynch as with Camillo Sitte or Ian Nairn. Frank Lloyd Wright would have considered it a travesty of Broadacre City, and Maki would probably find it a travesty of "group form." Perhaps Patrick Geddes might have understood and J.B. Jackson is very much attuned to it.

Although its buildings suggest a number of historical styles, its urban spaces owe nothing to historical space. Las Vegas space is neither contained and enclosed like medieval space nor classically balanced and proportioned like Renaissance space nor swept up in a rhythmically ordered movement like Baroque space, nor does it flow like Modern space around freestanding urban space makers.

It is something else again. But what? Not chaos, but a new spatial order relating the automobile and highway communication in an architecture which abandons pure form in favor of mixed media. Las

Vegas space is so different from the docile spaces for which our analytical and conceptual tools were evolved that we need new concepts and theories to handle it.

One way of understanding the new form and space is to compare it with the old and the different. Compare Las Vegas with Ville Radieuse and Haussmann's Paris; compare the Strip with a medieval market street compare Fremont Street, a shopping center, and the pilgrims' way through Rome. Compare a form that "just grew" with its designed equivalent and with "group forms" from other cultures.

Another way of understanding the new form is to describe carefully and then analyze what is there and, from an understanding of the city as is, to evolve new theories and concepts of form more suited to twentieth-century realities and therefore more useful as conceptual tools in design and planning. This approach provides a way out of the CIAM grid. But how does one describe new form and space using techniques derived from the old? What techniques can represent the 60mph form and space of the Strip? How does its desert site affect Las Vegas form and space?

Do Las Vegas public and institutional buildings show any influences from its recreational architecture?

LAS VEGAS AS A PATTERN OF ACTIVITIES

A city is a set of intertwined activities that form a pattern on the land. The Las Vegas Strip is not a chaotic sprawl but a set of activities whose pattern, as with other cities, depends on the technology of movement and communication and the economic value of land. We term it sprawl, because it is a new pattern we have not yet understood. The aim here is for us as designers to derive an understanding of this new pattern.

The questions are: How can the traditional city planning methods for depicting activity patterns (land-use and transportation maps) be adapted to a city such as Las Vegas? How can they be made useful as inspiration sources and design tools for urban designers? What other methods are there for coming to an understanding of the city as an activity system?

IMAGE OF LAS VEGAS: INCLUSION AND ALLUSION IN ARCHITECTURE

What is an urban designer's image, or set of images, for the Strip and the big low spaces of the casinos? What techniques – movie, graphic, or other-should be used to depict them? In the eighteenth and nineteenth centuries an integral part of an architect's education consisted of sketching Roman ruins. If the eighteenth-century architect discovered his design gestalt by means of the Grand Tour and a sketch pad, we as twentieth century architects will have to find our own "sketch pad" for Las Vegas.

1   Donald Appleyard, Kevin Lynch, and John R. Myer, *The View From the Road* (Cambridge, Mass.: The M.I.T. Press, 1964), p. 5.

Robert Venturi, Denise Scott Brown, and Steven Izenour, "Preface" and "Part 1: A Significance for A&P Parking Lots, or Learning from Las Vegas", *Learning from Las Vegas: The Forgotten Symbolism of Architectural Form* (Cambridge: MIT Press, 1972): xi–xvii; 3–4, 6, 8, 13, 18–19, 74–76, 83.

Reyner Banham, an English architecture critic, shared Venturi and Scott Brown's perspective on the importance of understanding cities through the lens of popular culture and everyday experience. He recognized Los Angeles as a city best understood through the dynamic experience of driving a car. He famously wrote, "I learned to drive so I could understand Los Angeles firsthand," comparing this experience to that of English intellectuals who learned Italian to read Dante's original works.[19] While Banham appreciated the unique urban fabric of Los Angeles, he was critical of certain architectural trends. In his book, *Megastructure: Urban Futures of the Recent Past* (1976), Banham declared the symbolic form of late Modernism, the megastructure, to be dead on the basis of its inflexibility and monotony.[20]

In 1983, Fredric Jameson reread Banham's eulogy for the megastructure in his essay, "Postmodernism and Consumer Culture," making reference to the postmodern characteristics of the interior urbanism of John Portman's Bonaventure Hotel in Los Angeles.[21] This project, resonating with the principles of "deep space" found in casino interiors, featured mesmerizing interior worlds characterized by dark and deep spaces and a vast atrium that almost obscured the time of day. Los Angeles became a model of a postmodern city, as further explored in Mike Davis' book, *City of Quartz* (1992). He sees the city's social inequity, spatial segregation, and fortification of affluent enclaves as a dystopian vision of postmodern urbanism.[22]

Whilst *Learning from Las Vegas* challenged designers to look at the existing world of contemporary commercial urbanism Rowe and Koetter, in *Collage City*, celebrated the gradualism of urban aggregation and accumulation of existing cities over time. The book articulated a framework for understanding and appreciating the city as a palimpsest of urban evolution.

Rowe and Koetter's book critiqued Modernism for what they called "total architecture." This is evident from the very beginning of their work, as they reference Walter Gropius' strong advocacy for this idea. In their chapter titled "Collision City and the Politics of 'Bricolage,'" they introduce Isaiah Berlin's concept of two contrasting approaches to the city: the fox, who knows many things, and the hedgehog, who knows one big thing. Rowe and Koetter recognize the hedgehog's "Total Architecture" as a fundamental aspect of all utopian visions.[23] In contrast to this single grand idea or a "complete unitary model" stands a more pragmatic and flexible approach, with a "seemingly disjointed accumulation of diverse enthusiasms."[24]

To illustrate their point, they draw a sharp contrast between the clear and purposeful design of the Palais de Versailles, described as "unambiguous and unabashed," and the haphazard collection of disparate ideal fragments found in Hadrian's Villa Adriana in Roman Tivoli.[25] Introducing the concept of bricolage, they articulate a distinction between a resourceful builder who uses whatever materials are available, in contrast to the methodical approach of a scientist. This comparison highlights the difference between a disciplined, rational approach and a more spontaneous mindset that embraces the serendipitous and the improvisational.[26]

Rowe and Koetter reject the notion of relying on "single central visions" and argue that the concept of Utopia, as a project of improvement and enhancement, becomes "unthinkable" in Postmodernism. They attribute this to the limitations of postmodern epistemology and its alignment with the world view of a new generation of urbanists who are skeptical of grand narratives.[27]

In Collage City Rowe and Koetter investigate collage as a pre-minent design technique of the twentieth century, which became a central method in the departure from Modernism. They celebrate collage for its ability to depict the complexity and diversity of urbanism, including its organizational intricacies and seemingly disparate elements. Although emerging in the early twentieth century, collage techniques gained prominence in the 1970s–80s as alternatives to the simplifications of Modernism. Later in this chapter, the profound influence of collage techniques on architects in the 1980s and 1990s will be further elucidate through an examination of the writing of architect Bernard Tschumi.

COLIN ROWE AND FRED KOETTER
"Collision City and the Politics of Bricolage"
Collage City

"... there exists a great chasm between those, on one side, who relate everything to a single central vision, one system less or more coherent or articulate, in terms of which they understand, think and feel – a single, universal, organizing principle in terms of which all that they are and say has significance – and, on the other side, those who pursue many ends, often unrelated and even contradictory, connected, if at all, only in some *de facto* way, for some psychological or physiological cause, related by no moral or aesthetic principle; these last lead lives, perform acts, and entertain ideas that are centrifugal rather than centripetal, their thought is scattered or diffused, moving on many levels, seizing upon the essence of a vast variety of experiences and objects, for what they are in themselves, without consciously or unconsciously seeking to fit them into or exclude them from any one. unchanging ... at times fanatical, unitary inner vision."

ISAIAH BERLIN

Scope of Total Architecture: such was the title which Walter Gropius affixed to a highly miscellaneous collection of, mostly, insubstantial essays. It was published in 1955; and, apparently, at that date, insistence on 'total architecture'—an obvious version of the Wagnerian *Gesamtkunstwerk* with all its promises of cultural integration—did not appear either unjustified or bizarre. Presumably, in 1955, a 'total architecture', an all controlling system which is yet not a system because it is a growth—'a new growth coming right from the roots up'[1] —a combination, probably, of both Hegelian freedom and Hegelian necessity, in any case an emanation from fundamentals, was still considered not merely a plausible but also a desirable possibility; and, no doubt, it is here, when such notions become expressed in the gentle voice of 'concerned' liberalism, that we may be encouraged to discern something of the still shining afterglow of a unitary and holistic utopian faith.

We have earlier attempted to specify two versions of the utopian idea: utopia as an, implicit, object of contemplation and utopia as an, explicit, instrument of social change; and it is, at this stage, that we must re-affirm how much the conceptions of 'total architecture' and 'total design' are present, of necessity, in all utopian projections. Utopia has never offered options. The citizens of Thomas More's Utopia *could not fail to be happy because they could not choose but be good*[2] and the idea of dwelling in 'goodness', without capacity for moral choice, has been prone to attend most fantasies, whether metaphorical or literal of the ideal society.

For the architect, of course, the ethical content of the good society has, maybe, always been something which building was to make evident. Indeed it has, probably, always been his primary reference; for, whatever other controlling fantasies have emerged—antiquity, tradition, technology—these have invariably been conceived of as aiding and abetting an in some way benign or decorous social order...

Filarete's Sforzinda, a quattrocento ideal city remained an idea and there was to be no question of its literal and immediate application. For the medieval city represented an intractable nucleus of habit and interest which could, in no way, be directly breached; and, accordingly, the problem of the new became one of subversive interjection (Palazzo Massimo, Campidoglio, etc.)

or of polemical demonstrations outside the city – the garden which discloses what the city ought to be.

The garden as criticism of the city—a criticism which the city later abundantly acknowledged—has not, as yet, received sufficient attention; but if, outside Florence, for instance, this theme is profusely represented, its most extreme affirmation can only be at Versailles, that seventeenth century criticism of medieval Paris which Haussmann and Napoleon III later so elaborately took to heart . . .

. . . Now, for present purposes, the obvious construct to mount alongside Versailles is the Villa Adriana at Tivoli. For, if the one is certainly an exhibition of total architecture and total design, the other attempts to dissimulate all reference to any controlling idea . . .

There is unambiguous, unabashed Versailles. The moral is declared to the world and the advertisement, like so many things French, can scarcely be refused. This is total control and the glaring illumination of it. It is the triumph of generality, the prevalence of the overwhelming idea and the refusal of the exception. And then, compared with this single-minded performance of Louis XIV, we have the curiosity of Hadrian—of Hadrian who is, apparently, so disorganized and casual, who proposes the reverse of any 'totality', who seems to need only an accumulation of disparate ideal fragments and whose criticism of Imperial Rome (configurationally much like his own house) is rather an endorsement than any protest.

But, if Versailles is the complete unitary model and the Villa Adriana the apparently uncoordinated amalgam of discrete enthusiasms and, if the shattering ideality of Versailles is to be compared with the relativistically produced 'bits' of Tivoli, then what opportune interpretations can be placed upon this comparison? The obvious ones no doubt: that Versailles is the ultimate paradigm of autocracy; that it assumes a complete political power, undeviating in its objectives and long sustained; that, fundamentally, Hadrian was no less autocratic than Louis XIV but that, perhaps, he was not under the same compulsion to make so consistent a display of his autocracy . . .

'The fox knows many things but the hedgehog knows one big thing.'[3] . . . here are the types of two psychological orientations and temperaments, the one, the hedgehog, concerned with the primacy of the single idea and the other, the fox, preoccupied with multiplicity of stimulus; and the great ones of the earth divide fairly equally: Plato, Dante, Dostoevsky, Proust, are, needless to say, hedgehogs; Aristotle, Shakespeare, Pushkin, Joyce are foxes . . .

. . . But the exigencies of 'the single central vision', palpitating with the sense of its own goodness, will not allow for any determination so obvious; and, as the architect became both messiah and scientist, both Moses and Newton, the consequences of this role playing were not be evaded . . . .

. . . And in our time the 'bricoleur' is still someone who works with his hands and uses devious means compared to those of the craftsman . . . The 'bricoleur' is adept at performing a large number of diverse tasks; but, unlike the engineer, he does not subordinate each of them to the availability of raw materials and tools conceived and procured for the purpose of the project. His universe of instruments is closed and the rules of his game are always to make do with 'whatever is at hand' . . . .[4]

Claude Lévi-Strauss

SPATIAL HETEROGENEITY, DIVERSITY, AND DIFFERENCE AFTER MODERNIST PLANNING

. . . For the 'bricoleur', who certainly finds a representative in 'the odd job man', is also very much more than this. 'It is common knowledge that the artist is both something of a scientist and of a 'bricoleur' . . . we have not only a confrontation of the 'bricoleur's' 'savage mind' with the 'domesticated' mind of the engineer . . .[5]

. . . For, if we can divest ourselves of the deceptions of professional *amour propre* and accepted academic theory, the description of the 'bricoleur' is far more of a 'real-life' specification of what the architect-urbanist is and does than any fantasy deriving from 'methodology' and 'systematics'.

Indeed, one could fear that the architect as 'bricoleur' is, today, almost too enticing a programme—a programme which might guarantee formalism, ad hocery, townscape pastiche, populism and almost whatever else one chooses to name. But . . . the savage mind of the bricoleur! The domesticated mind of the engineer/scientist! The interaction of these two conditions! The artist (architect) as both something of a bricoleur and something of a scientist! . . .

. . . For, if the notion of a 'final' solution through a definitive accumulation of all data is, evidently, an epistemological chimera, if certain aspects of information will invariably remain undiscriminated or undisclosed, and if the inventory of 'facts' can never be complete simply because of the rates of change and obsolescence, then, here and now, it surely might be possible to assert that *the prospects of scientific city planning should, in reality, be regarded as equivalent to the prospects of scientific politics.*

. . . Indeed, if we are willing to recognize the methods of science and 'bricolage' as concomitant propensities, if we are willing to recognize that they are – both of them – modes of address to problems, if we are willing (and it may be hard) to concede equality between the 'civilized' mind (with its presumptions of logical seriality) and the 'savage' mind (with its analogical leaps), then, in re-establishing 'bricolage' alongside science, it might even be possible to suppose that the way for a truly useful future dialectic could be prepared.

. . . the production of any spatial or temporal equivalent of the finite field is, characteristically, liable to be received with mistrust – again as a blockage of the future and as a dangerous impediment to the freedoms of open-endedness . . .

. . . the open society depends upon the complexity of its parts, upon competing group-centred interests which need not be logical but which, collectively, may not only check each other but may, sometimes, also serve as a protective membrane between the individual and the form of collective authority. For the problem should remain that of a tension between quasi-integrated whole and quasi-segregated parts; and, lacking the segregated parts; one can only imagine that 'open society' where, in despite of the theorems of liberty and equality . . . would break out yet again . . .

. . . in the absence of total design merely random procedures can be expected to flourish. Instead, whatever may be the empirical and whatever may be the ideal (and both positions can be distorted by intellectual passion or self-interest to appear their opposites), the ongoing thesis presumes the possibility and the need for a two-way argument between these polar extremes. To a point it is a formalist argument; but, then, to the degree that it contains formalist characteristics, this is not without intention . . .

> ...To terminate: rather than Hegel's 'indestructible bond of the beautiful and the true', rather than ideas of a permanent and future unity, we prefer to consider the complementary possibilities of consciousness and sublimated conflict; and, if there is here urgent need for both the fox and the 'bricoleur,' perhaps it can only be added that the job ahead should be envisaged as no matter of making the world safe for democracy. It is not totally different; but, certainly, it is not this. For, surely, the job is that of making safe the city (and hence democracy) by large infusions of metaphor, analogical thinking, ambiguity; and, in the face of a prevailing scientism and conspicuous *laissez-aller*, it is just possible that these activities could provide the true *Survival Through Design*.
>
> **1** Walter Gropius, Scope of Total Architecture, New York, 1955, p.91.
>
> **2** Thomas Moore, Utopia, 1516.
>
> **3** Isaiah Berlin, The Hedgehog and the Fox, London, 1953; New York, 1957, p.7.
>
> **4** Claude Lévi-Strauss, The Savage Mind, London, 1966: New York, 1969, p.16, 22.
>
> **5** Claude Lévi-Strauss, The Savage Mind, London, 1966: New York, 1969, p.19, 22.
>
> Colin Rowe and Fred Koetter, "Collision City and the Politics of Bricolage", *Collage City* (Cambridge MA: MIT Press, 1978): 86–117.

By the 1980s, several authors responded critically to Postmodernism in architecture. The philosopher Fredric Jameson, known for his analysis of postmodernity, claimed that Pop and Postmodernism sought "the effacement of boundaries between or separations, most notably the erosion of the older distinction between high culture and so-called mass or popular culture."[28] He argued that this represented the "logic of late capitalism": "By exploring the realms of differentiated tastes and aesthetic preferences, architects and urban designers have re-emphasized an important aspect of capital accumulation . . . symbolic capital." According to Jameson, late capitalism has evolved by incorporating cultural forms in order to accelerate turnover. He posits that by integrating aesthetics, capitalism can achieve further accumulation. Even when the material needs of a society are satisfied, constant consumption can be sustained since aesthetics become outdated with the fickle nature of fashion. Jameson's critique highlights the ways in which Postmodernism, despite its claims to pluralism and diversity, can be co-opted by the forces of consumer capitalism.

Other critics such as Michael Sorkin have also lamented the postmodern condition of the city "as a theme park" where "theming" was becoming increasingly dominant. His edited book, *Variations on a Theme Park: The New American City and the End of Public Space*, is considered the canonical work that describes this new urban condition of the American city. Disneyland is seen as transcending its physical site exerting an "all-pervasive" influence on American urbanism.[29] According to Sorkin, the city as a theme park is "ageographical," characterized by a "universal placelessness," lacking relations to local culture and physical geography, and often privatized. He claims these places are designed purely in visual terms, meant for visual consumption. The city is turned into a commodity, consumed as a spectacle. Sorkin's critique emphasizes the loss of authentic public space and the increasing privatization and commodification of the urban realm.[30]

Similar critiques of postmodern urban space are also expressed by Marc Augé in his book *Non-Places: Introduction to an Anthropology of Supermodernity* (1992). He observes the proliferation of generic "non-places," found in airports and shopping malls.[31] In his essay, *The Generic City* (1995), Rem Koolhaas also notes the expanding ubiquity of sameness in cities.[32] A decade later, David Grahame Shane, in his book, *Recombinant Urbanism: Conceptual Modeling in Architecture, Urban Design and City Theory* (2005), critiques the homogenizing tendencies of contemporary cities, as well, rejecting grand narratives in favor of urban mosaics of overlapping fragments. These authors share a concern for the loss of place identity and the increasing standardization of urban environments in the postmodern era.

Kenneth Frampton, a prominent architectural historian, also laments "the ubiquitous placelessness of our modern environment . . . . the endless processual flux of Megalopolis." He identifies "modern motopia"[33] as the culprit for the absence of a public realm. He noted, "The Megalopolis recognised as such in 1961 by the geographer Jean Gottman continues to proliferate throughout the developed world to such an extent that, with the exception of cities which were laid in place before the turn of the century, we are no longer able to maintain defined urban forms."[34]

Frampton criticizes the postmodernists, such as Charles Jencks, for their trajectory "towards pure technique or pure scenography."[35] He rejects the "communicative or instrumental sign" and opposes populism and what he calls its "conservative policies." He takes a position against the promotion of the image as referred to by Venturi and Scott-Brown. Instead, he favors tactile experience and tectonics over the visuality of the image. "The strong affinity of populism for the rhetorical techniques of imagery and advertising is hardly accidental," he wrote. "Unless one guards against such convergence, one will confuse the resistant capacity of a critical practice with the demagogic tendencies of populism."[36]

Frampton also declares how "optimized technology" limits creativity. He notes, "The restrictions jointly imposed by automotive distribution and the volatile play of land speculation serve to limit the scope of urban design to such a degree that any intervention tends to be reduced either to the manipulation of elements predetermined by the imperatives of production, or to a kind of superficial masking which modern development requires for the facilitation of marketing and the maintenance of social control."[37]

Frampton believes that instead of holding onto the idea that modernity would liberate us, like the avant-garde, we should take a more cautious approach, what he calls the "arrière-garde." Frampton's intent for architectural culture is that we should distance ourselves from "both the optimization of advanced technology and the ever-present tendency to regress into nostalgic historicism or the glibly decorative."[38] He states, "Architecture can only be sustained today as a critical practice if it assumes an arrière-garde position, that is to say, one which distances itself equally from the Enlightenment myth of progress and from a reactionary, unrealistic impulse to return to the architectonic forms of the preindustrial past."

Frampton's major contribution to the discourse is his stance against the "tabula rasa tendency of modernization,"[39] the homogenizing forces of consumer culture, and the universalizing tendencies of technology. He also sees the cultures of developing nations as being under threat by the forces of globalization. Frampton asks, "how to become modern and how to return to sources; how to revive an old dormant culture and take part in universal civilization."[40]

Frampton's answer to the universality of the global modern project was a search for the character of the region as a basis for expression. He promotes Critical Regionalism as a lens with which to better engage the specificities of place.

Frampton's impact has led to more sensitive regional and local approaches to urban design and architecture. This often includes a thorough analysis of urban morphology to promote urban historical continuity, as exemplified in the work of Anne Vernez Moudon, and others. These approaches aim to create more contextually responsive and culturally resonant urban environments that counteract the perceived placelessness of contemporary cities.

KENNETH FRAMPTON
"Critical Regionalism: Modern Architecture and Cultural Identity"
Modern Architecture: A Critical History

"The phenomenon of universalization, while being an advancement of mankind, at the same time constitutes a sort of subtle destruction, not only of traditional cultures, which might not be an irreparable wrong, but also of what I shall call for the time being the creative nucleus of great civilizations and great culture, that nucleus on the basis of which we interpret life, what I shall call in advance the ethical and mythical nucleus of mankind. The conflict springs up from there. We have the feeling that this single world civilization at the same time exerts a sort of attrition or wearing away at the expense of the cultural resources which have made the great civilizations of the past. This threat is expressed, among other disturbing effects, by the spreading before our eyes of a mediocre civilization which is the absurd counterpart of what I was just calling elementary culture. Everywhere throughout the world, one finds the same bad movie, the same slot machines, the same plastic or aluminum atrocities, the same twisting of language by propaganda. etc. It seems as if mankind, by approaching *en masse* a basic consumer culture. were also stopped *en masse* at a subcultural level. Thus we come to the crucial problem confronting nations just rising from underdevelopment. In order to get on to the road toward modernization, is it necessary to jettison the old cultural past which has been the *raison d'être* of a nation? . . . Whence the paradox: on the one hand, it (the nation) has to root itself in the soil of its past, forge a national spirit: and unfurl this spiritual and cultural revendication before the colonialist's personality. But in order to take part in modern civilization, it is necessary at the same time to take part in scientific, technical, and political rationality, something which very often requires the pure and simple abandon of a whole cultural past. It is a fact: every culture cannot sustain and absorb the shock of modern civilization. There is the paradox: how to become modern and to return to sources: how to revive an old, dormant civilization and take part in universal civilization. . . .

No one can say what will become of our civilization when it has really met different civilizations by means other than the shock of conquest and domination. But we have to admit that this encounter has not yet taken place at the level of an authentic dialogue. That is why we are in a kind of lull or interregnum in which we can no longer practice the dogmatism of a single truth and in which we are not yet capable of conquering the scepticism into which we have stepped. We are in a tunnel, at the twilight of dogmatism and the dawn of real dialogues."

Paul Ricoeur, 'Universal Civilization and National Cultures', 1961

The term 'Critical Regionalism' is not intended to denote the vernacular as this was once spontaneously produced by the combined interaction of climate, culture, myth and craft, but rather to identify those recent regional 'schools' whose primary aim has been to reflect and serve the limited constituencies

SPATIAL HETEROGENEITY, DIVERSITY, AND DIFFERENCE AFTER MODERNIST PLANNING

in which they are grounded. Among other factors contributing to the emergence of a regionalism of this order is not only a certain prosperity but also some kind of anti-centrist consensus – an aspiration at least to some form of cultural, economic and political independence.

The concept of a local or national culture is a paradoxical proposition not only because of the present obvious antithesis between rooted culture and universal civilization but also because all cultures, both ancient and modern, seem to have depended for their intrinsic development on a certain cross-fertilization with other cultures. As Ricoeur seems to imply in the passage quoted above, regional or national cultures must today, more than ever, be ultimately constituted as locally inflected manifestations of 'world culture'. It is surely no accident that this paradoxical proposition arises at a time when global modernization continues to undermine, with ever increasing force, all forms of traditional, agrarian-based, autochthonous culture. From the point of view of critical theory . . . we have to regard regional culture not as something given and relatively immutable but rather as something which has, at least today, to be self-consciously cultivated. Ricoeur suggests that sustaining any kind of authentic culture in the future will depend ultimately on our capacity to generate vital forms of regional culture while appropriating alien influences at the level of both culture and civilization . . .

. . . No-one has perhaps expressed the idea of a Critical Regionalism more forcefully than Harris, in 'Regionalism and Nationalism', an address which he first gave to the North West Regional Council of the AIA in Eugene, Oregon, in 1954. This was the occasion when he first advanced his felicitous distinction between restricted and liberated regionalism:

Opposed to the Regionalism of Restriction is another type of regionalism; the Regionalism of Liberation. This is the manifestation of a region that is *especially in tune with the emerging thought of the time.* We call such a manifestation 'regional' *only because it has not yet emerged elsewhere.* It is the genius of this region to be more than ordinarily aware and more than ordinarily free. Its virtue is that its manifestation has *significance for the world outside itself.* To express this regionalism architecturally it is necessary that there be building – preferably a lot of building – at one time. Only so can the expression be sufficiently general, sufficiently varied, sufficiently forceful to capture people's imaginations and provide a friendly climate long enough for a new school of design to develop.

San Francisco was made for Maybeck. Pasadena was made for Greene and Greene. Neither could have accomplished what he did in any other place or time. Each used the materials of the place: but it is not the materials that distinguish the work.

. . . A region may develop ideas. A region may accept ideas. Imaginations and intelligence are necessary for both. In California in the late Twenties and Thirties modern European ideas met a still developing regionalism. In New England, on the other hand, European Modernism met a rigid and restrictive regionalism that at first resisted and then surrendered. New England accepted European Modernism whole because its own regionalism had been reduced to a collection of restrictions.

Despite an apparent freedom of expression, such a level of liberative regionalism is difficult to achieve in North America today. Within the current proliferation of highly individualistic forms of expression (work which is often patronizing and self-indulgent rather than critical) only a few firms today display any profound commitment to the unsentimental cultivation of a rooted American culture. An atypical example of current 'regional' work in North America is the sensitively sited houses designed by Andrew Batey and Mark Mack for the Napa Valley area in California; another is the work of the architect Harry Wolf, whose activity has been largely restricted to North Carolina. Wolf's metaphorical approach to placemaking was polemically demonstrated in his 1982 competition entry for the Fort Lauderdale Riverfront Plaza. As his description indicates, the intention was to inscribe the city's history into the site through the incidence of light.

The worship of the sun and the measurement of time from its light reach back to the earliest recorded history of man. It is interesting to note in the case of Fort Lauderdale that if one were to follow a 26° latitudinal line around the globe, one would find Fort Lauderdale in the company of Ancient Thebes – the throne of the Egyptian sun god, Ra. Further to the East, one would find Jaipur, India, where heretofore. The largest equinoctial sundial in the world was built 110 years prior to the founding of Fort Lauderdale.

Mindful of these magnificent historical precedents, we sought a symbol that would speak of the past, present and future of Fort Lauderdale . . . To capture the sun in symbol a great sundial is incised on the Plaza site and the gnomon of the sundial bisects the site on its north-south axis. The gnomon of the double blade rises from the south at 26° 5' parallel to Fort Lauderdale's latitude . . . .

Each of the significant dates in Fort Lauderdale's history is recorded in the great blade of the sundial. With careful calculation the sun angles are perfectly aligned with penetrations through the two blades to cast brilliant circles of light, landing on the otherwise shadowy side of the sundial. These shafts of light illuminate an appropriate historical marker serving as annual historical reminders.

In Europe the work of the architect Gino Valle may be considered regional inasmuch as his career has always been centred on the city of Udine. Aside from his concern for the city, Valle made one of the earliest post-war reinterpretations of the rural vernacular of Lombardy in his Casa Quaglia, built at Sutrio in 1954-56.

It is surely understandable that in Europe, where the vestigial city-state was still very much alive, such a regionalist impulse would emerge spontaneously after the Second World War when a number of significant architects were able to contribute to the culture of their native cities. Among those of the post-war generation who remained committed to a regional inflection one may count Ernst Gisel in Zurich, Jorn Utzon in Copenhagen, Vittorio Gregotti in Milan, Sverre Fehn in Oslo, Aris Konstantinidis in Athens, and last but by no means least Carlo Scarpa in Venice . . .

. . . In their article on the Critical Regionalism of the Greek architects Dimitris and Susana Antonakakis, entitled 'The Grid and the Pathway' (*Architecture in Greece*, 1981), Alex Tzonis and Liane Lefaivre demonstrate the ambiguous role played by the Schinkelschuler in the building of Athens and the founding of the Greek state:

"In Greece historicist regionalism in its neoclassical version had already met with opposition before the arrival of the Welfare State and of modern architecture. It is due to a very peculiar crisis which explodes around the end of the nineteenth century. Historicist regionalism here had grown not only out of a war of liberation; it had emerged out of interests to develop an urban élite set apart from the peasant world and its rural 'backwardness' and to create a dominance of town over country: hence the special appeal of historicist regionalism, based on the book rather than experience, with its monumentality recalling another distant and forlorn élite. Historical regionalism had united people but it had also divided them."[1]

The various reactions which followed the proliferation of the 19th-century Greek Nationalist Neo-Classical style varied from the vernacular historicism of the 1920s to the committed modernism of the 1930s as this became manifest in the work of such architects as Stamo Papadaki and J.G. Despotopoulos. As Tzonis points out, a consciously regionalist modernism emerged in Greece with the earliest works of Aris Konstantinidis (his Eleusis house of 1938 and his Kifissia garden exhibition of 1940), and this line was developed further by Konstantinidis in the 1950s, in various low-cost housing schemes and in the hotels he designed for the Xenia national tourist organization between 1956 and 1966. In all of Konstantinidis's public work a tension appears between the universal rationality of the trabeated reinforced concrete frame and the autochthonous tactility of the native stone and blockwork which is used as infill. A much less equivocal regionalist spirit permeates the park and promenade that Dimitris Pikionis designed for the Philopappus Hill in 1957, on a site adjacent to the Acropolis in Athens. In this archaic landscape, as Tzonis and Lefaivre point out,

"Pikionis proceeds to make a work of architecture free from technological exhibitionism and compositional conceit (so typical of the mainstream of architecture of the 1950s), a stark naked object almost dematerialized, an ordering of 'places made for the occasion', unfolding around the hill for solitary contemplation, for intimate discussion, for a small gathering, for a vast assembly. . . . To weave this extraordinary braid of niches and passages and situations. Pikionis identifies appropriate components from the lived-in spaces of folk architecture, but in this project the link with the regional is not made out of tender emotion. In a completely different attitude, these envelopes of concrete events are studied with a cold empirical method, as if documented by an archaeologist. Neither is their selection and their positioning carried out to stir easy superficial emotion. They are platforms to be used in an everyday sense but to supply that which. In the context of contemporary architecture. Everyday life does not. The investigation of the local is the condition for reaching the concrete and the real, and for rehumanizing architecture."[2]

Tzonis sees the work of the Antonakakis partnership as combining the topographic path of Pikionis with the universal grid of Konstantinidis. This dialectical opposition seems to reflect once again that split between culture and civilization remarked on by Ricoeur. Perhaps no work expresses this duality more directly than their Benaki Street apartments built in Athens in 1975, a layered structure wherein a labyrinthine route drawn from the Greek island vernacular is woven into the regular grid of the supporting concrete frame.

As with the largely overlapping categories used in the previous chapter, Critical Regionalism is not so much a style as it is a critical category oriented towards certain common features, which may not always be present in the examples cited here. These features, or rather attitudes, may perhaps be best summarized as follows.

(1) Critical Regionalism has to be understood as a marginal practice, one which, while it is critical of modernization, nonetheless still refuses to abandon the emancipatory and progressive aspects of the modern architectural legacy. At the same time, Critical Regionalism's fragmentary and marginal nature serves to distance it both from normative optimization and from the naïve utopianism of the early Modern Movement. In contrast to the line that runs from Haussmann to Le Corbusier, it favours the small rather than the big plan.

(2) In this regard Critical Regionalism manifests itself as a consciously bounded architecture, one which rather than emphasizing the building as a free-standing object places the stress on the territory to be established by the structure erected on the site. This 'place-form' means that the

architect must recognize the physical boundary of his work as a kind of temporal limit – the point at which the present act of building stops.

(3) Critical Regionalism favours the realization of architecture as a *tectonic* fact rather than the reduction of the built environment to a series of ill assorted scenographic episodes.

(4) It may be claimed that Critical Regionalism is regional to the degree that it invariably stresses certain site-specific factors, ranging from the topography, considered as a three-dimensional matrix into which the structure is fitted, to the varying play of local light across the structure. Light is invariably understood as the primary agent by which the volume and the tectonic value of the work are revealed. An articulate response to climatic conditions is a necessary corollary to this. Hence Critical Regionalism is opposed to the tendency of 'universal civilization' to optimize the use of air-conditioning, etc. It tends to treat all openings as delicate transitional zones with a capacity to respond to the specific conditions imposed by the site, the climate and the light.

(5) Critical Regionalism emphasizes the tactile as much as the visual. It is aware that the environment can be experienced in terms other than sight alone. It is sensitive to such complementary perceptions as varying levels of illumination, ambient sensations of heat, cold, humidity and air movement, varying aromas and sounds given off by different materials in different volumes, and even the varying sensations induced by floor finishes, which cause the body to experience involuntary changes in posture, gait, etc. It is opposed to the tendency in an age dominated by media to the replacement of experience by information.

(6) While opposed to the sentimental simulation of local vernacular, Critical Regionalism will, on occasion, insert reinterpreted vernacular elements as disjunctive episodes within the whole. It will moreover occasionally derive such elements from foreign sources. In other words it will endeavour to cultivate a contemporary place oriented culture without becoming unduly hermetic, either at the level of formal reference or at the level of technology. In this regard, it tends towards the paradoxical creation of a regionally based 'world culture', almost as though this were a precondition for achieving a relevant form of contemporary practice.

(7) Critical Regionalism tends to flourish in those cultural interstices which in one way or another are able to escape the optimizing thrust of universal civilization. Its appearance suggests that the received notion of the dominant cultural centre surrounded by dependent, dominated satellites is ultimately an inadequate model by which to assess the present state of modern architecture.

1   A. Tzonis and L. Lefaivre, 'The Grid and the Pathway. An Introduction to the Work of Dimitris and Susana Antonakakis', Architecture in Greece, no. 15, 1981, 178.

2   L. Lefaivre and A. Tzonis, 'Dimitri Pikionis. Pathway up the Acropolis and the Philopappos Hill, Athens, Greece 1953–57', in Critical Regionalism. Architecture and Identity in a Globalized World (2003), 70.

Kenneth Frampton, "Critical Regionalism: Modern Architecture and Cultural Identity" Modern Architecture: A Critical History (London: Thames and Hudson, 1983, now 5th ed): 314–317, 320–321, 325–327.

Kenneth Frampton aimed to infuse architecture in a global context with a regional character. In contrast, other architects and urbanists sought a deeper disciplinary exploration of spatial practices, aiming to break from historical references. Along with Peter Eisenman and several other architects,

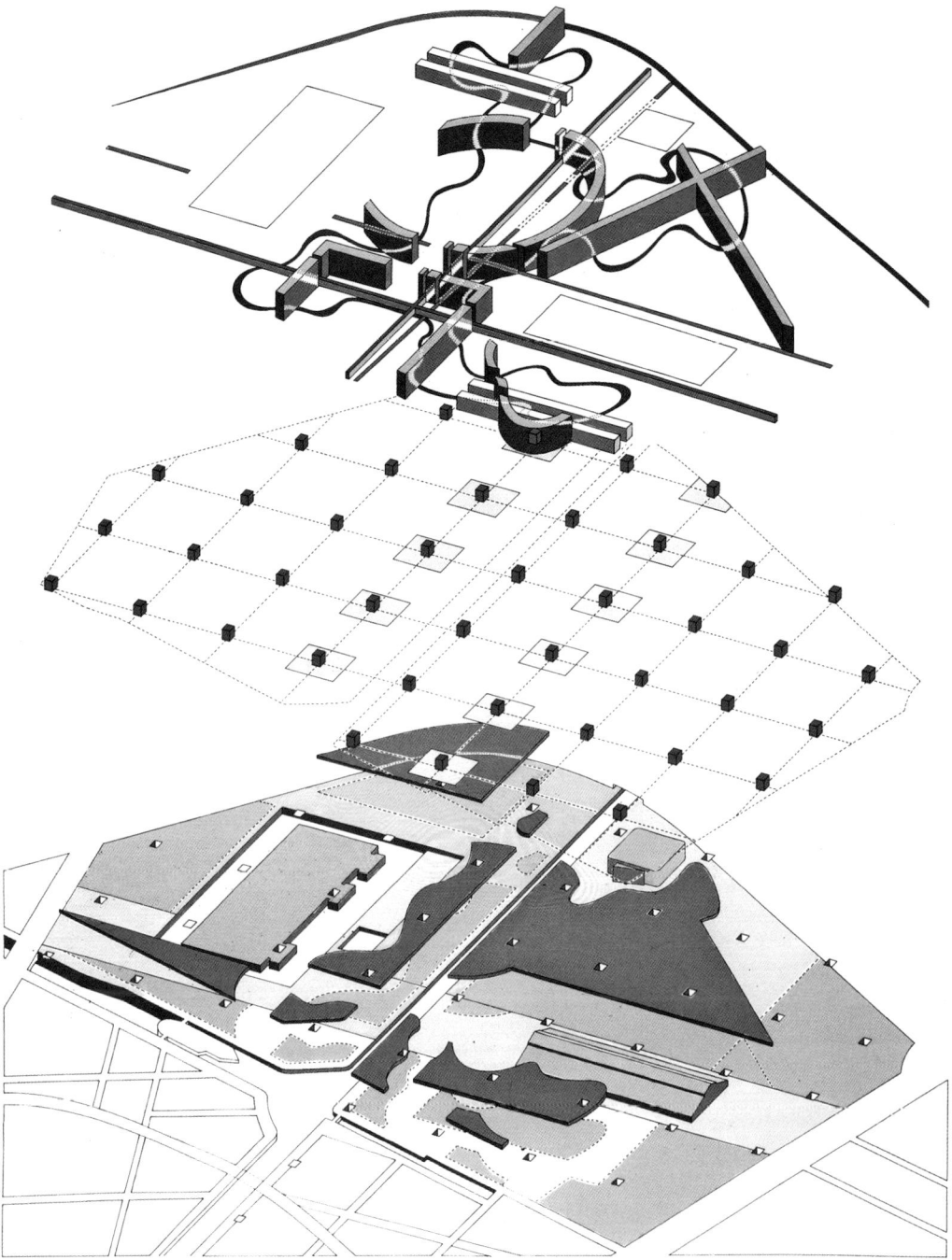

FIGURE 1.2 Axonometric drawing of systems deploying layers of points, lines, and surfaces, where the points represent recombinations of elements to form follies distributed in the landscape. Parc de la Villette, Paris. Bernard Tschumi Architects, 1982–7.

Bernard Tschumi had embraced the philosophy of Jacques Derrida, applying theories of deconstruction towards spatial design. Derrida's deconstruction is a philosophical method that seeks to reveal the inherent contradictions and ambiguities in texts and ideas by challenging the traditional binary oppositions and hierarchical structures upon which they rely. Tschumi's series of exhibition projects and eventual book, *Manhattan Transcripts* (1976–81), questioned the order and functionalist presumptions of space, in favor of dissociation and disjunction, drawing inspiration from the fragmented and layered nature of the urban experience.

Similar to *Learning from Las Vegas*, Tschumi also preoccupied himself with finding new media that could be associated with new ways of thinking about and diagramming the city, and he often used cinematic sequences and frames. His winning entry and subsequently constructed project for Parc de la Villette, completed in Paris in 1984, became an important example of this design approach. The design of Parc de la Villette rejected notions of unity and coherence, instead focusing on methods of repetition, distortion, and superposition, while advancing the narrative capacity of collage. Furthermore, Tschumi's design emphasized the juxtaposition of disparate elements and the creation of an open-ended spatial experience.

Tschumi recognized how "the concept of 'city' once implied a closed and finite entity."[41] But, he claimed, deregulation led the city to expand beyond its traditional boundaries. Much of the city does not belong to the realm of the visible anymore,"[42] he wrote. In addition, Tschumi theorized how the speed of the car "expands time by contracting space," thereby negating physical dimensions."[43]

In his writings and design projects, Bernard Tschumi has questioned the notions of "unity" and "stability."[44] His writings note the "crisis of the grand narratives of modernity" and of the "coherent totality" of the contemporary city, which, he noted, lacked "boundaries delineating a coherent and homogenous whole." Instead, he declared, "we inhabit a fractured space, made of accidents, where figures are disintegrated, *dis*-integrated."[45] He argued that it is through epistemological ruptures that new structures are brought forth, calling for "a need to discard established categories of meaning and contextual histories."

BERNARD TSCHUMI
"De-, Dis-, Ex-"
Architecture and Disjunction

The city and its architecture lose their symbols – no more monuments, no more axes, no more anthropomorphic symmetries, but instead fragmentation, parcellization, atomization, as well as the random superimposition of images that bear no relationship to one another, except through their collision.

1. DISJUNCTION AND CULTURE

The paradigm of the architect passed down to us through the modern period is that of the form-giver, the creator of hierarchical and symbolic structures characterized, on the one hand, by their unity of parts and, on the other, by the transparency of form to meaning. (The modern, rather than modernist, subject of architecture is referred to here so as to indicate that this unified perspective far exceeds our recent past.) . . .

4. STRATEGIES OF DISJUNCTION

Although, the notion of disjunction is not to be seen as an architectural concept, it has effects that are impressed upon the site, the building, even the program, according to the dissociative logic governing the work. If one were to define disjunction, moving beyond its dictionary meaning, one would insist on the idea of limit, of interruption. Both the *Transcripts* and La Villette employ different elements of a strategy of disjunction. This strategy takes the form of a systematic exploration of one or more themes: for example, frames and sequences in the case of the *Transcripts*, and superposition and repetition in La Villette. Such explorations can never be conducted in the abstract, *ex nihilo*: one works within the discipline of architecture-though with an awareness of other fields: literature, philosophy, or even film theory.

5. LIMITS

The notion of the limit is evident in the practice of Joyce, and Bataille and Artaud, who all worked at the edge of philosophy and nonphilosophy, of literature and nonliterature. The attention paid today to Jacques Derrida's deconstructive approach also represents an interest in the work at the limit: the analysis of concepts in the most rigorous and internalized manner, but also their analysis from without, so as to question what these concepts and their history hide, as repression or dissimulation. Such examples suggest that there is a need to consider the question of limits in architecture. They act as reminders (to me) that my own pleasure has never surfaced in looking at buildings, at the great works of the history or, the present of architecture, but, rather, in dismantling them. To paraphrase Orson Welles: "I don't like architecture, I like making architecture."

6. NOTATION

The work on notation undertaken in *The Manhattan Transcripts* was an attempt to deconstruct the components of architecture. The different modes of notation employed were aimed at grasping domains that, though normally excluded from most architectural theory, are indispensable to work at the margins, or limits, of architecture. Although no mode of notation, whether mathematical or logical, can transcribe the full complexity of the architectural phenomenon, the progress of architectural notation is linked to the renewal of both architecture and its accompanying concepts of culture. Once the traditional components have been dismantled, reassembly is an extended process; above all, what is ultimately a transgression of classical and modern canons should not be permitted to regress toward formal empiricism. Hence the disjunctive strategy used both in the *Transcripts* and at La Villette, in which facts never quite connect, and relations of conflict are carefully maintained, rejecting synthesis or totality. The project is never achieved, nor are the boundaries ever definite.

7. DISJUNCTION AND THE AVANT-GARDE

As Derrida points out, architectural and philosophical concepts do not disappear overnight. The once fashionable "epistemological break" notwithstanding, ruptures always occur within an old fabric that is constantly dismantled and dislocated in such a way that its ruptures lead to new concepts or structures. In architecture such disjunction implies that at no moment can any part become a synthesis or self-sufficient totality; each part leads to another, and every construction is off-balance, constituted by the traces of another construction. It could also be constituted by the traces of an event, a program. It can lead to new concepts, as one objective here is to understand a new concept of the city, of architecture . . .

. . . The concept of disjunction is incompatible with a static, autonomous, structural view of architecture. But it is not anti-autonomy or anti-structure; it simply implies constant, mechanical operations that systematically produce dissociation in space and time, where an architectural element only functions by colliding with a programmatic element, with the movement of bodies, or whatever. In this manner, disjunction becomes a systematic and theoretical tool for the making of architecture.

De-, Dis-, Ex-

Cities today have no visible limits. In America, they never had. In Europe, however, the concept of "city" once implied a closed and finite entity. The old city had walls and gates. But these have long ceased to function. Are there other types of gates, new gates to replace the gates of the past? Are the new gates those electronic warning systems installed in airports, screening passengers for weapons? Have electronics and, more generally, technology replace the boundaries, the guarded borders of the past?

The walls surrounding the city have disappeared and, with them, the rules that made the distinction between inside and outside, despite politicians' and planners' guidelines, despite geographical and administrative boundaries. In "*L'Espace Critique*", Paul Virilio develops a challenging argument for anyone concerned with the making of urban society: Cities have become *deregulated*. This deregulation is reinforced by the fact that much of the city does not belong to the realm of the visible anymore. What was once called urban design has been replaced by a composite of invisible systems. Why should architects still talk about monuments? Monuments are invisible now. They are *disproportionate* – so large (at the scale of the world) that they cannot be seen. Or so small (at the scale of computer chips) that they cannot be seen either . . .

. . . History, memory, and tradition, once called to the rescue by architectural ideologists, become nothing but modes of disguise, fake regulations, so as to avoid the question of transience and temporality . . .

. . . The crisis of these grand narratives, their coherent totality, is also the crisis of limits. As with the contemporary city, there are no more boundaries delineating a coherent and homogeneous whole. On the contrary, we inhabit a fractured space, made of accidents, where figures are disintegrated, *dis*-integrated. From a sensibility developed during centuries around the "appearance of a stable image" ("balance," "equilibrium," "harmony"), today we favor a sensibility of the disappearance of unstable images: first movies (twenty-four images per second), then television, then computer-generated images, and recently (among a few architects) disjunctions, dislocations, deconstructions. Virilio argues that the abolition of permanence – through the collapse of the notion of distance as a time factor – confuses reality . . . The city and its architecture lose their symbols – no more monuments, no more axes, no more anthropomorphic symmetries, but instead fragmentation, parcellization, atomization, as well as the random superimposition of images that bear no relationship to one another, except through their collision. No wonder that some architectural projects sublimate the idea of *explosion* . . .

. . . initially, the sciences were about substance, about foundation: geology, physiology, physics, and gravity. And architecture was very much part of that concern, with its focus on solidity, firmness, structure, and hierarchy. Those foundations began to crumble in the twentieth century. Relativity, quantum theory, the uncertainty principle: this shakeup occurred not only in physics, we know, but also in philosophy, the social sciences, and economics.

How then can architecture maintain some solidity, some degree of certainty? It seems impossible today – unless one decides that the accident or the explosion is to be called the rule, the new regulation, through a sort of philosophical inversion that considers the accident the norm and continuity the exception.

No more certainties, no more continuities. We hear that energy, as well as matter, is a discontinuous structure of points: punctum, quantum. Question: could the only certainty be the *point*?

The crises of determinism, or cause-and-effect relationships, and of continuity completely challenge recent architectural thought.

"To represent construction or to construct representation" (Virilio): this is the new question of our time. As Albert Einstein said, "There is no scientific truth, only temporary representations, ever-accelerating sequences of representation." In fact, we are forced to go through a complete reconsideration of all concepts of figuration and representation: the constant storm of images (whether drawings, graphs, photographs, films, television, or computer-generated images) increasingly negates any attempt to restore the Renaissance ideal of the unity of reality and its representation. The concept of double-coding was the last and futile attempt to keep some of that ideal intact by establishing a new relation between communication and tradition

. . . the problem is not a problem of images: gables and classical orders, however silly, are free to be consumed by whoever wishes to do so. But to pretend that these images could suggest new rules and regulations in architecture and urbanism by transcending modernism is simply misplaced.

There are no more rules and regulations. The current metropolitan deregulation caused by the dis-industrialization of European and American cities, by the collapse of zoning strategies, contradicts any attempt to develop new sets of regulating forces, however desirable it may be for some. The 1987 Wall Street "crash" and its relation to the economic deregulation that immediately preceded it is another illustration that an important change has taken place. Let me go back again to Virilio's argument. In the Middle Ages, society was self-regulated, auto-regulated. Regulation took place at its center. The prince of the city was the ruler; there was a direct cause-and-effect relationship between rules and everyday life, between the weight of masonry and the way that buildings were built.

In the industrial era, societies became artificially regulated. The power of economic and industrial forces took over by establishing a coherent structure throughout the whole territory: control was defined at the limits, at the edges of society. The relation between rules and everyday life ceased to be clear, and so large bureaucracies and administrators took over. Regulation was not at the center anymore but at the periphery. Abstract architecture used grids on its sheds International-style, before it discovered that one could decorate the same shed Multinational-style-regardless of what happened in them. Function, form, and meaning ceased to have any relationship to one another.

Today we have entered the age of deregulation, where control takes place *outside* of society, as in those computer programs that feed on one another endlessly in a form of autonomy, recalling the autonomy of language described by Michel Foucault. We witness the separation of people and language, the decentering of the subject. Or, we may say, the complete *decentering* of society.

> Ex-centric, dis-integrated, dis-located dis-juncted, deconstructed, dismantled disassociated, discontinuous, deregulated ... de-, dis -, ex-. These are the prefixes of today. Not post-, neo-, or pre-.
>
> Bernard Tschumi (1987). "De-, Dis-, Ex-" in *Architecture and Disjunction*. Cambridge: MIT Press. pp. 214–26.

This chapter covered a diverse set of theoretical stances in response to orthodox Modernism and their associated design approaches, surveying an era from the 1960s to the "pre-digital" early 1990s. These authors challenged the notions of universalization, unity, and the utopianism of modernist urbanism. Questioning the ways in which cities were understood and designed in the modernist paradigm, they embraced the pluralistic ethos associated with postmodernity, focusing on spatial heterogeneity, difference and diversity. Their work emphasized the importance of context, history, and local culture in shaping the urban fabric, and sought to create urban environments that celebrated the complexity and diversity of contemporary urban life. By rejecting the reductive and homogenizing tendencies of modernist urban design, these theorists and practitioners paved the way for more nuanced, contextually sensitive, and imaginative approaches to the design of cities.

2

Urbanism and Models of Design Complexity

This second chapter surveys the formation of new design theories and practices from the 1990s that address and express the complexities of urbanism. This era marks a transition towards the early digital era. The authors and designers featured in this chapter seek to both comprehend and create complex organizational structures in architecture and urbanism.

During the 1990s, a growing number of architects, landscape architects, and urban designers became fascinated by the city—not merely as a depository of history, culture, and civilization, but because of a newfound appreciation for the inherent complexity of urbanism. For instance, Zaha Hadid, the prominent architect, in a rare interview, said in 1995:

> Our interest is more about how you respond to the city, how through a new geometric plan for the ground you can open spaces, making them more public and more civic. How you manipulate the space, whether it's to be layered, whether it's to be compressed or expanded . . . The main issue is how you deal with building in the city, and in particular, how you deal with the ground. It is an issue that has not yet been resolved . . . One of the problems with the early moderns was that the ground condition was not programmed.[1]
>
> 1 Cecilia Fernando Marquez and Richard Levene Eds., Zaha Hadid 1983-1995, (El Croquis 52 + 73, 1995): 13

In another interview, she spoke of the complexity inherent in the city and nature:

> My ideas come from observation: of nature, of people, of the city. It's always about how people will use the space. We often look at the logic and coherence [of] nature's systems when we are working to create environments—as well as geological and landscape formations such as erosion, and the organic morphology of cells and biology. People do ask 'why are there no straight lines, why no 90 degrees in your work?' This is because life is not made in a grid. If you think of a natural landscape, it's not even and regular, but people go to these places and think it's very natural, very relaxing. We think that one can do that in architecture and design.[1]
>
> 1 "Queen of the Curve: An Interview with Zaha Hadid," available online: https://www.lumens.com/the-edit/the-makers/interview-with-zaha-hadid/. Accessed June 3 2024

The early digital era birthed a generation keen on understanding urban behaviors—their fluid transformations, crowd dynamics, and spatial manifestations. City design began to embrace urbanism's intrinsic complexity, recognizing cities as the interplay of various forces, systems, and agencies. Theorists and practitioners heralded urban complexity as a new design paradigm.

This shift in perspective traces back to earlier decades of the twentieth century. The Modernist perspectives of cities as rigid, machine-like constructs has evolved into a view that sees them as dynamic, intertwined systems. Influential texts such as Jane Jacobs' *The Death and Life of Great American Cities* (1961) challenged the established modernist urban planning models of the time.[1] Jacobs advocated for a more grass-roots, bottom-up approach to urban development, emphasizing community vibrancy and its "sidewalk ballet." Later that decade, Ian McHarg's *Design with Nature* (1969) introduced a pioneering approach to environmental planning, promoting the integration of natural processes and systems into urban design, viewing cities as part of larger ecological systems.[2]

New insights about cities and their design also stemmed from the field of mathematics, such as calculus, graph theory, and topology. One such example is "The City is Not a Tree" (1965), the seminal essay by Christopher Alexander, in which he introduces a fundamental critique of modernist urban planning.[3] At the core of Alexander's argument is a criticism of the modernist tendency to organize cities in clear-cut, hierarchical, and segregated ways. Modernist planners and architects, influenced by ideals of order, efficiency, and newness, often designed urban areas as isolated zones dedicated to specific functions: living, working, leisure, etc. Alexander argued that their layouts are too simplistic and do not reflect the rich complexity of organic cities.

Alexander's key argument revolves around the contrast between "tree" and "semi-lattice" structures. A tree is a hierarchical structure with singular connections, resembling branches on a tree that do not reconnect. A semi-lattice is a web-like network where points can have multiple overlapping connections. While trees have clear paths from top to bottom, semi-lattices feature crisscrossing, interconnected paths. Historic cities such as Siena or Kyoto have grown organically over time and exhibit the complex characteristics of a semilattice, whereas modern cities, like Chandigarh, are often designed with tree-like structures, which Alexander argues lack the richness and humanity of organic urban forms. He suggests that tree-like cities, while easier for designers to conceptualize and manage, significantly reduce the complexity and vibrancy of urban life, leading to fragmented and incoherent urban environments.

Alexander's work is significant for architecture and urban design as it challenges the modernist planning paradigm and highlights the need to embrace the complexity of overlaps in urban systems. By emphasizing the human dimension of cities and advocating for a more holistic approach that respects the intricate social relationships within urban environments, Alexander calls for a re-evaluation of how cities are conceived, understood, and designed. The semi-lattice structure, he argues, is more reflective of human needs and the multifaceted interactions that characterize vibrant urban life. The semilattice is "the structure of a complex fabric," Alexander writes. "It is the structure of living things, of great paintings and symphonies."[4]

CHRISTOPHER ALEXANDER
"The City is Not a Tree"

The tree of my title is not a green tree with leaves. It is the name of an abstract structure. I shall contrast it with another, more complex abstract structure called a semilattice. In order to relate these abstract structures to the nature of the city, I must first make a simple distinction.

I want to call those cities which have arisen more or less spontaneously over many, many years natural cities. And I shall call those cities and parts of cities which have been deliberately created by designers and planners artificial cities. Siena, Liverpool, Kyoto, Manhattan are examples of natural cities. Levittown, Chandigarh and the British New Towns are examples of artificial cities.

It is more and more widely recognized today that there is some essential ingredient missing from artificial cities. When compared with ancient cities that have acquired the patina of life, our modern attempts to create cities artificially are, from a human point of view, entirely unsuccessful.

Both the tree and the semilattice are ways of thinking about how a large collection of many small systems goes to make up a large and complex system. More generally, they are both names for structures of sets.

In order to define such structures, let me first define the concept of a set. A set is a collection of elements which for some reason we think of as belonging together. Since, as designers, we are concerned with the physical living city and its physical backbone, we must naturally restrict ourselves to considering sets which are collections of material elements such as people, blades of grass, cars, molecules, houses, gardens, water pipes, the water molecules in them etc.

When the elements of a set belong together because they co-operate or work together somehow, we call the set of elements a system . . .

. . . From the designer's point of view, the physically unchanging part of this system is of special interest . . . I define this fixed part as a unit of the city. It derives its coherence as a unit both from the forces which hold its own elements together and from the dynamic coherence of the larger living system which includes it as a fixed invariant part.

Of the many, many fixed concrete subsets of the city which are the receptacles for its systems and can therefore be thought of as significant physical units, we usually single out a few for special consideration. In fact, I claim that whatever picture of the city someone has is defined precisely by the subsets he sees as units . . .

. . . the choice of subsets alone endows the collection of subsets as a whole with an overall structure. This is the structure which we are concerned with here. When the structure meets certain conditions it is called a semilattice. When it meets other more restrictive conditions, it is called a tree.

The semilattice axiom goes like this: *A collection of sets forms a semilattice if and only if, when two overlapping sets belong to the collection, the set of elements common to both also belongs to the collection . . . .*

. . . However in this chapter we are not so much concerned with the fact that a tree happens to be a semilattice, but with the difference between trees and those more general semilattices which are not trees because they do contain overlapping units. We are concerned with the difference between structures in which no overlap occurs, and those structures in which overlap does occur.

It is not merely the overlap which makes the distinction between the two important. Still more important is the fact that the semilattice is potentially a much more complex and subtle structure than a tree. We may see just how much more complex a semilattice can be than a tree in the following fact: a tree based on 20 elements can contain at most 19 further subsets of the 20, while a semilattice based on the same 20 elements can contain more than 1,000,000 different subsets.

This enormously greater variety is an index of the great structural complexity a semilattice can have when compared with the structural simplicity of a tree. It is this lack of structural complexity, characteristic of trees, which is crippling our conceptions of the city . . .

. . . The units of which an artificial city is made up are always organized to form a tree. So that we get a really clear understanding of what this means, and shall better see its implications, let us define a tree once again. Whenever we have a tree structure, it means that within this structure no piece of any unit is ever connected to other units, except through the medium of that unit as a whole . . .

. . . Now, why is it that so many designers have conceived cities as trees when the natural structure is in every case a semilattice? Have they done so deliberately, in the belief that a tree structure will serve the people of the city better? Or have they done it because they cannot help it, because they are trapped by a mental habit, perhaps even trapped by the way the mind works – because they cannot encompass the complexity of a semilattice in any convenient mental form, because the mind has an overwhelming predisposition to see trees wherever it looks and cannot escape the tree conception?

I shall try to convince you that it is for this second reason that trees are being proposed and built as cities – that is, because designers, limited as they must be by the capacity of the mind to form intuitively accessible structures, cannot achieve the complexity of the semilattice in a single mental act . . .

. . . This is the problem we face as designers. While we are not, perhaps, necessarily occupied with the problem of total visualization in a single mental act, the principle is still the same. The tree is accessible mentally and easy to deal with. The semilattice is hard to keep before the mind's eye and therefore hard to deal with.

It is known today that grouping and categorization are among the most primitive psychological processes. Modern psychology treats thought as a process of fitting new situations into existing slots and pigeonholes in the mind. Just as you cannot put a physical thing into more than one physical pigeonhole at once, so, by analogy, the processes of thought prevent you from putting a mental construct into more than one mental category at once. Study of the origin of these processes suggests that they stem essentially from the organism's need to reduce the complexity of its environment by establishing barriers between the different events that it encounters.

It is for this reason – because the mind's first function is to reduce the ambiguity and overlap in a confusing situation and because, to this end, it is endowed with a basic intolerance for ambiguity – that structures like the city, which do require overlapping sets within them, are nevertheless persistently conceived as trees . . .

. . . You are no doubt wondering by now what a city looks like which is a semilattice, but not a tree. I must confess that I cannot yet show you plans or sketches. It is not enough merely to make a demonstration of overlap - the overlap must be the right overlap. This is doubly important because it is so tempting to make plans in which overlap occurs for its own sake. This is essentially what the high-density 'life-filled' city plans of recent years do. But overlap alone does not give structure. It can also give chaos. A garbage can is full of overlap. To have structure, you must have the right overlap, and this is for us almost certainly different from the old overlap which we observe in historic cities. As the relationships between functions change, so the systems which need to overlap in order to receive these relationships must also change. The recreation of old kinds of overlap will be inappropriate, and chaotic instead of structured . . .

. . . When we think in terms of trees we are trading the humanity and richness of the living city for a conceptual simplicity which benefits only designers, planners, administrators and developers. Every time a piece of a city is torn out, and a tree made to replace the semilattice that was there before, the city takes a further step toward dissociation . . .

. . . It not only takes from the young the company of those who have lived long, but worse, it causes the same rift inside each individual life. As you pass into Sun City, and into old age, your ties with your own past will be unacknowledged, lost and therefore broken. Your youth will no longer be alive in your old age – the two will be dissociated; your own life will be cut in two.

For the human mind, the tree is the easiest vehicle for complex thoughts. But the city is not, cannot and must not be a tree. The city is a receptacle for life. If the receptacle severs the overlap of the strands of life within it, because it is a tree, it will be like a bowl full of razor blades on edge, ready to cut up whatever is entrusted to it. In such a receptacle life will be cut to pieces. If we make cities which are trees, they will cut our life within to pieces.

Christopher Alexander, "The City is Not a Tree", Part 1, *Architectural Forum* 122, no. 1 (April 1965): 58–62; Part 2, *Architectural Forum* 122, no. 2 (May 1965): 58-61.

In the mid-twentieth century, complexity theory and the theory of nonlinearity emerged, following advances in mathematics, physics, and computer science. Nonlinearity refers to systems where output is not directly proportional to input, leading to complex behaviors and patterns. These would shape how we conceive of cities and their planning. Manuel De Landa's book, *A Thousand Years of Nonlinear History* (1997) researches various forms of nonlinear dynamics.[5] The key idea is that historical processes, whether in linguistics, economics, or biology, are not linear or determined by a few factors but are instead complex, with many interacting components leading to emergent phenomena. In the context of cities, urban environments exemplify nonlinear systems: small changes in policy, infrastructure, or demographics can lead to unexpectedly large shifts in urban dynamics, culture, and growth. The complex interplay of factors such as transportation, housing, social interactions, and economic drivers in cities often results in outcomes that are not immediately predictable, necessitating a nonlinear approach to urban planning and understanding.

De Landa's work is significant for architecture and urban planning because it challenges modernist narratives and encourages professionals to think of cities, buildings, and landscapes as evolving systems with many interconnected parts, rather than as static entities or the products of top-down modes of planning. Modernist urban planning often relied on master plans and overarching designs, assuming that cities could be organized and controlled in a linear order. However, by understanding cities as complex, evolving systems with emergent properties, urban planners can better appreciate the unpredictability and organic growth of urban environments. Instead of seeing cities as machines, as modernist Le Corbusier did, De Landa sees them as ecosystems, dependent on flows of organic materials, and often with a parasitic relationship to their hinterlands.

MANUEL DE LANDA
"Introduction"
A Thousand Years of Nonlinear History

Despite its title, this is not a book of history but a book of philosophy. It is, however, a deeply historical philosophy, which holds as its central thesis that all structures that surround us and form our reality (mountains, animals and plants, human languages, social institutions) are the products of specific historical processes. To be consistent, this type of philosophy must of necessity take real history as its starting point. The problem is, of course, that those who write history, however scholarly, do so from a given philosophical point of view, and this would seem to trap us in a vicious circle. But just as history and philosophy may interact in such a way as to make an objective assessment of reality impossible – when entrenched worldviews and routine procedures for gathering historical evidence constrain each other negatively – they can also interact positively and turn this mutual dependence into a virtuous circle. Moreover, it may be argued that this positive interaction has already begun. Many historians have abandoned their Eurocentrism and now question the very rise of the West (Why not China or Islam? is now a common question), and some have even left behind their anthropocentrism and include a host of nonhuman histories in their accounts. A number of philosophers, for their part, have benefited from the new historical evidence that scholars such as Fernand Braudel and William McNeil have unearthed, and have used it as a point of departure for a new, revived form of materialism, liberated from the dogmas of the past.

Philosophy is not, however, the only discipline that has been influenced by a new awareness of the role of historical processes. Science, too, has acquired a historical consciousness. It is not an exaggeration to say that in the last two or three decades history has infiltrated physics, chemistry, and biology. It is true that nineteenth-century thermodynamics had already introduced time's arrow into physics, and hence the idea of irreversible historical processes. And the theory of evolution had already shown that animals and plants were not embodiments of eternal essences but piecemeal historical constructions, slow accumulations of adaptive traits cemented together via reproductive isolation. However, the classical versions of these two theories incorporated a rather weak notion of history into their conceptual machinery: both classical thermodynamics and Darwinism admitted only one possible historical outcome, the reaching of thermal equilibrium or of the fittest design. In both cases, once this point was reached, historical processes ceased to count. In a sense, optimal design or optimal distribution of energy represented an end of history for these theories . . .

. . . And what is true of physical systems is all the more true of biological ones. Attractors and bifurcations are features of the system in which the dynamics are not only far from equilibrium but also *nonlinear*, that is, in which there are strong mutual attractions (or feedback) between components. Whether the system in question is composed of molecules or of living creatures, it will exhibit endogenously generated stable states, as well as sharp transitions between states, as long as there is feedback and an intense flow of energy coursing through the system . . .

. . . human history did not follow a straight line, as if everything pointed toward civilized societies as humanity's ultimate goal. On the contrary. At each bifurcation alternative stable states were possible, and once actualized, they coexisted and interacted with one another.

. . . In Chapter One I approach this synthesis through an exploration of the history of urban economics since the Middle Ages. I take as my point of departure a view shared by several materialist historians (principally Braudel and McNeill): the specific dynamics of European towns were one important reason why China and Islam, despite their early economic and technological lead, were eventually subjected to Western domination. Given that an important aim of this book is to approach history in a nonteleological way, the eventual conquest of the millennium by the West will not be viewed as the result of "progress" occurring there while failing to take place outside of Europe, but as the result of certain dynamics (such as the mutually stimulating dynamics involved in arms races) that intensify the accumulation of knowledge and technologies, and of certain institutional norms and organizations. Several different forms of mutual stimulation (or of "positive feedback," to use the technical term) will be analyzed, each involving a different set of individuals and institutions and evolving in a different area of the European urban landscape. Furthermore, it will be argued that the Industrial Revolution can be viewed in terms of reciprocal stimulation between technologies and institutions, whereby the elements involved managed to form a closed loop, so that the entire assemblage became self-sustaining. I refer to this historical narrative as "geological" because it concerns itself exclusively with dynamical elements (energy flow, nonlinear causality) that we have in common with rocks and mountains and other non-living historical structures.

Chapter Two addresses another sphere of reality, the world of germs, plants, and animals and hence views cities as ecosystems, albeit extremely simplified ones. This chapter goes beyond questions of inanimate energy flow to consider the flows of organic materials that have informed urban life since the Middle Ages. In particular, it considers the flow of food, which keeps cities alive and in most cases comes from outside the town itself. Cities appear as parasitic entities, deriving their sustenance from nearby rural regions or, via colonialism and conquest, from other lands. This chapter also considers the flow of genetic materials through generations – not so much the flow of human genes as those belonging to the animal and plant species that we have managed to domesticate, as well as those that have constantly eluded our control, such as weeds and microorganisms. Colonial enterprises appear in this chapter not only as a means to redirect food toward the motherland, but also as the means by which the genes of many nonhuman species have invaded and conquered alien ecosystems.

Finally, Chapter Three deals with the other type of "materials" that enter into the human mixture: linguistic materials. Like minerals, inanimate energy, food, and genes, the sounds, words, and syntactical constructions that make up language accumulated within the walls of medieval (and modern) towns and were transformed by urban dynamics. Some of these linguistic materials (learned, written Latin, for example) were so rigid and unchanging that they simply accumulated as a dead structure. But other forms of language (vulgar, spoken Latin) were dynamic entities capable of giving birth to new structures, such as French, Spanish, Italian, and Portuguese. This chapter traces the history of these emergences, most of them in urban environments, as well as of the eventual rigidification (through standardization) of the dialects belonging to regional and national capitals, and of the effects that several generations of media (the printing press, mass media, computer networks) have had on their evolution.

Each chapter begins its narrative in the year 1000 A.D. and continues (more or less linearly) to the year 2000. Yet, as I said above, despite their style of presentation, these three narratives do not constitute a "real" history of their subjects but rather a sustained philosophical meditation on some of the historical processes that have affected these three types of "materials" (energetic, genetic, and linguistic). The very fact that each chapter concentrates on a single "material" (viewing human history, as it were, from the point of view of that particular material) will make these narratives hardly recognizable as historical accounts. Yet, most of the generalizations to be found here have been made by historians and are not the product of pure philosophical speculation.

In the nonlinear spirit of this book, these three worlds (geological, biological, and linguistic) will not be viewed as the progressively more sophisticated stages of an evolution that culminates in humanity as its crowning achievement. It is true that a small subset of geological materials (carbon, hydrogen, oxygen, and nine other elements) formed the substratum needed for living creatures to emerge and that a small subset of organic materials (certain neurons in the brain) provided the substratum for language. But far from advancing in stages of increased perfection, these successive emergences were-and will be treated here as – mere accumulations of different types of materials, accumulations in which each successive layer does not form a new world closed in on itself but, on the contrary, results in coexistences and interactions of different kinds. Besides, each accumulated layer is animated from within by self-organizing processes, and the forces and constraints behind this spontaneous generation of order are common to all three.

In a very real sense, reality is *a single matter-energy* undergoing phase transitions of various kinds, with each new layer of accumulated "stuff" simply enriching the reservoir of nonlinear dynamics and nonlinear combinatorics available for the generation of novel structures and processes. Rocks and winds, germs and words, are all different manifestations of this dynamic material reality, or, in other words, they all represent the different ways in which this single matter-energy *expresses itself*. Thus, what follows will not be a chronicle of "man" and "his" historical achievements, but a philosophical meditation on the history of matter-energy in its different forms and of the multiple coexistences and interactions of these forms. Geological, organic, and linguistic materials will all be allowed to "have their say" in the form that this book takes, and the

> resulting chorus of material voices will, I hope, give us a fresh perspective on the events and processes that have shaped the history of this millennium.
>
> Manuel De Landa, "Introduction", *A Thousand Years of Nonlinear History* (Cambridge, MA: MIT Press, 1977): 11–13; 257–260; 271–274.

In the 1990s, many designers and design theorists turned to complexity theory as a guiding paradigm. Instead of understanding the city from a mechanical perspective, they understood it to be a biological one, in which the emergent properties of a whole are greater than the sum of the parts, exemplified by the dynamic swarming behavior of a flock of birds, school of fish, or pack of mammals. Various other examples, such as Gaia theory, René Thom's catastrophe theory, and Waddington's "Epigenetic Landscape" also exhibited an interest in self-organization, emergence and morphogenesis, and the autonomous generation of form.

Although the complexity sciences were not wholly new paradigms, they had more potential for designers by the 1990s, since computational technologies had accelerated, making possible the analysis and simulation of complex systems. Architectural theorist Sanford Kwinter explored how cities, just as living organisms, are complex, adaptive systems he called "soft systems."[6] Architecture critic Charles Jencks also turned to complexity theory for new design directions, inspired by "cosmogenic truths" of self-organization and emergence, in his book, *Architecture of the Jumping Universe* (1995).[7] Steven Johnson, in his book, *Emergence: the Connected Lives of Ants, Brains, Cities and Software* (2001), sought to associate similar dynamic patterns between the "emergent intelligence" of "a macrobehavior spawned by a million micromotives" of cities to the "higher level form . . . among the routers and fiber-optic lines of the internet.[8]

Kevin Kelly's book, *Out of Control: The New Biology of Machines, Social Systems, & the Economic World* (1992), popularized real-life consequences of complexity through examples, impacting how architects and urbanists were thinking about large collective and complex behavior. He wrote, "The marvel of the 'hive mind' is that no one is in control, and yet an invisible hand governs, a hand that emerges from very dumb members."[9]

With the new, or renewed, interest in organization during the 1990s, came the desire for developing and establishing appropriate design methods and techniques within the emerging culture of computational innovation. The authors selected in this chapter share ambitions to develop spatial expressions based on social and urban organizations, which they often mapped out as diagrams. They speculated on the formal generation of such organization models, such as a migration from a focus on the architectural *object* to the expanded *field* spaces of cities. Some authors, such as Greg Lynn, focus on how computation transforms urban design, leveraging the multifaceted nature of the city, as an extension of his interests in complex forms of architecture. He explores the design consequences of new digital capacities to create complex urban spaces and systems.

This shift was underpinned by a transition from the philosophy of Jacques Derrida to the ideas of Gilles Deleuze. This can be seen as a move from a focus on critique and deconstruction to a focus on affirmation, creativity, and the productive potential of multiplicity, as part of a heterogeneous and interconnected reality. For instance, Peter Eisenman's notion of "weak form" implies a multiplicity of meanings, displacing the perception of function and structure in architecture.[10] "Architecture has traditionally been a strong form discipline," he writes. Instead, he proposed architects should embrace "weak form". "Weak form derives from several ideas: that there is no single truth; that there is no decidability (things have to be undecidable, arbitrary); that things are no longer essential . . . that all is in the excess."[11]

Architecture and urbanism's newfound interest in design complexity was largely incubated and developed during the 1990s in academic contexts, particularly the *Paperless Studios* at the GSAPP at Columbia University in New York, and at the Architectural Association (AA) in London. Architecture critic Jeffrey Kipnis, initially in collaboration with Donald Bates of Lab Architecture Studio, and later in partnership with architect Bahram Shirdel, launched the Graduate Design Program (AAGDG) at the AA with the goal of discovering a new architectural language rooted in organizational heterogeneity. Kipnis critiqued Le Corbusier's modernist notion of architecture with its 'tabula rasa' approach that led to homogeneity. The AAGDG also pursued alternatives to the various techniques of collage, which many had come to view as exhausted. The technique of collage had remained a dominant design paradigm, as highlighted in Chapter 1. However, critics claimed that collage, despite its ability to create striking juxtapositions, ultimately fell short as a transformative design method. They contended that collage primarily functioned as a tool for recombination, limited to rearranging familiar forms rather than generating genuinely novel spatial configurations.

FIGURE 2.1 Aerial view of Melbourne's Federation Square, a vibrant cultural precinct and meeting place, with its distinctive architecture, laneways, and urban plazas. Designed by Lab Architecture Studio in 1997 and completed in 2002. Courtesy of Getty Images.

URBANISM AND MODELS OF DESIGN COMPLEXITY

> Phenomena such as flocking, schooling, swarming and crowd behaviours are characterized by transforming global patterns or organisations produced by 'populations' of elements in part-to-part relationships. Rather than being an a priori whole, each element communicates small differences of information to the rest. (Stan) Allen and (Jeffrey) Kipnis both associated these physical phenomena with new social orderings...Flocking may be the new figure for collective synchronization within a Post-Fordist economy.[1]
>
> 1 Michael Hensel, Christopher Hight, Achim Menges. "Forward", *Space Reader: Heterogeneous Space in Architecture*. Michael Hensel, Christopher Hight, Achim Menges, Eds. (London: John Wiley and Sons Inc., 2009); 31–32.

Kipnis, Shirdel, Lynn, and Eisenman, among others, developed the concept of "grafting" as a design methodology, offering greater potential for contextual integration and coherence than deemed possible through collage. Borrowing from horticulture, grafting refers to the process of joining two plants together so they grow as a single organism, integrating characteristics from each. In medicine, a "skin graft" involves transferring tissue from one part of the body to another. In architecture, grafting became a metaphor for the integration of disparate elements, forms, or styles into a cohesive organizational structure. It sought to maintain and subvert context simultaneously, employing a parallel that pursued both coherence and incongruity. The concept was relevant to urbanism, where grafting could generate typological and morphological diagrams to create provisional affiliations and ad hoc links within a given context, drawing attention to major and minor site influences.

Stan Allen, in his essay, "From Object to Field" (1997), also published in similar earlier titles, explores a shift in design thinking from viewing buildings as isolated objects and towards considering them as fields—dynamic, interconnected systems that engage with their environments. This approach emphasizes the relationships and interactions between different elements within a space, rather than focusing solely on the objectified form of discreet structures.[12]

Allen is concerned less by "the forms of things, as the forms between things," declaring Cubist compositional space of Modernism to be exhausted.[13] While painting and sculpture has moved beyond Cubist composition, he notes that architecture still adheres to Cubist compositional principles. Instead, he draws his inspiration from mathematical field theory, non-linear dynamics, and evolutionary change, while arguing for the capacity of fields to unify, from the bottom up, loosely connected aggregates. He shifts focus from top-down mechanisms towards a "more fluid, bottom-up approach," addressing "the dynamics of use, behavior of crowds and the complex geometry of masses in motion."[14]

Allen's approach rejects the notion of starting with a blank slate, or 'tabula rasa', advocating instead for harmonizing with pre-existing conditions. He argues that "working with not against the site, something new is produced by registering the complexity of the given."[15] Allen calls for the "logistics of context," as it is shaped over time and consisting of "multiplicities and collectivities." He calls on architecture to "learn to manage this complexity, which paradoxically, it can only do by giving up some measure of control. The logistics of context proposes a provisional and experimental approach to this task."[16]

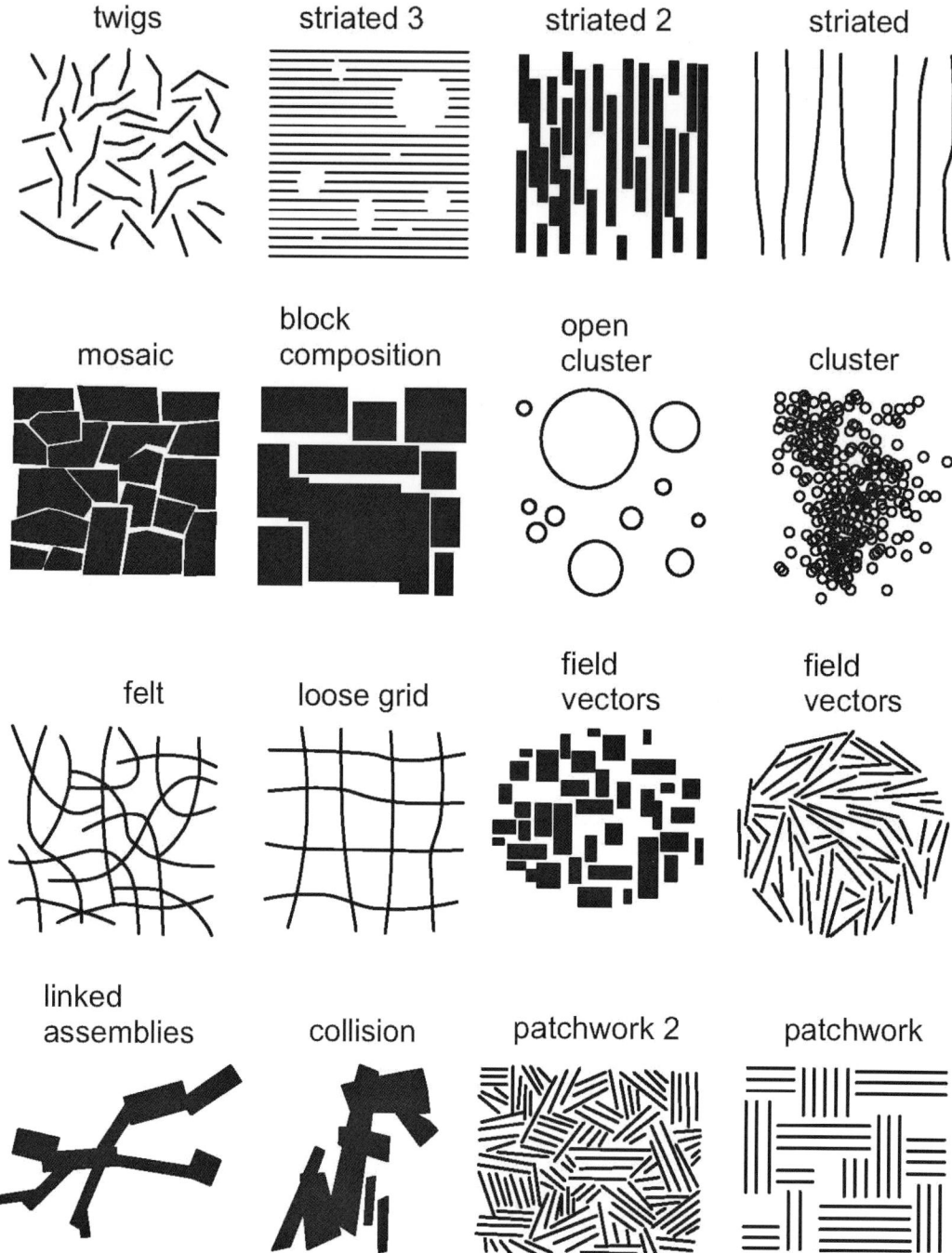

FIGURE 2.2 An array of organizational diagrams describing field conditions, articulating the relationship between space, form, and structure. Stan Allen, 1997.

Allen is concerned with systems which "operate at the edge of control" shifting attention from top-down regulatory mechanisms towards a "more fluid, bottom-up approach," addressing "the dynamics of use, behavior of crowds and the complex geometry of masses in motion."[17] He sees grids as one of many spatial arrangements that can be understood as fields. "All grids are fields but not all fields are grids,"[18] he declares.

Allen seeks to establish a dialectic between the figurative and the abstract, between "the figure not as a demarcated object but as an effect emerging from the field itself – as moments of intensity, as peaks or valleys within a continuous field."[19] As an example, he refers to Moiré patterns. This effect arises when two sets of uniform patterns or grids overlap, often slightly misaligned, yielding a newly emergent pattern. Characterized by the interaction between diverse layers, Moiré patterns epitomize for Allen the emergence of a pattern absent in any of the individual layers, exemplifying his thesis for design based on field theory.

STAN ALLEN
"From Object to Field"

The term "field conditions" is at once a reassertion of architecture's contextual assignment and at the same time a proposal to comply with such obligations.[1] Field conditions moves from the one toward the many: from individuals to collectives, from objects to fields. The term itself plays on double meaning. Architects work not only in the office or studio (in the laboratory) but in the field: on site, in contact with the fabric of architecture. 'Field survey', 'field office', 'verify in field': 'field conditions' here implies acceptance of the real in all its messiness and unpredictability. It opens architecture to material improvisation on site. Field conditions treats constraints as opportunity and moves away from a Modernist ethic – and aesthetics – of transgression. Working with and net against the site, something new is produced by registering the complexity of the given.

A distinct but related set of meanings begins with an intuition of a shift from object to field in recent theoretical and visual practices. In its most complex manifestation, this concept refers to mathematical field theory, to non-linear dynamics and computer simulations of evolutionary change. It parallels a shift in recent technologies from analogue object to digital field . . . The infrastructural elements of the modern city, by their nature linked together in open-ended networks, offer another example of field conditions in the urban context. Finally, a complete examination of the implications of field conditions in architecture would necessarily reflect the complex and dynamic behaviours of architecture's users and speculate on new methodologies to model programme and space.

To generalize from these examples, we might suggest that a field condition would be any formal or spatial matrix capable of unifying diverse elements while respecting the identity of each. Field configurations are loosely bounded aggregates characterised by porosity and local interconnectivity. The internal regulations of the parts are decisive: overall shape and extent are highly fluid. Field conditions are bottom-up phenomena: defined not by overarching geometrical schemas but by intricate local connections. Form matters, but nor so much the forms of things as the forms between things.

Field conditions cannot claim (nor does it intend to claim) to produce a systematic theory of architectural form or composition. The theoretical model proposed here anticipates its own irrelevance in the face of the realities of practice. These are working concepts, derived from experimentation in contact with the real. Field conditions intentionally mixes high theory with low practices. The assumption here is that architectural theory does not arise in a vacuum, but always in a complex dialogue with practical work.

PART 1 – FIELD CONDITIONS: ARCHITECTURE AND URBANISM

Geometric Versus Algebraic Combination

The diverse elements of classical architecture are organised into coherent wholes by means of geometric systems of proportion. Although ratios can be expressed numerically, the relationships intended are fundamentally geometric. Alberti's well-known axiom that 'Beauty is the consonance of the parts such that nothing can be added or taken away' expresses an ideal of organic geometric unity. The conventions of classical architecture dictate not only the proportions of individual elements but also the relationship between individual elements. Parts form ensembles which in turn form larger wholes. Precise rules of axiality, symmetry or formal sequence govern the organisation of the whole. Classical architecture displays a wide variation on these rules, but the principle of hierarchical distribution of parts to whole is constant. Individual elements are maintained in hierarchical order by extensive[2] geometric relationships to preserve overall unity.

PART 2 – DISTRIBUTIONS AND COMBINATIONS: TOWARDS A LOGISTICS OF CONTEXT

Distributions

'Field conditions' is opposed to conventional Modernist modes of composition as much as it is to classical rules of composition. My thesis here is that in Modernist composition by fragments – montage strategies that work to make connections between separate elements brought together at the site of composition – the classical assumption that composition is concerned with the arrangement of, and connections among, those parts persists . . . While painting and sculpture have gone beyond Cubism, architecture, I would argue, is by and large still operating with compositional principles borrowed from Cubism. The organisational principles proposed here suggest the new definitions of 'parts', and alternative ways of conceiving the question of relationships among those parts. What is required is a rethinking of some of the most familiar elements of architectural composition. Field conditions is not a claim for novelty, but rather an argument for the recuperation of an existing territory.

The American City: Open Field

The rectilinear grid is one of architecture's oldest and most persistent organising devices. From the outset, the grid supports a double valence: at once a simple and pragmatic means to partition territory or standardise elements and at the same time an emblem of universal geometries, with potential metaphysical er cosmological overtones. Hence the Jeffersonian grid, projected unconditionally over the open territories of the western United States is at once a symbol of democratic equality and an expedient means to manage vast quantities of territory; an attempt to impose measure on the immeasurable. But as Colin Rowe has remarked in a different context in America, the pragmatic tends to win out over the universal. Paraphrasing Rowe, we note that in this context, the grid is 'convincing as fact rather than as idea'.[3]

The earliest examples of gridded planning in the New World were Jesuit colonies, defensive enclaves organised hierarchically around the cathedral square in imitation of Spanish models . . . The town is an elaboration of the order applied to the farmland surrounding it. The grid is given as a convenient starting point, not as an overarching ideal. Over time, the accumulation of small variations establishes a counter principle to the universal geometry of the grid. In these American cities, pragmatics unpacks the ideality of the grid, in the same way as the unthinkable extent of the grid itself nullifies its status as an ideal object.

These cities are prototypical field conditions. Local variations of topography or history are smoothly accommodated within the overall order; borders are loosely defined and porous. They are connected with one another in larger networks. Organisation and structure display almost infinite variety within patterns that are publicly legible and institutionally manageable. Variation and repetition – individual and collective – are held in delicate balance . . .

. . . The field is a horizontal phenomenon – even a graphic one – and all of the examples described so far function in the plan dimension. Instead of refusing this characteristic, I would suggest examining it more closely. Although certain post-modern cities (Tokyo for example) might be characterised as fully three-dimensional fields, the prototypical cities of the late twentieth century are characterised by horizontal extension. What these field combinations seems to promise in this context is a thickening and intensification of experience at specified moments within the extended field of the city. The monuments of the past, including the skyscraper – a Modernist monument to efficient production – stood out from the fabric of the city as a privileged vertical moment. The new institutions of the city will perhaps occur at moments of intensity, linked to the wider network of the urban field, and marked not by demarcating lines but by thickened surfaces.

FLOCKS, SCHOOLS, SWARMS, CROWDS

The flock is clearly a field phenomenon, defined by precise and simple local conditions, and relatively indifferent to overall form and extent.[4] Because the rules are defined locally, obstructions are not catastrophic to the whole. Variations and obstacles in the environment are accommodated by fluid adjustment. A small flock and a large flock display fundamentally the same structure. Over many iterations, patterns emerge. Without repeating exactly, flock behaviour tends toward roughly similar configurations, not as a fixed type, but as the cumulative result of localised behaviour patterns.

Crowds present a different dynamic, motivated by more complex desires, interacting in less predictable patterns. Elias Canetti in *Crowds and Power* has proposed a broader taxonomy: open and closed crowds; rhythmic and stagnating crowds; the slow crowd and the quick crowd. He examines the varieties of the crowd, from the religious throng formed by pilgrims to the mass of participants in spectacle, even extending his thoughts to the flowing of rivers, the piling up of crops and the density of the forest. According to Canetti, the crowd has four primary attributes: the crowd always wants to grow: within a crowd there is equality; the crowd loves density; the crowd needs a direction.[5] The relation to Reynolds' rules outlined above is oblique but visible. Canetti, however, is not interested in prediction or verification. His sources are literary, historical and personal. Moreover, he is always aware that the crowd can be liberating as well as confining, angry and destructive as well as joyous . . .

. . . Crowds and swarms operate at the edge of control. Aside from the suggestive formal possibilities, I wish to suggest with these two examples that architecture could profitably shift its attention from its traditional top-down forms of control and begin to investigate the possibilities of a more fluid, bottom-up approach. Field conditions offers a tentative opening in architecture to address the dynamics of use, behaviour of crowds and the complex geometries of masses in motion.

A Logistics of Context

One of modern architecture's most evident failings has been its inability to address adequately the complexities of urban context. Recent debates have alternated between an effort to cover over the difference between old and new (the contextualism of Leon Krier or the so-called 'New Urbanists'), and a forceful rejection of context (deconstruction, and related stylistic manifestations). The potential of a well-developed theory of field conditions is to find a way out of this polarised debate, acknowledging the distinct capabilities of new construction, and at the same time recognising a valid desire for diversity and coherence in the city.

How to engage all the complexity and indeterminacy of the city through the methodologies of a discipline so committed to control, separation and unitary thinking? This is the dilemma of the architect working in the city today. Architecture and planning, historically aligned with technical rationality and committed to the production of legible functional relationships, have had tremendous difficulty thinking their roles apart from the exercise of control. This is all the more true today when the real power of architecture has been eroded everywhere by a swollen bureaucratic apparatus. Architecture and planning, in a desperate attempt to survive, have simply opposed their idea of order to chaos: planning versus uncontrolled growth. But this is a kind of zero-sum thinking, in which architecture can only be diminished in the measure to which it relinquishes control over the uncontrollable. We thrive in cities precisely because they are places of the unexpected, products of a complex order emerging over time.

Logistics of context suggests the need to recognise the limits of architecture's ability to order the city, and at the same time, to learn from the complex self-regulating orders already present in the city. Attention is shifted to systems of service and supply, a logic of flow and vectors. This implies close attention to existing conditions, carefully defined rules for intensive linkages at the local scale, and a relatively indifferent attitude toward the overall configuration. Logistics of context is a loosely defined working framework. It suggests a network of relations capable of accommodating difference, yet robust enough to incorporate change without destroying its internal coherence. Permeable boundaries, flexible internal relationships, multiple pathways and fluid hierarchies are the formal properties of such systems.

Above all it is necessary to recognise the complex interplay of indeterminacy and order at work in the city. 'This place, on its surface, seems to be a collage. In reality, its depth is ubiquitous. A piling up of heterogeneous places,' writes Michel de Certeau. These 'heterologies' are not arbitrary and uncontrolled, but rather 'managed by subtle and compensatory equilibria that silently guarantee complementarities'.[6] Even a very simple model of urban growth, ignoring large-scale accidents of history or geography, but incorporating fine-grained difference in the form of multiple variables and non-linear feedback, demonstrates how the interplay between laws and chance produces complex but roughly predictable configurations of a non-hierarchical nature. Field conditions and logistics of context reassert the potential of the whole, not bounded and complete (hierarchically ordered and closed), but capable of permutation: open to time and only provisionally stable. They recognise that the whole of the city is not given all at once. Consisting of multiplicities and collectivities, its parts and pieces are remnants of lost orders or fragments of never-realised totalities. Architecture needs to learn to manage this complexity, which, paradoxically, it can only do by giving up some measure of control. Logistics of context proposes a provisional and experimental approach to this task.

1   I first introduced the term field conditions'. and a version of the conceptual structure outlined here, in the context of a studio taught at Columbia University in spring 1995. As the articles collected here demonstrate. I am not alone in my interest in the techniques and phenomena associated with the field. Jeff Kipnis and Sanford Kwinter should be mentioned. Here is Kwinter, for example, writing in 1986: 'This notion of "the field" expresses the complete immanence of forces and events while supplanting the old concept of space identified with the Cartesian substratum and ether theory...The field describes a space of propagation, of effects. It contains no matter or material points, rather functions, vectors and speeds. It describes local relations of difference within fields of celerity, transmission or of careering points, in a word, what Minkowski called the world ('La Città Nuova: Modernity and Continuity'. Zone 1/2 (1986), pp88-89.
2   One of the essential characteristics of the realm of multiplicity is that each element ceaselessly varies and alters its distance in relation to the others . . . These variable distances are not extensive quantities divisible by each other: rather each is indivisible, or "relatively indivisible". In other words, they are not divisible above or below a certain threshold. they cannot increase or diminish without changing their nature [my emphasis]. Gilles Deleuze and Felix Guattari, A Thousand Plateaus. University of Minnesota Press (Minneapolis, MN), 1988, pp30–31.
3   Colin Rowe, 'Chicago Frame', in The Mathematics of the Ideal Villa and Other Essays, MIT Press (Cambridge, MA), 1995.
4   Linda Roy has studied swarm behaviour and its implications in greater depth.
5   Elias Canetti, Crowds and Power, Farrar, Straus and Giroux (New York, 1984): 29.
6   Michel De Certeau, 'Indeterminate', *In The Practice Of Everyday Life*, University of California Press (Berkeley, CA), 1984, p201.

Stan Allen, "From Object to Field" Donald Bates and Peter Davidson (eds.), Architecture after Geometry AD (*Architectural Design*) 127 (May–June, 1997): 24–31.

In *Diagram Diaries* (1999), Peter Eisenman explores the transformative potential of diagrams in architecture and urban design. He argues for diagrams to serve as instruments capable of uncovering perspectives beyond the author's biases, thus offering a more rational creation. Nevertheless, he acknowledges that diagrams are inherently quasi-objective. A diagram, he writes, "cannot help but be embodied. It can never be free of value or meaning, even when it attempts to express relationships of formation and their processes."[20]

Throughout *Diagram Diaries*, Eisenman shifts from the theorization of architecture's interiority— the intrinsic, self-contained aspects of structure and form — to a deeper investigation of architectural exteriority. This includes the relationships between a project and its site, context, and the ground. He refers to many of the diagrams of his projects shifting from Euclidean geometry toward topological operations and methodologies of grafting and folding. By shifting to exteriority, the application of diagrammatic design procedures to the site, or field, can be generative and inform the design process.

Eisenman presents his diagrammatic methods as both an analytical device and a generator, as the "mediation between a palpable object, a real building, and what can be called architecture's interiority."[21] In this understanding of the diagram, he draws upon the work of French philosopher Gilles Deleuze, who wrote how diagrams are "abstract machines." We tend to generate abstractions by simplifying substances, implying that abstractions are derived from substance. However, Deleuze proposes a reversal of this notion — suggesting that substance is formulated from abstract machines. This makes abstract machines, or diagrams, act as productive tools for design.

Eisenman introduces innovative diagrammatic concepts such as 'graft' and 'fold', which challenge traditional compositional methods and aim for a seamless transition between the existing site order and what is proposed as its transformation. The graft attempts to erase boundaries, amalgamating the old and new, while the fold reorients existing structures without destroying them. He borrows this concept of 'the fold' from Gilles Deleuze's work, "The Fold: Leibniz and the Baroque" (1988).[22] The fold, for Deleuze, as visible in baroque architecture, emphasizes fluidity, movement, and the integration of varying elements and spaces. It signifies a continuous process of varying and becoming, where the inside and outside, the visible and invisible, are intertwined and interrelated.

The concept of the fold has been particularly influential in architecture, inspiring architects to think beyond traditional forms and structures, and Euclidean geometry. The fold encourages architects to think of buildings and structures not as static and fixed entities but as continuous and transformable spaces. It enables the incorporation of variability, topological surfaces, and non-standard geometries into architectural design, thus allowing architects to explore novel spatial configurations, structural forms, and experiences. Applying folding in architecture often involves using digital design technology, computer-aided manufacturing, and innovative materials to realize the complexities and potentials inherent in a concept.

Greg Lynn, a key proponent of the application of Deleuze's theories of the fold in architecture, and a student of Peter Eisenman, has employed the fold to create a subtype: organic and amoeba-like architectural forms, also known as 'blobs', in the parlance of the 1990s. In his book *Animate Form* (1996), he introduces a transformative approach to architecture, pioneering the use of digital technology, particularly animation software, to explore novel forms and structures. The main concept in the book is "animate form," which Lynn describes as a design method where architectural forms are not perceived as static and inert but instead imbued with movement, dynamism, and potential for transformation.[23]

Lynn's approach to animate form involves utilizing computational tools to manipulate and animate geometric forms. Through this method, he examines how these animated forms can interact with various forces such as gravity, tension, and compression, resulting in architectures that appear dynamic, as though they are in a state of becoming, moving, or changing. This work exhibits characteristics of folding, and represents a further departure from the limitations of collage as a design technique, and the orthogonal organizational rigidity inherent to much of Modernism.

PETER EISENMAN
"Diagrams of Exteriority"
Diagram Diaries

. . . (The diagram) suggested an alternative relationship between the subject/author and the work. Such an alternative suggested a movement away from classical composition and personal expressionism toward a more autonomous process. Diagrams became a means to uncover something outside of my own authorial prejudices. In this sense, diagramming was potentially a more rational and quasi-objective means to understand what I was doing. It was also a means to move away from a subjective consciousness to an unconscious diagramming apparatus. Second, the process suggested that the built work could manifest the traces of the diagramming process as a means of relating built work to the interiority of its discourse.

As the diagrams progressed through the house, two issues concerning interiority became clear: (1) the diagram as assumed that interiority was an *a priori* condition of value, that is, a stable set of geometric icons, and (2) in transforming the geometry of the diagram into architecture, it was realized that geometry does not merely transform itself from a diagram to become architecture . . .

. . . the idea of a process of decomposition suggested that the interiority of architecture could be seen as a complex phenomenon from which a *less* complex condition of the object could be distilled. Interiority in this sense was no longer seen as either pure and stable or necessarily geometric. But because architecture is always based in geometry, the value of a formal universe as an embodiment of architecture was still present. In order to displace these embodied values, a series of other diagrams was introduced into the diagrammatic process that were not based in geometry, which could be seen in some way to relate to, but at the same time be distanced from, an interiority as it had been previously defined. Thus, a series of external texts was introduced in an attempt to displace that which seemed embodied, immanent, and ultimately motivated in architecture's interiority.

These outside texts questioned the pervasive value given to anything embodied, or immanent, in the interiority of architecture. If diagrams had to begin from such origins of value, whether from inside or outside architecture, they would always have an *a priori* embodiment – they would be motivated diagrams. At the same time, the question was asked: could such an embodiment ever be absent, without abandoning the discourse? Thus the idea of seemingly random and arbitrary texts from outside architecture was introduced in an attempt to overcome the immanence of architectural embodiment or the motivation of its signs. While there is no such thing as arbitrary – there is always some contingency – the diagrams began to look for the contingent structures in the arbitrary, structures which when inserted into real three-dimensional space would produce alternative conditions of the figural such as the interstitial, the affective, and the blurred, conditions which could open up the existing rhetoric and tropes sedimented in architecture's anteriority.

The Cannaregio housing project in Venice asked the following question: If interiority was no longer stable, then could the ground, an assumed architectural datum, also be questioned? This questioning of the ground datum would be the basis of many of the following projects. At Cannaregio, the surface of the ground was conceptualized as artificial, no longer a Euclidean datum but rather as a topological surface. In this context, any geometric form, whether Euclidean or topological, was seen to be artificial – that is, without any original value. A diagonal cut visually connecting the two major bridges on the periphery of the site was made in the surface, both to mark it as a surface and to mark the topological axis. It is interesting in this context that the axis became a cut rather than a pedestrian connection. Along the cut, the site was turned up like a rubber sheet to articulate the idea of it as a surface as opposed to a ground . . .

. . . After several projects working with superposition and registration, it was realized that while these projects dealt with the surface of the ground, none of them dealt with the edge of the intervention – how the new site dealt with the old. In the Frankfurt Rebstockpark master plan, that edge became a defining issue. The intention was to blur the distinction between old and new, to produce a seamless transition from old to new. This led to two new diagrammatic operations – one concerned the graft and the other the fold.

Graft is an operation similar to but different from collage. Whereas collage brings things from disparate contexts together in a new context, the juxtapositions – the edges – are necessarily articulated. The disjunctions of meaning rely on the fragmentation and the alien nature of the pieces to one another and to the whole. Graft, on the other hand, is more like montage, in that it involves time. Like the jump-cut in film, which makes seamless connections between events which are out of sequence, the graft also attempts to make a seamless connection between the new and the old. It attempts to erase the boundary or the frame of that which has been added in order to make the new project an amalgam of old and new. Such a graft was the basis of the Rebstockpark project; it was accomplished through the agency of the fold.

Folding is different from superposition in that superposition preserves the simultaneity of figure and ground, whereas folding provides for a groundless, smooth depth. Work on the fold originated from Rene Thom's catastrophe theory diagrams. As John Rajchman has said, "Rebstock is a smooth, folded space, rather than a striated, collaged one." For example, in origami, folds only figure the folding; at Rebstockpark, the frame is also folded. Origami is linear and sequential and ultimately involves a frame, whereas the folding at Rebstock is nonlinear and simultaneous. The folded surface does not look like the old, yet attempts a smooth transition, a between figure, between old and new. The site became the articulation of all the repressed immanent conditions. It does not destroy what is existing but rather sets it off in a new direction. In doing so, the fold gave to the edge a new dimension . . .

. . . The diagram is a tactic within a critical strategy – it attempts to situate a theoretical object within a physical object. It is the relationship between interiority and the theoretical object that is the critical content of the work displacing the functional, iconic, physical object of architecture. It is the embedded theoretical object which in a sense is the trace of the critical activity; it is this activity that becomes ideological.

All diagrams are both theoretical and ideological; they express an ideology about theory. The use of the diagram in a critical context has been recognized unconsciously by clients as an ideology. Ideology provokes a certain anxiety because it threatens the fundamental conditions of power; ideology deals with both super-structure and sub-structure, not as purely theoretical operations but as a critique of the relationship between them.

In order to practice critically an architect must develop, as the chameleon does, a form of camouflage, because clearly the motivation for all clients is some form of legitimation of power. Architects can never directly attack this power, but rather can only displace it through some form of mediation. While it is possible to teach ideology and to theorize ideologically, I am not convinced that the work in an office can ever be in the same ideological vein. That is, I no longer feel compelled to insist upon an ideological sub-structure in my own work.

If one looks back on the work, historically, thirty years from now, will it be said that this loss of ideology was a late period, a playing out of an endgame? Or will it be said that this publication marks a new opening to something else, a freeing of the work from an ideological necessity? In one sense the diagram has reached a certain denouement in the work of the office. As an endgame it can now

> be theorized after so many years of the work. It seems ironic that only now, in the last few years, when the diagram seems to have had a theoretical rebirth, that our work of thirty years on the same subject has become relevant. In one sense, this book stands as a critique of that rebirth, and in another sense, it is an acknowledgment that the larger the projects become, the less control that any architect has, no matter what the process. When politics and economics become the ruling factors, any critique – while perhaps more necessary – also becomes more problematic. Equally, in larger projects, it is not possible to displace function quite so easily. Therefore, if one cannot displace function, which is an ideological trope of the work, then the work itself must be re-examined . . .
>
> . . . The external diagram provided a series of formal relationships and organizations that when given form, structure, and function in an architectural context, did not permit these forms to be understood as coming from a known interiority – that is, a sedimented relationship between form and function. Lastly, and perhaps of equal importance, these diagrams shifted the focus of the reading strategy from its origin in formal relationships, and then linguistic and textual relationships, to the possibility of reading affective relationships in the somatic experience itself. This shift in the nature and use of the diagram has been critical in the evolution of the work. A critical analysis of these diagrams is crucial if one is to reexamine the work. This book, then, is a beginning of that process.
>
> Peter Eisenman, "Diagrams of Exteriority," in *Diagram Diaries* (London: Thames and Hudson, 1999): pp. 164–209.

In the essay, "Who's Afraid of Formalism?" (1994), Sanford Kwinter articulates the interests of the emerging digital, or algorithmic formalism, of the 1990s. He critiques the tendency to reduce formalism to a stylistic label and instead makes a distinction between poor and true formalism, by the degree to which "discernible patterns come to dissociate themselves from a less ordered field." He suggests ways in which formal explorations can engage with and reshape external factors such as the site, leading to richer and more meaningful architectural outcomes.[24]

In "Wildness: Prolegomena to a New Urbanism" (2007), Sanford Kwinter explores the concept of "wildness" in the context of urbanism. He illustrates the thesis of wildness through the tactics of the Vietcong guerrilla units in the Vietnam War and the principles governing complex adaptive systems. Kwinter argues that wildness, characterized by fluidity, adaptability, and lack of central control, is intrinsic to both natural and artificial systems, serving as an integral component in the creation and evolution of robust, adaptive, and flexible designs. Wildness, "the logic of animal societies" of packs, flocks and swarms, contrasts self-organization against the rigidity of "socially and behaviorally engineered urban space."[25] In such systems, "design does not come from the whole and trickle down to the parts, but rather travels in the opposite direction."[26]

He distinguishes between "the urban," which embodies this polygenetic and dynamic quality, and "the city," which may be restrictive and mechanically designed. Kwinter emphasizes that the majority of future urban development will not be traditionally designed or planned but will grow and evolve organically, driven by market forces and necessitating a re-evaluation of design approaches. Ultimately, Kwinter advocates for harnessing and emulating the ecological and morphogenetic processes inherent in wild nature to create living artificial environments, thereby redefining the practice of urbanism.

SANFORD KWINTER
"Wildness: Prolegomena to a New Urbanism"
Far from Equilibrium: Essays on Technology and Design Culture

. . . The Vietnam War was a case study in the futility of the classical Western strategy of holding space. The almost total super-fluidity of the Vietcong guerillas moving in and out of tunnels, changing sides and allegiances with every fall of the night, transforming the concept of "frontality" and "battle" by mastering a logic of the ambush, booby trap, and disappearance, made mincemeat of American techniques of waging war on a schedule and within a numbered, geographical grid. (It is a reflection of this same logic – the intuitive capacity to move fluidly between tactical and strategic modes in relation to fluctuating conditions – that computers may well never manage consistently to beat the human master at chess.) The Vietcong saturated the landscape and jungles, and even when they weren't literally present at all, the fraughtness of their threat persisted; indeed, they succeeded to "jungle-ize" even the city of Saigon. They did this, and prevailed, because they fought a *tactical* war in time, and so *strategically* rendered themselves unfindable in space.

***

The "wild" is the logic of animal societies (packs, flocks, and swarms), of the immixings and inadvertencies of the natural world (storms, quakes, abundance, extinctions), and of complex adaptive systems in general, even those of an entirely artificial kind. Since the mid-1980s Santa Fe, New Mexico, has become a main center for the study of such systems. The phrase "fast, cheap, and out of control" has become an unofficial slogan of scientists and systems designers working at the Santa Fe Institute for the Study of Complexity. The concept behind the slogan suggests that extremely intricate systems can most effectively be built up *messily*, in steps and layers, from approximate rather than finished and perfect parts, and incrementally over time, rather than in one fell swoop of assembly. *Indirectness*, it appears, is actually the secret to achieving a robust, adaptive, flexible, and evolving design. Such systems, until now, have been essentially self-designing. They are wild systems that range and explore and mine their environment, that capitalize on accidental successes, store them, and build upon them. They are densely layered systems, in which every layer functions and contributes – though in a totally unknown and untrackable way – to the shape, behavior, and stability of the whole. There is no central control, and the "design" does not come from the whole and trickle down to the parts, but rather travels in the opposite direction. Such bottom-up systems are called "subsumption architectures." The natural universe is itself a subsumption architecture utterly "out of (central, single) control." To give place to such out-of-control, adaptive, robust, selfdirected designs is to allow, or to install, a degree of wildness within them.

***

No real historical space – be it Central Park, the jungles of Vietnam, or, indeed, the new abstract modeling spaces being developed at Santa Fe – is ever univocal but always multiple and intertwined. This multiplicity and embeddedness, combined with the critical presence of a "thick" time, allows for the open-ended interactions of parts – the hybridizations, blendings, and conflicts – that effectively destroy a structure's determinism and that feed its wildness. (Wildness emerges in a system once we lose the ability to predict – from the outside – what it will do.)

This category of structure (which includes at least some architectures and most cities) can be thought of as *polygenetic* structures. One characteristic of such structures is that they are large – though in the qualitative and relative sense more than in the absolute. They are large in that they are complex (generated from an indeterminate number of distinct sources, distributed through many, or *n* dimensions), and fundamentally open (i.e., wild) and unfinished. The *urban* may be characterized precisely by this constellation of "polygenetic" qualities; it is a promiscuous, evolving manifold, to be distinguished whenever possible from the term "city," which, in its saddest form, may consist of nothing more than a stillborn, mechanical, man-made design.[1] The urban, in other words, may and often does exist at the scale of a piece of architecture, and conversely may fail to exist in city-sized agglomerates. Its existence depends only on whether a "computational" threshold has or has not been crossed. Approaching this computational threshold as a source or reservoir of work, information, and form is one of the central challenges of contemporary science, economics, and design. Over the next two decades the amount of urban substance that has existed on earth throughout all its history will double. Less than five percent of this will be designed or planned in the traditional manner. The rest will follow one-dimensional pathways of the market. Today's task is to induce – dare one say *grow*? – these polygenetic structures, or more accurately, to program the systems that enable such structures, in their turn, and at a sufficient wild distance, to assemble themselves.

Evolutionary process – the formation of organic meshes – was always built into urban matrices as the result of historical pressures and patterns embedding themselves into matter, in an open process over time. Design today must find ways to approximate these *ecological* forces and structures, to tap, approximate, borrow, and transform morphogenetic processes from all aspects of wild nature, to invent *artificial* means of creating living artificial environments. We must learn to see design algorithms everywhere we look. In time, we will earn the right to call ourselves urbanists again.

[1] If our culture has lost interest in "the city" it is because we no longer kribw what it is (or whether it exists at all). But this is no license for complacency or passive acceptance of what has come to replace it: exurb, garrison communities, middle landscape, edge, etc. The urban is the primordial modern human wilderness, currently under siege by laissez-faire ideology, and the new Republican-led feudalism that is striving to shape it. It is one thing to let go of the classical city, another entirely to abandon the emancipatory notion of the *urban*.

Sanford Kwinter, "Wildness: Prolegomena to a New Urbanism", *Far from Equilibrium: Essays on Technology and Design Culture* (Barcelona: Actar, 2007); 186–91.

In summary, the 1990s saw a shift in architectural and urban design thinking, as designers and architects drew inspiration from complexity sciences, nonlinear dynamics, and the philosophies of Gilles Deleuze. This transition led to a reconceptualization of cities as dynamic, complex, living systems, rather than static, machine-like entities. Key concepts such as grafting, folding, and animate form emerged, challenging traditional design approaches and embracing the inherent complexity of urban environments. Computational tools and digital tools played a crucial role in enabling designers to explore and generate these approaches and provided a new set of tools and techniques for simulating and generating urban complex forms and systems. This new paradigm advocated for designing in harmony with the city's intrinsic complexity, making a departure from the rigid, top-down planning approaches of Modernism and paving the way for a more nature-based, adaptive, and responsive approach to urban design in the 21st century.

FIGURE 2.3 Masses of people navigate the iconic Shibuya Crossing in Tokyo, famed for being one of the world's busiest pedestrian crosswalks. Courtesy of Getty Images.

3

Intensities, Flows, Connectivity, and Network Urbanism

Throughout the twentieth century, innovations such as electric and high-speed trains, the proliferation of automobiles, and the advent of air travel revolutionized the movement of raw materials, consumer goods, and vast populations. However, these advancements in mobility and connectivity did not come without their physical impact, leading to the construction of new railways, highways, and airport runways. Supplanting urban space with new infrastructure was a recurring theme throughout the twentieth century. In the early twentieth century, the Futurists dreamt of buildings enmeshed within this expanding infrastructure. By mid-century, such conceptualizations were no longer just fantasies but tangible realities, sometimes with tragic consequences. From the highways that cut through New York City built by modernist planner Robert Moses, to the segregated pedestrian and car lanes of roadways planned by traffic engineers, infrastructure had become a dominant force in shaping urban territories.

Historically, networks have had a close connection with the forces of globalization. From the initial trails carved by donkeys, horses, and camels, leading to the establishment of rudimentary settlements, to the vast interconnected highways and digital networks of the modern era, infrastructure has consistently driven human expansion, cooperation, and trade. Physical networks have not merely facilitated movement, they have shaped socioeconomic hierarchies, determined access to resources, and influenced cultural exchanges. For instance, it was only following the completion of the Erie Canal in 1825, which provided a cost-effective route into the heartland of America, that New York City rose to prominence as a significant commercial hub.

This chapter seeks to capture the ongoing transformation of modern cities through flows, connectivity, and networks. The selected texts from urban theorists also cover ground-breaking architectural initiatives that focus on infrastructure and movement as generators of urban organization. Their projects can be understood within the context of unbuilt work in the 1960s, when radical European architects such as Constant Nieuwenhuys, and collectives including Team X, Archigram, as well as the Metabolists in Japan, sought to create new systems of connectivity with which to shape new types of urban spaces.

This chapter examines how cities can be conceived and understood to be organized by flows and intensities, rather than only by their static spatial organization. It explores various theories related to the circulation of resources and information through mobility and connectivity systems. The focus is on the consequences and novel connections of integrating networks into cities and regions. The selected theorists in this chapter explore design strategies that revolve around network connectivity, such as innovative spatial designs that emerge through flow simulations and their synthesis. Additionally, they introduce the concept of single, continuous surfaces, which act as dynamic platforms hosting and distributing the transient nature of urban activities.

Infrastructural urbanism now extends our physical realm through the internet and online clouds, where computational systems monitor flows and mine data to improve efficiencies. This paradigm of the Network City seems to become ever more pervasive and ubiquitous. Keller Easterling, in her essay, "Extrastatecraft: The Power of Infrastructure Space," articulates the various systems that shape our cities.[1] From the underground cables and pipelines that sustain our cities to global financial systems and special economic zones (SEZs) that direct urban development, she recognizes a covert "extrastatecraft" shaping the built environment.

This chapter begins with an excerpt from engineer Frei Otto's book, *Occupying and Connecting: Thoughts on Territories and Spheres of Influence with Particular Reference to Human Settlement* (2009), in which he discusses the formation and evolution of path systems and their impact on settlements and urban development.[2] The text outlines how occupied territories, regardless of whether they are occupied by humans or other living organisms, necessitate connections for communication and survival. These connections, often initially formed based on geographical advantages, become path systems through repeated use and eventual occupation at strategic points, like forks or crossings. The excerpt illustrates how settlements grow around these paths, with path networks evolving and remaining relatively constant even with changes in population or colonization. These early path systems, independent of culture or religion, have even influenced forms of communal government and many still exist today.

Otto also explores human intervention in developing and utilizing path systems. Humans have significantly altered and constructed new path systems for various purposes, including energy transport and electronic communication, making them integral to technological development. The text details different kinds of path systems, each having distinct characteristics and methods of formation. In particular, minimal path systems are highlighted for their efficiency.

Ultimately, Otto's most famous contributions were his sustained experiments in soap film and bubbles, and "wet string" models, conducted at the Institut für Leichte Flächentragwerke (Institute for Lightweight Structures), Stuttgart University. These form-finding experiments were carried out with scientific precision, and are broadly understood as significant contributions to the development of material computation. Frei Otto used these models to theorize the behavioral efficiencies of "minimal path systems" allowing him to optimize the mass of structural systems, as well as the flow of people in urban environments.

FREI OTTO
Occupying and Connecting: Thoughts on Territories and Spheres of Influence with Particular Reference to Human Settlement

Connection
Occupied points, lines, surfaces and spaces have to be connected in several ways. This is especially true when surfaces are occupied by living organisms who wish to communicate with each other, or even need to communicate in order to survive.

Transport paths connect the occupied territories. Neither the occupations nor the transport paths have to be material. Often there are no or only temporary traces.

Animals and humans migrate, in groups or alone. The traces of their migration seldom remain. Often they disappear, although not always. Even when no permanent occupations result, path systems are created, which are used again and again. Initially they are created because they are simply favourable to migration, usually lying on collection lines such as rivers, shores and mountain ranges, or curving around obstacles such as lakes or mountains.

When they become etched in the Earth's surface through repeated use, then path systems are often occupied, especially at forks in the path or at crossings. Path systems therefore do not only connect mobile and stable occupations, but also become a grid network which encourages occupations: paths connect already occupied points, while themselves stimulating occupations.

Growing settlements
In the case of a high rate of human reproductive success and a correspondingly high availability of food, settlements will grow, as measured by the number of people, number of sites of habitation, kraals and houses, while the location itself, as a favoured place, especially the water source, is not abandoned.

Existing paths are favourable sites of habitation for arriving individual persons, pairs and families, especially those which are part of the long-distance path network. Higher-density settlements require intensive exploitation of the territory and also an intensifying of traffic to the neighbouring locations, that is, the long-distance path network.

The path networks of early pre-technological humans must have remained relatively constant over many 100,000s of years. Everything points to the established networks remaining even if the population of a whole expanse of land perished and were replaced by a new colonisation.

The food production of an expanse of land was constant. A path network created over the generations therefore corresponded to settlement density.

Early human forms of path network were independent of culture and religion. They did however influence the forms of communal government. In many places, early path networks remain today. They date from the earliest colonisation by homo sapiens.

The planning human being
In the case of both animals and people, a path system's effectiveness develops by itself. Only a small degree of intelligence is necessary for this. Presumably even a certain degree of so-called muscle memory is sufficient for orientation and finding a goal, food for instance, with the minimum of physical effort. In this, forks in the path are more conducive to orientation than path crossings.

Naturally, human beings apply their high degree of intelligence to the task of utilising path systems as effectively as possible. However, equally naturally, a forward-looking person who has been commissioned by his fellow citizens to lay out path systems on new ground makes use of his memory, that is, of the knowledge passed down through generations and influenced by different theories and cultures, thereby becoming increasingly distanced from the simple muscle memory.

With the construction of the path networks, the profession of the settlement, urban and regional planner begins, the two extremes of which are the path-seeking pioneer and the plan-maker.

Thought models of antiquity through to the modern age, according to which path networks were sometimes planned, thereby influencing cities, were very simple geometrical schemata, which are taught and, with the help of easily readable plans, could be realised by less educated people.

Path systems planned using planning theories, e.g. with the most simple geometrical knowledge of the last 8000 years can be instantly recognised on any map and are different from the still older path systems of the earliest settlements, but also from those of the transport path planners of today.

For instance, one can instantly recognise Egyptian and Greek paths and rampart layouts, and in particular those of the Roman military, who for power-political reasons among others preferred to lay out new paths rather than venture into the incomprehensible 'jungle' of existing paths.

Humankind is the most powerful changer of the Earth's surface. The procedures of occupation and connection are controlled, altered, influenced and triggered by humankind.

The natural path systems of streams, rivers and currents are altered, made serviceable for power stations and ships and overcome using fords, ferries, bridges and tunnels. Entirely new path systems are constructed: zinc water pipes, sewage outlets, purification plants, electrical supply systems, air ventilation systems for artificial aeration and ventilation in buildings.

Energy transport systems have a broad compass, as they are involved in the building of houses, bridges and towers.

Electronic communication networks have now become highly significant for technological development.

Path systems in general

Introduction

Suppose that a delimited area is occupied. It does not matter how the occupation took place, whether it was created in a random, attractive or distanced way or in any other way.

Connecting the occupied points (e.g., the territories' key points) with straight lines gives the direct path network.

An attempt to produce the connection with the shortest overall length produces the minimal path system. The minimising (optimum in terms of energy) detour network falls somewhere between the direct path network and the minimal path network.

The generative or expansion net is a special case. It is created when path connections are made sequentially and new points are connected taking the shortest route. Paths do not only connect occupied points, but also stimulate new occupations, especially at crossing points or forks.

The minimal path system

In a direct path system, every point is connected with every other point by the shortest route. This still applies if impassable obstacles deform some individual stretches.

A minimal path system constructed between the same points has a significantly shorter total length. The paths themselves are significantly more heavily used, that is, exploited, but the connection between one point and another involves a detour.

Minimal path systems are created when paths have a low level of use and/or are very expensive to construct, for instance, when three sites are situated in almost impassable swamp woodland.

They also occur where the detour is not considered disruptive, e.g. in heavily planted inner courtyards or in case of obstruction by snow, in which case a path already trodden clear is likely to be acceptable even when it is the longer option.

When new paths are being constructed, it is always instructive to know the minimal path system which would be required as well as the direct path system.

The minimal path network between three or four points can be constructed relatively easily with a pencil and protractor. If more than five points are involved, this becomes more difficult, even if computers are used. The roulette apparatus was created in my studio in Berlin around 1960. The soap bubble skin apparatus, in which a horizontal glass plate is held over the surface of water and the minimal path system forms itself from needles, followed in 1962. This work was continued at the Institut für leichte Flächentragwerke, and published in 1969. Minimal path systems are continuously open, that is, they have no closed units. At every junction, three arms connect at an angle of 120°. In practice one hardly ever finds exact minimal path systems. The system does not lose its properties if divergences are introduced, e.g. if the angles at the junction diverge ±10° from being 120°.

The occupation of paths and path networks – approaches to urban development

Path networks connect occupied territories, villages, cities or the concentrations of large surfaces. However, existing paths are also a significant incentive to occupation, especially where houses, workplaces, commercial operations or similar farmhouses are involved. Soap bubbles of the same size arrange themselves in dense occupation on a path.

At all their stopping places, railways increase the incentive to settle, while motorways have this effect in the areas around their exits. In the case of normal footpaths and cart roads, crossing and branching points encourage settlement. Soap bubbles occupying sticks in the minimal path apparatus form bulges at the branching points and often form a second layer. Vertical growth can be simulated using them.

Soap bubbles generally connect to linear elements at a right angle. The soap bubbles are closed minimal path systems.

> As described above, the paths of individual points and path systems also connect at a right angle to existing networks . . .
>
> . . . In experiments with small soap bubbles, the first small bubbles move towards the branching points and remain there. It is only after this that the open stretches are occupied. Soap bubbles have a double membrane. The distribution of fluid takes place between the membranes.
>
> The occupation of paths can progress to the point where all units of the network are fully occupied. However, this demands the continual construction of new paths in order to serve the occupied surface. However the centre remains free.
>
> Frei Otto, *Occupying and Connecting: Thoughts on Territories and Spheres of Influence with Particular Reference to Human Settlement*, Edited by Berthold Burkhardt (Stuttgart: Edition Axel Menges, 2009): 50, 58–60, 63, 74–75, 94.

Cities, according to Michael Weinstock in *The Architecture of Emergence: The Evolution of Form in Nature and Civilisation* (2010), are products of a deep evolutionary interplay between human cultural development, ecological conditions, and climatic shifts.[3] He posits that cities did not emerge in isolation but rather as nodal points within extensive metabolic networks, characterized by the flow of materials, energy, and information. These urban forms and their surrounding networks were influenced by both human-induced modifications to the environment and natural climatic fluctuations. As cities proliferated, they often approached their maximum metabolic capacities, rendering them sensitive to environmental changes and prone to periods of growth, collapse, and reorganization. Weinstock's analysis emphasizes the interconnectedness of ecological, climatic, and human sociocultural factors in the emergence and evolution of urban landscapes, highlighting the adaptability and resilience inherent in these complex systems.

According to Weinstock, the evolutionary development of city forms and their extended metabolic systems can also be traced to climate and ecological systems and their changes over long durations of time. His book chapter presents how human forms and culture had evolved alongside changes in the climatic context of the planet. He begins some 35,000 years ago, when humans had begun to modify their ecological context by domesticating wild cereals, as the "founding system of civilization."[4] He surveys the early deployment of tents and temporary structures, pit and cave dwellings, predating our recorded civilization some 12,000 years ago, as humans transitioned from nomadic to sedentary lifestyles while maintaining high logistic mobility. Yet, as human civilization is dependent on flows of energy, it was, and still is, "highly vulnerable to climatic and ecological changes."[5] The precariousness of early cities often led to system collapse, in which people abandoned the city and regrouped into smaller dispersed assemblies with lower levels of complexity. After the industrial revolution, people returned to cities with a higher complexity of associations. Weinstock touches on the ecological changes still occurring today within our era of accelerated climate change, as a direct consequence of the human footprint on the planet's ecology.

MICHAEL WEINSTOCK
"City Forms"
The Architecture of Emergence: The Evolution of Form in Nature and Civilisation

CITY FORMS
Cities simultaneously emerged from the collapse and reorganisation of the founding system of civilisation, in five geographically separated and ecologically stressed regions across the world. The evolutionary development of city forms and their extended metabolic systems was strongly coupled to multiple changes of the climate and ecological system within which they were situated, and to the rise in the flow of energy from intense cultivation, increased social complexity and to the evolution of information systems. The proliferation of cities, systems of cities and their extended metabolic systems across the world was characterised by episodic and irregular expansions and incorporations, collapse and subsequent reorganisation in more complex forms with greater flows of energy, information and material. The extensive modification of ecological systems at a variety of spatial and temporal scales is still evident in the arid and denuded landscapes that persist today.

Human forms and culture evolved over a period of extreme fluctuations in the climate, and consequent rapid variations in ecologies; a regime of natural selection that conserved and enhanced the ability to adapt their culture to a variety of climates and ecological conditions. The development of the elongated body plan and the large brain was strongly coupled to the increasing complexity of human culture, each acting as a positive feedback to accelerate the development of the other. Culture acts to transmit complex social and ecologically contextualised information down through the generations, and has tended to increase in complexity over time, a process that began over 130,000 years ago in east Africa with the emergence of anatomically modern humans, the diaspora 'out of Africa' and the spread of humans across the world.[1] By 35,000 years ago long-term settlements, complex spoken language, calendars and the material archiving of ecological information had emerged.[2]

Humans began to modify their local ecological systems about the same time, as the extinction of the megafauna and the use of fire to drive game and clear land produced changes in patterns of vegetation in steppe grasslands, in cool forests and in warmer grasslands. As the energetic returns from hunting were reduced, the increase in the gathering of grains initiated the genetic changes that over many thousands of years led to the domestication of wild cereals . . .

. . . . The founding system of civilisation continued to develop local and regional variations over tens of thousands of years, with long periods of population growth and local episodes of rapid declines. In many locations it had developed to its maximum metabolic capacity, and had become highly vulnerable to climatic and ecological changes. The collapse of the founding system in five ecologically distinct and geographically separated regions led to the emergence of linked hierarchical patterns of settlements. As the flow of materials, energy and information intensified through the integrated arrays of settlements, populations expanded and social and cultural complexity increased. Cities emerged through a process of nucleation, condensing into nuclei within the extended 'metabolic' networks of the linked settlements . . .

. . . VARIATIONS OF THE FOUNDING SYSTEM
Climatic and ecological changes induced change and an increase in complexity of the founding cultural system. Additional stresses were created by the continuous increase in numbers and the consequential greater extraction of food and material energy from their surroundings . . .

. . . COLLAPSE AND REORGANISATION
There has been a long held assumption that a benign 'interglacial' climatic regime was initiated 10,000 years ago and has persisted unchanged until today. That assumption was usually accompanied by the belief that it was the benign climate that enabled humans to 'invent' agriculture, cities and 'complex societies'. It is clear, however, that there have been many episodes of extreme variability in the climate, and that the effects have been far from benign . . .

. . . It is also clear that cultivation was not an 'invention', but a system that emerged out of a process that was at least 15,000 years long, and was achieved by the gradual genetic modification of wild cereals by human rather than natural selection . . .

. . . EMERGENCE OF THE CITY
Between 6,000 and 5,000 years ago, the latitudinal band of deserts around the world had broadened and developed the arid ecologies and spatial extent that they have today. Within the hot arid regions of the Levant and south-west Asia, Egypt and the Indus Valley of southern Asia; and in the cold arid regions of northern China, and the north-west coast of South America,[3] river valleys provided the only ecologically favourable locations for all living species, including humans. As recurrent episodes of severe climatic and ecological stresses continued,[4] cities emerged in all five regions within a few hundred years of each other. The relatively simultaneous emergence of city systems in five widely dispersed regions across the world, and the long distances between them, suggest that it is very unlikely that cities emerged first in one region and spread by cultural diffusion to the others. Cities emerged from the extended metabolic systems of dispersed settlements, condensing into nuclei within integrated arrays of settlements, with an amplified flow of materials, energy and information, and an increase in social and cultural complexity . . .

. . . EMERGENCE AND THE FORMS OF CITIES
Cities emerged from a process of nucleation in five topographically and ecologically defined regions within a latitudinal band characterised by either hot or cold arid climates. In each region recurrent episodes of climatic change induced further ecological stresses on the widely distributed pattern of settlements that had already made pronounced changes to local and regional ecological systems. River valleys were the most favourable areas, and the flow of migrants from the ecologically stressed territories into the valleys increased the population in topographically and ecologically delimited territories. The concentration of people, and the consequential increase in the volume of exchanges between settlements of food, fuel and materials, established the integration of the individual metabolic system of groups of settlements into larger systems. Severe climatic and ecological changes induced the process of nucleation and the subsequent emergence of cities.

City forms are material constructs that are composed of a spatial array of dwellings, a pattern of streets and public spaces together with differentiated buildings of varying sizes associated with the regulation of energy and material flow, and the extension of a metabolic network across the surrounding territory. City forms emerged within different topographies and ecological systems, evolving from regional variations of the founding system and the established patterns of settlements from which they condensed. The forms expanded and developed, strongly coupled to the dynamic changes of climate and ecology within which they were situated . . .

. . . As cities emerged within a latitudinal band characterised by arid climates, and arose from variations of the common founding system, their evolutionary development tended to be convergent, exhibiting many similar patterns, arrays and forms. Convergent evolution has occurred widely in living forms, and many animals and plants that emerge from quite different evolutionary trajectories exhibit strong similarities in their body plans and the processes of their organs.[5]

. . . As the populations in extended city systems continued to expand, plant cultivation and animal husbandry were intensified and the flow of materials and energy increased. In turn, the built area of cities expanded over the established patterns of cultivated fields, pastures and irrigation canals . . . .

. . . The growth and development of cities and systems of cities across the world was characterised by episodic and irregular expansions and incorporations, and by local and regional scale patches of collapse, the abandonment of cities and dispersal of the people, and subsequent reorganisation. Systems of cities all tended to develop and expand so that they were operating close to the limit of their capacity to extract energy and materials from their environment, and to manage the complexity of flows through their system. Systems of cities developed multiple processes, each with flows of energy and materials through them, and with critical thresholds at differing scales of distance and time. They developed and grew until they were delicately poised close to their critical threshold of stability, and were then extremely sensitive to changes within their environment.

The outcomes of system collapse can be: the abandonment and migration of the people and a complete loss of order; a regrouping of the 'components' of the system into smaller dispersed assemblies with fewer links and reduced flows of energy, materials and information; or reorganisation to a lower level of complexity and the reordering of the 'components' into a more integrated assembly with increased flows; or reorganisation to a higher level of complexity.

The ecological system of each of the five regions within which cities emerged and developed was modified by humans at a variety of spatial and temporal scales. The intensive cultivation of land supported large populations, but also resulted in the depletion of nutrients in the soil, and in some areas caused a marked salinisation of the soil. The use of timber for construction and for fuel, coupled to the clearance of land for agricultural use, resulted in deforestation at a regional scale, the spread of grassland savannahs and the extinction of animal and plant species. Successive cycles of drought, coupled to the elimination of tree root systems that bound the soil together, exposed the soil to further drying and erosion. The changes were cumulative and long lasting, and in many regions the modifications of ecological systems by humans are still evident in the arid and denuded landscapes that persist today.

1 Lahr, M. and R. Foley, 'Towards a Theory of Modern Human Origins: geography, demography, and diversity in recent human evolution', *Yearbook of Physical Anthropology,* vol. 41, 1998, pp. 137–76; and McBrearty, S. and A. Brooks, 'The Revolution that Wasn't: a new interpretation of the origin of modern human behavior', *Journal of Human Evolution,* vol. 39, 2000, pp. 453–563.
2 Noble, W. and I. Davidson, 'The Evolutionary Emergence of Modern Human Behaviour: language and its archaeology', *Man: Journal of the Royal Anthropological Institute,* vol. 26, 1991, pp. 223–53.

> 3. Solis, R.S., J. Haas and W. Creamer, 'Dating Caral, a Preceramic Site in the Supe Valley on the Central Coast of Peru'. *Science,* vol. 292, 2001, pp. 723–6.
> 4. Steig, E.J., 'Mid-Holocene Climate Change', Science, vol. 286, 1999, pp. 1485–7; and Brooks, N., 'Cultural Responses to Aridity in the Middle Holocene and Increased Social Complexity', *Quaternary International,* vol. 151, 2006, pp. 29–49.
> 5. Morphologists refer to the general anatomical architecture as the body plan, and similar or Sassen, Saskia. 1991. *The Global City,* New York, London, Tokyo. Related body plans are generally classified together in groups or 'phyla'. This taxonomy does not normally take into account metabolic processes.
>
> Michael Weinstock, "City Forms" *The Architecture of Emergence: The Evolution of Form in Nature and Civilisation,* (London: John Wiley and Sons Inc., 2010); 177, 184, 190, 202, 205, 206.

Several authors, theorists and urbanists have addressed the relationship of infrastructural connectivity, as well as informational networks, to global cities, megacities and urban regions. Saskia Sassen, in her work *The Global City* (1991), highlights the significance of select urban centers in the globalized world, where they function as command points in the global economy.[6] These "global cities," such as London, Tokyo, and New York, are interconnected through advanced infrastructural networks, facilitating the flow of information, capital, and people. Infrastructural connectivity and networks are thus essential for the operation and dominance of global cities, as they underpin the cities' role in global finance, commerce, and governance. Sassen also delves into the disparities and contrasts inherent within them. While they may be hubs of global finance and information networks, these cities also harbor marginalized populations, including migrants, the working poor, and others who are often excluded from the primary benefits of globalization. These less privileged and frequently overlooked areas within global cities highlight the socioeconomic inequalities that exist even in the heart of the world's most powerful urban centers.

Waldheim and Berger, in their article "Logistics Landscape" (2008), shed light on the critical, though sometimes overlooked, role of logistics in determining urban forms and architecture.[7] Historically, the transportation and prompt delivery of goods have been instrumental in shaping cities, but since the 1970s, new logistics systems have amplified these transformations, pushing the boundaries of storage and movement of goods. As a result, urban areas witness profound changes in response to shifts in global supply chains, as evident from sprawling Amazon distribution hubs to suburban retail giants. Jesse LeCavalier's *The Rule of Logistics* (2016) offers insights into Walmart's intricate operational methodologies and their architectural implications, demonstrating how logistics has revolutionized worldwide commerce and reshaped urban areas.[8] Through this lens, Walmart emerges as both a consequence of and a catalyst for this interconnectedness, underlining the transformative impact of these networks on urban structures. Reinhold Martin, in his book *The Urban Apparatus: Mediapolitics and the City* (2016), develops the notion of city-as-hardware. He understands cities as infrastructure networks, with an ability to shape power dynamics as well as the functional, aesthetic, and cognitive order of the city.[9]

Manuel Castells' seminal work, *The Network Society* (1996) from "The Information Age: Economy, Society, and Culture" trilogy, brings forth the "Space of Flows" concept—a foundational idea for grasping contemporary spatial dynamics, where intangible flows of data, images, and capital across global networks can surpass the importance of the mobility of physical goods and the geographical location of activities.[10] Castells defines the Space of Flows as having four layers, including electronic exchanges, nodes and hubs, the establishment of a technocratic elite, and the concurrence of globalization and localization.

Castells sees the Network Society as the dominant form of social organization in the Information Age. Amid this global, network-centric economy, cities and regions seamlessly integrated into the Space of Flows flourish, whereas isolated areas might wane. Such dynamics crucially inform urban strategies, urging cities to position themselves as vital global network junctions. By the 1990s, with IT advancements, Castells discerned the urban form of the "Informational City," as cities aim to become nodes or hubs in these global networks.[11] He recognized that such cities had a dual nature. For instance, while megacities are increasingly integrated into global networks, becoming centers of economic, political, and cultural power, they also exhibit stark contrasts. They are often characterized by significant socioeconomic disparities within, with vast wealth existing alongside sprawling informal settlements and marginalized populations. Castells notes, "they are connected externally to global networks and to segments of their own countries, while internally disconnecting local populations that are either functionally unnecessary or socially disruptive."[12]

In describing the new form of the informational city, he cautioned against assuming that it will not be a copy of Silicon Valley, just as the industrial city did not replicate Manchester. Each will develop its own unique characteristics.[13]

MANUEL CASTELLS
"Advanced Services, Information Flows, and the Global City"
The Rise of the Network Society: The Information Age: Economy, Society, and Culture

The informational, global economy is organized around command and control centers able to coordinate, innovate, and manage the intertwined activities of networks of firms.[1] Advanced services, including finance, insurance, real estate, consulting, legal services, advertising, design, marketing, public relations, security, information gathering, and management of information systems, but also R&D and scientific innovation, are at the core of all economic processes, be it in manufacturing, agriculture, energy, or services of different kinds.[2] They all can be reduced to knowledge generation and information flows.[3] Thus, advanced telecommunications systems could make possible their scattered location around the globe. Yet more than a decade of studies on the matter have established a different spatial pattern, characterized by the simultaneous dispersion and concentration of advanced services.[4] On the one hand, advanced services have substantially increased their share in employment and GNP in most countries, and they display the highest growth in employment and the highest Investment rates in the leading metropolitan areas of the world.[5] They are pervasive, and they are located throughout the geography of the planet, excepting the "black holes" of marginality. On the other hand, there has been a spatial concentration of the upper tier of such activities in a few nodal centers of a few countries.[6] This concentration follows a hierarchy between tiers of urban centers, with the higher-level functions, in terms of both power and skill, being concentrated in some major metropolitan areas. Saskia Sassen's classic study of the global city has shown the joint dominance of New York, Tokyo, and London in international finance, and in most consulting and business services of international scope.[7] These three centers together cover the spectrum of time zones for the purpose of financial trading, and work largely as a unit in the same system of endless transactions. But other centers are important, and even more pre-eminent in some specific segments of trade, for example Chicago and Singapore in futures' contracts (in fact, first practiced in Chicago in 1972). Hong Kong, Osaka, Frankfurt, Zurich, Paris, Los Angeles, San Francisco, Amsterdam, and Milan are also major centers both in finance and in international business Services.[8] And a number of "regional centers" are rapidly joining the network, as "emerging markets" develop all over the world: Madrid, Sao Paulo, Buenos Aires, Mexico, Taipei, Moscow, Budapest, among others.

As the global economy expands and incorporates new markets it also organizes the production of advanced services required to manage the new units joining the system, and the conditions of their everchanging linkages[9] . . .

". . . New activities concentrate in particular poles and that implies an increase of disparities between the urban poles and their respective hinterlands."[10] Thus, the global city phenomenon cannot be reduced to a few urban cores at the top of the hierarchy. It is a process that connects advanced services, producer centers, and markets in a global network, with different intensity and at a different scale depending upon the relative importance of the activities located in each area *vis-à-vis* the global network. Inside each country, the networking architecture reproduces itself into regional and local centers, so that the whole system becomes interconnected at the global level. Territories surrounding these nodes play an increasingly subordinate function, sometimes becoming irrelevant or even dysfunctional; for example, Mexico City's *colonias populares* (originally squatter settlements) that account for about two-thirds of the megapolitan population, without playing any distinctive role in the functioning of Mexico City as an international business center.[11] Furthermore, globalization stimulates regionalization. In his studies on European regions in the 1990s, Philip Cooke has shown, on the basis of available evidence, that the growing internationalization of economic activities throughout Europe has made regions more dependent on these activities. Accordingly, regions, under the impulse of their governments and business elites, have restructured themselves to compete in the global economy, and they have established networks of cooperation between regional institutions and between region-based companies. Thus, regions and localities do not disappear, but become integrated in international networks that link up their most dynamic sectors.[12]

Indeed, the hierarchy in the network is by no means assured or stable: it is subject to fierce inter-city competition, as well as to the venture of highly risky investments in both finance and real estate . . .

. . . This urban roller-coaster at different periods, across areas of the world, illustrates both the dependence and vulnerability of any locale, including major cities, to changing global flows.

But why must these advanced service systems still be dependent on agglomeration in a few large metropolitan nodes? Here again, Saskia Sassen, capping years of field work research by herself and other researchers in different contexts, offers convincing answers. She argues that:

> The combination of spatial dispersal and global integration has created a new strategic role for major cities. Beyond their long history as centers for international trade and banking, these cities now function in four new ways: first, as highly concentrated command points in the organization of the world economy; second, as key locations for finance and for specialized service firms . . .; third, as sites of production, including the production of innovation in these leading industries; and fourth, as markets for the products and innovations produced.[13]

These cities, or rather, their business districts, are information-based, value-production complexes, where corporate headquarters and advanced financial firms can find both the suppliers and the highly skilled, specialized labor they require. They constitute indeed networks of production and management, whose flexibility needs *not* to internalize workers and suppliers, but to be able to access them when it fits, and in the time and quantities that are required in each particular instance. Flexibility and adaptability are better served by this combination between agglomeration of core networks, and global networking of these cores, and of their dispersed, ancillary networks, via telecommunications and air transportation. Other factors seem also to contribute to strengthen concentration of high-level activities in a few nodes: once they are constituted, heavy investment in valuable real estate by corporations explains their reluctance to move because such a move would devalue their fixed assets; also, face-to-face contacts for critical decisions are still necessary in the age of widespread eavesdropping, since, as Saskia Sassen reports that a manager confessed to her during an interview, sometimes business deals are, of necessity, marginally illegal.[14] And, finally, major metropolitan centers still offer the greatest opportunities for the personal enhancement, social status, and individual self-gratification of the much-needed upper-level professionals, from good schools for their children to symbolic membership at the heights of conspicuous consumption, including art and entertainment.[15]

Nevertheless, advanced services, and even more so services at large, do indeed disperse and decentralize to the periphery of metropolitan areas, to smaller metropolitan areas, to less-developed regions, and to some less-developed countries.[16] New regional centers of service processing activities have emerged in the United States (for example, Atlanta, Georgia, or Omaha, Nebraska), in Europe (for example, Barcelona, Nice, Stuttgart, Bristol), or in Asia (for example, Bombay, Bangkok, Shanghai). The peripheries of major metropolitan areas are bustling with new office development, be it Walnut Creek in San Francisco or Reading near London. And in some cases, new major service centers have sprung up on the edge of the historic city, Paris's La Défense being the most notorious and successful example. Yet, in almost all instances, decentralization of office work affects "back offices"; that is, the mass processing of transactions that execute strategies decided and designed in the corporate centers of high finance and advanced services.[17] These are precisely the activities that employ the bulk of semi-skilled office workers, most of them suburbanite women, many of them replaceable or recyclable, as technology evolves and the economic roller-coaster goes on.

What is significant about this spatial system of advanced service activities is neither their concentration nor decentralization, since both processes are indeed taking place at the same time throughout countries and continents. Nor is it the hierarchy of their geography, since this is in fact tributary to the variable geometry of money and information flows. After all, who could predict in the early 1980s that Taipei, Madrid, or Buenos Aires could emerge as important international financial and business centers? I believe that the megalopolis Hong Kong-Shenzhen-Guangzhou-Zhuhai-Macau will be one of the major financial and business capitals in the early twenty-first century, thus inducing a major realignment in the global geography of advanced services.[18] But for the sake of the spatial analysis I am proposing here, it is secondary if I miss my prediction. Because, while the actual location of high-level centers in each period is critical for the distribution of wealth and power in the world, from the perspective of the spatial logic of the new system what matters is the versatility of its networks. The global city is not a place, but a process. A process by which centers of production and consumption of advanced services, and their ancillary local societies, are connected in a global network, while simultaneously downplaying the linkages with their hinterlands, on the basis of information flows.

1   For an excellent overview of current transformations of spatial forms and processes at the global level, see Hall (1995: 3-32).
2   Daniels (1993).
3   Norman (1993).
4   Graham (1994).

5   Graham (1994).
6   P. W. Daniels (1994).
7   Sassen (1991).
8   Daniels (1993).
9   Borja et al. (1991).
10 Cappelin (1991): 237.
11 Davis (1992).
12 Michelson and Wheeler (1994).
13 Sassen (1991: 3-4).
14 Personal notes, reported by Sassen over a glass of Argentinian wine, Harvard Inn, April 22, 1994.
15 For an approximation to the differentiation of social worlds in global cities, using New York as an illustration, see the various essays collected in Mollenkopf (1989); and Mollenkopf and Castells (1991); see also Zukin (1992).
16 For evidence on spatial decentralization of services, see Marshall et al.(1988); Castells (1989b: ch. 3); Daniels (1993: ch. 5).
17 See Castells (1989b: ch.3); and Dunford and Kafkalas (1992).
18 See Henderson (1991); Kwok and So (1992, 1995).

Manuel Castells, "Advanced Services, Information Flows, and the Global City", *The Rise of the Network Society: The Information Age: Economy, Society, and Culture* (Oxford: John Wiley & Sons, 2011); 409–417.

Jonathan D. Solomon's "Hong Kong – Aformal Urbanism," articulates the conclusions of a research project and earlier book publication, *Cities Without Ground: A Hong Kong Guidebook* (2011).[14] This project explored the spatial logic of Hong Kong's dense urbanism in a series of diagrams of intensely networked locations. These diagrams shed light on the multifaceted amalgamation of elements such as shopping malls, hotel atriums, corporate lobbies, dining spaces, educational institutions, religious centers, and the intricate transit links that bind them to the Mass Transit Railway (MTR), various stations, taxi stands, and bus depots. These expansive urban interiors, complete with their elevated footbridges and subway tunnels, have eclipsed the city's public spaces, asserting themselves as the foremost civic zones. Corridors and atriums within shopping malls in Hong Kong have evolved as key arteries, both facilitating pedestrian movement and fostering civic culture. This "interior urbanism," while nothing like traditional urban spaces such as outdoor plazas, is characterized by the effortless movement and intermingling of its inhabitants.

Earlier, Shelton, Karakiewicz and Kvan had analyzed Hong Kong's development of large interior spaces connected to its dense infrastructural network, in their book, *The Making of Hong Kong: From Vertical to Volumetric* (2011)[15]. Also relevant is a more recent body of research by Stefan Al, *Mall City: Hong Kong's Dreamworlds of Consumption* (2016), focusing on the typologies and network topologies of Hong Kong's shopping malls.[16]

Solomon and others traces the spatial complexity of Hong Kong's interior urbanism as an effect of the city's vast density, hot summer climate, and steep geography. Starting in 1965, Hong Kong's elevated pedestrian pathways developed incrementally, constructed by varied stakeholders to address immediate demands. Eventually extending and encompassing multiple discrete buildings, the network of elevated walkways quickly became a key aspect of large-scale urban development in Central Hong Kong. Earlier, and concurrently, similar transport-oriented approaches were also developed in Tokyo's Shinjuku Station, the "Reseau" (French for "network") also known as the "Underground City" in Montreal, and the "+15" or "+30" systems of above ground connections in Minneapolis, Calgary, and Atlanta.

Solomon explains how Hong Kong's network of pedestrian footbridges and subway tunnels, together with the malls, hotels, offices and transit hubs between which they connect, escape traditional legibility.[17] Hong Kong defies traditional urban hierarchies of public and private, and outside and inside. Unlike the insular interior urbanism of luxury hotels proposed by architect John Portman, argues Solomon, Hong Kong has a network of such places, which compresses economic classes, locals and expats, tourists, and foreign domestic helpers. In Hong Kong, connectivity is enhanced, notes Solomon, "to such a degree that it eliminates reference to the ground altogether. Hong Kong is a city without ground."

Solomon defines a new term, "aformal" to describe the figural qualities of Hong Kong's exterior volumetric landscape. This term captures how the characteristics of this network includes both aspects of formal planning as well as the informality of illegal, extra-legal, or bottom-up processes. This interplay of formal and informal has also been dissected by architectural critic Reyner Banham, notably in his distinction between "comprehensible design" and "self-determining systems," as explored in his 1976 book, *Megastructure*.[18] Interestingly, just at the time when Banham was eulogizing the demise of the Megastructure in the West, on the grounds of inflexibility, Hong Kong's network urbanism was developing and eventually thrived. One thing Banham did not

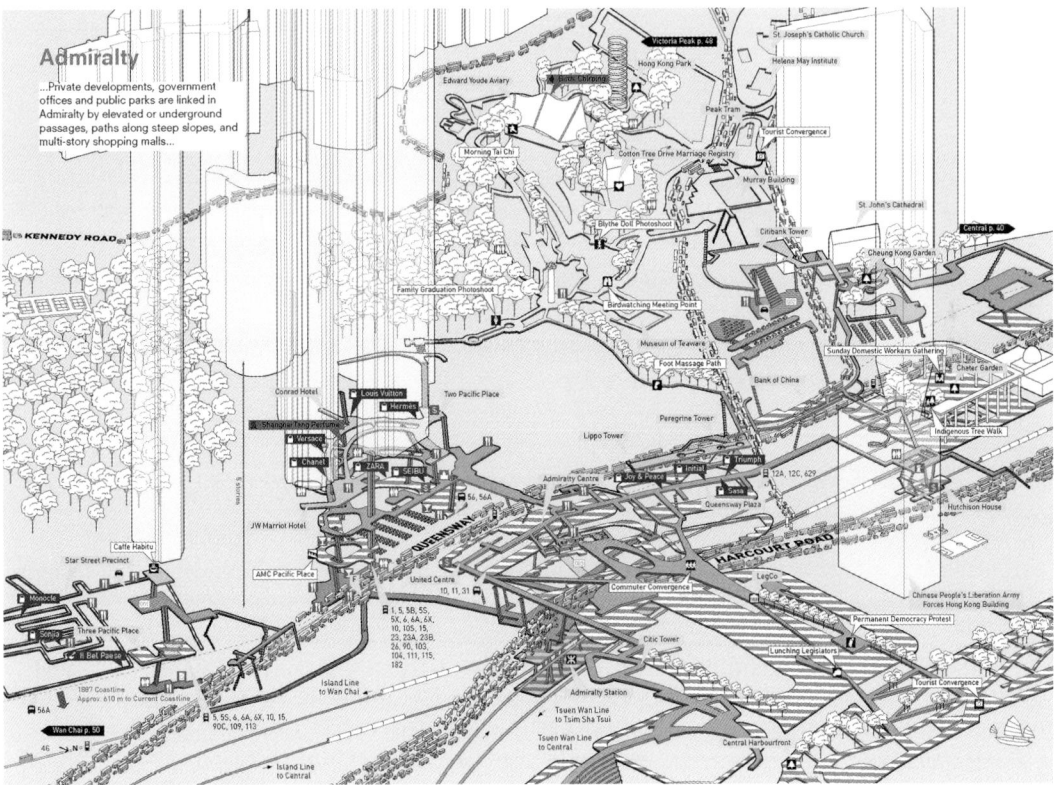

FIGURE 3.1 This axonometric diagram intricately maps the complex network of elevated walkways and subterranean passages that create a unique urban landscape in Hong Kong's Admiralty district, as featured in *Cities without Ground: A Hong Kong Guidebook* (Novato, CA: ORO Publishers, 2011). Courtesy of Jonathan Solomon.

foresee was Hong Kong's intense linking of large-scale, dense, and multiuse architectural complexes to the city's transport networks and to other massive buildings.

JONATHAN D. SOLOMON
"Hong Kong – Aformal Urbanism"

Hong Kong is an advanced form of the spatial logic of late capitalism; a shopping mall, a theme park or atrium hotel elaborated to the complexity of a city. Characterised by a three-dimensional publicly accessible network that facilitates propinquity and integration of diverse sectors, the city's unique take on a generic urbanism complicates understandings of the postmodern city and suggests exciting futures.

More than any site save Disneyland, John Portman's 1976 Bonaventure Hotel in Los Angeles established the spatial grammar of postmodernism. With its outwardly opaque spaces of international capital, its thoroughly disorienting interiors, its wholesale dismantling of any sense of exteriority in the city, and its lack of visual hierarchy and traditional urbanity, the building was characterized by Fredric Jameson as a "Postmodern Hyperspace."[1] In Hong Kong, Hyperspace is the norm, for there was never truly any traditional space in the city for it to supersede. If the Bonaventure, in Jameson's eyes, "aspires to being a total space, a complete world, a kind of miniature city,"[2] then Hong Kong succeeds. If the Bonaventure aspired to miniaturize the city in a building, in Hong Kong the city has coalesced into a single enlarged building.

The origins of this fascinating urban complex are unlikely: the shopping mall in Hong Kong serves as the medium both for pedestrian connectivity and of civic culture.[3] Typically located over busy public transit nodes, these malls are a development of the 1950s American dumb-bell mall, with two anchor department stores linked by 600-foot arcade of smaller shops, Hong Kong malls advance this model by adopting an inclusive approach to anchors, which can include office or hotel lobbies, transit stations, and residential estates; these malls also expand the network of anchors and arcades into three dimensions . . . The density, connectivity, and redundancy of these networks generate new forms of public space that, to function, require neither the images of classical European or Chinese urbanity to signify a street, a courtyard, a square, nor the underlying guarantees they suggest.[4]

While lacking traditional legibility, Hong Kong's pedestrian networks, when mapped as a seamless continuum uninterrupted by ownership, management, function, or vertical position, and describe a perceptible spatial logic . . .

. . . Aformal urbanism refers to a form of decision-making and design process in cities that falls between traditional understandings of the formal and the informal. Evidence of aformal urbanism can be found by examining the organizational structures it produces, which reject traditional form-based hierarchies that rely on visual legibility, such as solid-void or figure-ground relationships. "Aformal" thus has two meanings, one referring to the city's organization, the other to its spatial products.

Aformal logics

Discussions of the formal and the informal in architecture and urbanism, and particularly in areas experiencing rapid urbanization, tend toward polarization. On the one hand, the formal tends to be equated with the legal and specifically with the state apparatus either directly or through the application of codification or regulation to market forces. On the other hand, the informal, as explored by critic Mike Davis and others, tends to be equated with the illegal, or at least with the extra-legal solution-based results typical of less empowered operators.[5]

At the same time, the formal tends to be equated with the legible, and specifically with the kind of state-modernist visual legibility described by James C. Scott and others as ultimately ill-fated attempts to reduce complexity and unpredictability into models that better suit bureaucratic administration, while the informal tends to be equated with the illegible, and specifically with the express lack of precisely that type of bureaucratic clarity.[6]

In Hong Kong the impression of this dualism can be reinforced by other assumptions that rest on binary oversimplifications – residues of a colonial past neatly incorporated in the city's official slogan, "Asia's World City": East and West, rich and poor, fast and slow, old and new. In fact, all these assumptions are outdated. Hong Kong resists simple dualisms with surprising levels of integration in its spatial products. Its intense pedestrian connectivity is a result of a combination of top-down planning and bottom-up solutions, a unique collaboration between pragmatic thinking and comprehensive masterplanning, played out in three-dimensional space.

. . . This network is generated by the pressures and constraints of Hong Kong's context, not imported as an abstract idea. It is the result of neither top-down planning nor self-organizing systems. It is some new thing: an aformal urbanism.

Examples of aformal urbanism abound in Hong Kong, and not all of them are entirely anonymous. The Central and Midlevels escalator was envisaged by the Highways Department as a kind of pedestrian flyover linking the Central business district with residential neighborhoods in the Midlevels of Victoria Peak; it was proposed as a means to alleviate traffic on the region's narrow roads. By making the steep hills behind Central easier to access, the escalator had the unexpected effect of transforming a formerly sleepy neighborhood into a premier entertainment district, raising property values, and bringing new congestion . . . Like shortcuts taken across a formal quad that eventually create informal paths that the college paves, the Central and Midlevels Escalator and the Times Square Expresscalators formalize informal patterns and generate aformal urbanism.

The easy fluidity of public passage through diverse and apparently contradictory spatial and social complexes is a symptom of a more general and more fundamentally unlikely condition in Hong Kong with its origins in the city's extremes of geography and climate and unique historical circumstances . . .

A city without ground

Ground is a continuous plane and a stable reference point for the public life of the city. It is the surface on which the conflicts of urban propinquity – public and private, planned and impromptu, privileged and disadvantaged – are worked out. This stable reference point is what Hong Kong lacks.

A city built on steep slopes and vast areas of landfill at incredible density, Hong Kong's physical ground is equal parts elusive and irrelevant. Ground is never where you expect it. Nor is it often what it seems. What appears to be terra firma was likely water or air not so long ago. What appears to be a natural outcropping of rock is more likely a formed concrete retaining wall or even the side of a building. Often times a glance over a curb reveals not a gutter but several stories of descending platforms, drainage channels, and forested slopes, with no clear indication of datum. Even when a ground can be identified, such as the few blocks of urban grid in older areas of the city, it is often remarkably obfuscated, immersed in clouds of exhaust, or obstructed by major infrastructural programs like bus terminals or electrical substations.[7]

In place of a physical ground, Hong Kong has connectivity. On the North Shore of Hong Kong Island it is possible to walk from Sheung Wan through Central and Admiralty to Pacific Place 3 on the edge of Wanchai without ever having to leave a continuous network of elevated or submerged pedestrian passageways and interconnected malls, lobbies, and gardens . . .[8]

. . . Shun Tak Center cedes ground to connectivity. It is not seen so much as it envelops, not entered so much as moved through, on your way from a bus to a train. An elegant intermodal switch between land, sea, and air, it is almost primordial modernism – futurist in its ambitions . . . Legibility, however is absent. Spatial experiences like the sea approach to Hong Kong's edge are replaced by interior connective sequences that insure continuity and flow. Symmetry, centrality, axiality – the legible visual order that characterizes transit hubs envisaged by Garnier, St. Elia and Le Corbusier turns out to be unnecessary.

Figure-to-figure

Without a ground Hong Kong can have no figure-ground relationships. Rather, the city is a dense mass of figures abutting each other directly in three-dimensions. In this dense mass, even circulation becomes figural . . .

. . . The interiority is extreme, an environment that could be replicated anywhere, floating above the ground or burrowed beneath it. Intermittent breaks in the retail facade lead over short bridges to the podiums of the surrounding towers, past more shopping or directly into elevator lobbies . . .

A partial archeology of the present

. . . The same aformal logics can be observed in the development of the new district ample of aformal urbanism surrounding Tokyo's Shinjuku Station . . . An underground network of passageways leading from the station, the world's busiest, gradually spread to surrounding developments. Property owners, who saw profitability in connection to the network, financed portions of its later growth . . .

Hong Kong's aformal architecture holds out the promise of reconciling the formal and informal both in the city's decision-making process and its spatial products, yielding a unique urbanism with broad implications worldwide. Of particular interest are the possibilities for the aformal to generate civic culture, a goal that was famously elusive to modernism and megastructure alike. Hong Kong's aformal spaces – its shopping malls and footbridges – do just this. Art exhibitions and political protests occur in shopping malls, domestic workers gather on footbridges on their day off, sidewalks become salons or workshops, and streets become restaurants or dance halls. Hong Kong demonstrates the viability and even robustness of public spaces that do not resemble a street, a courtyard, a square.

1 Jameson, 1984.
2 Ibid.
3 Solomon, 2010, pp. 67–70.
4 For a deeper analysis of the IFC Mall and its role in the city of Hong Kong's access networks, see Solomon, 2012.
5 See Davis, 2004.
6 See Scott, 1998, for a complete review of this position.
7 For an alternative analysis of Hong Kong's "multiple grounds", see Shelton et al., 2010.
8 For an early analysis of the elevated walkways of Central Hong Kong, see Ohno, 1992, pp. 55–77. For a more contemporary analysis, see Frampton et al., 2012.

Jonathan D. Solomon, "Hong Kong – Aformal Urbanism" Rodolphe El-Khoury and Edwards Robbins (eds.), *Shaping the City: Studies in History, Theory and Urban Design* (New York: Routledge, 2013): 109–31.

In the 1960s, French architect Claude Parent and theorist Paul Virilio pioneered a radical method for creating urban and architectural effects, in their collaboration and 1966 pamphlet, titled "The Function of the Oblique." This concept provocatively re-envisioned the traditional realms of horizontal and vertical architectural dynamics. Where standard architecture and urban layouts have long been dominated by horizontal (floors) and vertical (walls) orientations, Parent and Virilio boldly embraced the oblique—a slanting plane. This resulted in architecture where ramps and inclined surfaces took precedence. The emphasis on obliqueness not only disrupted conventional architectural aesthetics but also posited a transformative way of experiencing and interacting with spaces, advocating for a more engaging and dynamic relationship between people and their environments. They had theorized the notion of "charged" spaces and surfaces through their drawings.[19] They demonstrated how the body is affected by the appearance of gravity of oblique surfaces, creating a sense of disequilibrium and continuous movement.

Decades later, the influence of Parent and Virilio's theory of the oblique, and more broadly, the notions of single surfaces and continuous surfaces, was vividly epitomized in the design of the Yokohama Ferry Port Terminal by Foreign Office Architects (FOA). Few competition projects, and their built outcomes, have had as much impact as this project. Resonating with the ideas of Parent and Virilio, the Yokohama project encapsulated the zeitgeist of the mid-1990s. As articulated by the designers themselves, they aspired to explore "the possibility of a transportation infrastructure that could operate less as a gate, as a limit, and more as a field of movements with no structural orientation."[20] At its core, the design aimed to morph the terminal into a complex terrain driven by the intertwined loops of circulation.

FOA were one of several design practices and authors in the 1990s who explored the potential for urban and architectural spaces to be organized by the channeling of flows. Ben van Berkel and Caroline Bos, in their trilogy of books, *Move* (1999), argue for the design concepts, techniques and effects related to "orientable" and "non-orientable structures", driven by tectonic surfaces acting as organizational structures connecting malleable programmatic ingredients.

FIGURE 3.2 Pedestrians on the publicly accessible rooftop of Yokohama International Ferry Terminal, affording urban views as this civic space projects into Tokyo Bay, by Foreign Office Architects, 1995–2002. Courtesy of Getty Images.

FOA's design for the Yokohama Ferry Port Terminal was a clear departure from the conventional modernist approach that focused on creating uniform and seamless spaces. Instead, they looked at architecture as "intensive space"—envisioning it akin to a large room where conditions such as temperature or light can vary across different areas. Advancing the conceptual framework of Parent and Virilio's oblique architectures, FOA used early computational modeling techniques to create a building that not only managed the movement of people efficiently but also made their experience more engaging and varied. In short, they aimed to design a space that was not just functional, but also spatially diverse and experientially dynamic.

MICHAEL KUBO, FARSHID MOUSSAVI, AND ALEJANDRO ZAERA POLO
The Yokohama Project

The Yokohama project actually started around the possibility of generating organisation from a circulation pattern, and as a development of an idea that we had already found in the Glass Centre project, which is basically a hybridisation between a shed – a more or less undetermined container – and a ground. Our interest in the circulation pattern was an attempt to move forward from similar approaches already developed during the 70's, where circulation was organized and then "architecture" deployed on the circulation diagram, but in a more consistent manner in which circulation can literally shape space. We had been involved in the past in designing transportation buildings and we were very interested in them precisely because of the brutal limitations they have, and the many determinations the program automatically imposes on space.

There was something very interesting about transportation buildings that we were interested in exploring. Usually, a transportation building works as an input-output device, with very clear orientation: departures and arrivals. We were more interested in exploring the possibility of a transportation infrastructure that could operate less as a gate, as a limit, and more as a field of movements with no structural orientation . . . Our first move was to set the circulation diagram as a structure of interlaced loops that allow for multiple return paths. The connection between the circulation paths was always set as a bifurcation, so that rather than setting the program as a series of adjacent spaces with more or less determined limits, we articulated them in the continuity of a branched sequence along the circulatory system. What we then called "the no-return diagram" was basically the first attempt to provide the building with a particular spatial performance. The second decision in the process was the thought that the building should not appear in the skyline, to be consistent with the idea of not making a gate on a semantic level as well, by avoiding the building becoming a sign . . . (and creating) an organisation that hybridises a pure enclosure with a topography. This immediately led to the idea of making a very flat building, and from there we moved into turning the building into a ground.

Once we decided that the building would be a warped surface, we needed to produce an argument of consistency between the no-return diagram and the surface as a geometrical argument. What we did was to associate a surface to every segment of the no-return diagram, and a surface bifurcation to every bifurcation of the line. As we wanted to spread the building mass as thin as possible, we occupied the maximum area possible within the site. This, and the requirement of placing straight boarding decks 15m from the pier's edge along both sides of the building to connect to moving bridges, is what determined the rectangular footprint of the building. This was also a decision devoid of meaning and external to the internal consistency of the project: almost a slice of a larger mille-feuille . . .

The association between segments of the diagram and surfaces gave us a basic metrics of the main chapters of the program: every segment of the no-return diagram had an associated size in square meters, which divided by the width of the pier provided the length of every surface between bifurcations. By proceeding in this manner we managed to produce the first approximation of the final form of the project, a three-dimensional version of the no-return diagram that resembled a kind of lasagne of warped surfaces. Obviously there were also some ergonomic determinations in the formal determination of that first scheme: the scale of the bifurcation was set so that it would produce inhabitable spaces of at least 3m height in section, etc . . .

. . . This would be a building without stairs and columns. The ramps became associated to the main longitudinal structural lines, running in two parallel lines along the pier, taking advantage of the depth of their bent to produce the largest structural elements. This association is extraordinarily important for the project, as it brings the structure and the circulation system together into the form in a complex whole, effectively achieving our primary goal of making the circulation affect directly the spatial definition. A very important battle took place in the project that is for us quite relevant in the production of the project as a complex entity rather than a sum of multiple linear orders: the circulatory diagram defined by the brief was perfectly symmetrical, as it required a duplication of the boarding facilities on both edges of the terminal, while the structural constraints were asymmetrical . . .

. . . If one looks at the plans of the competition entry, one can see still the struggle between symmetrical circulation and asymmetrical structure: the plans of the terminal levels are almost completely symmetrical topologically and geometrically, while the plans of the apron level are symmetrical topologically and asymmetrical geometrically.

There is another important geometrical trait at this point of the process, which is the introduction of the diagonal in plan as a consequence of the complexity introduced by making the circulation and the structure consistent. Already that association had proliferated the diagonal movement implicit in the bifurcation of the surface in the sectional dimension. The topological requirements that the ramps carried in virtue of their function made it impossible to place the landings along the same longitudinal axis, due to the limitations in the grounding conditions. This gave us the excuse for the exploration of the diagonal in plan. But the geometry of the ramps was straight between landings, producing a kind of geometrical inconsistency that we would later on correct during the basic design phase.

Some more materials were to be assembled into the project before it became a solid embryo of a building. A more refined level of programmatic determination was required. As opposed to what happened in the assemblage between structure and circulation, which blended in a metamorphic manner, the program was to become integrated in sedimentary form. (There was already a primary integration of large programmatic packages in the scale of the topography and the topology of the bifurcations.) The programmatic strategies used in the project can be related to an interest in exploring what we could roughly denominate as intensive space: that is, the kind of spatiality where the capacity of space is not directly related to its size, and where the quality of space varies differentially, rather than as a discontinuity. Intensive space is generally more effective at dealing with shifting programmatic conditions, evolution of programs, etc . . . A continuous and homogeneous space has been traditionally the instrument for flexibility, but intensive space is differentially flexible, which means that it offers multiple conditions in a continuum, in a similar way in which temperature, luminance, pressure or humidity tend to vary across a large room. Conventional programmatic distribution is fundamentally related to an extensive use of space and time: programs are allocated in particular extensions of space and time with well-defined limits. The traditional alternative to this traditional assignment is to avoid any determination of time and space, providing the maximum possible scale and openness. The potential of intensive space is to set up a degree of specificity without delimiting extensions.

There were three different programmatic strategies that were utilised in trying to exploit the potential of temporal change and programmatic instability within the circulatory/structural topography. On a primary level, the small blocks of program, shops, cafes, ticket desks, and control points were deployed as if they were furniture to be placed onto the warped surface, as if they were "confetti". So we would scan the resulting topography and detect areas where the flow of people would tend to become stagnant, to locate the furnished program in those areas, depending on their degree of "slowness". This would allow for the reconfiguration of the programmatic distribution to match the variable scenarios that a building of this nature would have, simply by assigning an order of slowness to each program in every functional scenario. As the cruise terminal functions have a very seasonal behaviour, the main advantage of the basic shed/landscape strategy and the deployment of program as furniture is that they would allow for a constant adjustment of the building to changing programmatic requirements. We often resorted to the metaphor of the picnic as a model to occupy this alienated topography . . .

. . . (A) strategy of shifting programmatic fields was designed for the design of the roof landscape: we went through a calendar with the main urban events to take place in the course of a year – the coming of age, the fireworks, the throwing of beans — and tried to locate them in ideal conditions within the roof topography, depending on views, wind protection, proximity to the city or to the water . . . This gave us a series of shifting domains that dictated the preliminary location of roof furniture – benches, canopies, fences – whose densities, orientation and quantity depended simultaneously on several programmatic conditions.

Michael Kubo, Farshid Moussavi, and Alejandro Zaera Polo, *The Yokohama Project* (Barcelona: Actar, 2002); 11, 13, 15, 17, 19.

This chapter aims to encapsulate how intensities, flows, connectivity, and networks shape cities. It brings together perspectives from urban theorists along with innovative architectural

FIGURE 3.3 Travellers walk past expansive glass walls and fluid surfaces within the train station's architecture, seamlessly linking multiple levels and forms of transit, in Arnhem Central Station, The Netherlands. Designed by UNStudio and completed in 2015. Courtesy of Getty Images.

projects that engage infrastructure and circulation. Throughout history, the formation of path systems and strategic infrastructural nodes have driven trade, communication, and the growth of human settlements. Contemporary global cities thrive as interconnected hubs in the world economy, underpinned by advanced transportation, digital networks, and financial flows. However, theorists point to disparities within global cities, where marginalized populations may be disconnected amidst such external connectivity. Meanwhile, logistics systems and supply chains have a substantial physical footprint, radically transforming urban landscapes.

However, such networked spaces can also create unique spatial experiences and urban places. Experimental architects like Foreign Office Architects pioneered new conceptions of architectural and urban space by using dynamic circulation systems, ramps, and oblique surfaces. The Yokohama Ferry Port Terminal project builds upon the diagrammatic methods introduced in Chapter 2, illustrating their application in creating innovative spatial effects. The various texts also reveal how infrastructure and networks don't just support the urban realm but actively sculpt it, with profound spatial, social, and economic implications. In the case of Hong Kong, vast elevated pedestrian networks have taken over traditional streets as civic spaces, creating a vertical compression of diverse populations and activities.

In conclusion, architects and urban planners are increasingly engaging with the complex interplay of infrastructure, networks, and urban life, recognizing their power to reshape cities and the lived experiences of their inhabitants.

4

Density, the Compact City, and Metropolitan Culture

Dense urban development offers several compelling benefits. By concentrating human activity and infrastructure within a relatively compact area, it helps preserve land for environmental conservation or agricultural use. Additionally, the proximity and interconnectedness inherent in high-density cities facilitates frequent social interactions and idea exchanges between people. These connections between people can lead to new ideas, innovation, social cohesion, and economic growth. However, when we examine the concept of density, several questions arise. How can we thoughtfully create density, utilizing urban design concepts such as the "compact city"? What unique, lifestyles communities, and cultural dynamics emerge from high-density environments? And how can architects and urban planners harness the potential benefits that can come with increased density?

In this chapter, "Density, the Compact City, and Metropolitan Culture," the authors of the selected texts explore the value of a high-density model of urban living. They consider how architects and urban designers can find benefits in urban density, such as by creating opportunities for people to interact and have meaningful experiences. Through their insights, we gain a deeper understanding of how density shapes city life and culture, and how it can be exploited to create vibrant and thriving urban spaces.

Historically, anti-urbanists resisted the dense city on the grounds of poor living conditions, detrimental health, overcrowding, and fear of crime. Up until the beginning of the twenty-first century, decentralization and suburbanization continue to be a driving force in cities around the world, fueled by transportation advances such as trains, trams, and most notably, cars allowing commuters access to less expensive land. After the Industrial Revolution, cities sprawled into vast conurbations across Europe and North America during the nineteenth and twentieth centuries, exemplified by regions such as the Ruhrgebiet and the Northeastern Seaboard.[1]

In the American context, Frank Lloyd Wright imagined his seminal low-density prototype, Broadacre City (1932), dispersing the spaces and functions of the city across a flat landscape, mixed with agricultural land. Wright saw suburbanization taking shape in 1958, as he noted, "America needs no help to build Broadacre City. It will build itself, haphazard." Ultimately, he forecast the car-based society which eventually developed most pervasively in the US.[2] Today, this suburban model can be observed worldwide from the "mega suburbs" in the periphery of most major Latin American and Mexican cities to the extended surroundings of Asian megacities—such

FIGURE 4.1 The Fok Cheong Building, a residential skyscraper in Quarry Bay, Hong Kong, features an array of protruding bay windows that extend over the courtyard, epitomizing the city's remarkable urban density and the residents' personalization of architectural spaces, 2019. Courtesy of Getty Images.

as the urbanized regions outside of Javan cities, referred to as *desakota* (*desa* meaning "village" and *kota* meaning "city"),[3] where urban and agricultural forms coexist.

By the late twentieth century, however, researchers had come to realize the overwhelming evidence of the environmental, social, and economic consequences of car-oriented suburban sprawl. In the book, *Cities and Automobile Dependence* (1989), Newman and Kenworthy popularized the link between human density and the per capita energy required for urban transportation in major cities.[4] They contrasted the dense urbanism of Hong Kong with the sprawling city of Houston, which has much higher per capita transportation energy consumption. Researchers today agree on the benefits of more closely packed human density: the proximity of more densely arranged programming and activities, reduces the per capita energy for transportation.[5] With people in closer proximity to their destinations, they can make more trips by foot or public transport. With more people per unit of land, cities can invest more tax resources in infrastructure such as public transportation and high-quality open space. And with people in compact multifamily buildings instead of single-family homes, there is less surface area per apartment, with less energy loss through air leakage. This can help reduce energy bills and carbon emissions related to heating and cooling.

The contrast between the dense urban fabric of Manhattan and the sprawling city of Phoenix illustrates the stark differences in land use and transportation patterns. In the sprawling city of Phoenix, cars seem indispensable. In Manhattan, people can ride public transportation, while dense urban development helps preserve rural and agricultural land. If Manhattanites were spread out as much as people in Phoenix, they would require twenty times more land.

By 2050, more than two thirds of the world's population is projected to be living in cities—2.5 billion more urbanites than today. To accommodate the increasing global urban population, the world's building stock will have to double by then. This is akin to building a new New York City every single month for the next 30 years.[6] If we were to build cities like Phoenix, we would waste much more energy related to transportation and use twenty times more land.

Nevertheless, it is common to encounter NIMBY (Not In My Backyard) responses towards higher-density residential living. Opponents of higher density development generally do not object to higher densities in other areas; they simply oppose it when it is planned near their current low-density residences. Additionally, some fears stem from worries about the consequences of perceived overcrowding and its potential impact on congestion, noise, and the overuse of public space. Urbanists counter these objections with core principles that can make higher density urban development desirable. These include densely mixing land uses, providing public transit, using permeable urban blocks optimized for walking, activating street frontages, providing quality public spaces, and promoting good architecture.

One key term to advocate for more dense, mixed-use development has been the notion of the "compact city." The compact city concept has historical roots, often attributed to Jane Jacobs and her influential work *The Death and Life of Great American Cities* (1961).[7] While the term "compact city" became commonly used academically and professionally only in the late 1980s, its principles align with the rising awareness of climate change and sustainable development following the 1987 Brundtland Report, *Our Common Future*.[8]

European governmental agencies played a significant role in promoting the compact city idea through documents like the EU's *Green Paper on the Urban Environment* published in 1990, which partially aimed to reduce sprawl. These documents recognized the role of urban planning and form in achieving environmental and urban sustainability and advocated for the compact city as a solution to challenges faced by European cities.

The compact city concept gained further momentum with publications like *Towards an Urban Renaissance* by the UK's Urban Task Force led by Sir Richard Rogers in 1999. By then, the British-Italian architect Richard Rogers had already made a name for himself as a champion of the compact city. Although Rogers was initially known for his architectural work such as the Centre Pompidou (co-designed with Renzo Piano), and as a proponent of High Tech architecture, in his later career he focused on issues surrounding urbanism and sustainability. In 1995, he delivered five talks for the BBC focused on sustainable cities. His fifth talk, titled *Cities for a Small Planet*, was later adapted into his eponymous book.

Roger's book, as well as the other sources, characterized the compact city as high-density, mixed-use development with an improved public realm, encouraging low-carbon lifestyles in walkable cities supported by public transit infrastructure. Largely focusing on the ecological benefits of the compact city, Rogers argues how dense cities "increase energy efficiency, consume fewer resources, produce less pollution and avoid sprawling over the countryside."[9] He notes how "dirty industry is disappearing from cities of the developed world," and sees this industrial change as an opportunity for greening manufacturing and cities as a whole.[10] He critiques the "dominant urban model" of the city zoned as the downtown office core, out-of-town shopping, and suburban living, all connected by highways. Implicitly, he rejects the segregated "single-function zoning" based on modernist urbanist principles established by CIAM in the 1930s.

Rogers attacks car-based cities, pointing towards the economic and social costs of traffic congestion and the impact of air pollution on public health. Instead, a reinvention of the model of high-density urbanism, the compact city, "grows around centres of social and commercial activity located at public transport nodes,[11]" endorsing the now prevalent Transit Oriented Development (TOD) model. Rogers also sees subsequent improvements in the "security and conviviality" of public space, and the reduction of congestion and pollution.[12] He sees the city as a condenser of human interaction and exchange, advocating for a "compact and overlapping approach" that "embraces complexity," in opposition to car-based, rigidly-zoned urban development.[13]

RICHARD ROGERS
Cities for a Small Planet

My own approach to urban sustainability reinterprets and reinvents the 'dense city" model. It is worth remembering why. In this century, this model was so categorically rejected. The industrial cities of the nineteenth century were hell: they suffered extremes of overcrowding, poverty and ill-health. Stinking open sewers spread cholera and typhoid: toxic industries stood side by side with overflowing tenements. As a result, life expectancy in many of the industrial cities of Victorian England was less than twenty-five years. It was precisely these hazards and basic inequities that led planners like Ebenezer Howard in 1898, and Patrick Abercrombie in 1944, to propose decanting populations into less dense and greener surroundings: Garden Cities and New Towns.

Today, by contrast, dirty industry is disappearing from cities of the developed world. In theory at least, with the availability of 'green' manufacturing, virtually clean power generation and public transport systems, and advanced sewerage and waste systems, the dense city model need not be seen as a health hazard. This means we can reconsider the social advantages of proximity, rediscover the advantages of living in each other's company.

Beyond social opportunity the 'dense city' model can bring major ecological benefits. Dense cities can through integrated planning be designed to increase energy-efficiency, consume fewer resources, produce less pollution and avoid sprawling over the countryside. It is for these reasons that I believe we should be investing in the idea of a 'Compact City' – a dense and socially diverse city where economic and social activities overlap and where communities are focused around neighbourhoods.

This concept differs radically from today's dominant urban model, that of the United States: a city zoned by function with downtown office areas, out-of-town shopping and leisure centres, residential suburbs and highways. So powerful is this image and so prevalent are the forces that motivate its creation (set by the market-driven criteria of commercial developers) that the less developed countries are now locked into a trajectory that has already failed the developed countries.

The pursuit of this approach is having quantifiably disastrous results. The reason for its continued adoption is economic expediency. If the compact and overlapping approach embraces complexity, the zoned approach rejects it, reducing the city to simplistic divisions and easily managed legal and economic packages. Even at the scale of individual buildings, developers both public and private are turning their backs on the concept of mixed use. Traditional city buildings, in which studios sit over family homes, which sit over offices, which sit over shops, bring life to the street and reduce the need for citizens to get into their cars to meet everyday needs. But these mixed-use buildings create complex tenancies which local authorities find hard to manage and developers find hard to finance and sell. Instead, public and private developers prefer single-function buildings. And when embarking on major projects they prefer large open sites or cheap 'green-field' ones which offer the possibility of constructing whole housing estates or business parks with minimal leasehold complications. Furthermore, these sites facilitate maximum standardisation of design and construction, thus furthering cost-effectiveness and the argument against mixed use. The search for short-term profit and quick results continues to turn investment away from complex mixed use urban development and its inherent social and environmental benefits.

But it is the car which has played the critical role in undermining the cohesive social structure of the city. There are an estimated 500 million cars in the world today. They have eroded the quality of public spaces and have encouraged suburban sprawl. Just as the elevator made the skyscraper possible, so the car has enabled citizens to live away from city centres. The car has made viable the whole concept of dividing everyday activities into compartments, segregating offices, shops and homes. And the wider cities spread out, the more uneconomic it becomes to expand their public transport systems, and the more car-dependent citizens become. Cities around the world are being transformed to facilitate the car even though it is cars rather than industry that are now generating the largest amount of air pollution, the very same pollution that the suburban dwellers are fleeing. In all, 2 trillion cubic metres of exhaust fumes per year are created, and the number of cars is likely to rise by 50 per cent by 2010 and to double by 2030. Paradoxically, from the perspective of the individual, the car remains the century's most liberating and most desired technological product. It is cheap because it is manufactured in volume and is subsidised; It is practical because cities have not been planned to rely on public transport; and it is an irresistible cultural icon that delivers glamour and status.

Simple logistics show how damage is caused by increasing car ownership. First the street, once the local playground and general meeting place, is taken over by parked cars. An efficient parking standard requires 20 square metres for a single car. Even supposing that only one in five inhabitants owns a car, then, a city of 10 million (roughly that of London) needs an area about ten times the size of the City of London ('the square mile'), just to park cars. But start up those 2 million cars and drive off, and you saturate the city with pollution and congestion that harass and divide communities. As transport by car becomes integral to city planning, the street corners and the shapes and surfaces of public spaces are all determined for the benefit of the motorist. Eventually the entire city, from its overall shape and spacing of new buildings to the design of its curbs, lamp posts and railings, is designed according to this one criterion.

Car ownership more than doubled in Europe between 1970 and 1995, and is about to soar in developing cities. It continues to be encouraged by those supporting both nationalised and privatised car industries. And the anticipation of astronomically high levels of car use in the future has led planners to design cities around road specifications, effectively encouraging ever-increasing car use.

Research in San Francisco has compared streets in different neighbourhoods to evaluate the impact of road traffic on the sense of local community. The movement of individuals between houses in busy and quiet streets was monitored in different neighbourhoods. The data reveals the shocking but predictable reality that the level of social interaction between neighbours in a given street, the sense of community in that street, is inversely related to the amount of traffic passing through. This study points the finger at urban traffic as a fundamental cause for the alienation of the urban resident, an effect at the heart of the erosion of modern-day citizenship.

Fortunately, the hidden cost of the zoned urban model is finally being recognised. In the United States the economic cost of traffic congestion, in terms of squandered energy and lost time, is about $150 billion per year, equivalent to the gross national product of Denmark. And this figure does not begin to address the social costs including health, recently estimated by the World Resources Institute (WRI) as a further $300 billion. Both figures exclude damage to the natural environment and, crucially, the social cost of isolation and disenfranchisement of those citizens left scratching a living in isolated and rotting city ghettos, while the city empties itself out into ever more exclusive suburbs. The *New York Times* recently headlined the dramatic problems of gridlock and pollution engendered by the sprawling 'paradise' cities of Phoenix, Denver, Las Vegas and Salt Lake City, Phoenix is now larger than Los Angeles with only a third of its population. Its quality of air ranks among the country's worst outside Southern California.

The creation of the modern Compact City demands the rejection of single-function development and the dominance of the car. The question is how to design cities in which communities thrive and mobility is increased – how to design for personal mobility without allowing the car to undermine communal life, how to design for and accelerate the use of clean transport systems and re-balance the use of our streets in favour of the pedestrian and the community.

The Compact City addresses these issues. It grows around centres of social and commercial activity located at public transport nodes. These provide the focal points around which neighbourhoods develop. The Compact City is a network of these neighbourhoods, each with its own parks and public spaces and accommodating a diversity of overlapping private and public activities. London's historic structure of towns, villages, squares and parks is typical of a polycentric pattern of development. Most importantly, these neighbourhoods bring work and facilities within convenient reach of the community, and this proximity means less driving for everyday needs. In large cities, Mass Transit Systems can provide high-speed cross-town travel by linking one neighbourhood centre with another, leaving local distribution to local systems. This reduces the volume and impact of through traffic, which can be calmed and controlled, particularly around the public heart of neighbourhoods. Local trams, light railway systems and electric buses become more effective, and cycling and walking more pleasant. Congestion and pollution in the streets are drastically reduced and the sense of security and conviviality of public space is increased.

Sustainable Compact Cities could, I contend, reinstate the city as the ideal habitat for a community-based society. It is an established type of urban structure that can be interpreted in all manner of ways in response to all manner of cultures. Cities should be about the people they shelter, about face-to-face contact, about condensing the ferment of human activity, about generating and expressing local culture. Whether in a temperate or an extreme climate, in a rich or poor society,

> the long-term aim of sustainable development is to create a flexible structure for a vigorous community within a healthy and non-polluting environment.
>
> Proximity, the provision of good public space, the presence of natural landscape and the exploitation of new urban technologies can radically improve the quality of air and of life in the dense city. Another benefit of compactness is that the countryside itself is protected from the encroachment of urban development. I will show how the concentration of diverse activities, rather than the grouping of similar activities, can make for more efficient use of energy. The Compact City can provide an environment as beautiful as that of the countryside.
>
> Richard Rogers, *Cities for a Small Planet* (London: Basic Books, 1998): 3–4.

The concept of the compact city has become a critical component of sustainable urbanism, combating suburban sprawl, and promoting a healthier environment and society. However, there are other aspects related to density that architects and planners have aimed to promote. One of these is related to social "collisions," augmenting the possible interactions between people. In *The City in History* (1961), Lewis Mumford, the noted urbanist, described cities as "containers" that help speed up civilization. "As with a gas, the very pressure of the molecules within that limited space produced more social collisions and interactions within a generation than would have occurred in many centuries if still isolated in their native habitats, without boundaries," he wrote.[14] From their very beginnings, cities accelerated the potential for innovation and the context conducive for social experiments. Ideas prosper in city centers, because cities concentrate people and offer them spontaneous and possibly fruitful encounters with others.

Researcher Thomas Allen, a former professor at MIT and author of *Managing the Flow of Technology* (1977), contributed some ground-breaking insights related to the university's "infinity corridor," the long hallway that connects most campus classrooms. Allen was known for the "Allen Curve," which found that collaboration increases as a function of proximity. He observed that in between classes, the crowded corridor became a social condenser of random and serendipitous encounters. These contributed to several inventions. The university eventually chose to plan future buildings around this corridor in order to further reap its rewards.

Knowledge-based industries benefit from spatial clustering to facilitate face-to-face interaction, where unpredictability and novelty can help stimulate the brain and spark innovation. The legendary innovator Steve Jobs, cofounder of Apple, famously played a role in designing Pixar's new headquarters with a large atrium at the center. He then located everything from the meeting rooms to the cafeteria, mailboxes, and even the bathrooms beside the atrium. This way, people would be more likely to run into each other serendipitously, increasing the possibility of fruitful encounters, like the perfect idea someone might never have thought of alone.

Collisions are central to the success of cities. Urban areas are known to exceed rural ones in innovation and economic output. US metropolitan areas alone generate 75 percent of the national GDP.[15] In the United States, large cities produce twice as many patents per person as small cities—plus those patents have more impact.[16] Cities capture the economic and intellectual benefits of agglomeration and physical proximity in a super linear way.[17] Double the city's size, and productivity and innovation more than doubles.

Similar to the metabolism of animals as they grow—such as the low metabolic rate of elephants, for example—large cities create massive economies of scale, as noted by the theoretical physicist

Geoffrey West and his colleagues. They found that when cities double in size, they only require a resource increase of 85 percent, such as the number of gas stations and the amount of road surface. This seems to be particularly true for dense cities, where resources are shared among more people, making them the champions of sustainability.

However, cities have also exacerbated problems from their very beginning. According to West, the bigger cities become, the bigger their problems. When a city doubles in size, there is a 15 percent per capita increase in violent crimes and traffic. The mathematics of social networks explain that the bigger the city, the more social connectivity per capita. However, while social connectivity fosters idea exchange and making financial transactions, it also speeds up more dubious activities and virus transmissions. During the Covid-19 pandemic and in the midst of social distancing, critics of cities called into question dense urban life.

While compact cities may have contributed to the rapid spread of the Covid-19 pandemic, its opposite, urban sprawl, may have been a cause. Zoonotic diseases, which spring from animals to humans, are a result of our increasing wildlife-human interface. They are partially a consequence of the destruction of nature through deforestation and unbridled suburbanization. If we can limit our human footprint by creating compact cities, we may be able to better protect our forests and wildlife.

Covid-19 was one of several instances in which density was considered a risk and a problem. In 2001, terrorists crashed two airplanes into New York's Twin Towers. The World Trade Center towers, which had been a symbol of the world's economic system, became emblematic of tragedy. The attacks raised difficult questions about dense urban life. "If there are to be new rules for the new warfare," wrote *Wired*, "one of the first is surely this: Density kills."[18]

The common perception of density in New York, at the time of architect's Rem Koolhaas 1978 book, *Delirious New York: A Retroactive Manifesto for Manhattan*, was that of a problem needing mitigation.[19] For instance, the 1961 Zoning Resolution of New York was aimed at promoting more open space and towers that were further set-back from the street. However, Koolhaas shows in his book that density was not a problem to be solved but an essential characteristic that contributed to the unique identity of New York City. Koolhaas contends that density is not just a practical solution to urban living but an essential catalyst for cultural and social development. Through historical analyses and visionary proposals, he showcases the potential of dense, hyper-concentrated urban spaces to foster innovation and dynamic interactions among people, leading to a "delirious" urban experience. Koolhaas' argument advocates for the embrace of density as a means to create more stimulating and culturally rich urban environments.

Koolhaas argues that density is essential to the city's vitality because it allows for a diversity of uses and activities to coexist in close proximity. This diversity, in turn, creates a sense of excitement and dynamism that is not possible in less dense environments. In particular, it is the juxtaposition of uses that could lead to unique cultures. He found examples in the phase of New York's early skyscrapers at the beginning of the twentieth century. Before a mature real estate market would push them to become standardized products, skyscrapers contained a kaleidoscope of activities, all under one roof. Koolhaas celebrated the skyscrapers of this age for their seemingly absurd juxtapositions of different uses, or their "culture of congestion." In *Delirious New York*, he focuses on the Downtown Athletic Club on West Street, a 518-foot-tall building that included an interior golf course. One floor featured a boxing club, a locker room, and an oyster bar. It was almost the set of a surrealist dream. "Eating oysters with boxing gloves, naked, on the 9th floor,"[20] Koolhaas wrote in *Delirious New York*. These skyscrapers were social condensers, with seemingly random juxtaposition of uses bringing people together in entirely new ways on their stacked "plots" in the sky. They created "unpredictable intrigue" through the surrender to "the definitive instability of life in the Metropolis."[21] They embodied the great promise of cities.

For Koolhaas, one of the projects representing New York City's potential for greatness was Rockefeller Center. Touted as a city within a city when it was first commissioned by John D. Rockefeller in the 1930s, it married commercial and cultural functions into a complex of nineteen buildings. The project includes a public plaza in front of the tallest skyscraper, which in the winter holds an ice-skating rink. Shorter buildings surround the center tower, each lavishly decorated with art, one of them housing Radio City Music Hall. An underground concourse has a shopping complex and connects to the subway system. Koolhaas writes:

> The Culture of Congestion proposes the conquest of each block by a Single structure. Each Building will become a "house" – a private realm Inflated to admit houseguests but not to the point of pretending universality in the spectrum of Its offerings. Each "house" will represent a different lifestyle and different ideology.
>
> On each floor, the Culture of Congestion will arrange new and exhilarating human activities in unprecedented combinations. Through Fantastic Technology it will be possible to reproduce all "situations" – from the most natural to the most artificial – wherever and whenever desired. Each City within a City will be so unique that it will naturally attract its own inhabitants.
>
> . . . The Culture of Congestion is the culture of the 20th century.[1]
>
> 1 Rem Koolhaas, Delirious New York: A Retroactive Manifesto for Manhattan (New York: Monacelli Press, 2014), 131

In the chapter, "The Skyscraper Theorists" in *Delirious New York*, Koolhaas investigates a number of illustrations from the early twentieth century which had served as predictions of the future of Manhattan. Tracing thinkers, theorists, and illustrators, he retroactively formulates a theory of *Manhattanism*, in what he calls, "the real enterprise of Manhattan's architects."[22] Ultimately, each Manhattan block is posited as a "City within a City." The sheer density of people and activities is a source of creativity, innovation, and cultural exchange. One year after publishing *Delirious New York*, Koolhaas summarized and synthesized its main themes in a follow up article, "The Future's Past" (1979).

REM KOOLHAAS
"The Future's Past"

"Why do we have a mind if not to get our way?"

Dostoevsky

In 1929, architect Ivan Leonidov designed an office building for the center of Moscow called the House of Industry. It was conceived as a tall, rectangular slab. Its facades consisted of a steel lattice with sliding glass panels that could "disappear" in the summer, making the walls, in effect, a transparent scaffold of human activity. Two-thirds of the way up, several floors were omitted: The gap formed a park in the air. An exposed elevator-stairwell tapered toward the top to reflect the diminishing volume of vertical traffic; a separate, freestanding lift led directly from the ground to the roof to make it easily accessible to Moscow's inhabitants.

But the most unusual feature of the building was the floorplan, a drastic architectural revision of the idea and mechanics of work itself. A square grid divided two-thirds of each floor into identical areas for every worker. These subdivisions were marked on the ground by white lines on a cushion-like rubber surface meant to combine psychological comfort with acoustic control. Potted plants further demarcated individual territories.

The remaining third of each floor was conceived by Leonidov as an *antithetical zone*, an area for non work that included a swimming pool, a sauna and high-pressure shower, kiosk for news and announcements, a lavish arrangement of *chaises-longue*s, a small library, an acoustic console, and a TV-like screen.

Leonidov was convinced that a human being could concentrate on any given task for only about 20 minutes. Then fatigue would begin to erode performance. He built on this thesis by making each floor of the office complex into a *recuperative plane*, where work is only one of many possible activities, each erasing the exhaustion left by the previous effort. The "office" thus became a cultural apparatus, holding out to its occupants the promise of a perpetual peak condition. (Soviet officials rejected the whole idea, and Leonidov's building was never constructed.)

Not long afterward, in Manhattan, several architects, whose names have not come down to us, conceived the Downtown Athletic Club. Like Leonidov's House of Industry, the Club, built in 1931, is essentially a stack of therapeutic planes. But where each of the floors in the Moscow building was to have offered identical combinations of activities, each story of the Downtown Athletic Club is emphatically different, and the building as a whole strives not so much for an efficiency of work as for an efficiency of pleasure.

An Incubator for Adults

Each floor is devoted to a particular interpretation of "athletic" activity. But as a climb through the structure demonstrates, the layout transcends athletics.

The lower 15 floors are accessible only to men. Their sequence from ground to top corresponds to an ever-increasing refinement of activity. Floor 7 is an interior golf course, a synthetic English landscape with grassy hills (real) and a small stream that curls invitingly across the terrain. After nature's near-total eclipse in the Metropolis, it is now re-created as merely one of the city's congested layers. Stopping on the ninth floor, the guest finds himself in a vestibule leading directly to a locker room. There he undresses, puts on trunks and boxing gloves, and enters an adjoining space equipped for boxing and wrestling. On the southern side of the locker room, there is also a small oyster bar.

Eating oysters with boxing gloves, near naked, on the ninth floor – such is the "plot" of this rectangle.

The 10th floor is devoted to preventive medicine. There are sections for massage and rubbing, an 8-bed station for artificial sun-bathing, and a 10-bed rest area, all arranged around a Turkish bath.

In one corner, there is a medical facility, with a capacity of five patients. A doctor here is in charge of the procedure of "colonic irrigation" – the literal invasion of the human body with cultured bacteria to modify and improve its natural metabolism.

From the 17th to the 19th floors, the men, perfected in the lower part, are allowed to communicate with the opposite sex. The final 20 floors are devoted to hotel accommodations.

Such fanatical pursuit of a transcendent peak physical and mental condition amounts to a form of human redesign. The Downtown Athletic Club provides its clients with traditional athletic pastimes that have been crossbred with modern technology. The result is an incubator for adults, who, impatient with the pace of evolution, can reconstruct themselves into new beings . . .

. . . Return to Disneyland

. . . To establish a world totally fabricated by man, to live inside fantasy – this was the ambitious program they had set themselves, a program that to be realized could never be openly stated. Who would allow it?

This view of architecture was triggered by a specific mutation in the forms of human coexistence: hyperdensity, the simultaneous explosion in certain parts of the world of both modern technology and human population. From this mutation, modern architects derived their vision of an architecture equally mutant, and perhaps compensatory and retaliatory as well. Their object – dangerous, manipulative, artificial, experimental, and behavioralist in the extreme – was the transformation of the Metropolis into a colossal laboratory . . . of life itself.

But there are opportunities commensurate with the dangers of this approach. It claims for architecture a role in human experimentation, not just in designing the laboratory. If the Metropolis is already transforming its inhabitants, why not take the process into our own hands? Only in this way can we invent the "plots" for the disinherited, scriptless urban masses, the drifting castaways of the 20th century.

At this moment, however, a persistent if unspoken coalition of the two major architectural avant-gardes – the Rationalists in Europe and the Post-Modernists in America, both of them susceptible to a misguided "historicism" in their designs – threatens this 50-year-old Architecture of Congestion with deliberate extinction. The best minds in modern architecture are ready to abandon the claims staked out in the 1920s for an activist profession with a capability, and indeed a responsibility, for redesigning the human environment. The new architects are determined to pose the issues of architecture in traditional terms once more. Doric columns, pediments, moldings, piazzas – all are making their prodigal return.

This conflict makes it both simple and difficult to predict architecture's future. If this reactionary coalition wins, there will be no future – only an empty imitation of the past that will make Disneyland a monument to authenticity. If the coalition loses, the future of architecture will be as unpredictable as ever.

Rem Koolhaas, "The Future's Past," *Wilson Quarterly* 3, no. 1 (Winter, 1979): 135–40.

But how should we design for this dense world? In the work of the Dutch firm OMA, the firm cofounded by Rem Koolhaas, it is simply to harness the power of density. Packing and juxtaposing contrasting uses on a site became a core design philosophy of OMA. Even in their design for a proposal for Parc de la Villette, a park in Paris, OMA proposed to activate the park with bands of different programs, almost like a horizontal skyscraper. In their museum for Rotterdam, the Kunsthal, the spatial juxtapositions included a public service road going through the museum, and the building itself acting as a bridge between a roadway and a park.

Rem Koolhaas' concept of "Bigness," articulated in his essay "Bigness or the Problem of Large,"[23] refers to the transformative scale at which architecture starts to impact and intertwine with urbanism. For Koolhaas, once buildings reach a certain scale, they begin to operate beyond traditional architectural principles and start affecting urban environments in unique ways. "Bigness no longer needs the city," Koolhaas writes. "It competes with the city; or better still, it is the city. If urbanism generates potential and architecture exploits it, Bigness enlists the generosity of urbanism against the meanness of architecture."[24] While cities can benefit from "Bigness" in handling infrastructure and programmatic requirements, it also challenges urban continuity.

Are serendipity and surprise possible within the context of a crowded landscape of competing forms that is the city? Is there a way in which we can densify even more, and achieve self-sufficiency? And how can we extend urbanism into the third dimension to overcome the problem that most cities are regulated through zoning, generally limited to two dimensions? These are the challenges addressed by MVRDV, another Dutch firm, and its cofounder, Winy Maas.

The firm's work is driven by a desire for land-use maximization and densification. Early on, they became interested in stacking landscapes, despite their associated horizontality. This led to the design for the Netherlands pavilion for the Expo 2000 in Hanover, a pavilion with stacked functions of six different landscapes, titled "Holland Creates Space." In their project "Silodam," completed in 2003, they stacked different housing types into one ten-story compact mass, complete with interior mini neighborhoods. In their dense three-tower skyscraper project "The Valley," completed in Amsterdam in 2022, they included elevated common landscapes, shared among residents.

Several of their books further expanded their argument around density. In *Farmax: Excursions on Density* (1998), MVRDV critiqued the suburban "grayness" of the Dutch landscape and proposed to intensify density.[25] Their later book *KM3: Excursions on Capacities* (2005) built on this work while delving deeper into the implications of global population growth and resource consumption.[26] As a potential solution, it proposed different scenarios of hyper-dense urban environments to accommodate the needs of a growing population. "KM3 is a story about a world that is getting dense. Very dense. It constructs its logical response: a city that is denser," MVRDV wrote. The book rang the alarm that if everyone on earth "behaved with U.S. citizen-like consumption" it would require four planet Earths to sustain.

The firm's key contribution to the design debate is centered around their concept of the "datascape," first put forward in the early 1990s. Maas argued that in an era of technological advancement, everything can be made and nothing seems strange or extravagant anymore. This proliferation of form making has led to a "sea of uniqueness" in which the individual object has become meaningless. Maas argues that architecture should embrace this massiveness, or

FIGURE 4.2 In this competition entry by OMA for the redevelopment of Les Halles, Paris, a playful cluster of tapering buildings appears to sprout from the subterranean layers of an underground shopping center, blending retail with innovative architectural form, landscapes, and urban spaces. Courtesy of OMA.

vastness of possibility, and use it as an opportunity to explore the "datascapes" of our world, such as the statistical information related to behavioral and lifestyle preferences. Maas writes: "In this massiveness, architecture becomes synonymous with urbanism."[27] Asking what aspects of the material world can be informed by facts, MVRDV had developed a design method through which information is expressed in spatial terms.

Maas argues that by understanding these datascapes, architects can create buildings that are both pragmatic and critical. They can use their work to challenge the norms and morals of our society and construct possible "arguments" for a better future.

A historical precedent for this approach can be found in architect and artist Hugh Ferriss' drawings. Ferriss visualized New York's 1916 Zoning Resolution, illustrating how regulatory mechanisms like setback requirements shaped the city's skyline over time. Ferriss' large charcoal drawings showcased the pure expressions of the zoning code's impact on the built environment and served as a precursor to the modern datascape concept. His dark, evocative drawings, later published in his 1929 book *The Metropolis of Tomorrow*, would later inspire Gotham City in the *Batman* comics and movies.[28]

This method, like Hugh Ferriss' visualizations of zoning codes, substitutes artistic intuition with data. MVRDV's "Pig City" epitomizes this approach, which is a stacking of pig landscapes based on pork consumption statistics. MVRDV proposed skyscrapers filled with pigs, akin to a statistical diagram. In response to the desire for single family homes, they promoted a vertical suburb, called *The Vertical Village* (2012). Challenging traditional horizontal cityscapes, they stacked single family homes in a new configuration of vertical density.

In their 1999 publication, *Metacity / Datatown*, MVRDV applied this method on a global level.[29] "The world has shed the anachronism of the 'global village' and is transforming into the more advanced state of the 'metacity.' More and more regions have become more or less continuous urban fields," writes Maas:

> How to study this Metacity? Initially, one can describe its vastness and explore its contents perhaps only by number or data. Its web of possibilities – both economical and spatial – seems so complex that statistical techniques seem the only way to grasp its processes. By selecting or connecting data according to hypothetical prescriptions, a world of numbers turns into diagrams . . . A 'datatown' appears that resists the objective of style. One way to study the world of numbers is through the use of 'extremizing scenarios'. They lead to frontiers, edges, and therefore to inventions. If we imagine the most extreme state of the Metacity's enlargement of urban conditions – and thus the reduction of available space – new urban inventions might start to emerge. Looking at the world's available territories, only a scant percent of the earth's total surface currently can be imagined as usable urban space– for living, for industry, for agriculture, for water-cleaning, and so on.[1]
>
> 1 Winy Maas and MDRDV, *Metacity / Datatown* (Rotterdam: 010 Publishers, 1999).

"Datatown" was an extrapolation of Dutch statistics. Meant to be a self-supporting city, it housed all its own needs, including energy and agriculture. "Datatown is based only upon data," writes Maas, "a city of 400 by 400 km . . . Datatown is dense . . . In fact, with 1,477 inhabitants per square kilometre, Datatown is the densest place on earth. It is a city for 241 million inhabitants. It is the USA in one city."[30]

What would be the spatial implications of different social preferences at this level of density? For instance, what if everyone wanted to live in urban blocks, or in detached houses? And where would the waste go? And what, with current eating habits, would this mean for agriculture? Would it be possible to locate pig production into vertical farms to reduce transportation costs? The project became about visualizing different scenarios.

FIGURE 4.3 In their design for the Markthal in Rotterdam, MVRDV arranged 228 apartments into a vast arch, allowing a covered market space and an expansive public art work by Arno Coenen and Iris Roskam, colorfully depicting fruits, vegetables, and fish. Completed in 2014. Courtesy of Getty Images.

Datascapes are both a serious inquiry as well as a provocation, showing the spatial implications of our habits and choices. They are an investigation into the socio cultural and economic forces that shape our built environment. MVRDV typically begins design projects with an assembly of all relevant information, from demographic information to zoning laws and building views. Instead of seeing this as a bureaucratic burden, they use this as an opportunity. The datascape becomes the design, making for buildings and urban spaces that are dense and iconic in their diagram-likeness.

WINY MAAS
"Datascape: The Final Extravaganza"

Massive Uniqueness: the final extravaganza

Everything can be made, every object is imaginable, nothing seems strange or extravagant anymore. What should one make under such circumstances? Do we still aspire to the ultimate extravaganza? Are we suffering from "object fatigue," a consequence of the multitude of objects competing for our attention, all these buildings clamoring to tell us something?

In our search for the "one-off" in a veritable slew of the "unique," the expression of the individual object has become ridiculous: in a massive "sea of uniqueness" the individual object simply ceases to exist. In this massiveness, architecture becomes synonymous with urbanism.

Majorities

The lion's share of building production is concerned with the banal and the ordinary. The desire to be avant-garde signifies an all-absorbing massiveness, a prescribed experience, a pasteurized reality. Why is there still no interest in it? Are we afraid of the banal in ourselves?

It has become the emblem of something that is past its peak, a vivid illustration of the twentieth century dilemma: in our search for the unique we all make or find the same things; desiring *en masse* the authentic and exceptional, it all turns banal.

If we regard this phenomenon ironically, we are denying all its humanity. The way we look down on it, must be the same as the way the Victorian bourgeoisie looked down on the working classes, with contempt, mixed with shame. Now, as then, a Dickensian type is needed to return that human face to banality.

Urbanism

When architecture becomes urbanism, it enters the realms of quantities and infrastructure, of time and relativism. Things come, things go. Events take place in apparently unorganized patterns, the very chaos of which possesses hidden logics, allowing "gravities" to emerge from within this endless tapestry of objects.

These gravities reveal themselves when sublimated beneath certain assumed maximized circumstances or within certain maximized constraints.

Because of tax differences, the borders between Belgium and the Netherlands are occupied with vast numbers of villas generating a linear town along the frontier. In Holland market demands have precipitated a "slick" of houses-with-a-small-garden. Political constraints in Hong Kong generate "piles" of dwellings around its boundaries. The popularity of white brick in Friesland causes a "white cancer" of housing estates alongside all the villages. In its desire for a cosmetic nineteenth-century identity, Berlin forces its new buildings into tight envelopes. This pushes larger programs underground, turning the streets into mere components in the midst of vast programs. Monumental regulations in Amsterdam limit the demand for modern programs, generating "mountains of program" invisible from the street behind the medieval facades. Throughout the Ruhr, demands of accessibility create virtually enclosed types of infrastructure, precipitating a string of linear towns. In La Defense in Paris, to avoid the high-rise regulations massive programs have manifested themselves as ziggurats with 18-meter high accessible "steps" so that all offices can be entered by the maximum length of the fire ladders.

Psychological issues, anti-disaster patterns, lighting regulations, acoustic treatments. All these manifestations can be seen as "scapes" of the data behind it.

Extremities

If "progress" remains the main reason for "research," the hypothesis remains the most effective way to deal with it. In order to understand the behavior of massiveness, we have to push it to the limits and adopt this "extremizing" as a technique of architectural research.

Assuming a possible maximization (the word "maximum" already implies rules), society will be confronted with the laws and by-laws that it has set up and that are extrapolated with an iron logic. It will begin questioning these regulations.

The protection of certain areas push programs to the remaining corners of our countries. Do we want that? More comfort raises the issue that we are becoming dependent on it. Do we want that? More massiveness and higher densities leads to the question of whether we still should use our light and air regulations. Or if we should cope with noise in another way.

Datascapes: sublimized pragmatism?

Under maximized circumstances, every demand, rule, or logic is manifested in pure and unexpected forms that go beyond artistic intuition or known geometry and replace it with "research."

Form becomes the result of such an extrapolation or assumption as a "datascape" of the demands behind it. It shows the demands and norms, balancing between ridicule and critique, sublimizing pragmatics.

It connects the moral with the normal. Having found the opportunity to criticize the norm and the moral behind it, it constructs a possible "argument."

Artistic intuition is replaced by "research": hypotheses that observe, extrapolate, analyze and criticize our behavior.

Winy Maas, "Datascape: The Final Extravaganza", *Daidalos*, 69/70 (1998): 48–54.

As the global population continues to gravitate toward cities, the concept of the compact city becomes increasingly relevant and crucial in shaping sustainable and vibrant urban environments. As explored in this chapter's readings, the valorization of urban density may also be a point of departure for design strategies, such as by promoting a unique "culture of congestion" in Rem Koolhaas' theories on Manhattanism, in which unexpected interactions take place due to proximity, adjacency, and complexity. In addition, MVRDV's thesis of the "datascape" as an expression of a site's accessible data can create unexpected results, enabling their concept of massive architecture becoming urbanism. Through the work of architects and urban designers like Koolhaas, Rogers, and MVRDV, we see how density can be harnessed as a creative force, shaping the physical and social fabric of our cities. By understanding the implications, challenges, and opportunities associated with density, we can pave the way for a more sustainable and exciting urban future.

5

Ecology, Resilience, and Green Infrastructure

This chapter examines urbanity through an ecological lens, advocating for a greater alignment between the built and natural environments. In response to pressing environmental challenges such as climate change, an increasing number of architects, urban designers and landscape architects increasingly embrace environmental principles. They champion "designing with nature," reintroducing natural elements into urban settings through initiatives such as green infrastructure, and proposing new design concepts and methods for large territories, as exemplified by Landscape Urbanism.

Advocates of these approaches argue for a synthesis of environmental planning, water management, landscape architecture, and architecture. Landscape Urbanism integrates ecology, infrastructure, and engineering, synthesizing diverse expertise to design urban environments. Proponents not only recognize the practical benefits of greater synergies with nature, such as managing stormwater through diverting it through green areas instead of concrete drains, but also value the indeterminacy and absence of formal unity which ecological systems present. Moreover, some designers seek inspiration from indigenous knowledge, which offer time-tested strategies attuned to local ecosystems. These approaches seek to harmonize human settlements with their natural surroundings, fostering sustainability and resilience.

Since the advent of the agricultural revolution, which allowed for permanent settlements instead of nomadic hunter-gatherer lifestyles, our ancestors inadvertently placed themselves in the path of natural disasters. Uncontrollable events such as floods, droughts, and hurricanes posed considerable risks to their well-being. Furthermore, they also significantly modified the natural environments, such as through deforestation, which led to soil erosion. This marked the beginning of an adversarial relationship with nature, where human habitation and cities became subject to its forces and sometimes contributed unintentionally to the occurrence and severity of such "natural" events. These challenges served as harsh reminders of the increased vulnerability and responsibility that came with settled living—and, as Jared Diamond showed in his eponymous 2005 book, they occasionally led to societal *Collapse*.[1]

The Industrial Revolution appeared to offer an advantage in our relationship with nature. With access to more resilient materials and advanced technologies, we gained new powers to control and shape our environment. Steel, concrete, and various engineering innovations allowed us to reshape landscapes, dam rivers, deforest land, and even reclaim land from oceans. Air conditioning made inhabiting the harshest desert environments viable. However, this newfound control was not without consequences, as climate change and a higher frequency of disasters began to manifest themselves. Trees were cleared, hillsides were bulldozed for urban development, and homes with ocean views were built on vulnerable beachfronts. This disregard for natural flora and topography led to adverse outcomes such as landslides and flooding in urbanized territories. The larger repercussions include a warming planet with much hotter cities and generally more erratic and extreme weather.

However, since the mid-twentieth century, our perception of the relationships between cities, natural ecologies, and our energy paradigm, has evolved significantly. In the 1950s, as it became evident that the planetary oil supply was finite, interest in solar homes and neighborhoods grew. Architects like Victor and Aladar Olgyay promoted "bioclimatic" architecture, which considered environmental conditions in design.[2] The 1960s brought Rachel Carson's book *Silent Spring* (1962),[3] highlighting the dangers of pesticides, the first Earth Day protest march in 1970, and important major environmental legislation such as the Clean Air Act and Clean Water Act. Buckminster Fuller's *Operating Manual for Spaceship Earth* (1969)[4] argued for the need for responsible resource management, while the iconic "Blue Marble" (1972) photograph raised global awareness of Earth's fragility.

Theorist Sanford Kwinter, later commented on the power of these Apollo photographs from outer space:

> The earth, seen now in uncanny perspective rising as an exterior orbiting planet, was simply astonishing. More than simply an inert yet hospitable system of thermal and energy flows, the earth appeared in its distance both strange and exuberant – like a slow stirring animal artfully forging and cultivating its lair. The shimmering complexity of movement and color was at once awe-inspiring and disturbing. As a system or spectacle it appeared strangely moist, layered, and kinetic, saturated with pattern and nuance, at once fragile in its kaleidoscope of shifting hues and textures, and visibly robust against the crystalline void of deep space.
>
> A Soviet cosmonaut witnessing firsthand this same view commented that only through an embarrassing misconception could we have come to call our planet 'Earth', for it is plain for anyone to see that in fact it ought really to be called 'Water'. This massive liquid object, struck us, too, as a terrible surprise. It seemed so elegantly and uncannily poised between stability and instability . . .[1]
>
> **1** Sanford Kwinter, "Soft Systems", Culture Lab 1, Brian Boigon Ed. New York: Princeton Architectural Press. p.209–210.

Also in 1972, the Club of Rome forewarned of the imminent limits on urbanization, in their influential report, *The Limits to Growth*.[5] People began to recognize Earth as a finite and interconnected ecosystem, motivating action to address pollution, deforestation, and habitat destruction.

In 1969, Ian McHarg, a Scottish landscape architect, and founder of the Landscape Architecture Department at Penn, published the seminal book, *Design with Nature*. He argued that human activities should be designed to fit into the natural environment, rather than the other way around. He advocated for the preservation of the natural environment because it serves essential functions for humanity, such as flood control and pollution dispersion. McHarg developed a method for preserving land based on the value of natural features, prioritizing surface water, floodplains, marshes, and other ecological elements. Unfortunately, this message often fell on deaf ears, with planners, designers, and developers continuing to ignore the importance of designing with nature.

One such example was the disrespect for a coastal dune system in New Jersey, which when left intact, can provide a natural barrier to the sea. McHarg noted, "Houses are built upon dunes, grasses destroyed, dunes breached for beach access and housing, groundwater is withdrawn with little control, areas are paved, bayshore is filled and urbanized, ignorance is compounded with anarchy and greed to make the raddled face of the Jersey shore,"[6] commenting on oceanside urban development. Sadly, McHarg was vindicated in 2012, when Superstorm Sandy had devastated hundreds of thousands of homes, particularly in coastal areas of New Jersey that lacked a protective dune system. Designing against nature can have catastrophic consequences, raising the question of whether floods and landslides in cities can truly be considered "natural" disasters when they result from human decisions to settle in vulnerable areas.

Anne Whiston Spirn, a distinguished landscape architect, authored *The Granite Garden: Urban Nature and Human Design* in 1984. This influential work emerged during a transformative period of environmental awareness in urbanism. American cities were grappling with urban decay, pollution, and the loss of green spaces, while the environmentalist movement was on the rise. Spirn's book provided a fresh perspective on urban landscape design, advocating for sustainable approaches that accommodate both human needs and the natural world. Similar to McHarg, Sprin claimed that urban design should be based on an understanding of the natural processes of the city. She had introduced the concept of "urban ecology" and underscored how cities are integral parts of larger ecological systems. Positing the city as "part of nature," Spirn critiqued the notion of the city being opposed to nature and nature being opposed to the city. She also distanced herself from the view of landscape as a "superficial embellishment, as a luxury, rather than as an essential force that permeates the city." City, suburbs and countryside, she argued, "must be viewed as a single, evolving system with nature." Her work highlighted the various ways in which natural ecologies can be maintained and integrated into urban areas, and the benefits of doing so.

ANNE WHISTON SPIRN
The Granite Garden

Seen from space, the earth is a garden world, a planet of life, a sphere of blues and greens sheathed in a moist atmosphere. At night, lights of the cities twinkle far below, forming constellations as distinct and varied as those of the heavens beyond. The dark spaces that their arcs embrace, however, are not the voids of space, but are replete with forests and farms, prairies and deserts. As the new day breaks, the city lights fade, overpowered by the light of the sun; blue seas and green forests and grasslands emerge, surrounding and penetrating the vast urban constellations. Even from this great distance above the earth, the cities are a gray mosaic permeated by tendrils and specks of green, the large rivers and great parks within them.

Homing in on a single constellation from hundreds of miles up, one cannot yet discern the buildings. But the fingers and patches of green – stream valleys, steep hillsides, parks, and fields – swell and multiply. The suburban forest surrounds the city; large lakes and ponds catch the sunlight and shimmer. Swinging in, now only a few miles up, the view is filled by a single city. Tall buildings spring up toward the sky, outcrops of rock and steel, and smaller homes poke up out of the suburban forest. Greens differentiate themselves into many hues. Silver ribbons of roadway flash across the landscape, and stream meanders Interrupt and soften the edges of the city's angular grid.

Flying low, one skims over a city teeming with life. The amount of green in the densest part of the city is astonishing; trees and gardens grow atop buildings and in tiny plots of soil. On the ground, a tree-of-heaven sapling is thriving in the crack between pavement and building, and a hardy weed thrusts itself up between curb and sidewalk. Its roots fan out beneath the soil in search of nutrients and water. Beneath the pavement, underground rivers roar through the sewers.

The city is a granite garden, composed of many smaller gardens, set in a garden world. Parts of the granite garden are cultivated intensively, but the greater part is unrecognized and neglected.

To the idle eye, trees and parks are the sole remnants of nature in the city. But nature in the city is far more than trees and gardens, and weeds in sidewalk cracks and vacant lots. It is the air we breathe, the earth we stand on, the water we drink and excrete, and the organisms with which we share our habitat. Nature in the city is the powerful force that can shake the earth and cause it to slide, heave, or crumple. It is a broad flash of exposed rock strata on a hillside, the overgrown outcrops in an abandoned quarry, the millions of organisms cemented in fossiliferous limestone of a downtown building. It is rain and the rushing sound of underground rivers buried in storm sewers. It is water from a faucet, delivered by pipes from some outlying river or reservoir, then used and washed away into the sewer, returned to the waters of river and sea. Nature in the city is an evening breeze, a corkscrew eddy swirling down the face of a building, the sun and the sky. Nature in the city is dogs and cats, rats in the basement, pigeons on the sidewalks, raccoons in culverts, and falcons crouched on skyscrapers. It is the consequence of a complex interaction ~between the multiple purposes and activities of human beings and other living creatures and of the natural processes that govern the transfer of energy, the movement of air, the erosion of the earth, and the hydrologic cycle. The city is part of nature.

Nature is a continuum, with wilderness at one pole and the city at the other. The same natural processes operate in the wilderness and in the city. Air, however contaminated, is always a mixture of gasses and suspended particles. Paving and building stone are composed of rock, and they affect heat gain and water runoff just as exposed rock surfaces do anywhere. Plants, whether exotic or native, invariably seek a combination of light, water, and air to survive. The city is neither wholly natural nor wholly contrived. It is not "unnatural" but, rather, a transformation of "wild" nature by humankind to serve its own needs, just as agricultural fields are managed for food production and forests for timber. Scarcely a spot on the earth, however remote, is free from the impact of human activity. The human needs and the environmental issues that arise from them are thousands of years old, as old as the oldest city, repeated in every generation, in cities on every continent.

The realization that nature is ubiquitous, a whole that embraces the city, has powerful implications for how the city is built and maintained and for the health, safety, and welfare of every resident. Unfortunately, tradition has set the city against nature, and nature against the city. The belief that

> the city is an entity apart from nature and even antithetical to it has dominated the way in which the city is perceived and continues to affect how it is built. This attitude has aggravated and even created many of the city's environmental problems: poisoned air and water; depleted or irretrievable resources; more frequent and more destructive floods; increased energy demands and higher construction and maintenance cost than existed prior to urbanization; and, in many cities, a pervasive ugliness. Modern urban problems are no different, in essence, from those that plagued ancient cities, except in degree, in the toxicity and persistence of new contaminants, and the extent of the earth that is now urbanized. As cities grow, these issues have become more pressing. Yet they continue to be treated as isolated phenomena, rather than as related phenomena arising from common human activities, exacerbated by a disregard for the processes of nature. Nature has been seen as a superficial embellishment, as a luxury, rather than as an essential force that permeates the city. Even those who have sought to introduce nature to the city in the form of parks and gardens have frequently viewed the city as something foreign to nature, have seen themselves as bringing a piece of nature to the city.
>
> To seize the opportunities inherent in the city's natural environment, to see beyond short-term costs and benefits, to perceive the consequences of the myriad, seemingly unrelated actions that make up daily city life, and to coordinate thousands of incremental improvements, a fresh attitude to the city and the molding of its form is necessary. The city must be recognized as part of nature and designed accordingly. The city, the suburbs, and the countryside must be viewed as a single, evolving system within nature, as must every individual park and building within that larger whole. The social value of nature must be recognized and its power harnessed, rather than resisted. Nature in the city must be cultivated, like a garden, rather than ignored or subdued.
>
> Anne Whiston Spirn, *The Granite Garden* (New York: Basic Books, 1984): 3–5.

By the twenty-first century, overwhelming scientific consensus confirmed that the actions of the human species were directly responsible for the warming of the Earth's climate, primarily due to carbon dioxide emissions. The natural planetary systems lost their stable equilibrium, with temperatures warming, sea levels rising, and extreme weather events becoming more recurring and intense. Meanwhile, increased saltwater intrusion and rising temperatures put the world's freshwater supply under pressure.

In the spirit of McHarg and Spirn's work, more designers, theorists and writers grew more environmentally conscious and adopted ecological design principles. One significant milestone in this journey was the publication of *Ecological Urbanism*, co-edited by Mohsen Mostafavi and Gareth Doherty in 2010.[7] This hefty book, following an exhibition at the Harvard Graduate School of Design, explores the integration of ecological principles and systems thinking into urban design and planning to counter urbanization's negative impact on the environment. With 117 essays, the contributing authors place a strong emphasis on designing for biodiversity, habitat preservation, and resilience to environmental challenges. A central component of this philosophy involves the restoration of urban green spaces and the integration of sustainable water management practices into urban environments.

Some years earlier in 2003, Mohsen Mostafavi and Ciro Najle co-edited, *Landscape Urbanism: A Manual for Machinic Landscapes*. In this collection of essays landscape, was understood as a mode through which to comprehend, conceive and design in urbanism, with greater sensitivity to temporal processes and multiple systems and scales. The editors contrasted how modern cities "emphasized regularity," whereas the "temporal characteristics" of the landscape tradition were unexplored. "The temporality of landscapes renders them forever incomplete, and this incompletion can be seen as an antidote to the implicit finitude of zoning."[8]

James Corner's essay, "Landscape Urbanism" in Mostafavi and Najle's book, argued how Landscape Urbanism, as a "hybrid" discipline, "brings together two previously unrelated terms," similar to the fusion of biology and technology in "biotech."[9]

A later influential work in this tradition was the *Landscape Urbanism Reader* published in 2006 and edited by Charles Waldheim. Landscape Urbanism, a now prominent design theory, challenges conventional notions of urban design by prioritizing the role of the landscape in the design process. Instead of perceiving urban areas as isolated built environments, landscape urbanism recognizes the landscape—whether natural, ecological, or cultural—as a foundational element that shapes and informs the structure and function of cities. As a "model for contemporary urbanism," Waldheim notes how landscape had emerged as having the capacity to describe complex conditions of urbanism, especially when considered in relation to "complex natural environments."[10] His text critiques "architecture and urban design's inability to offer coherent, competent, and convincing explanations of contemporary urban conditions." Further, he suggests a "disciplinary realignment" in which architecture's "historic role as the basic building block of urban design" is supplanted by landscape. He notes how projects at the scale of landscape urbanism synthesize various areas of knowledge and professional expertise, "at the intersection of ecology and engineering, social policy and political processes." At its core, landscape urbanism asserts that landscapes do not need to be passive backdrops but can be active agents that drive urban development and regeneration.

Waldheim has been a leading advocate and thinker behind the landscape urbanism movement. He claims that landscapes, more than buildings, will impact urbanization in the twenty-first century. Many of the landscape urbanism projects are aimed at cleaning up and repurpose former industrialized sites, such as Freshkills Park, a former landfill in Staten Island, New York City, and Downsview Park, a former military base in Toronto, Canada. These projects showcase the transformation of former industrial sites into vibrant and ecologically rich public spaces, while integrating sustainable design principles, green infrastructure, and cultural programming.

Prominent protagonists of landscape urbanism include practitioners such as James Corner of the design firm Field Operations, Adriaan Geuze of West 8, Eva Castro and Holger Kehne of Plasma Studio, as well as Kotchakorn Voraakhom, founder of the non-profit Porous City Network based in Bangkok.

The comparison of two iconic green spaces in New York City, the High Line and Central Park, helps illuminate the principles of landscape urbanism. Central Park, designed by Frederick Law Olmsted and Calvert Vaux in the 1850s, represents a park designed in the English Landscape tradition, in which wilderness is simulated. It is a carefully planned and manicured oasis within the city, creating a distinct separation between the built environment and the natural landscape.

In contrast, the High Line, an elevated linear park co-designed by the landscape architects James Corner Field Operations and architects Diller Scofidio + Renfro, and completed in 2009, exemplifies landscape urbanism principles. It repurposed an abandoned railway line, integrating

FIGURE 5.1 An aerial view captures The High Line as it attracts crowds above New York City's streets, transforming a disused freight rail line into an elevated park and infrastructural artery. Courtesy of Getty Images.

the existing industrial infrastructure into a new urban landscape. The High Line celebrates the dynamic interplay between nature and urbanity, weaving plantings, walkways, and public spaces through the fabric of the city. In addition, it uses native plants in the design, reducing its reliance on artificial irrigation. In short, it embraces the idea of adaptive reuse and ecological design, and aims for the integration of nature and culture within the urban context.

In summary, landscape urbanism presents a new approach to urban design, putting landscapes at the forefront of urban revitalization. Successfully integrating ecologies, infrastructure, and programming, landscape urbanism synthesizes the categories of the artificial and the natural. It demonstrates how contemporary designers of urban landscapes are evolving to embrace nature not as a static, isolated pastoral scene but as a dynamic and integrated process that encompasses ecological sustainability and cultural vibrancy.

CHARLES WALDHEIM
"Landscape as Urbanism"

Over the past decade landscape has emerged as a model for contemporary urbanism, one uniquely capable of describing the conditions for radically decentralized urbanization, especially in the context of complex natural environments. Over that same decade the landscape discipline has enjoyed a period of intellectual and cultural renewal. While much of the landscape discipline's renewed relevance to discussions of the city may be attributed to this renewal or to increased environmental awareness more generally, landscape has improbably emerged as the most relevant disciplinary locus for discussions historically housed in architecture, urban design, or planning.

Many of the conceptual categories and projective practices embodied in landscape urbanism and documented in this publication arise from outside those disciplines traditionally responsible for describing the city. As such, landscape urbanism offers an implicit critique of architecture and urban design's inability to offer coherent, competent, and convincing explanations of contemporary urban conditions. In this context, the discourse surrounding landscape urbanism can be read as a disciplinary realignment in which landscape supplants architecture's historical role as the basic building block of urban design. Across a range of disciplines, many authors have articulated this newfound relevance of landscape in describing the temporal mutability and horizontal extensivity of the contemporary city. Among the authors making claims for the potential of landscape in this regard is architect and educator Stan Allen, Professor in the School of Architecture at Princeton University:

> "Increasingly, landscape is emerging as a model for urbanism. Landscape has traditionally been defined as the art of organizing horizontal surfaces . . . By paying close attention to these surface conditions – not only configuration, but also materiality and performance – designers can activate space and produce urban effects without the weight apparatus of traditional space making."[1]

This efficiency – the ability to produce urban effects traditionally achieved through the construction of buildings simply through the organization of horizontal surfaces – recommends the landscape medium for use in contemporary urban conditions increasingly characterized by horizontal sprawl and rapid change. In the context of decentralization and decreasing density, the "weighty apparatus" of traditional urban design proves costly, slow, and inflexible in relation to the rapidly transforming conditions of contemporary urban culture.

The idea of landscape as a model for urbanism has also been articulated by landscape architect James Corner, who argues that only through a synthetic and imaginative reordering of categories in the built environment might we escape our present predicament in the cul-de-sac of post-industrial modernity, and "the bureaucratic and uninspired failings" of the planning profession.[2] His work critiques much of what landscape architecture has become as a professional concern in recent years – especially its tendency to provide scenographic screening for environments engineered and instrumentalized by other disciplines.[3] For Corner, the narrow agenda of ecological advocacy that many landscape architects profess to is nothing more than a rear-guard defense of a supposedly autonomous "nature" conceived to exist *a priori*, outside of human agency or cultural construction. In this context, current-day environmentalism and pastoral ideas of landscape appear to Corner, and many others, as naive or irrelevant in the face of global urbanization.[4]

Landscape urbanism benefits from the canonical texts of regional environmental planning, from the work of Patrick Geddes and Benton MacKaye to Lewis Mumford to Ian McHarg, yet it also remains distinct from that tradition.[5] Corner acknowledges the historical importance of McHarg's influential *Design with Nature* yet, himself a student and faculty colleague of McHarg's at the University of Pennsylvania, rejects the opposition of nature and city implied in McHarg's regionally scaled environmental planning practice[6] . . .

. . . Several recent international design competitions for the reuse of enormously scaled industrial sites in North American cities have used landscape as their primary medium. Downsview Park, located on the site of an underutilized military airbase in Toronto, and Fresh Kills, on the site of the world's largest landfill on Staten Island, New York, are representative of these trends and offer the most fully formed examples of landscape urbanism practices to date applied to the detritus of the industrial city.[7] While significant distinctions exist between these two commissions, as do questions regarding their eventual realization, the body of work produced for Downsview and Fresh Kills represents an emerging consensus that designers of the built environment, across disciplines, would do well to examine landscape as the medium through which to conceive the renovation of the post-industrial city. James Corner's projects for Downsview (with Stan Allen) and Fresh Kills are exemplary in this regard, illustrating mature works of landscape urbanism through their accumulation and orchestration of absolutely diverse and potentially incongruous contents. Typical of this work, and by now standard fare for projects of this type, are detailed diagrams of phasing, animal habitats, succession planting, and hydrological systems, as well as programmatic and planning regimes. While these diagrams initially overwhelm with information, they present an understanding of the enormous complexities confronting any work at this scale. Particularly compelling is the complex interweaving of natural ecologies with the social, cultural, and infrastructural layers of the contemporary city.

While both Koolhaas/OMA (in partnership with designer Bruce Mau) and Tschumi submitted entries as finalists at Downsview, they found their historical fortunes reversed, more or less precisely. The imageable and media friendly Mau and Koolhaas/OMA scheme "Tree City" was awarded first prize and the commission; while the more sublime, layered, and intellectually challenging scheme of the office of Bernard Tschumi will doubtless enjoy greater influence within architectural culture, particularly as the information age transforms our understandings and limits of the "natural." Tschumi's "The Digital and the Coyote" project for Downsview presented an electronic analog to his longstanding interest in urban event, with richly detailed diagrams of succession planting and the seeding of ambient urbanity in the midst of seemingly desolate prairies. Tschumi's position at Downsview is symmetrical with his original thesis for la Villette. Both projects were based on a fundamental indictment of the nineteenth-century Olmstedian model, offering in its place an understanding of landscape conflated with a pervasive and ubiquitous urbanism. As Tschumi put it in his project statement for Downsview:

"Neither theme park or wildlife preserve, Downsview does not seek to renew using the conventions of traditional park compositions such as those of Vaux or Olmsted. The combination of advanced military technologies with water courses and flows and downstreams suggest another fluid, liquid, digital sensibility. Airstrips, information centers, public performance spaces, internet and worldwide web access all point to a redefinition of received ideas about parks, nature and recreation, in a 21st century setting where everything is "urban," even in the middle of the wilderness."[8]

The Downsview and Fresh Kills projects are notable for the presence of landscape architects on interdisciplinary teams of consultants, whereas the la Villette competition named a single lead architect to orchestrate the entire project. Striking and consistent in this regard are the central involvement of ecologists as well as information or communication designers on virtually all teams. This is clearly distinct from the overarching role of architects in previous regimes of urban design and planning, where these concerns were either absent altogether (ecology) or simply subsumed within the professional practice of the architect (information design).

While it remains unclear if either of the winning schemes by Mau and Koolhaas/OMA for Downsview and Corner and Allen/Field Operations for Fresh Kills will be fully realized, we must see this as a challenge of political imagination and cultural leadership rather than as a failure of the competition processes or the projects they premiated. These projects and the work of their competitors, taken collectively, point to transformations currently underway which are profoundly changing the disciplinary and professional assumptions behind the design of the built environment. Particularly evident is the fact that projects of this scale and significance demand professional expertise at the intersections of ecology and engineering, social policy and political process. The synthesis of this range of knowledge and its embodiment in public design processes recommend landscape urbanism as a disciplinary framework for reconceiving the contemporary urban field.

1   Stan Allen, "Mat Urbanism: The Thick 2-D," in Hashim Sarkis (ed.), *CASE: Le Corbusier's Venice Hospital* (Munich: Prestel, 2001), 124.
2   See James Corner, "Terra Fluxus," in *The Landscape Urbanism Reader*. See also James Corner, ed., *Recovering Landscape* (New York: Princeton Architectural Press, 1999).
3   See Corner's introduction to *Recovering Landscapes*, 1–26.
4   One marker of a generational divide between advocacy and instrumentalization has been the recent emergence of complex and culturally derived understanding of natural systems. An example of this can be found in the shift from pictorial to operational in landscape discourse that has been the subject of much recent work. See for example James Corner, "Eidetic Operations and New Landscapes," in *Recovering Landscape,* 153–69. Also useful on this topic is Julia Czerniak, "Challenging the Pictorial: Recent Landscape Practice," in *Assemblage* 24 (December 1997): 110–20.
5   Ian McHarg, *Design with Nature* (Garden City, New York: Natural History Press, 1969). For an overview of Mumford's work, see Mark Luccarelli, *Lewis Mumford and the Ecological Region: The Politics of Planning* (New York: Guilford Press, 1997).
6   See: Corner, "Terra Fluxus" in *The Landscape Urbanism Reader*.
7   Downsview and Fresh Kills have been the subject of extensive documentatlon, including essays in *Praxis*, no. 4, *Landscapes* (2002). For additional information see Julia Czerniak, ed., *CASE: Downsview Park Toronto* (Cambridge/Munich: Harvard/Prestel, 2001), and Charles Waldheim, "Park=City? The Downsview Park Competition," in *Landscape Architecture Magazine* vol. 91, no. 3 (March 2001): 80–85, 98–99.
8   Bernard Tschumi, "Downsview Park: The Digital and the Coyote," in Czerniak, ed., *CASE: Downsview Park Toronto,* 82–89.

Charles Waldheim, "Landscape as Urbanism", *The Landscape Urbanism Reader* (Princeton, NJ: Princeton Architectural Press 2006): 37–9, 46–51.

Up until recently, urbanization was seen as in conflict with nature. For example, in the twentieth century, numerous cities concealed culverts, streams, and even rivers. However, a shift has occurred in the twenty-first century, with some cities working to undo this environmental damage and restore their waterways. A paradigmatic case is Seoul, South Korea, where a 6-kilometer elevated freeway once obscured a stream within the city. In 2003, the city's mayor opted to remove the aging expressway, revitalize the polluted stream, and establish a park along its banks.

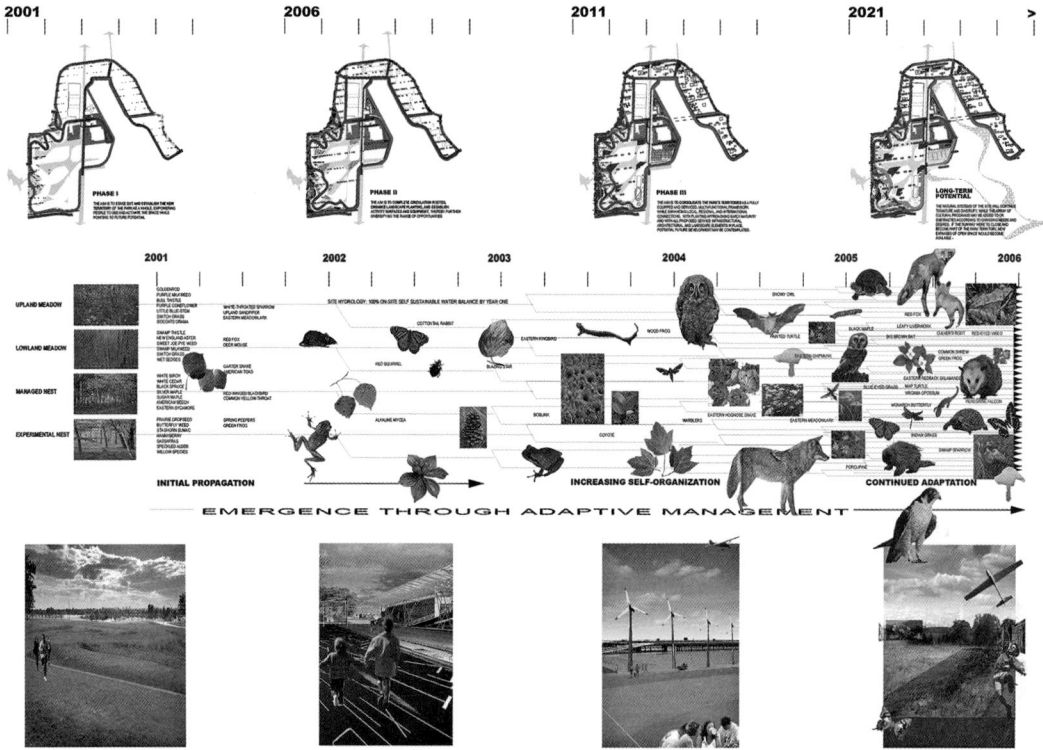

FIGURE 5.2 In their competition proposal for Downsview Park, Toronto, Field Operations crafted a diagram that illustrates the potential adaptive growth and evolution of the park's non-human flora and fauna over time, 1999. Courtesy of Field Operations.

By 2005, the rejuvenated Cheonggyecheon stream and linear greenway welcomed the public, now serving as a vibrant recreational space while mitigating the urban heat island effect.

Central to this approach is the concept of "green infrastructure," which offers innovative solutions to various challenges. Publications such as *Green Infrastructure: Linking Landscapes and Communities* (2006)[11] have popularized these ideas, promoting strategies such as bioswales, rain gardens, and permeable pavers to replace traditional stormwater pipes. Notably, Seattle's adoption of permeable pavement for streets resulted in a 50 percent reduction in paving costs, and the city incentivizes green features like rainwater harvesting, large trees, green walls, and green roofs.[12] These initiatives not only decrease stormwater runoff but also contribute to energy savings, as water and wastewater systems account for 3 percent of total energy consumption in the United States.

The concept of "green infrastructure" stands in contrast to traditional "grey" infrastructure, as it offers multiple benefits beyond single-use systems like water pipes. Green infrastructure, when integrated into urban networks, can purify water, reduce runoff, manage floods, and promote sustainable stormwater management. Moreover, it fosters biodiversity, supports urban agriculture, conserves energy by cooling and insulating buildings with green roofs, and mitigates air pollution, noise, and wind loads through appropriate tree planting.

Greening neighborhoods and building, playgrounds, parks, and community gardens also contribute to healthier living. Greener communities also have a reduced urban heat-island effect and a reduced amount of polluted stormwater run-off. Locally grown crops, moreover, shrink the environmental footprint as well as improve food security.

Research supports the positive impact of greenery on human well-being, showing that exposure to green foliage enhances attention spans and reduces stress levels. A study of 20,000 individuals revealed that those spending at least 120 minutes in green spaces reported significantly better health and psychological well-being.[13] Even hospital patients with views of trees recover more swiftly than those facing brick walls.[14] People residing near open green spaces tend to perform better in cognitive tasks and cope more effectively with major life issues This finding underscores the importance of practices like "forest bathing," which is prescribed by doctors in Japan.

Singapore stands as a prime example of integrating green spaces into urban development. With over a million trees planted since 1967, more than 50 percent of the city's landmass is now populated with vegetation, harmoniously coexisting with its high-rise skyline. This extensive green cover not only reduces the need for air conditioning but also enables the city to capture and recycle two-thirds of its rainfall, bolstering its freshwater supply. Singapore's unwavering commitment to green infrastructure exemplifies an innovative approach to sustainable urban development. This aligns with its self-designation as a "Biophilic City in a Garden," referencing the biophilia concept introduced by biologist E. O. Wilson in 1984, and put forward in his 1986 book, *Biophilia*.[15] The biophilia hypothesis theorizes that humans are hardwired to connect with nature, even urbanites who may have never visited a forest.

Urbanization often exacerbates flooding due to impervious surfaces preventing water from seeping into the ground. In response, designers are increasingly integrating green infrastructure into plaza design, addressing urban flooding by enhancing ground surface infiltration. Implementing stormwater management infrastructure also enhances recreational opportunities, as demonstrated by Portland, Oregon's urban parks such as Tanner Springs Park. These parks absorb water and reduce runoff while providing a serene natural retreat.

Yu Kongjian, a distinguished Chinese landscape architect and founder of Turenscape, is celebrated for pioneering ecological and sustainable landscape design principles. He elaborates on this approach in his writings such as the "Big Foot Revolution," seeing a parallel between unnatural modern cities and the ancient Chinese practice of foot-binding.[16] Instead, he emphasizes the harmonious integration of natural systems, culture, and urban environments to create resilient, ecologically vibrant spaces. Houtan Park in Shanghai, designed by Turenscape, serves as a prime example, functioning as a constructed wetland that treats contaminated water from the Huangpu River, making it suitable for non-potable uses in the landscape, including urban agriculture. This innovative approach demonstrates the potential of performative landscapes to address environmental challenges while enhancing urban liveability.

In the 2010s, Yu had pioneered the "Sponge City" model of working with water flows, topography, and permeable surfaces towards the mitigation of flood risks in cities. In Turenscape's projects in China for "The Floating Gardens of Yongning," in Taizhou, in 2004, and "Jinhua Yanweizhou Park," in Jinhua City, Zhejiang Province, in 2014, Yu's ecological approach to stormwater management was honed—not preventing, but working synergistically, with flooding. By 2017, the Sponge City model was adopted as a national urban planning and design policy.

FIGURE 5.3 The aerial view shows the Xi'an Horticultural Expo, by Plasma Studio, a prime example of landscape urbanism principles and methods, highlighting its network of pedestrian pathways, horticultural basins, and architectural pavilions, in Xi'an, China, 2011. Courtesy of Plasma Studio.

KONGJIAN YU
"Beautiful Big Feet: Toward a New Landscape Aesthetic"

Little feet/big feet: sustainability and aesthetics in China

For almost 1,000 years, young Chinese girls were forced to bind their feet so they could marry citified elites, since their natural "big" feet were associated with provincial people and rustic life. At first, foot-binding was the sole privilege of the high class. The practice flourished until the collapse of the Qing Dynasty in 1911. Respected intellectuals had written poems and created paintings to praise artificial tiny feet that today would be considered grotesque and abused. Painters portrayed classic Chinese beauties with small feet, flat breasts, tiny waists, and white skin, in complete contrast to strong and healthy peasant girls. For a long time, in other words, the beautiful has been seen as necessarily unproductive, above the "crude," survival-oriented processes of nature.

This definition of beauty and its connection with high-status urbanites is not unique to Chinese culture. Pre-Hispanic Mayan priests and nobles deformed their children's bodies in a quest for social status. Their "beautiful" features—sloping foreheads, almond-shaped eyes, large noses, and drooping lower lips—today seem as grotesque as bound feet.[1]

For thousands of years, the urban elite worldwide has maintained the right to define beauty and good taste as part of its assertion of superiority and power. Bound feet and deformed heads are among the thousands of cultural practices that, in trying to elevate city sophisticates above rural bumpkins, have rejected nature's inherent goals of health, survival, and productivity.

Pearl S. Buck vividly depicted this process of urbanizing and denaturalizing taste in her novel about Chinese village life, *The Good Earth* (1931). Early on we meet Wang Lung, a poor man who could marry only a slave from the local aristocrat's Great House. The slave was very productive, giving birth to three sons and two daughters. She was not beautiful, but she was hardworking, cooked and kept house well, and begged in the streets to relieve her family's poverty. Wang Lung eventually became so wealthy that he didn't need to labor himself but instead hired farmers. He could even afford to leave his land unfruitful, buy from others, and build rooms to accommodate a slender beautiful woman as his concubine, who was prevented from working or having children. As Wang Lung's property increased, he was able to rent the Great House as his family's residence and live in town. His unproductivity was the measure of his social "success."

Mixed into in the evolution of the Chinese idea of beauty are people's changing ideas of urbanity and good taste in landscape design. For thousands of years, farmers had managed living landscapes using the survival skills passed on by their ancestors through endless trial and error. Generations had adapted to both the threat and the results of natural disasters—floods, droughts, earthquakes, landslides, and soil erosion—while honing their abilities in field grading, irrigation, and food production. A popular story arose: Our ancestors created and maintained "The Land of Peach Blossoms," a lost paradise, a productive and harmonious basin discovered by a fisherman.[2] Efforts to survive were what engendered the skills and artistry of rendering the landscape productive and durable. People found this land beautiful because it had the order and integration with natural processes that resulted from working with the given.

But as China has become more urbanized and "civilized," this vernacular landscape has gradually been deprived of its productivity, its support to and of life, and its natural beauty. Like the peasant girls whose footbinding crippled them, it has gradually been adapted by the minority urban upper class and transformed into artificial decorative gardens. The aesthetic of uselessness, leisure, and adornment has taken over as part of a larger overwhelming urge to appear "modern" and sophisticated.

But designed landscapes and gardens in different cultures have roots in the agricultural landscapes that were the first expressions of civilization: Islamic gardens evolved from dry fields that needed irrigation. Italian terraced gardens originated as vineyards adapting to steep slopes. Picturesque English landscapes began as pastures. And Chinese gardens have roots in agricultural farms. But the owners and designers of urban gardens didn't appreciate the vernacular peasant landscapes, which were associated with the disheveled working class.

Using ornamental plants and artificial rocks for 2,000 years, emperors and nobles created a fake Land of Peach Blossoms for the pursuit of indolent pleasures. Irrigation ditches and ponds were turned into ornamental water features. Fish farms were stocked with mutant ornamental goldfish. Green plants were replaced with golden- or yellow-leafed ones; vegetables and herbs were ousted by ostentatious peonies and roses. Healthy trees were pruned, twisted, dwarfed, and damaged to make bonsai. Only "delicate" Small-Foot rocks were arrayed. Peach trees unable to bear fruit were planted. Like tiny-footed women, these urbane ornaments produced little and survived only with constant human upkeep. They were watered, pruned, weeded, and artificially reproduced. Most of the "great gardens" in history decayed soon after their owners passed on. What survives or has been revived today requires endless maintenance.

Please don't misunderstand me: In one sense all art, music, and dance is "unproductive"—it is useless for sustaining biological life. I am not arguing for the end of all this or for any demeaning of the value of beauty and pleasure in our lives. What I am arguing is that in our resource-depleted and ecologically damaged and threatened era, the built environment must and will adapt a new aesthetic grounded in appreciation of the beauty of productive, ecology-supporting things. Our desire for beauty detached from utility is weakening, and it should be. In our new world, survival is at stake. Wastefulness becomes viscerally unattractive, if not immoral. But there is plenty of opportunity for joyful pleasure in useful things.

THE PRACTICE OF THE BIG-FOOT AESTHETIC

Make friends with floods: The Floating Gardens of Yongning River Park, Taizhou

This project demonstrates how we can live and design with nature, enacts an ecological approach to flood control and storm-water management, educates people about solutions to flood control other than engineering, and reveals the beauty of native vegetation and the ordinary landscape.

The site occupies 21 hectares (52 acres) along the Yongning River, the mother river of the historical city of Huangyan on the east coast. Most of the site was already embanked with concrete as the result of the local flood control policy and before a landscape architect was asked to "beautify" it. Our firm successfully convinced the local decision-maker to stop the conventional flood control engineering along the remaining part of the river and to create instead an ecological flood control and stormwater management system.

A water process analysis dictated a regional drainage approach; concrete embankments were removed and replaced with wetlands that provided flood mitigation, biodiversity conservation, outdoor recreation, environmental education, and local historical and cultural demonstrations. Native grasses—"ugly weeds" most thought—were used to stabilize the riverbanks. On the recovered natural landscape is a network of straight paths and informational mounted texts to help people enjoy the natural processes and learn about local history. The results have been remarkable: Flood problems were successfully addressed; frogs, fish, and birds have returned; local television celebrated the "weed" grass in blossom on prime time; and hundreds of thousands of people visit to appreciate what would have been considered a messy and uncouth landscape.[3]

Revalue common culture and the beauty of weeds: Zhongshan Shipyard Park

This park covers eleven hectares (twenty-seven acres) in Zhongshan in Guangdong Province. It is built on the site of an abandoned shipyard that was originally constructed in the 1950s and went bankrupt in 1999, seemingly insignificant in Chinese history, and therefore likely to be razed to give space for urban development and a grand "Baroque" garden. But the shipyard reflected the remarkable fifty-year history of socialist China, including the Cultural Revolution of the 1960s and '70s, and recorded the experiences of common people.

The principle of reducing, reusing, and recycling natural and man-made materials is followed. Original vegetation and natural habitats were preserved, just as only native plants were used throughout. Machines, docks, and other industrial structures were recycled for educational, aesthetic, and functional purposes. The design addresses several challenges of the site, including accommodating variable water levels and balancing river-width regulations for flood control with protecting old riverbank banyan trees.

Completely different from the classical Chinese scholar's gardens, this park, since its inauguration in 2002, has become an attraction to tourists and local residents. It has been used all day and yearlong, has become a favored site for wedding photographs, and has even been used for a fashion show. It demonstrates how landscape architects can create environmentally friendly public places full of cultural and historical meaning but not on sites previously singled out for attention and preservation. It supports the common people and the environmental ethic "Weeds are beautiful."

The productive landscape: The Rice Campus of Shengyang Architectural University

This project demonstrates how agricultural landscape can become part of the urbanized environment and how cultural identity can be created through an ordinary productive landscape. The overwhelming urbanization of China is encroaching upon much arable land. With a population of over 1.3 billion people and limited tillable land, food production and sustainable land use is a survival issue that landscape architects must address.[4]

The site of about 80 hectares (198 acres) forms the new campus of Shengyang Architectural University. The design and construction had to contend with a small budget and a short construction timeline (six months), but the university still wanted the landscape to provide a strong identity. My firm proposed creating productive rice fields (along with other native crops) while fulfilling the need for new functions. Storm water is collected in ponds to irrigate the fields. Frogs are raised to control insects, and fish are cultivated to double the productivity of the field. Sheep "cut" the grass, eliminating the pollution of mowing machines.

Student involvement is part of the landscape's productivity. Each year a planting festival and a harvesting festival are held on campus, which bring Chinese culture alive. Farming processes become an attraction to the students of the university and the nearby middle school. The crop is packaged as "Golden Rice," which is sold in the university canteen and presented as souvenirs to visitors. Now Golden Rice has become the university's identity marker, well-known across universities nationwide.

The Rice Campus increases sensitivity about the environment and farming among the mostly urban students. It demonstrates that inexpensive and productive agricultural landscapes can also become, through careful design and management, pleasurable social spaces. And finally this working landscape is a clear example of the new Big-Foot aesthetic—unbound but beautiful.

1 Vera Tiesler, "Head Shaping and Dental Decoration Among the Maya: Archeological and Cultural Aspects," *Society of American Anthropology* 64 (1999), pp. 1–6.
2 This is, in essence, the original story of Shangri-La, a mystical, harmonious valley described in the 1933 novel *Lost Horizon* by British writer James Hilton.

> 3   For a detailed review of this park, see Graham Johnstone and Xiangfeng Kong, "Making Friends with Floods: An Ecological Park Reclaims a Degraded Stretch of a Chinese River," *Landscape Architecture*, April 2007, 106–15.
> 4   For a detailed review of this project, see Mary G. Padua, "Touching the Good Earth: An Innovative Campus Design Reconnects Students to China's Agricultural Landscapes," *Landscape Architecture*, December 2006, 100–7.
>
> Kongjian Yu, "Beautiful Big Feet: Toward a New Landscape Aesthetic," *Harvard Design Magazine* (Fall/Winter 2009): 48–59.

The concept of sustainability is often associated with building science and environmental engineering. However, it must be acknowledged that many of the ecological practices put forward today are simply old knowledge repackaged in new ways. Prior to the Industrial Revolution, building practices were more sustainable by necessity, rooted in local ecosystems, climate, and available resources. For instance, vernacular building materials such as rammed earth and bamboo have a minimal environmental impact. By embracing the principles of vernacular and indigenous architecture, contemporary urban designers and architects can draw upon the wisdom of indigenous communities to create urban environments that prioritize ecological balance, resilience, and cultural continuity.

For example, in arid and hot climates, vernacular structures often employ massive walls and roofs to absorb heat, while small, strategically placed windows provide sufficient interior lighting without unwanted heat gain. Light-colored exterior surfaces minimize solar radiation absorption, while flat roofs often double as living and sleeping spaces during cooler nights. These buildings are clustered closely to offer mutual shading and promote a sense of community. Conversely, in humid climates, vernacular architecture typically prioritizes shading, ventilation, and lightweight wood construction, with high ceilings facilitating larger windows and efficient air circulation for cooler interiors. Overhangs, shutters, and light-colored walls protect against solar radiation and rain, while building layouts maximize exposure to cooling breezes.

This harmonious integration of climatic considerations and sustainable design principles underscores the ingenuity of pre-industrial architecture. One of the first to acknowledge the value of vernacular architecture was Bernard Rudofsky. His influential MOMA exhibition and subsequent 1964 book, *Architecture without Architects: A Short Introduction to Non-Pedigreed Architecture*, challenged conventional architectural norms by highlighting the beauty and wisdom found in vernacular and indigenous building practices.[17] His book ignited a re-evaluation of what constitutes "architecture" and emphasized the importance of local context.

More recently, Julia Watson in her work *Lo-TEK: Design by Radical Indigenism* (2019)[18] examines indigenous technologies and sustainable design strategies employed by various traditional cultures worldwide. Watson's research and advocacy focus on the innovative ways in which indigenous communities have adapted to and thrived within their local environments, offering valuable lessons for contemporary ecological urbanism. In the excerpt below, Watson and her co-authors lament our planet's "strained relationship with water," arguing against the universality of technology as a result of urban globalization, echoing Kenneth Frampton's position towards technology, as argued in his writing championing Critical Regionalism.[19] They question how "north knows best," in its apparent imposition of technology upon the global south.

One of Watson's most well-known case studies is the Jingkieng Dieng Jri Living Root Bridges, found in the northeastern state of Meghalaya in India. These indigenous "living bridges" are created by guiding the aerial roots of the *Ficus elastica* (rubber) tree across streams and rivers, allowing them to grow and fuse together over time. This organic construction method not only harnesses the strength of nature but also ensures the bridges' longevity and minimal environmental impact. Watson suggests these living bridges could grow in cities as canopies over streets to reduce the heat island effect.

In the world's current state of climate change, the study of vernacular and indigenous approaches to architecture and urbanism has gained renewed relevance. These traditional design approaches can offer valuable lessons for a more sustainable and resilient future for our cities.

J. WATSON, H. ABUKHODAIR, N. A. NAEEMA ALI, A. ROBERTSON, ISSAOUI, AND C. SUN
"Design by Radical Indigenism: Equitable Underwater & Intertidal Technologies of the Global South"

This article retells an ancient mythology—that humankind can and must live symbiotically with water. It is an indispensable part of life on earth, and essential to healthy ecosystems. In the past, civilizations and settlements were built on the availability of water resources. Today, this is reversed as humans manipulate the course of water bodies for their benefit. This has fractured our innate connection to the earth's water systems and we have become blind to the strain it is putting on the planet and our livelihoods. Climate change is forcing us to rethink this strained relationship with water and how it has led to disasters and a rising sea. Today, the existential risk of climate change is a global challenge, evidenced by universal metrics and approached with universal solutions. If we continue this generic approach of universality, we perpetuate the thinking that led to this climate crisis. We need to prepare ourselves to face the increasing climatic extremes by turning to complex solutions that have been in existence for centuries and acknowledge an adaptive relationship with the earth's water resources.

With wealthier nations causing climate change, poorer nations are suffering in a crisis that disproportionately affects people living in the global south, a term used for regions that are identified as lower wealth or undeveloped. An increasingly contentious term, however, the ideology behind identifying certain regions as less developed in the western sense is still maintained in discussions of technological progress and resilience. In specifically referring to regions that have been identified as part of 'the global south' the intention is to reverse the stereotype of less valuable and present the innovations and knowledge present in these overlooked areas. In the wealthier nations of the global north, homogeneous, high-tech infrastructures are being deployed in response to climate events. Designed primarily by and for affluent communities, these single-purpose solutions, considered 'best practice,' are so often counterintuitively incompatible with local conditions and the living water systems that have been evolved by local communities.[1] This current practice fails to acknowledge that an immediately available and more equitable typology of solutions already exists. In the global south, there are thousands of sustainable Lo—TEK living water solutions that have evolved by continual adaptation over millennia in response to climate extremes. Instead, the south is sold a belief that the high-tech solutions of developed nations are superior to their own local innovations, even though the latter embody the intelligence of the environments and cultures that have evolved them.

This article challenges this 'north knows best' narrative on the topic of climate solutions that disregards traditional knowledge and frames the need for high-tech and costly infrastructures. Many of the cities and coastal communities in the global south that will be greatly affected by a rise in sea level are already living with these climate extremes, and have developed ecologically intelligent resilient living water systems. This research argues for the imminent need to recognize these overlooked climate solutions, which are inspired by indigenous innovation and embedded with the traditional ecological knowledge (TEK) of communities working with ecological systems thinking.

The research presented here documents the traditional, indigenous responses to coastal resilience found across the global south that amplify local cultural, ecological, economic, and agricultural resilience. These indigenous innovations acknowledge the human relationship to water, through both built infrastructure and cultural practices. The following chapter examines three systems written in collaboration with local indigenous experts. These technologies have evolved from traditional ecological knowledge and work with local conditions and culture. The examples explored are the *Kuttanad Kayalnilam* Farming System in India, the *Sangjiyutang* Mulberry Dyke and Fish Ponds in China, and the *Ramli* lagoon farms in Tunisia. While indigenous peoples and their responses to coastal resilience remain largely excluded in global discussion on design solutions, these studies, reframed through an architectural lens, intend to inform the future of design for climate resilience . . .

. . . Lo—TEK

Lo—TEK, a term coined by designer and author Julia Watson, is defined as resilient infrastructures developed by indigenous people through traditional ecological knowledge (TEK).[2] The movement to bring these innovations to the forefront of the design field counters the idea that Lo—TEK indigenous innovation is *low-tech*, a term often incorrectly applied to indigenous innovation that means unsophisticated, uncomplicated, and primitive. Instead, Lo—TEK aligns to today's sustainable values of low-energy, low-impact, and low-cost, while producing complex nature-based innovations that are inherently sustainable. Forming the foundation of indigenous technologies, TEK is a field of study in anthropology defined as a cumulative body of knowledge, practice, and belief, handed down through generations by traditional songs, origin stories, and everyday life. By using TEK, humans have been able to harness the energy of ecosystems and adapt to environmental obstacles using soft and symbiotic living systems. Developed through direct contact with nature, TEK is engineered to sustain, rather than exploit resources. It fosters symbiosis between species, while making biodiversity the building block used to construct sustainable technologies.

Lo—TEK innovations come from a deep understanding of working with nature and are evolved from the philosophy of radical indigenism. Coined by a citizen of the Cherokee Nation, Professor Eva Marie Garoutte, radical indigenism argues for a rebuilding of knowledge and understanding of indigenous philosophies from their roots.[3] For design, this rebuilding can expand our understanding of nature-based technologies and generate new, sustainable, and resilient infrastructures informed by TEK. Lo—TEK is how humans have been dealing with the extremes of the climate for millennia, by harnessing the energy and intelligence of complex ecosystems. It is eminently possible to weave ancient knowledge on how to live symbiotically with nature into the ways in which we shape the cities of the future. We can rewild our urban landscapes and apply Lo—TEK ecological thinking to climate solutions for sanitation, storm surge, sea level rise, drought, deluge, wildfire, food supply, and water, that have worked for indigenous peoples for thousands of years. Lo—TEK expands the definition of contemporary technology by rebuilding our understanding of climate resilient design using indigenous knowledge and practices that are sustainable, adaptable, and borne out of necessity . . .

. . .Kuttanad Kayalnilam Farming System by the Malayalis in India

Kuttanad, a low-lying wetland at the mouth of the Vembanad Backwaters in India, is the only place in the country where paddy farming has been practiced below sea level for more than two centuries. Due to this area's unique geographical phenomenon, life here revolves around water with the daily activities like commuting, bathing, washing, and their livelihoods and seasonal celebrations like the snake boat race festivals . . .

. . . In this system, the artificially created landforms are called *Kayalnilams*, where *kayal* means backwaters and *nilam* means ground, implying that they were lifted out of water.[4] The *Kayalnilam* system intelligently accommodates seasonal flooding and salinity intrusion, allowing the Malayalis to grow rice, coconut, and other fruit trees through the local technology and water management practices associated with the *Kayalnilams*.

Existing as a striated topographical undulation rising and falling above the backwaters, the system is composed of bio-bunds and canals. The constructed module forms a two-tier system, making it adaptable to seasonal precipitation. The bio-bunds, known as *kuttiyum chirayum*, are made of local materials including coconut poles, bamboo mats, sand, twigs, and sedges like cattail (*Typha latifolia*) and common three square (*Schoenoplectus pungens*), interspersed with high quality clay dug from a lake depth of 20–25m.[5] The bunds separate the canals which hold water used for irrigation. The water enters the paddy fields through a flexible opening in the bund called a *thoomba*. However, to avoid excess water entering the paddy fields, dewatering technologies called *pettiyum parayum* that periodically remove water, are placed at strategic junctures between the bunds and the canals. To block the seasonal entry of salt, temporary barriers called *orumuttu*, made of sand bags and twigs are built above the salt level allowing only fresh water to enter the paddy fields. The entire system is lined with an exterior bund two metres above the intertidal level, which acts as a sea defence barrier against fluctuating tidal levels.

Beyond climate resilience and agricultural optimization, these bunds and canals also improve water quality and structure a complex habitat. As a permeable structure, the bunds act as a favourable ground for freshwater prawns and other aquatic species while the canals serve both as a fish nursery and hunting ground. Fish venturing upstream during high tide are trapped in the system by a detachable net fitted inside the dewatering technology. The introduction of fish into the system creates opportunities for aquaculture with some fish that seek refuge under the roots of the paddy crops. Stirring movements of the fish aerates the planting bed improving the surface soil conditions both in terms of porosity and fertility. This accelerates the growth of paddy crops which in turn provide oxygen and food for fish, as their roots favour the growth of microorganisms which are natural fish food. This symbiosis between rice and fish is further enhanced by the recurring movement of salt and water in the system . . .

> **... Lo—TEK for Climate Resilience ...**
>
> ... Scientists have acknowledged that the world is in the midst of the earth's sixth mass extinction, but species extinction alone will not be the twenty-first century's greatest loss. Those same forces that drive species extinction endanger the local, nature-based technologies—not yet recognized as technologies—that may hold a key to the survival of the world's population in the global south. These are technologies that have evolved and passed through generations in response to flood, fire, drought, sea level rise, and severe weather—the same crises we face today. These are incredibly well adapted to their environments and play an important role in conserving global biodiversity.
>
> 1   Nunn, P. D., Runman, J., Falanruw, M, & Kumar, R. (2017). Culturally grounded responses to coastal change on islands in the Federated States of Micronesia, northwest Pacific Ocean. Regional Environmental Change, 17, 959–971. doi:10.1007/s10113-016-0950-2.
> 2   Watson, 2019.
> 3   Garroutte, E. M. (2006). Defining Radical Indigenism and Creating an American Indian Scholarship. Culture, Power, and History: Studies In Critical Sociology. Brill.
> 4   Chandran, S. & Purkayastha, S. (2021). History Of Reclaimed Kayals. In: Kuttanad Wetland And Associated Social Divide In Alappuzha District, Kerala. Ijrar, 5(3), pp.573–581.
> 5   Nagarajan, S., Bhavani, R.V. & Swaminathan, M.S. (2014). Operationalizing the concept of farming system for nutrition through the promotion of nutrition-sensitive agriculture. Current Science, pp.959–964.
>
> J. Watson, H. Abukhodair, N. A. Naeema Ali, A. Robertson, H. Issaoui, and C. Sun, "Design by Radical Indigenism: Equitable Underwater & Intertidal Technologies of the Global South", *SPOOL* 8, no. 3 (2021): 57–74 doi.org/10.7480/spool.2021.3.6217.

In the current epoch, named by several geologists as the Anthropocene, humanity's indelible mark on Earth's ecosystems, particularly through greenhouse gas accumulations, suggests a seemingly irreversible alteration of our planet. As we move away from Anthropocentric worldviews, it becomes evident that the long-standing nature-culture binary must be reframed.

This chapter traces the shift in design disciplines over the past six decades, revealing a trend towards a more holistic, sensitive, and respectful approach to designing with greater synergy with nature. For all the merits of sustainable, resilient, and green design solutions, the professions of landscape architecture, architecture, and urban design, must engage directly with the dynamism of our natural world. Effective urban design aligns with natural processes and embraces nature's temporal and seasonal shifts—where "going with the flow," particularly in terms of water management, is paramount. By recognizing the intricate interconnectedness of human activities and natural systems, designers can create more harmonious and adaptive urban environments that not only mitigate the negative impacts of human development but also potentially regenerate natural systems.

6

Health, Equity, and Livable Cities

During the nineteenth century, cholera, typhoid, yellow fever, and other epidemics of infectious diseases, often stemming from inadequate sanitation facilities among the poor, acted as catalysts for the improvement of sewage drainage and water purification systems in urban areas. Today, architects and urban designers remain deeply concerned about the equity and health of all people. This chapter, titled "Health, Equity, and Livable Cities," covers architects and urban designers who focus on the various ways in which the built environment can exacerbate inequality and foster behavior detrimental to our physical and mental well-being. Their vision advocates for cities and landscapes that are walkable, sociable, equitable and just.

The Covid-19 pandemic triggered concern for healthy urban environments. It forced cities to swiftly adapt to new challenges, effectively placing urban life on pause in much of the world.

FIGURE 6.1 In 2020, San Francisco restaurateurs expanded outdoor dining to Main Street and its parking spaces, a move permitted amidst the Covid-19 pandemic to safely serve guests. Courtesy of Getty Images.

HEALTH, EQUITY, AND LIVABLE CITIES

Temporary measures, such as pop-up bike lanes, outdoor dining spaces, and widened sidewalks were implemented in many cities to allow for social distancing, while simultaneously improving the quality of urban life. These changes highlighted the importance of flexible and adaptive urban planning in response to health crises. Reflecting on the historical progression from combating infectious diseases to contemporary health crises, this chapter highlights how the pursuit of health and equity remains a cornerstone of urban design.

The built environment should be expected to augment the physical and spiritual welfare of people and society as a whole, through more positively impactful effects upon our bodies and minds. However, urban and architectural space is generally designed with an ableist bias towards a narrow definition of "normative bodies," creating mobility challenges for persons with a disability, for equity of mobility and access. This is especially problematic given the demographic trend of an aging population in developed countries. In response, universal design addresses issues of reduced mobility, injury and disability, challenging the ingrained ableist biases in the built environment. The search is on for healthier, more inclusive, and equitable approaches to city design, architecture and interiors that promote universal well-being.

The effects of interior spaces upon our well-being is important, as Emily Anthes shows in her book, *The Great Indoors: The Surprising Science of How Buildings Shape our Behavior, Health and Happiness* (2020), since Europeans and North Americans spend over 90 percent of their time in interior environments. However, even as many spend only 10 percent of their time in exterior environments, these places play a major role in our health and happiness as well.[1]

In her essay, "Emergency Urbanism and Preventative Architecture," which forms part of a co-edited book titled, *Imperfect Health: The Medicalization of Architecture* (2012), Hilary Sample writes, somewhat prophetically, on the impact of the SARS epidemic on cities. She argues how the built environment, shaped by rules made to protect public health, is constantly reshaped by outbreaks such as the Covid-19 pandemic. As disease emerges, cities adapt – spaces are redefined, and rules rewritten, leading to a dynamic interplay between health governance and urban architectures. Sample asks how our built environment can be designed to better absorb and mitigate health crises.[2]

Although Covid-19 underscored the relationship between public health and the built environment, the significance of health in city design and architecture traces its roots to antiquity. Two millennia ago, Vitruvius, in his work *The Ten Books on Architecture*, represents the Romans' meticulous consideration of "healthy" air when selecting settlement sites. Vitruvius wrote,

> Such a site will be high, neither misty nor frosty, and in a climate neither hot nor cold, but temperate; further, without marshes in the neighbourhood. For when the morning breezes blow toward the town at sunrise, if they bring with them mists from marshes and, mingled with the mist, the poisonous breath of the creatures of the marshes to be wafted into the bodies of the inhabitants.[1]
>
> **1** Vitruvius Pollio, "The Site of a City," edited by Morris Hicky Morgan, *The Ten Books on Architecture*, (New York: Dover, 1960).

During the rapid unfolding of the second industrial revolution, cities experienced explosive growth and industrialization, and escalating pollution levels. Friedrich Engels, in his book *The Condition of the Working Class in England* (1845) described nineteenth-century Manchester as, "hell upon earth," defying "all considerations of cleanliness, ventilation, and health." He noted, "If any one wishes to see in how little space a human being can move, how little air—and *such* air!—he can breathe, how little of civilization he may share and yet live, it is only necessary to travel hither."[3] By 1900, most of London's five million people endured these dreadful horrendous conditions as smog and pollution shrouded the city, leading a Victorian poet to coin the moniker of the "city of dreadful night."[4]

The early twentieth century introduced technological advancements that negatively impacted our built environments and health, with the widespread adoption of the automobile. Henry Ford's Model T, first mass-produced in 1908, made car travel accessible to many. Just four years later, New York City saw more cars than horses on its roads. Soon, car-related infrastructure, including gas stations, car washes, and parking garages, began to proliferate.

Once vibrant hubs of social interaction, streets gradually transformed into mere "traffic machines," as envisioned by Le Corbusier in his 1929 work, *The City of To-morrow and Its Planning*.[5] He championed a cityscape dominated by a gridded network of highways. Modernist urban planners viewed the city as a machine delineating separate elements for housing, commerce, transportation, and recreation as discreet parts. Le Corbusier's *City of To-morrow* envisioned vast grand plazas as spaces for socialization.

However, Jane Jacobs, in her seminal work *The Death and Life of Great American Cities* (1961), contested this view, campaigning against the effects of New York's car-oriented superblocks and highways on communities. Recognizing that the importance of streets extended beyond traffic, she celebrated streets and sidewalks as "the main public spaces of the city"[6] that fostered social interaction, play, shopping and entrepreneurship. Jacobs understood the street network as a "nervous system" and "a major point of transaction and communication."[7] Well-designed streets offer more than just transportation; they create spaces for social engagement, memorable experiences, and economic activity. Her ideas emphasized the importance of mixed land uses, short blocks, and pedestrian-friendly streets.

In the Global South, plazas, sidewalks, and residual urban spaces, often serve as vital arteries of city life, hosting food and market stalls. In places such as Jakarta many pedestrians are engaged in activities such as street vending.[8] Annette Kim's *Sidewalk City: Remapping Public Space in Ho Chi Minh City* (2015) uncover the cultural facets of sidewalk life, often overlooked in official planning studies.[9]

Ironically, standards intended to enhance safety had eroded the vitality of streets. Michael Southworth and Eran Ben-Joseph, in *Streets and the Shaping of Towns and Cities* (1997) documented how these standards dictated increased street width and parking requirements, allocating the most space for cars rather than people.[10] Pedestrian sidewalks not only became less inviting but also started disappearing. When sidewalks were present, the lack of curb cuts made them hard to navigate for people with disabilities and parents pushing strollers. In some American cities, parking spaces account for over a third of the metropolitan footprint,[11] reducing potential social spaces, privileging cars over people.

As cars congested cities, they further fuelled the suburban exodus. By the late 1960s, more people in the United States lived in suburbs than in cities. Federal highways, cheap rural land, and government mortgage insurance programs supported suburban growth, associated with "the good life," as documented by Kenneth T. Jackson in *Crabgrass Frontier: The Suburbanization of the United States* (1985). Importantly, minority groups were grossly under-represented in these new neighborhoods, unable to buy homes through mortgage discrimination and redlining.

A vicious cycle began. The car made suburban sprawl possible, which then made the car a necessity. Subway and inter-city train networks failed to mature in North American cities, leaving few alternatives to automobiles. Highways frequently dissected neighborhoods, contributing to traffic congestion, and often leading to further segregation based on racial and economic distinctions. Instead of building rail lines, governments had built highways cutting through urban communities, such as the Bronx Expressway in 1953, also known as "Heartbreak Highway." But even the widest highways are no match to the subway trains' capacity for transporting people. One highway lane can carry only about 2,000 cars per hour, whereas subways can carry almost 36,000 people.

This car-centric lifestyle exacted an environmental toll. Cars disproportionately contribute to smog and climate change, with a car trip consuming about five times more transport energy per passenger kilometre than public transit.[12] In 2016, the global transport sector was responsible for 23 percent of the global carbon emissions, and the vast majority of this came from road vehicles.[13]

Each year, road traffic accidents kill 1.25 million people. The car impacted public health in other sinister ways as well. A century ago, we used to walk to school or to pick up groceries. Today, trips like this are often made by motorized means. With each additional hour spent in a car, there is a 6 percent increase in the likelihood of obesity.[14] Weight gains lead to obesity-related illnesses such as strokes and diabetes.[15] Mental well-being suffered as well, with longer car commutes associated with decreased job satisfaction, increased stress, and reduced community engagement. One survey reported 42 percent of commuters felt heightened stress levels as a result of driving in congestion, while 35 percent indicated it made them angrier.[16]

In the 1990s, researcher Robert D. Putnam found that for each additional 10 minutes spent commuting to work, there was 10 percent less involvement in community affairs, such as volunteering and even voting. In addition, informal socializing activities also dropped from 85 minutes in 1965 to 57 minutes in 1995.[17] Where Americans used to play in leagues, he noted, in his eponymous book, they were increasingly, *Bowling Alone* (2000).[18]

The car also reshaped social interactions in cities. In Don Appleyard's pioneering book *Livable Streets* (1981), he conducted a study comparing streets with varying levels of vehicular traffic, from 2,000 to 16,000 vehicles daily. The results revealed that streets with lower traffic volumes fostered three times as many local connections among residents. Appleyard demonstrated that less congested streets were more conducive to interpersonal interactions.

Authors like Don Appleyard, Jan Gehl and Jeff Speck have focused on designing cities that prioritize walking and cycling. Their books—respectively *Liveable Streets* (1981), *Life between Buildings* (1971), and *Walkable City* (2012)—advocate for pedestrian-friendly urban environments that promote physical activity and reduce reliance on cars. These works have been influential in implementing more pedestrian-friendly streets through traffic calming, shared streets, or even pedestrianization. They emphasize the promotion of "liveability," a term used to describe the quality of life in a particular place or community.[19]

The work of urban designer Jan Gehl from Denmark has had a global impact. His book *Public Spaces, Public Life* (2011) documents how the city of Copenhagen has gradually transformed from a car-dominated to a pedestrian-oriented city. Over several decades, the city removed parking spaces in the urban center. These spaces were transformed into open-air cafés and neighborhood parks. Social activities increased fourfold.[20]

Copenhagen was able to remove parking spaces because commuters had the option to take a train instead of a car. In 1947, the city had announced its new "five-finger plan" for future expansion, with a railway structuring development within each finger. Transit-oriented plans like Copenhagen's are known to bring health benefits for citizens. Nine separate studies from across the world showed that people walked between eight and thirty-three minutes more a day when using public transit, since it typically requires walking to and from a bus stop or a train station.[21]

Gehl makes a number of insightful analyses regarding the promotion of sociability. He distinguishes between necessary activities, such as walking to work, which will likely always happen regardless of the quality of public space. On the contrary, optional activities (such as stopping to talk) will only happen more frequently in a high-quality public space . He advocates for buildings with "soft edges," with lots of doors, windows, and semi-private areas like stoops and porches to make streets more lively and invite optional activities. His firm, Gehl Architects, has created people-centered spaces in cities around the world, including pedestrianized plazas in New York City. Lively cities increase social interaction amongst citizens, augmenting how we learn from each other, stay informed, and find inspiration. By contrast, lifeless cities are generally lacking vitality due to segregated zoning which causes cities "to become duller and more monotonous." Gehl argues for creating spaces for people to congregate and interact, in which he sees

FIGURE 6.2 A child strolls through a pedestrian zone, part of Barcelona's expanded "superilla" (superblock) initiative, which fosters cycling and car-free areas for a greener city. Courtesy of Getty Images.

opportunities for human spectacle, rather than spectacular architecture. "Life between buildings," for Gehl famously stated, is more "essential and relevant than the spaces and buildings themselves."

Donald Appleyard and Allan Jacobs, in their influential article, "Towards an Urban Design Manifesto," (1987) highlight physical characteristics that promote sociable neighborhoods. These include: walkable streets; a minimum residential density; many and varied activities within proximity to each other; and numerous buildings rather than just a few large buildings.[22] This is a counter to the mono-use, low-density, and car-centric characteristics of much of suburban sprawl.

However, even in suburban neighborhoods, thoughtful planning can optimize social interaction by promoting visual contact and creating enjoyable communal spaces where people can spend time together.[23] Peter Calthorpe, Andres Duany, and Elizabeth Plater-Zyberk are proponents of New Urbanism and Smart Growth principles, promoting mixed land use, compact cities, and sustainable development. However, critics have noted that New Urbanism, despite its good intentions, has also promoted suburban sprawl, because several neighborhoods lacked the essential public transportation infrastructure required to sustain them.[24] While several projects may have been limited to beautifying suburbia and small towns, New Urbanism has nevertheless positively impacted urban planning by promoting walkable neighborhoods and environmentally sustainable practices.

By considering the physical characteristics that promote sociability and by creating enjoyable communal spaces, urban environments can be enhanced, fostering physical health and mental well-being. The future of urban planning lies in designs that prioritize people over cars, creating cities and suburbs where everyone can thrive.

JAN GEHL
Life between Buildings: Using Public Space

LIFE BETWEEN BUILDINGS

The opportunity to see and hear other people in a city or residential area also implies an offer of valuable information, about the surrounding social environment in general and about the people one lives or works with in particular.

This is especially true in connection with the social development of children, which is largely based on observations of the surrounding social environment, but all of us need to be kept up to date about the surrounding world in order to function in a social context.

Through the mass media we are informed about the larger, more sensational world events, but by being with others we learn about the more common but equally important details. We discover how others work, behave, and dress, and we obtain knowledge about the people we work with, live with, and so forth. By means of all this information we establish a confident relationship with the world around us. A person we have often met on the street becomes a person we "know."

In addition to imparting information about the social world outside, the opportunity to see and hear other people can also provide ideas and inspiration for action.

We are inspired by seeing others in action. Children, for example, see other children at play and get the urge to join in, or they get ideas for new games by watching other children or adults.

The trend from living to lifeless cities and residential areas that has accompanied industrialization, segregation of various city functions, and reliance on the automobile also has caused cities to become duller and more monotonous. This points up another important need, namely *the need for stimulation*.[1]

Experiencing other people represents a particularly colorful and attractive opportunity for stimulation. Compared with experiencing buildings and other inanimate objects, experiencing people, who speak and move about, offers a wealth of sensual variation. No moment is like the previous or the following when people circulate among people. The number of new situations and new stimuli is limitless. Furthermore, it concerns the most important subject in life: people.

Living cities, therefore, ones in which people can interact with one another, are always stimulating because they are rich in experiences, in contrast to lifeless cities, which can scarcely avoid being poor in experiences and thus dull, no matter how many colors and variations of shape in buildings are introduced. If life between buildings is given favorable conditions through sensible planning of cities and housing areas alike, many costly and often stilted and strained attempts to make buildings "interesting" and rich by using dramatic architectural effects can be spared.

Life between buildings is both more relevant and more interesting to look at in the long run than are any combination of colored concrete and staggered building forms . . .

. . . If given a choice between walking on a deserted or a lively street, most people in most situations will choose the lively street. If the choice is between sitting in a private backyard or in a semiprivate front yard with a view of the street, people will often choose the front of the house where there is more to see. In Scandinavia an old proverb tells it all: "people come where people are."

A series of investigations illustrates in more detail the interest in being in contact with others. Investigations of children's play habits in residential areas show that children stay and play primarily where the most activity is occurring or in places where there is the greatest chance of something happening.[2]

Both in areas with single-family houses and in apartment house surroundings, children tend to play more on the streets, in parking areas, and near the entrances of dwellings than in the play areas designed for that purpose but located in backyards of single-family houses or on the sunny side of multi-story buildings, where there are neither traffic nor people to look at.

Corresponding trends can be found regarding where people choose to sit in public spaces. Benches that provide a good view of surrounding activities are used more than benches with less or no view of others.

An investigation of Tivoli Garden in Copenhagen, carried out by the architect John Lyle, shows that the most used benches are along the garden's main path, where there is a good view of the particularly active areas, while the least used benches are found in the quiet areas of the park.[3] In various places, benches are arranged back to back, so that one of the benches faces a path while the other "turns its back." In these instances it is always the benches facing the path that are used.

Comparable results have been found in investigations of seating in a number of squares in central Copenhagen. Benches with a view of the most trafficked pedestrian routes are used most, while benches oriented toward the planted areas of the squares are used less frequently.[4]

At sidewalk cafes, as well, the life on the sidewalk in front of the cafe is the prime attraction. Almost without exception cafe chairs throughout the world are oriented toward the most active area nearby. Sidewalks are, not unexpectedly, the very reason for creating sidewalk cafes.

The opportunity to see, hear, and meet others can also be shown to be one of the most important attractions in city centers and on pedestrian streets. This is illustrated by an attraction analysis carried out on Strøget, the main pedestrian street in central Copenhagen, by a study group from the School of Architecture at the Royal Danish Academy of Fine Arts.[5] The analysis was based on an investigation of where pedestrians stopped on the walking street and what they stopped to look at.

Fewest stops were noted in front of banks, offices, showrooms, and dull exhibits of, for example, cash registers, office furniture, porcelain, or hair curlers. Conversely, a great number of stops were noted in front of shops and exhibits that had a direct relationship to other people and to the surrounding social environment, such as newspaper kiosks, photography exhibits, film stills outside movie theaters, clothing stores, and toy stores.

Even greater interest was shown in the various human activities that went on in the street space itself. All forms of human activity appeared to be of major interest in this connection.

Considerable interest was observed in both the ordinary, everyday events that take place on a street – children at play, newlyweds on their way from the photographers, or merely people walking by – and in the more unusual instance – the artist with his easel, the street musician with his guitar, street painters in action, and other large and small events.

It was obvious that human activities, being able to see other people in action, constituted the area's main attraction.

The street painters collected a large crowd as long as their work was in progress, but when they left the area, pedestrians walked over the paintings without hesitation. The same was true of music. Music blaring out on the street from loudspeakers in front of record shops elicited no reaction, but the moment live musicians began to play or sing, there was an instantaneous show of lively interest.

The attention paid to people and human activities was also illustrated by observations made in connection with the expansion of a department store in the area. While excavation and pouring of foundations were in progress, it was possible to see into the building site through two gates facing the pedestrian street. Throughout this period more people stopped to watch the work in progress on the building site than was the case for stops in front of all the department store's fifteen display windows together.

In this case, too, it was the workers and their work, not the building site itself, that was the object of interest. This was demonstrated further during lunch breaks and after quitting time – when no workers were on the site, practically nobody stopped to look.

A summary of observations and investigations shows that people and human activity are the greatest object of attention and interest. Even the modest form of contact of merely seeing and hearing or being near to others is apparently more rewarding and more in demand than the majority of other attractions offered in the public spaces of cities and residential areas.

Life in buildings and between buildings seems in nearly all situations to rank as more essential and more relevant than the spaces and buildings themselves.

1 Gehl, Ingrid. *Bo-miljø* (Living Environment-Psychological Aspects of Housing). Danish Building Research Institute, report 71. Copenhagen: Teknisk Forlag, 1971.
2 Kjærsdam, Finn. *Haveboligområdets fællesareal*. Parts 1 and 2. Part 1 published by: Den kongelige Veterinær og Landbohøjskole, Copenhagen, 1974. Part 2 by: Aalborg Universitetscenter, ISP, Aalborg, 1976. Morville, Jeanne. *Planlægning af børns udemiljø i etageboligområder* (Planning for Children in Multistory Housing Areas). Danish Building Research Institute, report 11. Copenhagen: Teknisk Forlag, 1969.
3 Lyle, John. "Tivoli Gardens." Landscape (Spring/Summer 1969): 5 – 22.
4 Gehl, Jan. *Attraktioner på Strøget*. Kunstakademiets Arkitektskole. Studyreport. Copenhagen, 1969. Gehl, Jan. "Mennesker til fods" (Pedestrians). *Arkitekten* (Danish) 70, no. 20 (1968): 429–46. Kao, Louise. "Hvor sidder man på Kongens Nytorv?" (Sitting Preferences on Kongens Nytorv). *Arkitekten* (Danish) 70, no. 20 (1968): 445.
5 Gehl, Jan. *Attraktioner på Strøget*. Kunstakademiets Arkitektskole. Studyreport. Copenhagen, 1969. Gehl, Jan. "Mennesker til fods" (Pedestrians). *Arkitekten* (Danish) 70, no. 20 (1968): 429–46.

Jan Gehl, *Life between Buildings: Using Public Space*, (Washington, DC: Island Press, 2011); 21–23, 27–30.

Modernist design ideals often stood in the way of the creation of sociable and equitable spaces. In *The Social Life of Small Urban Spaces* (1980), urbanist William H. Whyte critiqued the modernist plazas which emerged from the 1961 Zoning Resolution in New York. This resolution offered incentives for builders to provide adjacent privately owned public spaces (POPS), resulting in the construction of about 1.1 million square feet of new urban open space in New York City by 1973, surpassing all other US cities combined.[25] However, these plazas were often under-programmed and underutilized.

Whyte declared that "the city was being had"[26] and led an investigation into the issue. His research revealed that these plazas lacked adequate seating and sometimes even featured deterrents to sitting such as spikes on horizontal surfaces. Developers and designers prioritized visual appeal over public use. He wrote,

> Benches are artifacts the purpose of which is to punctuate architectural photographs. They're not so good for sitting. There are too few of them; they are too small; they are often isolated from other benches or from whatever action there is on the plaza. Worse yet, architects tend to repeat the same module in plaza after plaza, unaware that it didn't work very well in the first place.[1]
>
> 1 William H. Whyte, *The Social Life of Small Urban Spaces* (New York: The Conservation Foundation, 1980), 33.

Whyte demonstrated that people want to sit near others, instead of sitting in isolation in segregated areas. "What attracts people most, it would appear, is other people," he noted. Whyte argued for sociable places with abundant seating, ideally near busy and accessible locations. "This might not strike you as an intellectual bombshell," Whyte said, "but people like to sit where there are places for them to sit." Whyte's advocacy led to a 1975 amendment, forcing plazas to be "amenable" to the public, eventually leading to better open spaces with more seating. Today, the city's public plaza provision includes many standards including specifying vegetation, external lighting and seating requirements, with a minimum of one linear foot of seating for every 30 square feet of plaza.[27]

The sociability in public spaces promoted by authors like Whyte and Gehl are also better suited for aging populations. The World Health Organization (WHO) has advocated for "active aging" and age-friendly cities. Unfortunately, most urban spaces are not designed for people at all stages of human life. In response, "age-friendly" cities are designed to cater to the needs of all residents, including the elderly. An article titled "Towards Global Age-Friendly Cities: Determining Urban Features that Promote Active Aging" (2010) by Louise Plouffe and Alexandre Kalache highlights the importance of urban features and design principles that support active aging, such as accessible public spaces, walkability, safety, social engagement opportunities, and healthcare access.[28]

Additionally, modernist design has been criticized for its embedding of sexist elements. It often bases its concepts on the male body, resulting in buildings and furniture that are uncomfortable or inaccessible for women and people with disabilities. For example, the Modulor, a system of proportions developed by Le Corbusier, is based on the height of a hypothetical man. In addition, Modernism prioritized rationality and efficiency over comfort and livability, which can make modernist spaces feel cold and unwelcoming.

Moreover, Modernism frequently overlooked the different needs of all people. For example, in the 1920s, proponents of the modernist Bauhaus school, championed "efficiency" in design. Their vision of the "Frankfurt kitchen," a clean and cubist marvel, offered users a streamlined kitchen following scientific management. Yet the tailored compactness of this domestic future, meant for a single purpose only, would further perpetuate the isolation of women. These were designed not only as single-purpose rooms, but also as single-person rooms, isolating the cook, most often a woman.

Dolores Hayden, an architect and historian, has argued for a more gender-equitable built environment in her seminal article, "What Would a Non-sexist City Be Like?" (1980).[29] She finds good examples of housing projects with daycare and other services, which would reduce the domestic burden that often falls on women. Hayden's critique of "the conservative and male-dominated design professions" demands, she contends, "a new paradigm of the home, the neighborhood, and the city" which can better accommodate employed women. Through a feminist agenda, she addresses the dismantling of "the conventional division between public and private space." Her own design proposal to interconnect single family homes with communal services would extend these ideas to suburban areas. Not dissimilar to projects in the Soviet Union in the 1920s, or the Israeli kibbutz, Hayden's proposition is for "collective houses" with the provision of daycare. More broadly, Hayden calls for new types of housing that are demographically diverse, and dense, and integrated to overcome the gender coding in cities, architecture, and interiors.

In contrast, Elizabeth Wilson, a feminist theorist, in her book *The Sphinx in the City: Urban Life, the Control of Disorder, and Women* (1991) writes about the liberating potential of urbanism for women. She points to nineteenth-century department stores in Paris where, as an urban form of exhibitionism, goods were displayed, inviting touch and sight. Inside stores, women were allowed to see and be seen, to admire themselves, and move without constraint. She cautions against "the worst of all worlds: danger without pleasure, safety without stimulation, consumerism without choice, monumentality without diversity."[30]

Aaron Betsky, in *Queer Space* (1997), shows how gay men and women have played a pioneering role in architectural and urban innovation.[31] They have revitalized neglected neighborhoods and transformed inhospitable environments into a canvas for artistic expression. These spaces, often referred to as "queer spaces," serve as reflections of LGBTQ+ experiences in a predominantly heterosexual society. Constrained by societal norms that compelled them to conceal their true identities, gay men and women created interior environments characterized by theatricality and festivity, where they could define and express themselves without the fear of judgement or persecution.

Despite their different areas of concern, proponents of feminism gender studies, and queer theory share common goals: creating more inclusive and equitable cities that cater to everyone's needs. In the following excerpt from the book *She City* (2024), Nicole Kalms articulates a participatory feminist design approach which aims for the dismantling of systemic barriers in traditional urban settings. It highlights the adversities girls and women endure in public spaces, such as discrimination, threats and violence. Kalms critiques conventional city planning for neglecting the female experience, thereby solidifying patriarchal norms and marginalization. Advocating for a fundamental transformation of urban spaces that foreground women's safety and autonomy, the book argues against the 'neutral' urban design paradigm and instead proposes a gender-sensitive framework that seeks to engage with women across the design process. *She City* provides research-backed strategies for targeting an inclusive urbanism which can serve all residents, advocating for gender equity in urban design.

KALMS, NICOLE
She City: Designing Out Women's Inequity in Cities

Women in Cities: An Introduction

Cities are always on the cusp of transformation and change. As the scale and density of cities increase, so too does the inequity of the women and girls who live and work within them. Understanding the challenges faced by women in cities requires understanding how sex and gender shape both the practicalities of designing cities and the gendered experiences of those living within them. Some practitioners struggle to recognize how cities impact women's experiences of sexism, of discrimination or their fear of men's violence. There may be resistance to deepening their understanding or they may believe that feminism is passé and does not warrant their serious consideration.[1] For those that are curious, questions commonly asked indicate uncertainty and ambiguity, and often include:

> How and why do women experience cities differently?
> What does the built environment have to do with women's oppression?
> Why do women feel more at risk in cities than men do?
> Can design address the complex concerns of women moving through cities?

These questions have been the focus of research by feminist planners, urban geographers and architects for many decades. Despite their interrogation of these questions—and their agitation for alternative approaches to policy, practice and design — evidence reiterates time and again that women' use and occupation of public space continues to be inhibited. The barriers women face when trying to freely access public space include hetero/sexism encountered in cities, discrimination and bias, which result in a lack of attention to their practical daily urban needs, as well as in the social tolerance toward and normalization of men's violence . . .

. . . . Activating a feminist-focused, women-centered approach to designing cities for women's rights and needs is more critical than ever. Women have the right to be part of their cities and their communities, and of all the culture that cities might offer, including access to education, training and employment, to health care and social services, as well as to leisure and recreation. This requires that women and girls move freely and safely in public spaces and transport networks, as these rights are critical for ensuring a cycle of social and economic inclusion for women and girls into the future. Addressing women's needs means recognizing that cities are not simply defined by materiality and infrastructure, but that the urban environment is equally defined by its capacity to shape the interactions which take place within it. And yet, without these foundational concepts most practitioners will fall short when asked to address inequity in cities.

Understanding how gender impacts urban experience and, in turn, policy, planning and practice, is not a core part of the education of engineers, architects, planners and designers, yet there is increasing pressure from communities and governments alike to align with local and national targets for gender equality in cities. While many will agree that identifying and fiercely challenging the tendency to create androcentric, heterosexist and heteronormative urban places is vital, they may also concede that they lack confidence to enact change, and they view the task as anything but straightforward . . .

. . . Public Space, Private Hell

Women's perceptions of risk and vulnerability are a recurring theme in this book. And for good reason. The impact of men's violence against women dominates women's lives, is an enduring public health issue, and is devastatingly and disproportionately perpetrated by men against women. Some will counter that "women are also perpetrators" and while this statement may be true, the statistics that make any claim for parity are nothing short of ridiculous.[2] Political theorist and feminist Carole Sheffield wrote about "sexual terrorism" over thirty years ago, and in a recent updated edition of the same book, she maintains that the issues are as relevant as ever. Sheffield suggests that in the face of cultural change, and despite greater understanding of men's violence against women and girls, her position on sexual terrorism "has proven to be remarkably adaptable and sustainable".[3] Importantly, whether women are direct victims of violence or not, the mere *threat* of violence is a form of social control that impacts *all* women in cities. As Sheffield writes, "The difference between men's and women's experiences of fear underscores the fact that women's lives are bounded by both the reality of the pervasive danger of men's violence and the fear that reality engenders"[4]. Similarly, Dora Epstein writes about fear and the burden of staying safe in urban space.[5] She states:

> There is a story to this fearing, this fearing that maps the cityscapes into places I will go and places I will not. As speaking subjects, sentient members of urban terrains, we can narrate our cartographies of avoidance, our fearing, far better than we can narrate how the fearing came to be. We know, can articulate, what we have deemed "unsafe"—the strange, the unfamiliar, the supposedly violent "other" against which we have insulated and barricaded ourselves—and what we have deemed as "safe" — the lit, the populated, the orderly, or seemingly controlled to which we have clung. We felt justified when violence occurred in the realm of our "unsafe"; felt shock when it occurred in our "safe."

These insights serve to demonstrate how women's fear of men's violence can be defined by "sensed risk, concern, anxiety, worry, and fear" and as such is held by women in subjective ways that defy definition and result in "many sub-constructs, each with large variations".[6] As such, management of the fear of men's violence zaps energy from women and girls and decreases their participation in public life, and will almost certainly negatively impact their social, economic and educational outcomes.[7] The degree of that impact will be markedly increased if a woman's experience includes additional intersectional factors and systemic disadvantage . . .

. . . Activating the City . . .

. . . For more equitable cities, designers must engage with women and girls across the design process to examine the concepts and complexity of inequality and work, in order to understand how design practice can contribute to (and positively shape) cultural narratives. By opposing the limitation of top-down approaches, the politics of space can progress women's agency through design processes and practice. This requires design practitioners to employ methods and modes that engage diverse stakeholders, including the people who will benefit from the outcomes of design. Foundational is the understanding that broader participation in the design process that includes the perspectives of women and girls can transform urban experiences.

Participatory design (also broadly referred to as co-design) is a common tool used across multiple stages of the design process with the aim of democratizing urban development. Increasingly (and unfortunately) it is also a buzzword within the public sector, where the method is reinforced by increasing pressure on communities to involve members of the public in decision-making processes.[8] It has come to represent a wide range of techniques and has been subsumed as a "problem solving technique" that is "easily adopted in different context, both to positive and negative effects".[9] This may mean that some of the uses of participatory design are not participatory at all, particularly if aspects of the process are overlooked (such as sketching, modeling, prototyping, etc.) within the research method.[10]

Inherent in the methodology is the co-production of knowledge, where the perceived "expert" (usually the policymaker, planner or designer) is required to share the privileges of power via co-learning.[11] This moves the design process away from design "for" communities and engages with methods that privilege the process of "designing with" communities.[12] In this practice, this means that the designer must relinquish their perceived expertise within the hierarchical modes of traditional design practice, with a shared participation intercepting the hegemony of the ambitious and all-knowing "expert."

The process is a means to address the ways that design reproduces "dysfunctional ideologies, coming from a traditionally white hetero-patriarchal and capitalist narrative," as participatory co-design can "be a tool" that questions assumptions, assists in reflection, and be a mode for "positive change".[13] The evidence for inviting policymakers, planners and designers to work alongside women and girls suggests that participatory co-design is a mode to foster outcomes that are "supportive of the spectrum of gender and intersectional identities".[14]

As a process of "mutual learning," and with the aim to challenge "top-down power structures"[15] participatory co-design "intertwines" the act of designing a method for "questioning and reconfiguring power relations and notions of expertise".[16] When properly implemented in the context of urban placemaking projects, the project outcomes will be more equitable and will center local communities not only as participants in the design process but as evaluators and co-producers of solutions.[17]

Participatory *feminist* placemaking examines relevant urban issues specifically about women and girls and provides a framework to understand their perspectives. Drawing on their experiential knowledge, the process actively positions women and girls at the center of the design process to reconfigure the dynamics that tend to exclude women from urban design and placemaking. This means that design "about" or "for" women and girls moves to a design "with" women and girls, where collaborative tasks between designers and women stakeholders resist assumptions and biases in the design process. The method confronts the assumed disciplinary "expertise" in order to recognize the importance or "using women's experiences as a resource for social analysis",[18] which, when centered in placemaking, can progress women's social and political equity . . .

A Better Standard than This[19]

This book has shown how feminists continue to intervene across government policy, urban design planning and community activism to encourage the uptake of a women-centered approach to cities and with the aim to accelerate equity in the built environment. For some, it may seem passé to engage a feminist-focused approach, as many will be persuaded that these concerns are somehow resolved in the rhetoric of "equality".[20] And yet, insisting on an appraisal of women's experiences of urban space and the necessity to create cities that prioritize the diverse needs of women and girls is more important than ever.

Assessing the effects of feminist frameworks on women's experiences and equity in cities and communities takes time and is an area that is under-researched. The short-, medium- and long-term impact must be measured through qualitative and quantitative modes with a focus on benefits to women's and girls' quality of life and a fairer distribution of community resources in their cities and communities. It is likely that this measure is dynamic and able to respond to the changing needs of women and girls across their life course. The financial cost of implementing the frameworks as well as the aligned engagement and training need to be appraised in relation to the overwhelming negative impacts on women's health, wellbeing and economic position which is overlooked when cities continue to engage with neutral policy and practice.

To challenge women's exclusion in cities, practitioners need to consider how and why women experience cities differently and how to overcome "cultural and attitudinal bias toward women".[21] Through clear and considered understanding of how the built environment contributes to women's oppression—and by engaging with frameworks that are sensitive to women's needs— policymakers, planners and designers will positively impact women's experiences in public life. The integration of participatory feminist co-design can ensure that practitioners understand why women feel at risk in cities, where barriers exist, and what women believe will enable their participation. Centering women to the process will transform design approaches to address inequity in cities.

1 Gamble, Sarah (2006), *The Routledge Companion to Feminism and Postfeminism,* London: Routledge, 38.
2 In Australia, for example, during 2018-19, 97% of sexual assault offenders were men (Australian Institute of Health and Welfare 2020: 1) and likely even higher, given that underreporting is estimated to be around 80%.
3 Sheffield, Carole J. (2020), "Sexual Terrorism in the Twenty-first Century", in Jennifer M. Brown & Sandra L. Walkate (eds), *Book on Sexual Violence*, 190-211, London: Taylor & Francis Group, 2011, 191. Accessed May 16, 2022. ProQuest Ebook Central.
4 Ibid, 192.
5 Epstein, Dora (1997), "Abject Terror: A Story of Fear, Sex, and Architecture" in N. Ellin (Ed.), *Architecture of Fear*, 132-142, New York: Princeton Architectural Press, 134.
6 Struyf, Pia (2020), "Fear in the Dark: The Potential Impact of Reduced Street Lighting on Crime and Fear of Crime", in Vania Ceccato & Mahesh K. Nalla (eds), "Crime and Fear in Public Places: An Introduction to the Special Issue", *International Journal of Comparative and Applied Criminal Justice*, 44(4): 261–264.
7 World Bank (2020), *Book for Gender Inclusive Urban Planning Design.* https://www.worldbank.org/en/topic/urbandevelopment/publication/handbook-for-gender-inclusive-urban-planning-and-design
8 Thinyane, Mamello., Karthik Bhat, Lauri Goldkind, & Vikram Cannanure (2020), "The Messy Complexities of Democratic Engagement and Empowerment in Participatory Design – An Illustrative Case with a Community-Based Organisation", *CoDesign*, 16(1): 29–44.
9 Edwards, Allison & Hannah Korsmeyer (2017), "Communication with Self, with Others, and with Futures: Making Artefacts in Design Thinking Workshops", LEA – Lingue e Letterature D'Oriente e D'Occidente, 6(6): 157–798.
10 Ibid.
11 Caretta, Martina A. & Yvonne Riaño (2016), "Feminist participatory methodologies in geography: Creating spaces of inclusion", *Qualitative Research*, 16(3): 258–266.
12 Gheerawo, Rama (2016), "Socially Inclusive Design: A People-Centred Perspective", in Penny Sparke & Fiona Fisher (eds), *The Routledge Companion to Design Studies*, 326–338, London: Routledge.
13 Benbrahim, Dina (2021), "Co-designing Meaningful Dialogues on Sexual Harassment," *Temes de Disseny*, 37: 106–131.
14 Kalms, Nicole & Gene Bawden (2021) "Lived Experience: Participatory practices for gender-sensitive spaces and places", in Jess Berry, Timothy Moore, Nicole Kalms & Gene Bawden (2020), *Contentious Cities: Design and the Gendered Production of Space*. Abingdon, Oxon: Routledge, 107.
15 Fuad-Luke, Alastair (2009), *Design Activism: Beautiful Strangeness for Sustainable World*, London: Earthscan, 147; Winschiers-Theophilus, Heike., Bidwell, Nicola J., & Blake, Edwin (2012), "Community Consensus: Design Beyond Participation," *Design issues*, 28(3): 89–100.
16 Huybrechts, Liesbeth, Henric Benesch, & Jon Geib (2017), "Institutioning: Participatory Design, Co-Design and the Public Realm", *CoDesign*, 13(3): 148–159.
17 Gheerawo (2016), 304.
18 Harding, Sandra G., (1987), *Feminism and Methodology: Social Science Issues*, Bloomington: Indiana University Press, 7.
19 Excerpt from the closing statement of former Australian Prime Minister Julia Gillard's "Misogyny Speech" delivered October 9, 2012.
20 Gamble, Sarah (2006), *The Routledge Companion to Feminism and Postfeminism*, London: Routledge, 38.
21 Greed, Clara (2006), "Making the Divided City Whole: Mainstreaming Gender into Planning in The United Kingdom", *Tijdschrift Voor Economische En Sociale Geografie*, 97(3): 267–280.

Nicole Kalms, "Chapter 1: Women in Cities: An Introduction" and "Chapter 11: Run the World: Co-design in a Feminist World." In She City: Designing Out Women's Inequity in Cities (London: Bloomsbury Publishing, 2024): 1, 2, 4, 7–8, 230–232, 241.

Cities have not only exhibited inequalities based on gender, sexuality, age, and ability, but have also been scarred by racial disparities. In recent decades, heightened awareness of these injustices has been catalyzed by movements such as the Civil Rights Movement, and more recently, the Black

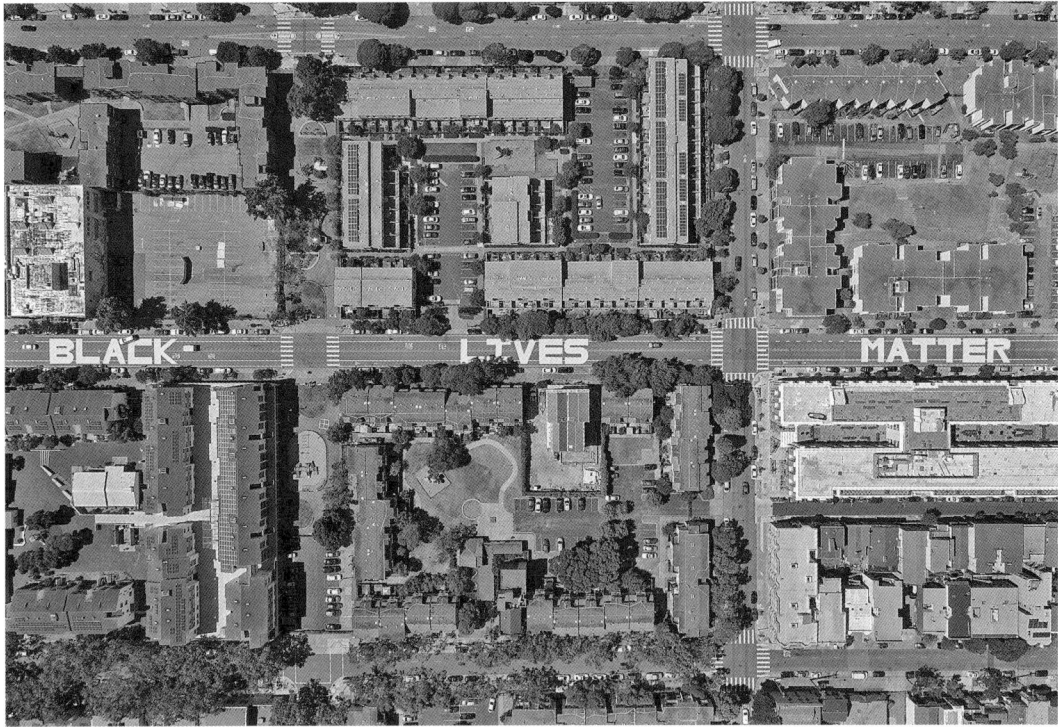

FIGURE 6.3 Drone view of a three-block-long "Black Lives Matter" mural painted in yellow along Fulton Street, with a direct view of City Hall in San Francisco, 2020. Courtesy of Cmichel67, Wikimedia Commons

Lives Matter movement. However, the racial inequality that was at the heart of the George Floyd protests in 2020 can be traced back to the legacy of slavery and the postcolonial history of redlining, and other dubious governmental practices, which have not yet reached reconciliation. Richard Rothstein, in his book *The Color of Law* (2017), demonstrates how, since the abolition of slavery in the 1860s, the American government and its judiciary system have actively upheld racist policies to perpetuate segregation.[32] And despite the Fair Housing Act of 1968 putting an end to redlining as a government sanctioned practice, its repercussions are still acutely felt today.

Evicted: Poverty and Profit in the American City (2016) by Matthew Desmond delves into the housing crisis and eviction practices, which are closely related to the historical consequences of redlining. This Pulitzer Prize-winning work exposes how the system often favors landlords, who are even legally allowed to provide substandard housing, while housing subsidies remain scarce.[33]

In the realm of environmental justice, authors like Robert Bullard have brought to light how marginalized communities often bear the brunt of environmental pollution and have advocated for the equitable distribution of environmental burdens and benefits. Among Bullard's works, *Dumping in Dixie: Race, Class, and Environmental Quality* (1990) shows how communities of color, particularly in the American South, have been disproportionately burdened with toxic waste dumps, landfills, and other environmental hazards.[34] Conversely, underlying this unequal distribution of environmental and health risks are disparities in environmental benefits as well. Predominantly black communities often have smaller, less accessible, and lower-quality parks than their white counterparts, potentially impacting their health.[35] In addition, black communities are more likely to live in "food deserts," or to be victimized by digital injustice.

Meanwhile, much of the American economy and landscape has been shaped through the exploitation of black labor and land. As landscape architect Walter Hood asserts, "The American landscape is a product of its colonial institutions and practices that have never been reconciled and resolved. At this country's core looms the legacy of slavery."[36] The American vernacular, from plantation fields to cabins and houses, is inexorably tied to an "ugly and unforgivable memory." The urban and rural landscape bears "the detritus of diverse origins," of memories of slavery encoded into architecture and patterns of settlement.[37]

In recent times, some places, such as Monticello, Thomas Jefferson's home, have begun to acknowledge this past, including by new tours that highlight his relationship with Sally Hemings, an enslaved woman at Monticello. In his co-edited volume with Grace Mitchell Tada, titled *Black Landscapes Matter* (2020), Hood reflects on this history. He also contemplates the path forward. Examples such as at Monticello show what can be done to bring back some of the erased black spaces. As another example of the legacy of history in the southern United States, he refers to the debates on whether to remove civil war statues of Confederate generals. He argues how memory, as embedded in urban space, can serve as prophecy, giving a voice to the underrepresented.

In addition, the authors call upon designers to create new black spaces and a fresh language of landscape design that prioritizes inclusivity and equity. Finally, increasing black representation in the design professions is essential. These initiatives offer the potential to build a more just and equitable society for all.

WALTER HOOD AND GRACE MITCHELL TADA (EDS.)
Black Landscapes Matter

"Traditional Africans did not look forward to radical change or to a messianic age, but rather they 'remembered' the homes of their forefathers, reestablished after death by their spirits and awaiting the souls of the living. . . . In this traditional African sacred cosmos, time was viewed as having scale of value. There were good times and bad times, times that were favorable for an activity and times that were inauspicious for that special action. These particular events that were tied to time were also tied further to place. Events should and have occurred at particular places on the earth, places that were auspicious for and tied to the event."

—**Mechal Sobel, *The World They Made Together***

Black landscapes matter because they are prophetic. They tell the truth of the struggles and the victories of African Americans in North America. The landscape bears the detritus of diverse origins: from the plantation landscape of slavery, to freedman villages and new towns, to agrarian indentured servitude. To northern and western migrations for freedom, to segregated urban landscapes, and to an integrated pluralist society. Black landscapes illuminate the diaspora of free Africans from the Southern Hemisphere to North America. These landscapes are the prophecy; they tell us our future. Their constant erasure is a call to arms against concealment of the truth that some people don't want to know or see. Erasure is a call to arms to remember. Erasure allows people to forget, particularly those whose lives and actions are complicit.

HEALTH, EQUITY, AND LIVABLE CITIES

The question "Do Black landscapes matter?" is intertwined in the colonial story of the Americas and their shadowed past. It is shared by all Americans, deeply ingrained in America's subconscious, and its landscapes. In the United States, the landscapes of my ancestors exist all around: from ocean to ocean, border to border, the diaspora of African Americans on the North American continent reaches far.

Imagine if the United States had built a monument to the end of the Civil War—to the end of slavery. Instead, as soon as the Civil War ended, the battlefield was declared a monument to the tens of thousands of soldiers who died. Not the war itself, or its causes, or its "heroes." At the dawning of freedom for African Americans, their emancipation was not imagined or viewed as something worthy of memorializing.

In the heterogeneous society of the United States, it takes time to work through memories. J. B. Jackson presents a framework that could help understand memory here. In The Necessity for Ruins, he writes:

> "But there has to be that interval of neglect, there has to be discontinuity; it is religiously and artistically essential. That is what I mean when I refer to the necessity for ruins: ruins provide the incentive for restoration, and for a return to origins. There has to be (in our new concept of history) an interim of death or rejection before there can be renewal and reform. The old order has to die before there can be a born-again landscape. Many of us know the joy and excitement not so much of creating the new as of redeeming what has been neglected, and this excitement is particularly strong when the original condition is seen as holy and beautiful. . . . That is how we produce the cosmic scheme and correct history."[1]

Jackson is describing the landscape of preservation and commemoration, which can also provide ways for cultures to deal with cultural change and adaptation.

In previous times, Jackson writes, commemoration "determine[d] our actions in the years to come . . . For centuries that is what monuments and feast days had been for: to remind us of obligations, religious or political, and keep us on the beaten path, loyal to tradition."[2]

Gettysburg, Jackson argues, is where the monument and the commemorative landscape changed. In the several decades following the war's end, monuments dedicated to the unknown soldiers from the North and South proliferated, and even to the Confederacy itself. These new monuments celebrate a different past, "not the past which history books describe, but a vernacular past, a golden age where there are no dates or names, simply a sense of the way it used to be, history as the chronicle of everyday experience."[3] It is this comment that offers a distinct lens through which we observe Black landscapes.

Here a second question emerges: are the places that I inhabit valued? Much of my life I have seen them mostly devalued. All around me, it is not these landscapes that are remembered, but the vernacular ones that Jackson mentions. In 2017, a southern politician, elucidating this view, remarked that the Black family under slavery was better off than they are presently, claiming that, in the past, Black people were "united" and "strong."[4] This vernacular past is celebrated in many manners, and, in many cases, the Black landscape is not a part of it. Middleton Place in Charleston, South Carolina, remembers its colonial gardens before it remembers its enslaved population and their contributions. The current conflicts surrounding the removal of the Civil War statues—those to which Jackson refers—celebrate the vernacular past. And the insistence on a vernacular past at the Lorraine Hotel in Memphis is manifest in the preference to talk about the African slavery diaspora rather than the murder of Dr. Martin Luther King Jr.

The past persists today as difficult burdens: the memory and guilt of institutionalized slavery, and the emancipation heritage. Memories document our historical presence in landscapes as subservient human beings, as segregated communities in a separate but equal cultural setting, and as integrated into the melting pot culture. Within this triad it is possible to see resilience, faith, optimism, and invention in the places and landscapes that African Americans made and occupy, but mostly these actions and places go forgotten. Are these memories too much for the country to bear? Are they too dark and heavy to bring forward for reconciliation?

Over the past 155 years, there have been moments when the country remembered. To name a few: the creation of the Freedmen's Bureau at the beginning of Reconstruction, the promise of forty acres and a mule, *Brown v. Board of Education*, the Civil Rights Act of 1964, and the Voting Rights Act of 1965. But there has always been a lag, a period of forgetting. Reconstruction's end, in 1877, by President Rutherford Hayes, immediately created a Jim Crow landscape in the South that persisted until the civil rights movement. Maybe a way to understand this pendulum of remembrance and neglect is through a 155-year timeline that begins with emancipation in 1865. Nearly forty years later, the National Association for the Advancement of Colored People was founded, and, in 1919, at the end of World War I, we were remembered for our service in the war. In the late 1980s and early 1990s, multiculturalism and hip-hop made us remember how "cool" Black is—until the neglect that followed. The election of Barack Obama, in 2008, demonstrated another period of remembrance followed by neglect, which led to the Black Lives Matter movement. But during these pauses or lapses we become apathetic, drunk from recent victories. Consequently, we are now in the midst of another period of neglect. The actions of some, who desire to erase the past, from immigration to civil rights, are forcing us to remember.

Black landscapes matter because they can be "born again." They exist all around us and are continuously resuscitated. Doing so requires care in how we exhume and resuscitate these landscapes to ensure that their resonance and power are not lost. Maybe some Black landscapes have become vernacular: we now have a Malcolm X Plaza, a Frederick Douglass Circle, an *Invisible Man* sculpture in Harlem, an MLK memorial in Washington, DC, and a plethora of new landscapes conserved to correct history. But we need something more powerful—not simply pedagogical, not a vernacular past, and not merely a chronicle. To correct history, we must see the original condition as "holy and beautiful." We must be audacious in what we bring forward.

Black landscapes matter because they are renewable. We can uncover, exhume, validate, and celebrate these landscapes through new narratives and stories that choose to return us to origins. The contested and the forgotten landscapes, renewed through a myriad of expressions, can give us incentives to obligations for years to come.

The period of neglect can be seen as a powerful "pregnant pause." It can be a time to develop new concepts of history without being thwarted by the old, which must die and be rejected. Culturally, this relates to the people and objects that preserve these memories. The interval of time is where memories are stored through reflexive borrowing, mimetic appropriations, exchanges, and inventions within the cultural landscape. Thus, when these memories are "born again," they can be prophetic. The nascent and latent landscapes that necessarily emerge from the neglected bear these memories and are mnemonic devices that can be triggered when we want to remember. Black voices are emerging today because we are in a period of neglect. How do we articulate and promote the acceptance and reconciliation of the cultural atrocities that accompany the American experiment? It is up to us to help America remember through our collective speech, writings, art, music, architecture, and landscapes.

Here is a call for new expressions that force reconciliation. I would argue that the times when opposition is loud—the periods of neglect—are the times when we renew. In these times, we must find ways to be outspoken, more audacious, and prophetic. Instead of being reactive, we should be proactive, preserving, conserving, and making more landscapes that are for us—Black landscapes that are resilient and forward-looking. Black landscapes that tell alternative stories and forge a new language for landscapes. Black landscapes that build on our local knowledge, a knowledge that attests to creativity and passion for inclusion. . .

. . . As the global context of place and culture becomes less distinct as heterogeneity blurs boundaries, it is crucial that we validate and nurture the existence of Black landscapes and spaces. Specific to the postcolonial landscapes that we inhabit, Black landscapes are forged within contested space, improvised and reshaped to allow Black people to thrive within a context of marginality and exclusion. But as our history assures us, Black people have built and shaped the American landscape in ways that we will never know. It is up to those of us in the field to continue to articulate and, most of all, develop a "prophetic aesthetic" to counter the colonial malaise so that we can remember and develop new futures from the power of the past.

1   J. B. Jackson, The Necessity for Ruins (Amherst: University of Massachusetts Press, 1980), 102.
2   Jackson, The Necessity for Ruins, 93.
3   Jackson, The Necessity for Ruins, 94–95.
4   German Lopez, "Roy Moore: America 'Was Great at the Time When Families Were United—Even Though We Had Slavery,'" Vox, December 8, 2017, www.vox.com/policy-and-politics/2017/12/7/16748038/roy-moore-slavery-america-great.

Walter Hood, "Introduction" in Walter Hood and Grace Mitchell Tada eds., *Black Landscapes Matter* (Charlottesville, VA: University of Virginia Press, 2020): 1–5, 7, 8.

This chapter explored how architects and urban designers are working to create cities that are more accessible, promote greater social interaction, and are more equitable and just.

The rise of the automobile in the early twentieth century had transformed urban environments, leading to sprawling vehicular infrastructure and a decline in pedestrian-friendly spaces, negatively impacting health and social interactions. Urban thinkers and designers, from Jane Jacobs to Jan Gehl, have since advocated for cities that prioritize walking, cycling, and communal spaces, emphasizing the importance of fostering social connections and physical well-being over car-dominated landscapes.

Modernist design, despite its aesthetic appeal, often lacked sociability and inclusiveness in urban spaces, leading to critiques from urbanists like Whyte who demonstrated the underutilization and inadequacy of public seating in Manhattan's private owned public spaces. Other critiques expanded to highlight age-unfriendly designs, the gender biases rooted in Modernism's male-centric concepts, and the need for diverse, safe, and inclusive spaces that accommodate the experiences of marginalized groups, such as women, the elderly, and the LGBTQ+ community.

Finally, racial disparities in American cities, rooted in the legacy of slavery, colonialism, and redlining, are still evident in housing and environmental injustices. Authors such as Walter Hood expose these inequalities and advocate for acknowledgment and a new design language aiming to reshape urban landscapes in the spirit of justice and reconciliation.

7

Emergent, Tactical, and Informal Urbanism

In reality, cities and neighborhoods across the globe often diverge from grand designs. Informal settlements, for instance, follow an alternative logic. They emerge through collective individual actions, devoid of an overarching design, resulting in incremental expansion. This chapter, "Emergent, Tactical, and Informal Urbanism," explores the context of informal urban settlements and methods targeting their upgrading. In addition, it looks at the ways in which designers have harnessed self-organizing processes in cities as an alternative to rigid top-down city planning. These endeavors, such as tactical urbanism, seek to benefit from emergent behaviors and tap into local knowledge and spontaneity for evolutionary growth and adaptation.

The first cities in history did not adhere to blueprints, but instead formed without a preconceived plan. For instance, recent findings from ancient Mesopotamian settlements dating back to 4000 BCE suggest initial urban formations had a decentralized nature. In Brak, located in northeastern Syria, clusters of households and open spaces were interspersed, devoid of any signs of ruling elites or centralized planning. Urban agglomerations had seemingly sprung up through self-organization, where individual households adhered to certain unwritten rules. The motivation of individual households may have been to feed dependents, expand their membership, and increase prestige. These collective rules inadvertently led to significant population agglomerations, even though this probably was not the conscious intent of the household leaders who had initiated the process.[1]

These phenomena align with the concept of emergence, where new structures arise from interactions among various agents. As explored in Chapter 2, "Urbanism and Models of Design Complexity," these behaviors and phenomena are observed in natural systems such as schools of fish, flocks of birds, ant colonies, weather patterns, and other complex, agent-based systems. In such systems, simple rules generate a higher order of complexity in the same way fractal patterns manifest in snowflakes or termites construct intricate "cathedrals." Local "rules" among households likely yielded organized growth, akin to the flocking behavior of birds guided by simple directives such as moving in the same direction, maintaining distance, and avoiding collisions.

Today, this process is most evident in informal settlements. A substantial portion of global urbanization unfolds within the informal sector, beyond the bounds of institutional structures such as building codes, zoning laws, or land tenure. According to the United Nations, there are over 1 billion people living in informal settlements across the world. This number is expected to grow to 2 billion by 2030.

Countless millions worldwide lack access to formal housing, leading to various unique types of informal settlements, including *barrios* in Mexico, "villages in the city" in southern China, and shantytowns in India and Africa.[2] For instance, Rio de Janeiro's informal settlements, or *favelas*, have grown alongside urban expansion, many of them on the city's steep hillsides. By the 1990s, over a million residents, a quarter of the city's urban population, inhabited the favelas. Even developed nations have their versions of unplanned communities, such as the colonias border settlements in Texas, as documented by Peter Ward in his 1999 book, *Colonias and Public Policy in Texas and Mexico: Urbanization by Stealth*.[3]

Many attribute the rise of informal settlements globally to the weakened state under neoliberal capitalism, as Mike Davis argues in *Planet of Slums* (2006).[4] While Davis uses the catchall term "slums," it is essential to clarify the distinctions between a "slum" and an "informal" settlement. According to the UN, "slums are the most deprived and excluded form of informal settlements."[5] UN-Habitat (2003) defines a "slum" based on inadequate living conditions, such as lacking durable housing, clean water, sanitation, sufficient space, and secure tenure. The term often refers to dilapidated or overcrowded inner city tenements. In contrast, "informal settlements" is a wider term that refers to "unplanned" development, often referring to squatter settlements where communities settle on land without permission or land tenure. The term "urban informality" was popularized by Ananya Roy and Nezar AlSayyad in their 2003 edited volume, *Urban Informality: Transnational Perspectives from the Middle East, Latin America, and South Asia*.[6]

FIGURE 7.1 This view of a sprawling informal settlement in Caracas, Venezuela, reveals tightly clustered homes cascading down a steep mountainside. Courtesy of Getty Images.

FIGURE 7.2 Illustration of Xiasha Village, Shenzhen, China, a rapidly urbanized former rural settlement that has transformed into a densely populated and lively urban village, emblematic of rapid urbanization and urban informality. Drawing by Daniel King Him Fung

A major misconception to dispel is that informal settlements are marginal to society. Janice E. Perlman's *The Myth of Marginality: Urban Poverty and Politics in Rio de Janeiro* (1976) was one of the first to challenge this view, revealing favelas' profound ties to the city's economic, social, and political fabric.[7] Informal settlements are integrated into the economy, often supporting formal sectors through informal labor.

Informal settlement communities typically face stigmatization. Local media often describe them in negative terms, equating them to medical ailments like "eyesores," "scars," or even "cancer" in the city. Such portrayals fuel hostilities from governments, justifying their aversion to these settlements as a disruption to a sanitized vision of modernity, or a "world class aesthetic" as Asher Ghertner illustrated in his 2015 book *Rule by Aesthetics: World-Class City Making in Delhi*.[8] Government planners often disparage informal "squatters" as encroachers who disrespect the law; but it is this refusal of formal authorities to recognize and integrate these settlements that often perpetuates their informal status.[9] Informal urbanism, while not illegal, is rather the product of extra-legal processes and actions. Stigmas associated with slums overlook the complexities of these communities, exacerbating marginalization, discrimination, and perpetuating cycles of poverty.

For instance, in some places in China even white collar workers and students are known to reside in informal settlements, known as "urban villages," as a result of a lack of affordable housing. Several authors have contributed to recording and assessing China's urban villages, especially in Shenzhen, where hundreds of traditional villages had been densified in the past forty years, serving newly arrived migrants as rental housing. These include Thomas J. Campanella's book, *The Concrete Dragon: China's Urban Revolution and What It Means for the World* (2008),[10] Stefan Al's book, *Villages in the City: A Guide to Southern China's Informal Settlements* (2014),[11] and *The Shenzhen Experiment: The Story of China's Instant City* (2020), by Juan Du.[12]

How can the lives of residents in informal settlements be enhanced? Despite economic growth, many remain unemployed or underemployed. Informal economy jobs, while common, offer uncertain pay and scant security. This impedes entry into the formal economy, limiting access to loans and insurance. Health issues without access to medical coverage can lead to financial devastation.

However, improving the physical environment can also make a significant difference. Better transportation links, such as metro stations, paved roads, staircases, and cable cars, enhance resident accessibility. Storm drains, sewage networks and toilets improve safety and sanitation. Place-making efforts contribute as well, as many new areas lack the distinctive character of established districts. Diverse, appealing neighborhoods attract residents, jobs, tourists, and shoppers.

These strategies are often termed "slum upgrading." They generally aim to provide essential infrastructure, such as water and roads, alongside offering opportunities such as microfinancing and community centers. Despite the emphasis on mobility and sanitation infrastructure, interventions to upgrade social, health, and educational services and facilities also have the potential to transform the lives of people living in informal settlements.

Some notable initiatives, like Rio's *Favela-Bairro* program, received substantial support from institutions like the World Bank. This widely replicated program has transformed lives since 1994 by introducing improved water access, sewage facilities, roads, open spaces, social services, and secure tenure for hundreds of thousands. Similarly, Vietnam's Urban Upgrading Project elevated local infrastructure, benefiting millions in cities like Ho Chi Minh City. This undertaking prioritized flood control, including measures including expanding drainage systems, dredging water bodies, constructing dual-purpose roadways as stormwater barriers, and relocating vulnerable households.[13]

However, assessing such projects poses challenges. Ananya Roy, a leading scholar on urban informality and the underlying systems of global poverty, warns against the "aestheticization of poverty." Slum upgrading efforts, especially when led by external experts, can risk becoming an exercise in aesthetics, failing to address fundamental needs. One example receiving such criticism is the Indore Habitat Improvement project. Although it was honored with a 1993 World Habitat Award and 1998 Aga Khan Award for Architecture, the on-the-ground impact was limited. Surface-level improvements were devised without considering the willingness of local residents to allocate limited water resources for new landscaping or flushing the newly installed toilets,[14] as found by Gita Dewan Verma, author of *Slumming India: A Chronicle of Slums and Their Saviors* (2002).[15] In response to such mistakes, Roy advocates for a "politics of shit," which involves engaging with locals to fully understand the practicalities and merits of potential upgrades, delving into details like feces management in toilets. Ultimately, Roy's aim is "enablement," to help those living in poverty to help themselves.

Roy also points out how the developing world is host to much of the urban growth in this century, yet the theories of urbanism continue to be rooted in the developed world.[16] Roy puts forth three "policy epistemologies" for more sustainable urban futures, including "moving from land use to distributive justice, rethinking the object of development, and replacing best practice models with realist critique." The emergence of informal settlements and the challenges they present have prompted strategies like slum upgrading, aimed at improving living conditions. However, it is essential that these efforts are approached with a deep understanding of local dynamics and needs, ensuring that improvements extend beyond surface aesthetics to address fundamental issues.

ANANYA ROY
"Urban informality: Toward an Epistemology of Planning"

The study of cities is today marked by a paradox: much of the urban growth of the 21st century is taking place in the developing world, but many of the theories of how cities function remain rooted in the developed world. There is much discussion in academic circles about whether the time has come to move from the Chicago school of urban sociology to the Los Angeles school of postmodern geography,[1] and yet, as urban sociologist Douglas Massey[2] recently commented, the urban future lies neither in Chicago nor Los Angeles; it instead lies in "Third World" cities like Rio de Janeiro, Mumbai, Hong Kong. Beyond this mundane fact of urban growth is also the pressing issue of what might be learned by paying attention to the urban transformations of the developing world. This is not simply an issue of the inappropriateness of Euro-American ideas for Third World cities. Planning practices are constantly borrowed and replicated across borders. To attempt to stem this tide is rather useless and indeed under some circumstances can mark a turn to isolationism. Instead, I am interested in what it means to locate the production of theory and policy in the cities of the developing world.

In an important article, Jennifer Robinson[3] shows how the field of urban studies is constituted through a duality: global cities versus megacities. Global cities are conceptualized as First World command nodes of a global system of informational capitalism, "models" for the rest of the world. In contrast, megacities, located primarily in the Third World, are conceptualized in terms of crisis—"big but not powerful." There is an urgency for urban studies and planning to move beyond the dichotomy of First World "models" and Third World "problems." One possible route is through policy approaches that seek to learn from Third World cities.[4]

In this article, I trace such a route by discussing one key theme of Third World research: urban informality and policy responses to informality, such as slum upgrading and land titling.[5] My goal is not so much to evaluate these policies as it is to highlight some of the distinctive challenges and paradoxes that they present for planners. . .

. . . Policy Epistemology 1: The Politics of Shit

In the 1990s, the harsh rhetoric of austerity and privatization gave way to a new generation of poverty alleviation programs that recycled the populist ideas of an earlier era: self-help housing, microenterprises, community initiatives. There is, however, a distinctive signature to today's policies: they emphasize the moral capacity of the poor. De Soto's trope of the Third World poor as "heroic entrepreneurs" can be seen as the mirror image of American discourses about the "dependent" poor. The latter diagnoses poverty as the absence of a work ethic; the former poses the solution of entrepreneurship facilitated through participation in the market.

The key element of today's paradigm of "Sustainable Human Development" is the idea of enablement, helping the poor help themselves. To this end, there has been considerable emphasis on urban upgrading strategies. Upgrading is a welcome change from previous policies that sought to eradicate informal settlements or relocate them to urban peripheries. Like the favela-bairro program of Brazil, they are predicated on the notion that providing services on site is much cheaper than relocating residents of informal settlements to new housing on the periphery. Initiated in the mid 1990s with financing from the InterAmerican Development Bank, the favela-bairro program seeks to transform squatter settlements (favelas) into officially-recognized neighborhoods (bairros) through physical upgrading. However, it is also important to note the limitations of urban upgrading. In a recent study of the Rio de Janeiro favelas tracking residents of the informal settlements that she studied in the early 1970s, Janice Perlman shows that while there have been considerable physical improvements, other dimensions of life in the favela have drastically worsened.[6] The favelas have been taken over by international drug bosses who have created a de facto state of domination by violence. Favela residents are also the target of the militarized violence of the state. Indeed, as Zaverucha-notes, Rio de Janeiro's riot police, the Special Group for Urban Control, trained by the army and using military weaponry, has repeatedly been deployed against squatters and street vendors.[7] What does democracy mean in the face of this militaristic control of cities? What does democratic citizenship mean in the face of systemic unemployment when, as Perlman notes, the bowl of fruit on the table that was once always full is now always empty? What do physical improvements mean when the majority of favela residents feel marginalized, a world apart from the *asfalto* or formal city? Perlman's work resonates with that of Auyero who makes note of the structural exclusion that marks informal settlements in Buenos Aires.[8] He argues that the provision of services and upgrading, while perhaps well meaning, is a bit like rearranging the chairs on the deck of the Titanic.[9]

The limitations of urban upgrading are the limitations of the ideology of space. In such policy approaches, what is redeveloped is space, the built environment and physical amenities rather than people's capacities or livelihoods. I have argued elsewhere that such an emphasis on the physical environment is an "aestheticization of poverty,"[10] one that equates upgrading with aesthetic upgrading rather than the upgrading of livelihoods, wages, political capacities.[11] It is an expression of what Scott calls high modernism: the search for rational order in aesthetic terms, the belief that an efficient city is one that *looks* regimented and orderly in a geometrical sense.[12] Quoting Jane Jacobs, he warns urban planners not to infer functional order from purely visual order. The ideology of space is not unique to Third World policies. As Modarres points out, the American war on poverty can be understood as a project that equated poverty with the failure of geographically defined communities.[13] Not only were these spaces seen as places of disorder, but also a series of area-based policies were introduced in the attempt to "improve" and "integrate" these spaces into the city.

The issue at stake here is not simply the limits of upgrading strategies but rather the question of who sets the upgrading agenda. A provocative example is provided by the Alliance, a group of nongovernmental organizations (NGOs) in Bombay that have organized around land tenure, housing rights, and urban services for slum dwellers. The Alliance encourages the poor to design and conduct their own census. It also holds housing festivals and toilet festivals where the poor design their own model homes and model public toilets and where these designs are then passed on to professionals. While it is important not to romanticize such self-help efforts, this is nevertheless an intriguing model. Designating this as a form of "deep democracy," Arjun Appadurai calls it the "politics of shit":

> "When a World Bank official has to examine the virtues of a public toilet and discuss the merits of faeces management with the defecators themselves, the poor are no longer abject victims, they become speaking subjects, they become political actors."[14]

The shift from aesthetic considerations to the politics of shit, I would argue, is a useful policy epistemology. It recognizes the importance of infrastructure but indicates that the provision and distribution of infrastructure is not a technical issue but rather a political process. The politics of shit also disrupts models of expertise, making it possible to generate knowledge about upgrading and infrastructure from a different set of experts: the residents of informal settlements...

Conclusion

... Finally, international planning today is constituted through models and best practices. These blueprint utopias are seen to be the key to the universal replicability of "good" planning. In this article, I have advanced critique as an important policy epistemology, arguing that there is also quite a bit to be learned from what goes wrong. Confronting the failures and limitations of models provides a more realistic sense of politics and conflicts, and also forces planning to face up to the consequences of its own good action. Such outcomes must be seen as something more than simply "unintended consequences." This vocabulary of planning not only has the flavor of a casual shrug but also implies the inability to think about the complex social systems through which plans must be implemented.

These three pressing issues—moving from land use to distributive justice, rethinking the object of development, and replacing best practice models with realist critique—are not just policy epistemologies for dealing with informality. Rather, they indicate that informality is an important epistemology for planning.

1. Dear, Michael. *From Chicago to LA: Making sense of urban theory*. Sage, 2001.
2. Massey, D. (2001, August). Opening plenary session, Annual Conference of the American Sociological Association, Atlanta, GA.
3. Robinson, Jennifer. "Global and world cities: a view from off the map." *International journal of urban and regional research* 26.3 (2002): 531–554.
4. Roy, Ananya. "Paradigms of propertied citizenship: Transnational techniques of analysis." *Urban affairs review* 38.4 (2003): 463–491; Sanyal, Bishwapriya. "Knowledge transfer from poor to rich cities: A new turn of events." *Cities* 7.1 (1990): 31–36.
5. My discussion draws upon a recently concluded Ford Foundation funded project on Urban Informality that I led along with my colleague, Nezar AlSayyad. Intended to "cross borders," the project brought together scholars and practitioners working in Latin America, the Middle East, and South Asia. It revealed new processes of informality and fostered cross-regional conversations and comparisons. These findings are presented in a forthcoming co-edited volume. *Urban Informality: Transnational Perspectives from the Middle East, South Asia, and Latin America* (Roy & AlSayyad, 2004). This article supplements the book by placing the project's findings within the larger context of urban research and discussing some key policy debates.
6. Perlman, Janice. "Marginality: from myth to reality in the favelas of Rio de Janeiro, 1969–2002." *Urban Informality: Transnational Perspectives from the Middle East, Latin America, and South Asia*. New York: Lexington (2004): 105–146.
7. Zaverucha, Jorge. "Fragile democracy and the militarization of public safety in Brazil." *Latin American Perspectives* 27.3 (2000): 8–31.
8. Auyero, Javier. '"This is a lot like the Bronx, isn't it?' Lived experiences of marginality in an Argentine slum." *International Journal of Urban and Regional Research* 23.1 (1999): 45–69.
9. A similar analogy was used by Burgess (1982) in his critique of selfhelp policies.
10. Roy, Ananya. "Transnational trespassings: The geopolitics of urban informality." *Urban Informality: Transnational Perspectives from the Middle East, Latin America, and South Asia* (2004): 289–317.
11. These aesthetic approaches to upgrading also confuse informality with poverty, suggesting that (a) physical upgrading can end informality, and (b) ending informality can end poverty. At the 2003 ACSP-AESOP conference, Joe Nasr therefore commented that the aestheticization of poverty is the pauperization of informality.
12. Scott, James C. *Seeing like a state: How certain schemes to improve the human condition have failed*. Yale University Press, 2020, p.183.
13. Modarres, Ali. "The dialectic of development in US urban policies: An alternative theory of poverty." *Cities* 20.1 (2003): 41–49.
14. Appadurai, Arjun. "Deep democracy: urban governmentality and the horizon of politics." *Environment and urbanization* 13.2 (2001): 37.

Ananya Roy, "Urban informality: Toward an Epistemology of Planning", *Journal of the American Planning Association* 71, no. 2 (2005): 147–58.

Until recently, only a small number of architects and urban designers were willing to engage with informal settlements, often relegating their work to the confines of the formal sector. However, a notable shift has taken place as several prominent architects challenge this narrow perspective on their role. Among them are Alfredo Brillembourg from Venezuela and Hubert Klumpner from Austria. They co-founded Urban Think Tank in Caracas—an interdisciplinary design collective aimed at dissecting and reimagining informal cities. Emphasizing conceptual thinking alongside practical action, they embedded themselves in Caracas to study and eventually directly intervene in informal settlements. Many of their projects are self-initiated, and they work with "pencil and hammer" to ignite change.[17]

Brillembourg and Klumpner challenge the "informal" label, asserting that these settlements are formally shaped reactions to historical and current socio-economic dynamics. They also debunk the notion of these settlements being "exceptional," since such urban areas have become integral components of major Latin American cities, shaped in part by their postcolonial history and contemporary economic policies. They also point out how the economy of informal urbanism not only impacts its host city, but is an "integral part" of the global economy.

Brillembourg and Klumpner observe a pattern that emerges with a certain logic in informal urbanization, "unlike that taught by conventional architecture or planning," locating order within seeming disorder.[18] Informal urbanism arises by itself with its residents as makers. It simply functions with different rules and procedures than those in recognized urban territories. In addition, informal settlements reveal a complex symbiotic relationship between regulated and unregulated urban land use.

Their contributions extend to highlighting the unique phenomenon of the "vertical slum" in Caracas. Since 2007, squatters have repurposed a vacant 45-story skyscraper, nicknamed *Torre David*. The skyscraper, meant to be a commercial center and office tower, now includes a makeshift hair salon, gym, grocery stores, and even unlicensed dentists, alongside hundreds of residents. This narrative is documented in the book *Torre David: Informal Vertical Communities* (2013), edited by Brillembourg and Klumpner,[19] as well as *Radical Cities: Across Latin America in Search of a New Architecture* (2014), by Justin McGuirk.[20]

Among Brillembourg and Klumpner's most notable design projects are four "vertical gyms," the first one built in 2004, which rise above the favelas of Caracas. The gyms, all non-profit entities, foster community through exercise and health initiatives. However, the pair's most lasting legacy may well be their initiation of a cable car system connecting informal settlements to the formal city center of Caracas. Brillembourg and Klumpner created five station designs which combined cultural, social and office functions with the stations, such as public space, a daycare, and a gym. Instead of building roads, which would have led to the demolition of many homes, the cable car travels above the settlements, causing minimal demolitions while enhancing accessibility.

This approach resonates with similar initiatives worldwide. In Medellín, Colombia, rapid urban expansion led to informal settlements on steep hillsides. To address accessibility disparities and improve conditions in disadvantaged suburbs, the Medellín Metrocable was introduced in 2004—a system of aerial gondolas facilitating movement across the hills. This project was complemented by investments in education, public spaces with lighting, pedestrian pathways and bridges, and support for social housing around the stations. The Metrocable helped improve access and stimulate urban regeneration. Nevertheless, the replicability of such systems is uncertain. Rio de Janeiro's attempt at a Metrocable failed due to underuse. The project was designed with a lack of community engagement and understanding of the residents' true mobility needs.

Projects like the vertical gyms and metrocable stations are aptly termed "urban acupuncture." This term refers to a strategy in urban planning that involves precise, small-scale interventions to generate larger transformative effects. Similar to the insertion of needles in traditional Chinese medicine, these interventions target specific urban issues, through the creation of community buildings, public spaces, pocket parks, pedestrian pathways, or cable car stations. The goal is to initiate broader revitalization, increase social interaction, and improve resident well-being. These interventions are often cost-effective and quick to implement, making them more accessible to communities, local governments, and grassroots organizations than grand plans. The concept emphasizes the importance of community engagement and participation in the decision-making process, as well as the need to consider the unique context and characteristics of each locale.

Urban acupuncture has faced criticism. Critics argue that it tends to focus on isolated interventions rather than tackling systemic issues more comprehensively. There is also the potential for gentrification, where original inhabitants can be displaced by wealthier newcomers drawn to upgraded areas. Nevertheless, urban acupuncture offers an alternative bottom-up approach to traditional top-down urban planning by promoting incremental, community-driven improvements that can contribute to more vibrant and equitable cities.

ALFREDO BRILLEMBOURG AND HUBERT KLUMPNER
"Rules of Engagement: Caracas and the Informal City"

In Caracas, a city ringed by verdant mountains and blessed with abundant rainfall, petrol is cheaper than drinking water. Caracas is flooded with oil money, but it has the largest, densest barrios relative to its size of any city of Latin America. Barrio, which literally means 'neighbourhood' in Spanish, is commonly used in Caracas to refer to the low-income urban settlements in which 55 per cent of the population lives on 33.5 percent of the city's geographical footprint, in homes ranging from cardboard shacks to well-constructed, multi-storey buildings. The sites are often hazardous, and all have serious problems of access. Those homes built on the hillsides are highly vulnerable to mudslides. Those settlements encircling existing fixtures of city infrastructure – a water tank, market, sports venue, or industrial complex – are difficult to access and often have limited space for expansion which makes them extremely crowded. A third zone of housing runs along and just above the city's rivers and small creeks, which are prone to flooding, or follows the line of a highway, all of them hazards which must be negotiated by residents accessing their homes.

This is the informal city in Caracas. If one looks at it from a distance, one sees sprawling, rhizome-like shapes; one searches in vain for an ordering principle, a clear beginning and end, for ways to separate the whole into comprehensible elements. But close up, patterns begin to emerge and a certain logic – unlike that taught by conventional architecture or planning – can be discerned.

We do not believe 'informal' means 'lacking form'. It implies, for us, something that arises from within itself and its makers, whose form has not yet been recognised, but which is subject to rules and procedures potentially as specific and necessary as those that have governed official, formal city-making. Our work sets out to identify and describe that particular logic, to locate the order within the apparent disorder, so as to open up a productive dialogue about the relevance and the role of the informal city in the world.

In this chapter we wish to discuss Caracas and the informal city, and to position Caracas as an ideal laboratory for architecture and urbanism research in the 'global South'. We will describe the new urban context of informality in Latin America and the rest of the global South. We will describe informality's implications for urban theory, reimagining the barrio. We will talk about architectural practice in the informal city – what we call 'performative architecture' – using specific examples from our own architectural practice, Urban Think Tank. And we will conclude by presenting a rough agenda for architecture and design in the informal city, positioning architecture at the intersection of the economic, social, political and sustainable. Throughout we focus on the Caracas urban region because it is where we work and what we know, but we hope that our observations can be generalised to a certain extent to the rest of the global South, and specifically to Latin America. Moreover, we believe the lessons of the informal city extend to the developed world as well, where informality can also be observed.

Informal Globalisation

. . . The informal city, long treated as an aberration or an exception to the standard of urbanism, is actually becoming the norm throughout the global South, and it does so as an integral part of the global economy.

Our research shows that in Caracas a growing majority of the city's inhabitants live in informal zones, and 80 per cent of new housing is self-built. The improvisation that characterises these zones resembles the 'plug-in, tune-up, clip-on' architecture of Yona Friedman.[1] Unsurprisingly, this often collides with ordinances and laws, for example in Caracas where public spaces have been transformed into commercial strips and barrio houses project like rhizomes into the valleys. The informal city has generated its own modular design logic, and it needs to be better understood rather than ignored or treated like an aberration. This is a central tenet of our ongoing architectural practice and research . . .

. . . It is important to recognise that when we talk about the informal city we are not simply talking about something criminal. By and large it is not illegal. It is simply extra-legal, outside the regulatory apparatus. It is also important to distinguish informal globalisation from the older idea of informalism as temporary, transitional, small-scale and concerned only with strategies for survival. The new informal concept is completely different, although it can sometimes look similar. It is permanent, established and large-scale. Sixty percent of the jobs in the global South are located here; they are products of informal globalisation . . .

. . . Our Work

Urban Think Tank is our attempt to put these ideas into practice. After we left Columbia University in New York we were faced with the urban reality of Caracas. Through first-hand experience we discovered that not enough is being done to address the increasingly exacerbated urban condition. The city we experience has very little in common with the myth of the progressive modern Latin American city propagated by architects such as Carlos Raul Villanueva in Caracas and Oscar Niemeyer in Brazil. In the informal city we have the ability to challenge the materialistic treadmill of progress and object architecture and look for a practice of architecture based on other ideals – like real structural change for the global South.

We are immersed in what we call 'and/and' projects: the norm is adaptation to constantly changing conditions, building in a country under extreme economic and political circumstances. Uncertainty is the only constant in our daily routine as architects and, thus, we habitually begin many lines of work simultaneously – writing, mapping, researching, building and networking – that sustain one another, that interact synergistically and multiply. We are increasingly dissatisfied with an excess of computer-generated design and in our office we encourage first-hand, on-site experience. We find ourselves moving toward the pencil and the hammer, the physical three-dimensional model, the experiment combined with electronic tools.

Our practice is committed, first, to placing the social reality of a site at the forefront of political discussion. We are committed to building and sustaining dialogue between stakeholders and policy makers. Our non-profit research branch has developed into a school without the formalities of a school where interns from around the world mix with local community leaders in order to explore strategies for sustainable urban development in the global South. But our work does not merely contemplate the city. Rather, we initiate change in the city through direct intervention. The following are a few examples.

The Vertical Gym

Sports facilities stacked in the extremely dense environments of the informal settlements of Caracas offer the chance for integration and cooperation among the city's diverse communities. The Vertical Gym is dedicated to the belief that a physical structure can have a profound positive impact on social and physical interactions and a clear reduction in gang crime and health issues. It stands immediately outside the entrance to a barrio in Caracas's most affluent municipality and offers free services to all residents. It is a working alternative to the massive – and failed – social projects that sought to integrate citizens, but created just the opposite effect. Since the Vertical Gym's inception, crime has dropped sharply in the neighbourhood, exemplified by the astounding decrease in homicides from twenty-five each weekend to only five. The links between sports recreation and social well-being is so well established that it is mandatory by law in Venezuela that sports facilities be offered to neighbourhoods. But in great part due to urban space limitations, these facilities have not been provided. The Vertical Gym manoeuvred around these obstacles and its positive effects are being thoroughly recognised.

House Core Unit

Caracas's informal city has spread through a region of dangerous, unstable and contaminated hills surrounding the main valley. Here one of the most pressing problems is the scarcity of water, and especially the lack of sewers and sewage treatment. A truly useful toilet in the barrio must meet certain requirements: it must be adaptable, functional despite resource deficiency, and built, altered and maintained self-sufficiently by the dwellers of the informal sector. Urban Think Tank's Core Unit is the culmination of each of these seemingly incongruous factors. With the incorporation of solar panels, a rain-catching roof and a storage tank, the design solution becomes a Core Unit from which the barrio house can grow. The toilet inside the unit is designed to separate off solid matter or sludge from the water, which, treated with chemicals, can be used as compost for growing medicinal herbs and vegetables on the roof of a single or communal home. Because of the lack of a proper collection system in the barrios and the fact that the sheer density of the urban landscape make even septic tanks impossible, the prototype is a solution that can feasibly be built and used by neighbourhood residents.

Prefab Modular Stairs

The issue of mobility within the barrios is both a cause for concern – in the case of lack of access – and a stimulus for community-building – in the case of the culture maintained within the boundaries of the informal city. Given the hilly geography of the barrios, stairs are central to this issue. But, overwhelmingly, the current stair systems within the barrios are old, worn and crumbling, where they still exist at all. Often there is no direct access between contiguous zones, and the lack of plumbing means that stairs often serve as drainage routes, to the detriment of the residents' health and safety. Urban Think Tank is implementing a prefabricated stair system to address these issues, in addition to issues such as cost, ease of construction, versatility and self-sustainability. The basis of the system is a familiar one in Venezuela: stilts, or *palafitos*. With the stairs raised off the ground the problem of rain and waste drainage is avoided, while the support tubing offers a way to run electrical wires and any other piping necessary. Barrio residents can install the stairs easily and cost-effectively as they are prefabricated and can be brought up the hills in pieces. Moreover, given the unstructured layout of the barrios, the versatility of the stairs allows them to be fitted to the neighbourhoods, not the other way around.

Conclusion: Transition to an Urban World

As we have shown in the projects described above, rather than producing a symbolic or autonomous architecture, our practice adopts concrete strategies that tend toward physical appropriation and production. It reflects our belief in politicising the urban sphere, and our interest in the performative elements of cultural-political practices. Moreover, we aim to reverse the top-down hierarchy of governance in the public sphere in favour of bottom-up, locally-driven action. Our clients are not corporations; they are cooperatives. This reversal sets up new paradigms for the dynamics of urban growth, the configuration of built form and social activities. Hence, we are not concerned with ideal situations because our work is about avoiding catastrophe.

We do not believe it possible to separate the concern for people from the concern for urbanism. The city's fate today is closely linked with virtually every aspect of human life. What is required is that people from a great many cities and a wide variety of disciplines consider evolutionary scenarios that lead from the present urban context of conflict and collision to a more just and sustainable future. We are not calling simply for open-ended or unfocused speculation; we live in an age of increasing specialisation, and for good reason. But the city is a complex system and specialisation must be supplemented by integration if we are going to adequately understand it. Architects, we think, are particularly well trained to integrate disciplines.

At Urban Think Tank we try to offer a platform for all disciplines to work. We meet to do research and to develop and build pilot projects aimed at making the city a better and more equitable place to live for all its citizens. In recent years we have invited people from a range of disciplines and from more than twenty countries to join us in taking a broad look at the whole as well as developing precise, acupuncture-like urban interventions.

We believe that in addition to the architectural and design dimensions, more and more we will need to consider environmental, economic and social questions as we intervene in the city.

1 Friedman, Y. 1999. Structures Serving the Unpredictable. Rotterdam: NAi Publishers, pp.9–13.

Alfredo Brillembourg and Hubert Klumpner, "Rules of Engagement: Caracas and the Informal City" Felipe Hernández, Peter Kellett, and Lea Knudsen Allen (eds.), *Rethinking the Informal City: Critical Perspectives from Latin America* (New York and Oxford: Berghahn Books, 2022): 119, 120, 123–5, 131–3.

Slum clearance and eviction have been dominant responses to informal urbanism. Among the first to conceptualize solutions away from these approaches were John Turner and Robert Fichter in their co-edited book *Freedom to Build: Dweller Control of the Housing Process* (1972).[21] The authors argue that traditional top-down housing approaches often fail to meet the needs of residents, particularly in informal settlements and low-income communities. The book proposes a participatory approach where residents have greater control over the planning and construction of their homes, which can result in better and cheaper housing.

Several notable approaches to informal urbanism in Latin America follow in this tradition. One of these is "sites and services," a strategy developed in the 1970s for improving informal settlements. Instead of offering traditional housing projects, it offers land plots with basic infrastructure to households, such as roads, water supply, sanitation, and sometimes electricity. Individual households would then develop their homes independently and at their own pace on their land plots. This was seen as a more cost-effective way for the government, allowing it to provide housing to more people. An example of the "sites and services" approach in Latin America is the "Villa El Salvador" project in Lima, Peru. Built in the early 1970s by the Peruvian government, the project aimed to address the rapid influx of rural migrants into Lima's informal settlements. Villa El Salvador provided residents with electricity, water, sewage, and land tenure. Residents were involved in the planning and development process. Over time, the community continued to develop along this backbone of infrastructure, and Villa El Salvador became a model for similar initiatives across the region.

Sites and services schemes offer plots with essential infrastructure and services, leaving the construction of the actual housing entirely to the residents. In contrast, "core housing" provides residents with basic, essential structures, allowing them to expand and customize their homes over time based on their needs and financial capacity. More recently, the work of Chilean architect

FIGURE 7.3 Quinta Monroy housing in Iquique, Chile, designed by Elemental and completed in 2003, highlights an innovative core-housing strategy for the low-income sector, enabling incremental expansion and personalization over time. Photo by Cristóbal Palma.

Alejandro Aravena continues these principles. He gained international recognition for his low-cost housing work with Elemental, an architecture firm that focuses on addressing social and economic challenges through design solutions. One of his notable projects is the concept of "Half a House," an initiative that emerged as a response to the housing needs of low-income families in Chile. "Half a House" provides families with a basic structure that is designed to accommodate future expansion. The initial construction provides essential amenities and space, while residents have the flexibility to complete the construction of the second half of the house as they are able to save more money for construction.[22]

The "Half a House" concept is a creative solution to the problem of inadequate housing for disadvantaged communities. It acknowledges the economic realities of residents while providing them with a foundation to build upon over time. By having to build only "half a house," the budget was able to cover essential housing for more people. This approach not only addresses immediate housing needs but also empowers residents to gradually improve their living conditions. Aravena engages in informal urbanism by enabling citizens to self-organize through bottom-up self-build homes and expansions. His "Half a House" neighborhoods demonstrate how urbanism can result from the direct actions of everyday people, gradually shaping the city over time.

ALEJANDRO ARAVENA
"Elemental: A Do Tank"

Elemental is a for-profit company with a social conscience working on projects that capitalise on the city's capacity to create wealth and provide a short cut to equality by improving quality of life without having to wait for income redistribution. Elemental has been operating since 2002, and since 2006 has worked in partnership with Universidad Catolica de Chile (Chile's Catholic University) and the Chilean oil company, COPEC. This unusual combination of academic excellence, corporate vision and entrepreneurship has been instrumental in enabling Elemental to expand its scope in the city. It is currently engaged in upgrading urban infrastructure, transportation networks, services and housing.

Elemental Housing

When Elemental first took off at Harvard University in 2000, social housing was associated with a dearth of economic and professional resources that meant limited options for poor families. Elemental sought to change this negative association, using professional skills to work with social housing providers. The aim was to generate a technical scenario that would guarantee value gain over time without the need to change existing policies or market conditions.

'There have been perhaps two major moments in the history of social housing. The first came in 1927, when, in the Weissenhofsiedlung of Stuttgart, the best architects at the time, made built contributions to try to solve the problem of low-cost housing. The second came in 1970, after the PREVI-Lima project (1968–75), when attempts by avantgarde architects to help overcome a housing deficit came to an end. We are planning to write the third chapter of this story by again bringing the best architects to solve that most difficult of architectural issues: extremely low-cost housing that can be a real means to overcoming poverty.'[1]

Elemental Iquique (2003) was the first project in Chile to apply the company's design criteria and confirm that the methodology worked. Five years after its construction, there was an overall increase in the value of both houses and neighbourhood. The project, in a city in the North Chilean desert, involved settling 93 families on the site – where they had been squatting for the last 30 years in the heart of Iquique´s downtown – instead of displacing them to the periphery. The budget was US$7,500 per family. The opportunity to develop this site allowed Elemental to test its own developed design criteria for ensuring that each unit appreciated in value so that social housing could become a social investment instead of a social expense. Success was achieved by clearly identifying the restrictions and then working with the families themselves in participative workshops, proving feasibility on a local level. The results? People were able to double the area of their original homes (36 square metres/387.5 square feet) at a cost of only $1,000 each. Today, five years later, any house in the Elemental Iquique project is now valued at over $20,000.

Scale and Speed

By 2030, the population of the world living in cities will have increased from 3 to 5 billion, with 2 billion of these living below the poverty line. The problem the world needs to solve is to build a 1-million-inhabitant city per week for the next 20 years for $10,000 dollars per family. Elemental is working on a 'scale and speed strategy' to share its experience and quality standards with poor communities around the globe.

Scale

Resolving the housing problem of the world's poor requires action on a massive scale that can only be achieved by worldwide cooperation in the transfer of technology. Elemental is committed to developing projects together with local builders and governments around the world, transmitting its experience through specific projects. For example, the company has worked in partnership with the Make It Right Foundation-New Orleans, the City of São Paulo and the government of Nuevo León, Mexico, to develop projects using Elemental's design principles. In Mexico, the Housing Institute of Nuevo León commissioned a group of 70 homes on a site of 0.6 hectares (1.48 acres) in a middle-class neighbourhood in Monterrey (2010). This project demonstrates the adaptability of the design criteria abroad, empowering local builders by giving them the knowledge that allows them to take these same innovations and apply them themselves.

Speed

The key to increasing the speed of construction lies in prefabrication. Historically, prefabricated systems have been criticised for their inability to adapt to varied situations. However, if the goal is to prefabricate only half a house, this problem no longer exists. Each owner, when building the second half of his or her house, is responsible for customising the final solution. Moreover, while the first half becomes more strategic (ie, concentrating on the difficult parts of the house), it achieves a more universal application, justifying and confirming the advantages of prefabrication. These concepts were implemented in the Milan Triennale prototype (2008) that can be assembled in 24 hours, successes which then led to the second phase development of the E-block, a second-generation of prefab prototypes that with speed and flexibility can generate housing for whole neighbourhoods where resources are scarce.

Elemental's Response to the Chilean Earthquake

On 27 February 2010, an earthquake measuring 8.8 on the Richter scale, and resultant tsunami hit Chile, affecting the greater part of the country. Two days after the incident, Elemental began work on three different projects, at varying speeds and scales, to assist the people and cities of Chile.

1st-Day Response

The process of collecting water from a central distribution tank is inefficient for two reasons: water is heavy, making it impossible to carry large quantities at any one time, and containers that can efficiently hold and carry water are not readily available. Under normal circumstances, a family needs between 20 and 25 litres (5.5 gallons) of water daily to meet their basic drinking, cooking and washing needs. Obviously, these simple tasks will require much more time if water has to be collected several times rather than once.

Referencing methods of transporting water in Africa, Elemental proposed rolling water instead of carrying it. Rolling water is a more efficient means of transporting this necessity. The process, which is so easy that even a child can do it, consists of: 1) filling plastic bottles with water; 2) packing the bottles tightly inside a tyre; 3) lifting the tyre into an upright position; and 4) rolling the tyre alongside you.

10th-Day Response

Each 32-square-metre (344.4-square-foot) Elemental emergency housing unit was designed to utilise natural light and cross-ventilation and to be assembled within 48 hours by a team of three people. Made from 14 structurally insulated panels (SIPs) that can later be reused for constructing permanent accommodation, it is possible to build 50 units daily. The goal was to buy time so that the quality of reconstruction was of a higher standard; otherwise the urgency and pressure to provide solutions would compromise the end result.

100th-Day Response

The municipality and government of Constitución contacted Elemental inviting the company to join a team of Chilean organisations and the international engineering firm Arup to work on PRES, a masterplan for the sustainable reconstruction of this coastal city. About 80 per cent of the city was destroyed by the earthquake and resultant tsunami; the team had 90 days to completely redesign the city including its infrastructure, energy distribution systems, waste management, housing, public spaces and facilities.

One part of the masterplan consisted of a 7-kilometre (4.3- mile) long park to be situated along the river and coastal edge of the city. Not only does this provide much-needed green space, but a heavily wooded area serves to mitigate the effects of future tsunamis, with a modeled potential reduction in the force of the water of up to 41 per cent and of its height by up to 28 per cent.

PRES also plans for increased density at the city centre while transforming certain streets into pedestrian walkways. In addition to the reconstruction of keynote public buildings, different housing typologies were designed to take account of variables such as surface area and to allow for the possibility of expansion. And with reconstruction came the opportunity to capture the city's renewable energy potential. Photovoltaic lights were incorporated into the new pedestrian walkways and, rather than electricity, solar panels are used to heat water for homes. Also, the residual heat produced by the cellulose plant near the city centre would be harnessed to heat public buildings and facilities.

Citizen Participation

Implementing PRES involved meshing the know-how and experience of professionals and local authorities with the views and aspirations of the citizens. Utilising the design of Elemental's emergency housing unit, a town hall was built in the city centre that housed various forums and discussion groups on the city's development. During the 90 days within which the redesign of the city had to be completed, the town hall received 6,300 visitors, more than 1,200 ideas were deposited in its mailbox, and 4,230 votes were counted in community polls. It was an unprecedented level of participation that allowed the vision and priorities of the city's citizens to be incorporated within the final proposal.

Chile has a history of destructive earthquakes, but each one has left behind a legacy of improved construction standards. In part due to the latest disaster, Elemental believes it is now necessary to design coastal cities with an inherent ability to withstand tsunamis, and to consider seismic isolation for basic services and utilities serving all cities.

One last point. Under normal circumstances, Chilean (and other Latin American) cities do not grow at the same rate as per capita income. Which is why the process of reconstruction with its emphasis on public space within the city's natural and geographic setting is an opportunity to improve upon the city's potential for growth.

1   Alejandro Aravena, 'Elemental: Building Innovative Social Housing in Chile', Harvard Design Magazine 21, Fall/Winter 2004/5.

Alejandro Aravena, "Elemental: A Do Tank", AD (Architectural Design) 81, no. 3 (2011): 32–7.

Despite the prevailing crisis of socioeconomic inequity inherent in informal urbanization, there exists a unique opportunity for designers in formal contexts to glean insights from emergent and grassroots urbanism. In recent history, designers and activists have aimed to harness the self-organizing dynamics present within several major cities, from New York to Quito. One such innovative approach is known as tactical urbanism. This concept draws inspiration from Michel de Certeau's seminal work, *The Practice of Everyday Life*, in which he highlights the dichotomy between "strategies"—the top-down exercises of power—and "tactics"—the calculated actions individuals employ to subvert or navigate these power structures. De Certeau contends that the theater of everyday life is a constant battleground where strategies and tactics collide.[23]

Margaret Crawford further extends these ideas in her book, *Everyday Urbanism*, championing an approach that reveres the spontaneous acts of appropriation and adaptation that people undertake to shape spaces according to their needs.[24] Examples include impromptu garage sales and street vendors setting up shop on chain-link fences. Even attempts by certain municipalities to regulate garage sales have proven futile, as these activities often unfold on private property.

Mike Lydon and Anthony Garcia, in their book *Tactical Urbanism*, build on this work by de Certeau and Crawford. Tactical Urbanism refers to a strategy defined by "short-term, low-cost, scalable interventions and policies," implemented by various actors, from governments and businesses to non-profits and individuals. They, paradoxically, mainly show examples from the formal sector. Yet, the book argues for the value of Tactical Urbanism in its capacity to bypass what they call "the Big Planning process" with more granular, time-based projects and policies. These are, they note, "adjusted on the fly while never losing sight of long-term and large-scale goals."[25] One of their prime examples is the pedestrianization of Times Square, spearheaded by Janette Sadik-Khan, a former New York City Department of Transportation commissioner, in 2009. Up until then, the iconic intersection in Manhattan had most of its space dedicated to car travel. Using mostly paint and folding chairs, the temporary pedestrian plaza proved successful. It was made permanent in 2017 by the firm Snøhetta.

Tactical urbanism interventions, by nature, are experimental, serving as a way to test new concepts and involve communities in the urban planning and design process. Tactical urbanists claim to be creative, opportunistic, entrepreneurial and civic-minded. They encompass endeavors like pop-up parks, temporary bike lanes, street art installations, and community-led events. In a world grappling with the complexities of urban development and social equity, the concept of tactical urbanism offers a dynamic platform for designers to harness the potential of bottom-up urban practices. In Lydon and Garcia's words: "Tactical urbanism doesn't propose one-size-fits-all *solutions* but intentional and flexible *responses*."[26]

MIKE LYDON AND ANTHONY GARCIA
Tactical Urbanism

Disturbing the Order of Things

"The lack of resources is no longer an excuse not to act. The idea that action should only be taken after all of the answers and the resources have been found is a sure recipe for paralysis. The planning of a city is a process that allows for corrections; it is supremely arrogant to believe that planning can be done only after every variable has been controlled."

–Jaimie Lerner
Architect, former mayor of Curitiba, Brazil

If you visited Times Square on the Friday before Memorial Day in 2009, you, along with approximately 350,000 others, would have found a hostile urban environment. Walking into the district, you'd find the famed public space dominated by trucks spewing noxious fumes, impatient taxis blaring horns, and cars turning across your feet despite a pedestrian signal in your favor. You'd lament the false advertising: Times Square is not a square at all but a traffic-clogged bowtie wound tightly around midtown Manhattan's bulging neck. It's likely you never would have found a momentary reprieve from the chaos to observe what draws so many tourists there in the first place: the energy, the bright lights of Broadway, the spectacle of it all.

Yet if you returned *after* the same Memorial Day weekend, you would have experienced a very different place. The sidewalks, still full of life, would be noticeably less congested. The noise from the street would no longer seem as deafening. And to your astonishment, you would discover hundreds of people smiling, chatting, and taking photographs while they sat in foldable lawn chairs placed in the middle of the street. With space to look up and around to admire the lights you would realize that the new and somewhat makeshift public space is where, just days before, cars and trucks battered all senses. Even if you didn't know the term, you would have just discovered the power and potential of Tactical Urbanism.

What Is Tactical Urbanism?

Merriam-Webster's defines tactical as "of or relating to small-scale actions serving a larger purpose" or "adroit in planning or maneuvering to accomplish a purpose." Translated to cities, Tactical Urbanism is an approach to neighborhood building and activation using short-term, low-cost, and scalable interventions and policies. Tactical Urbanism is used by a range of actors, including governments, business and nonprofits, citizen groups, and individuals. It makes use of open and iterative development processes, the efficient use of resources, and the creative potential unleashed by social interaction. It is what Professor Nabeel Hamdi calls making plans without the usual preponderance of planning.[1] In many ways, Tactical Urbanism is a learned response to the slow and siloed conventional city building process. For citizens, it allows the immediate reclamation, redesign, or reprogramming of public space. For developers or entrepreneurs, it provides a means of collecting design intelligence from the market they intend to serve. For advocacy organizations, it is a way to show what is possible to garner public and political support. And for government, it's a way to put best practices into, well, practice—and quickly!

Because the places people inhabit are never static, Tactical Urbanism doesn't propose one-size-fits-all *solutions* but intentional and flexible *responses*. The former remains the fixation of numerous and overlapping disciplines in the urban development fields, which assume that most variables affecting cities can be controlled now and into the distant future. The latter rejects this notion and embraces the dynamism of cities. This reframing invites a new conversation about local resiliency and helps cities *and* citizens together explore a more nuanced and nimble approach to citymaking, one that can envision long-term transformation but also adjust as conditions inevitably change . . .

. . . Of course we recognize that not all city-building efforts lend themselves to the tactical approaches we outline in this book; we don't advocate using temporary materials to pilot-test bridges or prototype skyscrapers. When done well, large-scale projects can be catalytic, if not iconic. The value of Tactical Urbanism is in breaking through the gridlock of what we call the Big Planning process. . .with incremental projects and policies that can be adjusted on the fly while never losing sight of long-term and large-scale goals.

Tactical Urbanism can be used to initiate new places or help repair existing ones. For example, when Boston's $22 billion "Big Dig" buried the Central Artery expressway and made room for the 15-acre Rose Kennedy Greenway, the new public green space needed to be activated.[2] In a 2010 editorial, the *Boston Globe* asserted, "What could be a monument to Boston's collective spirit is instead a victim of the region's parochial rhythms."[3] Architecture critic Robert Campbell put it this way: "There are things to look at but nothing to do."[4] In response to his critique, and many others, the Rose Kennedy Greenway Conservancy began activating the forlorn spaces;

demonstration gardens, street art, food trucks, and low-cost movable tables and chairs have breathed new life into the greenway. These low-cost modifications were never part of the master plan per se but demonstrate that improving otherwise lifeless public spaces need not cost millions of dollars.

Tactical Urbanism is not alone in its use of lower-cost, iterative development processes. The manufacturing industry, for example, often holds up the famed Toyota Way, which uses a continuous improvement process to achieve long-term goals.[5] Similarly, tech entrepreneurs look to the tenets of The Lean Start-Up, which is a product development method advocating rapid prototyping as the inception of the deliberately agile "Build—Measure—Learn" product development cycle. The idea is that each revolution quickly improves on the last until a product is ready for the market, if only in beta form.[6] These concepts have gained currency in other professional disciplines including urban planning . . .

. . . Through our research and work, we have identified a burgeoning catalogue of Tactical Urbanism projects that respond to outdated policies and planning processes with innovative transportation, open space, and small-scale building initiatives. These projects often result from the direct participation of citizens in the creation and activation of their neighborhood, or the creative work of formal entities, such as nonprofits, developers, and government. Collectively, they demonstrate time and again that short-term action can create long-term change.

Tactical Urbanism is frequently applied to what urban sociologist William "Holly" Whyte called the "huge reservoir of space yet untapped by imagination."[7] Today's reservoirs—vacant lots, empty storefronts, overly wide streets, highway underpasses, surface parking lots, and other underused public spaces—remain prominent in our towns and cities and have become the targets of entrepreneurs, artists, forward-thinking government officials, and civic-minded "hacktivists." Such groups increasingly view the city as a laboratory for testing ideas in real time, and their actions have led to a variety of creative and entrepreneurial initiatives realized in the rise of food trucks, pop-up stores, better block initiatives, chair bombing, parklets, shipping container markets, do-it-yourself (DIY) bike lanes, guerrilla gardens, and other hallmarks of the Tactical Urbanism movement. These interventions were never anticipated by a master plan but provide a needed dose of whimsy and also help users and passersby not only envision a different future but experience it too. And therein lies the seductive power of Tactical Urbanism: It creates tactile proposals for change instead of plans or computer-generated renderings that remain abstract.

1   Nabeel Hamdi, *The Placemaker's Guide to Building Community*, Earthscan Tools for Community Planning (London: Routledge, 2010).
2   Ethan Kent, "Rose Kennedy Greenway 'A Design Disaster,'" Project for Public Spaces blog, April 30, 2010, http://www.pps.org/blog/rose-kennedy-greenway-a-design-disaster/.
3   Editorial, "How to Fix the Greenway," *The Boston Globe*, April 18, 2010, http://www.boston.com/boston-globe/editorial_opinion/editorials/articles/2010/04/18/how_to_fix_the_greenway/.4.
4   Robert Campbell, "How to Save the Greenway? Make It a Neighborhood," *The Boston Globe*, April 25, 2010, http://www.boston.com/ae/theater_arts/articles/2010/04/25/how_to_save_the_rose_kennedy_greenway_from_emptiness_and_disconnection/?page=full.
5   http://en.wikipedia.org/wiki/The_Toyota_Way (accessed 7/21/14).
6   http://theleanstartup.com/principles (accessed 7/21/14).
7   William H. Whyte, *City: Rediscovering* the Center (New York: Doubleday, 1989).

Mike Lydonww and Anthony Garcia, *"A Tactical Urbanism How-to" Tactical Urbanism* (Washington, DC: Island Press: 2015): 1–8.

This chapter explored design approaches diverging from formal planning processes, each advocating for the agency of emergent and informal actions and interventions. With over a billion individuals living in informal settlements, situated beyond the purview of formal planning frameworks, often in marginal and undesirable areas, architects and urban designers are aiming to improve their living conditions. Strategies such as slum upgrading, "sites and services," and core housing aim to uplift these communities. While the context of tactical urbanism projects in formal cities differs from informal communities' dire needs addressed by slum upgrading and incremental housing, both challenge the entrenched norms of top-down urban planning. Instead, they empower communities to address their needs in adaptable and innovative ways. In essence, these approaches harness the complexity of bottom-up urban dynamics, recognizing citizens or users as the true agents of design, thereby enabling communities to adapt and innovate in response to their own needs.

8

Evolutionary, Computational, and Parametric Urbanism

For millennia, most cities developed organically, shaped by the cumulative decisions of countless residents, builders, and leaders over many generations. This led to a rich tapestry of spatial variety, unguided by the singular authority of designers or planners. This incremental process contrasted with the advent of Modernism in the early 20th century, which often emphasized centralized control, standardization and efficiency. However, since the late 20th century, many architects and urban designers aimed to create controlled, designed environments while maintaining the spatial diversity inherent in pre-modernist cities. With new computational design tools becoming available in the 1990s, urban designers began to experiment with new ways to generate spatial diversity.

This chapter delves into "computational urbanism"—the integration of computational methods, algorithms, and data analytics into urban design. By marrying computer science with urban design, this approach facilitates the modeling, simulation, and visualization of temporal urban dynamics.

Jane and Mark Burry, in their book *The New Mathematics of Architecture* (2010), demonstrate how advanced mathematics has become crucial to modern architectural design due to technological advances. They explore how mathematical concepts allow architects to create innovative structures previously deemed unattainable. This synergy between mathematics and design, they suggest, is pivotal for the future of architecture. In addition, this allows designers to "engage with the city from the bottom-up, from the discrete granular forces from which it unfolds, rather than top-down."[1]

Modern urban design benefits from innovations such as 3D modeling, generative algorithmic coding, parametric design, and artificial intelligence. These computational techniques empower designers to interpret city data, simulate scenarios, and produce adaptive algorithmic designs.

This chapter further discusses the various facets of computational design, its proponents and critics, and its technical potential. Delving into cybernetic theories, Gordon Pask's groundbreaking insights open the chapter. Other notable contributors include John and Julia Frazer, Tom Verebes, Patrik Schumacher, and Benjamin H. Bratton, each exploring different aspects of computational architecture and urbanism.

Gordon Pask was a British cybernetician and psychologist known for his pioneering work in the field of cybernetics—the study of systems, control, and communication in both animals and machines. Pask's work largely revolved around the concepts of learning systems and processes, particularly human-machine interaction and adaptive systems. One of his most notable contributions was "Conversation Theory," which elucidated the ways in which interactions (or "conversations") lead to learning and understanding. This theory emphasizes the importance of understanding, agreement, and learning through conversation, whether between humans, machines, or a combination of both. Throughout his career, Pask collaborated with various professionals, including architects, to explore the application of his theories in various domains.

Pask understood architecture as one of the fundamental conversational systems in human culture.[2] To Pask, architects are not just builders but "system designers" who focus on organizational properties such as development, communication, and control. He viewed architecture as a "social control" medium, inherently linked to broader systems.

Pask's theories found resonance in projects such as the *Fun Palace*, conceived in the 1960s by British architect-engineer Cedric Price and theatre director Joan Littlewood. Though never built, its design was revolutionary—adaptable, dynamic, and user-centric. Pask envisioned cities as expansive versions of such adaptive systems. He believed urban designs should be evolutionary, prompting architects to interact with a city's ever-changing nature and to leverage predictive modeling and the principles of self-organization to attain deeper urban insights.

GORDON PASK
"The Architectural Relevance of Cybernetics"

The argument rests upon the idea that architects are first and foremost system designers who have been forced, over the last 100 years or so, to take an increasing interest in the organisational (i.e., nontangible) system properties of development, communication and control. . .

Historical Roots

. . . architects were asked to solve problems entailing the regulation and accommodation of human beings; hence, to design systems. But, in a sense, their brief was quite narrow. The problems could all be solved by the judicious application of pure architectural rules . . . Consequently, architects did not need to see themselves as systems designers, even though they designed systems, and the evidence suggests that they did not do so . . .[1]

Evolutionary ideas in architecture

Systems, notably cities, grow and develop and, in general evolve. Clearly, this concept is contingent upon the functionalist/mutualist hypothesis (without which it is difficult to see in what sense the system itself does grow), though the dependency is often unstated. An immediate practical consequence of the evolutionary point of view is that architectural designs should have rules for evolution built into them if their growth is to be healthy rather than cancerous. In other words, a responsible architect must be concerned with evolutionary properties; he cannot merely stand back and observe evolution as something that happens to his structures . . .

. . . The machinery of architectural production

Just as a functionally interpreted building constitutes a system, so also the *construction* of this building is a *system*. The new techniques developed in the last century and the general mechanization of production facilities led to sub-theories concerned with the achievement of forms (the most important centred around the Bauhaus) and these, in turn, restricted the forms that could be produced.

The widening brief

As a result of these essentially cybernetic, sub-theoretical developments, many architects *wanted* to design systems but, on the whole, they were *expected* to design buildings . . .

. . . It is, nowadays, legitimate to enter the design process much earlier, even for a conventional project. For example, it is quite commonplace to design (or at least to plan) cities as a whole with provision for their evolution . . .

. . . The point I wish to establish is that nowadays there is a *demand* for system-orientated thinking whereas, in the past, there was only a more or less esoteric *desire* for it. Because of this demand, it is worthwhile collecting the isolated sub-theories together by forming a generalization from their common constituents. As we have already argued, the common constituents are the notions of control, communication and system. Hence the generalization is no more nor less than abstract cybernetics interpreted as an overall architectural theory . . .

. . . Status of the new theory

In common with the pure architecture of the 1800s, cybernetics provides a metalanguage for critical discussion. But the cybernetic theory is more than an extension of 'pure' architecture. As we noted somewhat earlier, pure architecture was descriptive (a taxonomy of buildings and methods) and prescriptive (as in the preparation of plans) but it did little to predict or explain. In contrast, the cybernetic theory has an appreciable predictive power.[2] For example, urban development can be modelled as a self-organizing system (a formal statement of 'evolutionary ideas in architecture') and in these terms it is possible to predict the extent to which the growth of a city will be chaotic or ordered by differentiation. Even if the necessary data for prediction is unavailable we can, at least, pose and test rational hypotheses. Much the same comments apply to predictions in which time is not of primary importance; for instance, in predicting the influence of spatial and normative constraints upon the stability of a (functionally interpreted) structure.

The cybernetic theory can also claim some explanatory power insofar as it is possible to mimic certain aspects of architectural design by artificial intelligence computer programs[3] (provided, incidentally, that the program is able to learn *about* and *from* architects and by experimenting in the language of architects, i.e. by exploring plans, material specifications, condensed versions of clients' comments, etc.). Such programs are clearly of value in their own right. They are potential aids to design; acting as intelligent extensions of the tool-like programs mentioned at the outset. Further, they offer a means for integrating the constructional system (the 'machinery of production') with the ongoing design process since it is quite easy to embody the constraints of current technology in a special part of the simulation. However, I believe these programs are of far greater importance as evidencing our theoretical knowledge of what architecture is about. Insofar as the program can be written, the cybernetic is self-explanatory . . .

. . . A simple cybernetic design paradigm

In the context of a reactive and adaptive environment, architectural design takes place in several interdependent stages.

i Specification of the purpose or goal of the system (with respect to the human inhabitants). It should be emphasized that the goal *may* be and nearly always *will* be underspecified, i.e. the architect will no more know the purpose of the system than he really knows the purpose of a conventional house. His aim is to provide a set of constraints that allow for certain, presumably desirable, modes of evolution.

ii Choice of the basic environmental materials.

iii Selection of the invariants which are to be programmed into the system. Partly at this stage and partly in ii above, the architect determines what properties will be relevant in the man environment dialogue.

iv Specification of what the environment will learn about and how it will adapt.

v Choice of a plan for adaptation and development. In case the goal of the system is *underspecified* (as in i) the plan will chiefly consist in a number of evolutionary principles.

Of course, this paradigm applies to systems which adapt over rather short time intervals (minutes or hours). In contrast, the adaptation in a project such as the Fun Palace system took place over much longer time intervals (for instance, an 8-hourly cycle and a weekly cycle formed part of the proposal). Depending upon the time constraints and the degree of flexibility required, it is more or less convenient to use a computer (for example, the weekly cycle is more economically programmed by a flexible office procedure). But exactly the same principles are involved.

Urban planning usually extends over time, periods of years or decades and, as currently conceived, the plan is quite an inflexible specification. However, the argument just presented suggests that it need not be inflexible and that urban development could, perhaps with advantage, be governed by a process like that in the dialogue of a reactive environment (physical contact with the inhabitants giving place to an awareness of their preferences and predilections; the inflexible plan to the environmental computing machine). If so, the same design paradigm applies, since in all of the cases so far considered the primary decisions are systemic in character, i.e. they amount to the delineation or the modification of a control program. This universality is typical of the cybernetic approach.

One final manoeuvre will indicate the flavour of a cybernetic theory. Let us turn the design paradigm in upon itself; let us apply it to the interaction between the designer and the system he designs, rather than the interaction between the system and the people who inhabit it. The glove fits, almost perfectly in the case when the designer uses a computer as his assistant. In other words, the relation 'controller/controlled entity' is preserved when these omnibus words are replaced either by 'designer/system being designed' or by 'systemic environment/inhabitants' or by 'urban plan/city'. But notice the trick, the designer is controlling the construction of control systems and consequently design is control *of* control, ie. the designer does much the same job as his system, *but* he operates at a higher level in the organizational hierarchy.

Further, the design goal is nearly always underspecified and the 'controller' is no longer the authoritarian apparatus which this purely technical name commonly brings to mind. In contrast the controller is an odd mixture of catalyst, crutch, memory and arbiter. These, I believe, are the

> dispositions a designer should bring to bear upon his work (when he professionally plays the part of a controller) and these are the qualities he should embed in the systems (control systems) which he designs.[4]
>
> **1** There are two important sorts of exception:
>   (i) Architects of genius, with a breadth of vision that impels them to see things in a systemic and interdisciplinary fashion. They have existed over the years: Sir Christopher Wren and Sir John Soane, for example.
>   (ii) Men like John Nash, whose talents lay in conceiving an urban development as a functional and aesthetic whole. But, within the tenets of the early 1800s, such men are probably "organizers with a vision," rather than "architects."
> **2** The impact of cybernetics upon architecture is considerable just because the theory does have much more predictive power than pure architecture had. Cybernetics did relatively little to alter the shape of biochemistry for instance, because although these concepts are bound up with everything from enzyme organisation to molecular biology, the discipline of biochemistry already had a *predictive* and *explanatory* theory of its own. I made the same point for engineering in an earlier footnote.
> **3** I have the work of Negroponte's group (see pp 78-85) chiefly in mind, though there are other exemplars.
> **4** The cybernetic notions mooted in this article are discussed in *An Approach to Cybernetics,* Hutchinson (London), 1961 (paperback 1968) and, in a lighter vein, in 'My Predictions for 1984' in Prospect, The Schweppes Book of the New Generation, Hutchinson (London), 1962.
>
> Gordon Pask, "The Architectural Relevance of Cybernetics", *AD* (*Architectural Design*) 7/6 (1969): 949–6.

In his foreword to John Frazer's book, *An Evolutionary Architecture* (1995), Gordon Pask encapsulates the book's core premise: architecture is a living entity with the capacity to evolve.[3] He emphasizes how human-made structures are intertwined with the lives of their inhabitants. The book delves deeply into generative evolutionary spatial patterns, showcasing John and Julia Frazer's significant contributions to concepts and methods of computational design, especially their work on generative growth and evolutionary models. This perspective sees architecture not as a mere craft but as an advanced digital practice.

Frazer's methods for generating forms suggests correlations with the evolutionary processes of nature. Under the umbrella term "natural and artificial biologies," John Frazer begins by postulating that life's foundation is information. His work underscores the notion that humans and the built environments we create are part of nature, echoing Gordon Pask's views. The idea that genetically coded information propels evolution becomes central to Frazer's computational and generative approach to architecture.

Frazer claims architectural constructs should act as evolving models that acclimate to their surroundings, much like natural organisms. By leveraging computer models, he believes we can expedite this architectural evolution. Echoing Nicholas Negroponte, Frazer introduces the notion of "soft architecture," advocating for a design approach that is both adaptive and evolutionary.[4] This concept integrates architectural innovation with nature's complexities, proposing a holistic theory that unites nature, science, and construction. Even though Frazer's pioneering efforts in architectural computation preceded the rise of genetic coding and 3D modeling, his visionary work remains a guiding light, illuminating the evolutionary nature of our constructed surroundings.

JOHN FRAZER
An Evolutionary Architecture

An Evolutionary Architecture investigates fundamental form-generating processes in architecture, paralleling a wider scientific search for a theory of morphogenesis in the natural world. It proposes the model of nature as the generating force for architectural form. The profligate prototyping and awesome creative power of natural evolution are emulated by creating virtual architectural models which respond to changing environments. Successful developments are encouraged and evolved. Architecture is considered as a form of artificial life, subject, like the natural world, to principles of morphogenesis, genetic coding, replication and selection. The aim of an evolutionary architecture is to achieve in the built environment the symbiotic behaviour and metabolic balance that are characteristic of the natural environment . . .

. . . Architectural concepts are expressed as generative rules so that their evolution may be accelerated and tested. The rules are described in a genetic language which produces a code-script of instructions for form-generation. Computer models are used to simulate the development of prototypical forms which are then evaluated on the basis of their performance in a simulated environment. Very large numbers of evolutionary steps can be generated in a short space of time, and the emergent forms are often unexpected . . .

. . . The Nature of the Analogy

Architecture has frequently drawn inspiration from nature – from its forms and structures, and, most recently, from the inner logic of its morphological processes . . .

. . . We can say that architecture is literally part of nature in the sense that the man-made environment is now a major part of the global eco-system, and man and nature share the same resources for building. In turn, our description of an architectural concept in coded form is analogous to the genetic code-script of nature. Analogies, particularly biological, bedevil architectural writing. Sullivan, Wright and Le Corbusier all employed biological analogies, and the concept of the organic is central to the twentieth century. In our case, the primary inspiration comes from the fundamental formative processes and information systems of nature . . .

. . . The Inspiration of Nature

The perfection and variety of natural forms is the result of the relentless experimentation of evolution. By means of profligate prototyping and the ruthless rejection of flawed experiments, nature has evolved a rich biodiversity of interdependent species of plants and animals that are in metabolic balance with their environment. Whilst vernacular architecture might occasionally share some of these characteristics, the vast majority of buildings in our contemporary environment most certainly do not . . .

. . . Natural and Artificial Models

The modelling of these complex natural processes requires computers, and it is no coincidence that the development of computing has been significantly shaped by the building of computer models for simulating natural processes . . . The Church-Turing hypothesis stated that the Turing Machine could duplicate not only the functions of mathematical machines but also the functions of nature. Von Neumann, the other key figure in the development of computing, set out explicitly to create a theory which would encompass both natural and artificial biologies, starting from the premise that the basis of life was information . . .

. . . Artificial Life

In nature it is only the genetically coded information of form which evolves, but selection is based on the expression of this coded information in the outward form of an organism . . .

. . . Generative Systems

An essential part of this evolutionary model is some form of generative technique. Again this is an area charged with problems and controversy . . .

. . . From our point of view, there are several problems with this approach. All of (the past) generative systems are essentially combinatorial or configurational, a problem which seems to stem from Aristotle's description of nature in terms of a kit of parts that can be combined to furnish as many varieties of animals as there are combinations of parts. Fortunately, nature is not actually constrained by the limitations implied by Aristotle . . .

. . . The Environmental Case

Natural ecosystems have complex biological structures: they recycle their materials, permit change and adaptation, and make efficient use of ambient energy. By contrast, most man-made and built environments have incomplete and simple structures: they do not recycle their materials, are not adaptable, and they waste energy. An ecological approach to architecture does not necessarily imply replicating natural ecosystems, but the general principles of interaction with the environment are directly applicable . . .

. . . Responsive Environments

Another important issue for our model of an evolutionary architecture is that it should be responsive to evolving in not just a virtual but a real environment. In his article, 'The Design of Intelligent Environments', Warren Brodey proposed an evolutionary, self-organizing, complex. predictive, purposeful, active environment. He asked: can we teach our environments first complex, then self-organizing intelligence which we can ultimately refine into being evolutionary? These issues preoccupy us too.

. . .and Soft Architecture

Brodey went on to describe in enthusiastic terms some of the hypothetical implications of intelligent environments, and to introduce the concept of 'soft architecture'.

The idea of a soft, responsive architecture also preoccupied Nicholas Negroponte, author of *The Architecture Machine*. He suggested that the design process, considered as evolutionary, could be presented to a machine, also considered as evolutionary, to give a mutual training resilience and growth. Negroponte placed high expectations first on computer hardware, then on software through artificial intelligence. Neither delivered any answers.

The Role of the Computer

Christopher Alexander dismissed the use of computers as a design aid: 'A digital computer is, essentially, the same as a huge army of clerks, equipped with rule books, pencil and paper, all stupid and entirely without initiative, but able to follow exactly millions of precisely defined operations . . . In asking how the computer might be applied to architectural design, we must, therefore, ask ourselves what problems we know of in design that could be solved by such an army of clerks . . . At the moment, there are very few such problems.'[1]

Our evolutionary approach is exactly the sort of problem that could be given to an army of clerks – the difficulty lies in handing over the rule book . . .

. . . The Electronic Muse

I see computers not as an army of tedious clerks who will thwart all creativity with their demands for precise information, but as slaves of infinite power and patience. However computers are not without their dangers. If used unimaginatively, they have a tendency to: dull critical faculties, induce a false sense of having optimized a design which may be fundamentally ill conceived, produce an atmosphere where any utterance from the computer is regarded as having divine significance, distort the design process to fit the limitations of the most easily available program, distort criticism to the end-product rather than to an examination of process, and concentrate criticism and feedback on aspects of a problem which can be easily quantified.

'Imaginative use' in our case means using the computer – like the genii in the bottle – to compress evolutionary space and time so that complexity and emergent architectural form are able to develop. The computers of our imagination are also a source of inspiration – an electronic muse . . .

. . . Problems of Complexity . . .

. . . I shall examine polyautomata in order to show that even very simple local rules can generate emergent properties and behaviour in a way apparently unpredicated by the rules. Collections of small actions ripple upwards, combining with other small actions, until a recognizable pattern of global behaviour emerges. When a certain critical mass of complexity is reached, objects can self-organize and selfreproduce in an open-ended fashion, not only creating their equals but also parenting more complicated objects than themselves. Von Neumann recognized that life depends upon reaching this critical level of complexity. Life indeed exists on the edge of chaos, and this is the point of departure for our new model of architecture.

The New Model of Architecture

There is so far no general developed science of morphology, although the generation of form is fundamental to the creation of all natural and all designed artefacts. Science is still searching for a theory of explanation, architecture for a theory of generation – and it is just possible that the latter will be advanced before the former. In other words, form-generating models developed for architectural purposes (or based on unorthodox or incorrect scientific views) may be valuable if they model a phenomenon that scientists are seeking to explain . . .

> **...The Urge for a Unified Theory**
>
> In the meantime the approach of the end of the century is signalled by a frantic scramble in all fields to formulate a holistic view of the universe – the great unification theory, or GUT. In the natural sciences this takes the form of two juxtaposed tendencies. One is to embrace everything under the umbrella of evolution (or at least evolution in the form of neo-Darwinism). Evolution of the chemical elements, evolution of physical constants, evolution of information, cultural evolution – evolutionary theory is somehow made to explain all phenomena. The other tendency is to recruit all other developments in science, such as self-organizing systems, to expand the theory of evolution to make a new meta-theory.
>
> Overall there is a tendency to deal with complexity, chaos and catastrophe in the same way; to treat natural and artificial systems equally. The optimistic view is that the current debate about the possibility of a new holistic understanding of nature and science will make a significant contribution to current environmental and social problems . . .
>
> **1** C. Alexander, 'The Question of Computers in Design', *Landscape*, Autumn 1967, pp. 8–12
>
> John Frazer, "Introduction", *An Evolutionary Architecture* (London: AA Publications, 1995); 9–21.

In his book *Masterplanning the Adaptive City* (2013), Tom Verebes shifts the discussion in computational design from its impact on architectural design towards a more comprehensive exploration of urban planning and design. Verebes delves into the complexities of incorporating self-organization, automation, and intelligence into urban development processes. He is particularly fascinated with the intricate balance between planned city development and spontaneous, informal changes that arise during what he terms the "age of indeterminacy." This encompasses a transition from top-down directives to a more organic, bottom-up approach. Through this lens, Verebes perceives cities as perpetually evolving entities, their future trajectories being unpredictable. Computational design becomes a tool to navigate and frame these fluid concepts.

Verebes probes the fascination many architects have with evolutionary growth patterns, using historical examples such as medieval European cities, Islamic cities, and even sprawling contemporary informal settlements to illustrate evolutionary trajectories. Much like Pask, he critiques the rigidity inherent in traditional urban planning methodologies, pointing out their often static, predefined nature. Verebes concedes that no design plan can ever be flawless; there is always room for adjustments due to the unpredictability of the future. This brings to the fore the challenge for designers and planners: how can they shape the future while grappling with a myriad of shifting variables and uncertainties?

Echoing Pask's perspective that architects essentially design systems rather than mere spaces, Verebes broadens the idea of mastery. Instead of seeing it as asserting control, he likens it to the seamless interplay between user interfaces and underlying coding, raising intriguing questions about the essence of design and control in an age of self-organizing systems.

Verebes extends Frazer's architectural theories to urbanism, recognizing the unpredictable nature of modern cityscapes. He emphasizes the importance of viewing complex natural systems not merely as muses but as fundamental shifts in approach—where computational techniques do not just replicate intricate emergent behaviors, but also genuinely model their dynamics.

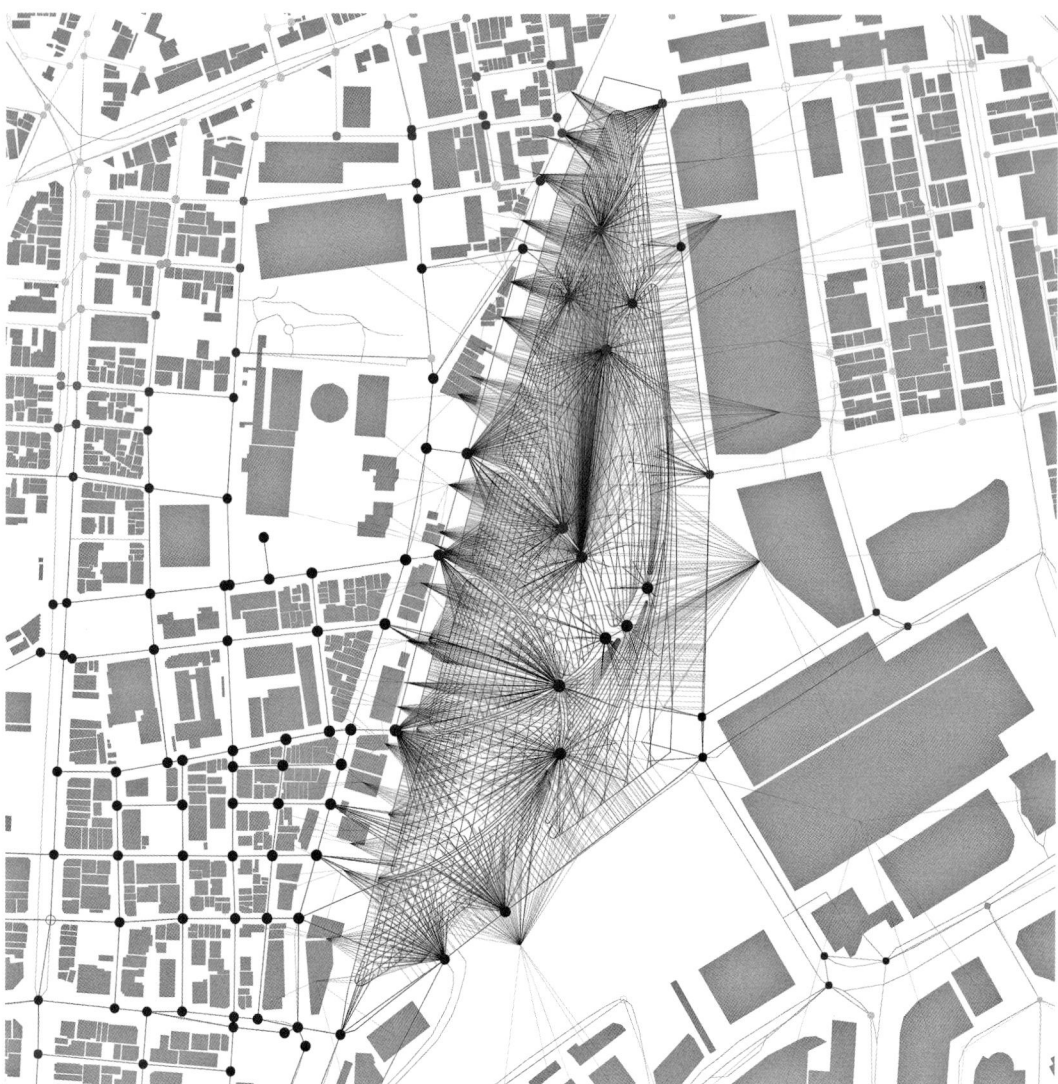

FIGURE 8.1 Diagram created by simulating future pedestrian flows, used to determine a new project's urban massing, open spaces, and connecting paths, as the 'back end' of a model capable of producing differentiated outcomes from different inputs. Umekita Second Development Area Masterplan, invited competition. OCEAN CN and Arup Transportation, 2011–13. Courtesy of OCEAN CN.

TOM VEREBES
Masterplanning the Adaptive City: Computational Urbanism in the Twenty-first Century

PLANNING AND/OR EMERGENCE...

... Architects are often enamoured of evolutionary patterns of urbanization, of urban entities that appear as though they were not designed but rather just happened, with some seemingly invisible intelligence at work. Medieval European towns and cities appear as though they were not designed, but evolved gradually through the playing out of the rules of a dynamic game. Such cities, "far from being messy, disorganized forms, have rather well defined spatial structures."[1] ...

... Self-organized, emergent systems in biological and physical processes parallel the ways in which collective human activity unfolds in real time, including how cities grow and evolve over the years, decades, or centuries ... emergent order occurs precisely when control is relinquished, and here lies the essential contradiction between planned cities and evolutionary forms of urbanism ...

... Conventional techniques of masterplanning, as we have seen, are inflexible in the face of changing requirements and limited in their adaptability to new contextual criteria, and therefore less intelligent than they ought to be. The most-used planning tools inherently lack feedback mechanisms, or the ability to process information and learn from input–output relationships. And it is an oversimplification to set top-down design in opposition to bottom-up growth and development of urbanism—both approaches understand and project the city as a coherent whole. The central question to address is how coherent, compelling evolutionary patterns can be embedded in our existing planning processes ...

TELEOLOGICAL FALLACIES OF THE MASTERPLANNNER

... The conventional tools and techniques of city design are fundamentally unable to manage change. Static plans have traditionally been one of the primary communication tools for presenting images of the city, as final, completed, and stable urban organization, often several years in the future ... This overreliance on narrow, singular, inflexible pictures of the future ignores the inherent complexity of the modern world, and the manifold forces, agents, and contingencies which shape the future. During the course of implementation of a masterplan, the basis upon which decisions are made in response to apparent requirements tends to evolve, or even shift catastrophically, for example according to economic or demographic changes, and hence the process of planning for a stable endgame is ideologically and practically flawed ...

... The inclusion of the term "master" in the title "masterplanner" implies not only a coordinating role, as "master" of a team, but also "mastery," the control of a design outcome—the masterplan ....

... Here is a significant shift from designing as an immediate authorial action, done by hand on paper, to coding for a "back-end" modeling environment, with a "front-end" user interface engaging the designer to produce not one "original" but potentially a series of outcomes, through the negotiation of relationships in a constraints-based experimental approach to design ...

... The decision to reject one paradigm is always simultaneously the decision to accept another, and the judgment leading to that decision involved the comparison of both paradigms with nature and with each other."[2] If one extends this thesis to masterplanning the city, then the inadequacy of the preeminent concepts and methodologies of masterplanning in dealing with an unstable, dynamic world suggests that techniques need to be developed to provide new interfaces of dynamic control . . .

. . . In a world which is increasingly uncertain, information about the world can be embedded in cities and buildings, giving them a metabolic capacity to absorb and process it, and hence to change in relation to dynamic contextual or environmental conditions. In a century when urbanization is occurring at unprecedented rates, the notion of the masterplan as a conclusive document with which to determine the future is in crisis. Uncertainty can indeed be integrated into planning methodologies, though the predominant tendency in nearly all past approaches to urbanism has been to eliminate indeterminacy.

COMPLEX SYSTEMS, EQUILIBRIUM, AND EMERGENCE

. . . Theories of complex natural systems have proliferated in the discipline of architecture. Nature is so complex, "there is no single 'natural landscape' to be found, no ideal state of nature that can be reconstructed or modelled."[3] Far from finding analogs in the behaviors of species, and hence being isolated from the behavior of "man-made" constructs, systems, and networks, cities have behaviors similar to other complex natural phenomena . . .

. . . Over the last two decades, natural systems have increasingly been seen as a source of inspiration for the formal organization of design work, drawing on parallels between natural geometries and their equivalents in three-dimensional modeling environments. Computation is also opening up new design arenas for working with material performance, forces, and effects, which "marks a significant transformation from the primacy of representations to the use of computation as a simulation and map of performativity."[4] The potential of performance-driven computation for urbanism is yet to be theorized, yet there has been some research and practice based on an understanding of the growth of the city, as well as its quotidian routines, as essentially dynamic . . .

. . . The paradigm of dynamic equilibrium, a term associated with thermodynamics, can be interrogated for equivalence within discourses on urbanism . . .

. . . A central issue in dynamics is the idea of equilibrium; and in contrast to the idea of the city has having a stable, enduring nature, "In fact, disequilibrium [is the] more characteristic state of urban systems."[5] The term "far-from-equilibrium" originates from the field of thermodynamics, where it has come to refer to "the special states of a system in which it is most likely to produce radical, productive and unforeseeable behaviours.". . .

. . . Self-organizing systems "raise questions of control" and of the position of the designer.[6] Self-organization is a compelling understanding of the city, for the ways in which dynamic systems arise from rule-based component parts, and simplicity gives rise to a coherent but complex whole. In establishing new paradigms and practices with respect to the self-organization which occurs within all cities, De Landa argues that "what matters is not the planned results of decision making, but the unintended collective consequences of human decisions," arguing that the "best illustration of a social institution that emerges spontaneously from the interaction of many human decision makers is that of a pre-capitalist market, a collective entity arising from the decentralized interaction of many buyers and sellers."[7] . . .

... The principles of evolution in biological systems outline the ways in which order relates to a set of functional criteria, and through successive generations the order is adjusted toward increasingly optimal configurations. According to Marshall, "When we say that evolution has happened, we mean that there was a transformation, via successive intermediates, or descent with modification."[8] Marshall's thesis indicates that evolution is a "generic effect" of a series of non-biological processes of adaptation and transformation, allowing readings of the city to be dissociated from a notion of it as a living organism. In this light, he argues for the idea of design as an evolutionary process, for an approach to design which assumes evolution is linked to "adaptive emergence," as the process of change reflecting incremental local decisions and actions. The term "evolution" is thus used loosely to denote dynamic transformative processes. Questions arise as to whether it can be used to refer to non-biological processes of variation and selection through descent. If "evolution" can be described as any process which aims for long-term transformations resulting from selection and adaptation, to what extent can it be applied to a discussion about urbanism? . . .

PARAMETRIC PATTERNS AND MODELS OF EVOLUTIONARY URBANISM

Without variability, the evolution of an organism would not be possible. In this lies the potential for the architecture of the city to be driven by information to achieve high degrees of local specificity. Whether designed or planned, grown or evolved, cities are undeniably variable over time, and this is not limited to a spatial model of differentiation. The challenges lie in employed visions without determinism . . .

. . . In which ways can cities be said to evolve? Questions arise about the means by which designers can produce generated organizational structures, and, critically, why these kinds of patterns are so compelling. In the following chapters we will investigate the methodologies and projects which enable the phenomena involved in biological evolution analogically to drive tomorrow's architecture and urbanism.

1 M. De Landa (2009) "The Limits of Urban Simulation," *Architectural Design* 53.
2 W.J. Mitchell (1994) *City of Bits: Space, Place and the Infobahn* (Cambridge, MA: MIT), 107.
3 M. Weinstock, *The Architecture of Emergence*, 14.
4 C. Hight, M. Hensel, and A. Menges (2009) "En Route: Towards a Discourse on Heterogeneous Space beyond Modernist Space-Time and Post-Modernist Social Geography," in *Space Reader* (London: Wiley), 10.
5 M. Batty (2005) *Cities and Complexity* (Cambridge, MA: MIT Press), 30.
6 J. Burry and M. Burry, *The New Mathematics of Architecture*, 55.
7 M. De Landa, *A Thousand Years of Nonlinear History*, 19.
8 S. Marshall, *Cities, Design, Evolution*, 172.

Tom Verebes, "The Death of Masterplanning in the Age of Indeterminacy", *Masterplanning the Adaptive City: Computational Urbanism in the Twenty-first Century* (New York: Routledge, 2013); 87, 91–7, 100, 103–4, 113–14.

Patrik Schumacher, principal of the renowned firm Zaha Hadid Architects, is a key advocate for parametricism, an architectural and urban design theory based on parametric design. Parametric design relies on algorithms, primarily derived from parameters defined by the designer, to generate architectural forms and spatial organizations. These parameters can include elements related to site-specific data, material properties, or desired outcomes. The defining characteristic of parametric design is its ability to easily adjust and modify designs by simply changing underlying parameters.

In his chapter, "Parametricist vs. Modernist Urbanism," from *The Autopoiesis of Architecture: A New Agenda for Architecture* (2010), Schumacher explores the potential of Parametricism as an alternative to the shortcomings of both Modernist and Postmodernist urban designs. He critiques Modernism for its monotony, leading to a lack of spatial variety, and Postmodernism for failing to provide a coherent order. In contrast, he claims Parametricism offers both complexity and order, making the multifaceted processes of urban life more legible.

Schumacher revisits Le Corbusier's emphasis on the straight line and right angle as symbols of human purpose, contrasting it with the random paths of a pack-donkey. He critiques Le Corbusier's limited understanding of order, advocating instead for the recognition of complex patterns that emerge from processes of self-organization, which can now be understood through complexity theory and computational tools. In Parametricism, the traditional sharp boundaries and clear geometries give way to fluid fields filled with movement and interaction, like swarms or fluid dynamics, suggesting a more relational urban fabric.

Schumacher concludes by highlighting Parametricism's potential in urban design, emphasizing its aesthetic coherence and ability to manifest rich, adaptive, and varied urban life-processes. This shift, from modernist urban planning to a more dynamic, adaptive approach, resonates with the work of Zaha Hadid Architects and extends to design research at the AA Design Research Lab (AADRL). Here, parametric tools, typically used for single-building variations and differentiated building systems, are applied on an urban scale, highlighting the potential of Parametricism as an urban design method.

FIGURE 8.2 Aerial view of Munich's Olympiapark, showcasing the innovative tension structures of its stadiums and facilities set against the landscaped grounds, designed by Behnisch & Partners and Frei Otto, completed in 1972. Courtesy of Getty Images.

PATRIK SCHUMACHER
The Autopoiesis of Architecture: A New Agenda for Architecture, vol. 2

Parametricist vs Modernist Urbanism

The work of Frei Otto is the only true precursor of Parametricism.

In its urban application, Parametricism offers a convincing alternative to both Modernist monotony and Postmodernist laissez-faire. The former produces order without complexity and the latter produces complexity without order. Both result in disorientation. Parametricist urbanism offers orientation within a complex order. Modernist monotony obliterates the social complexity of Post-Fordist network society. Postmodernist laissez-faire urbanism allows the richness of societal life-processes to be accommodated, albeit without being able to order and articulate this rich complexity. Parametricism can indeed deliver something that produces a decisive advantage. Laissez-faire urbanism proceeds via arbitrary juxtapositions that lack all aesthetic rhyme and reason. This process always results in visual chaos, even if the pragmatic logics of urban life are accommodated within this chaos. The contemporary choice of typologies, construction options and styles is simply too large to expect pragmatic logics to become legible. The result is a cacophony of pure difference.

Parametricism affords the build up of a complex visual and semiological order that facilitates orientation by making the complex order of the urban life-processes legible. Parametricism is able to coordinate pragmatic concerns and articulate them with all their rich differentiations and relevant associations. The danger of overriding real life richness is minimized because variety and adaptiveness are written into the very genetic make up of Parametricism.

SIMPLE ORDER, DISORDER, COMPLEX ORDER

Le Corbusier's first great theoretical statement on urbanism starts with a eulogy on the straight line and the right angle as means by which man conquers and goes beyond nature. The first two paragraphs of the book famously contrast man's way with the pack-donkey's way: 'Man walks in a straight line because he has a goal and knows where he is going; he has made up his mind to reach some particular place and he goes straight to it. The pack-donkey meanders along, meditates a little in his scatter-brained and distracted fashion, he zig-zags in order to avoid larger stones, or to ease the climb, or to gain a little shade; he takes the line of least resistance.'[1] Le Corbusier admires the urban order of the Romans and rejects our sentimental attachment to the picturesque irregularity of the medieval cities: 'The curve is ruinous, difficult and dangerous; it is a paralyzing thing.'"[2]

Le Corbusier insists that: 'the house, the street, the town . . . should be ordered; . . . if they are not ordered, they oppose themselves to us.'[3] Le Corbusier's limitation is not his insistence upon order but his limited concept of order in terms of Classical geometry. Complexity theory (or chaos theory) in general, and the research of Frei Otto[4] in particular, have since taught us to recognize, measure and simulate the complex patterns of order that emerge from processes of self-organization. Phenomena like the 'donkey's path' and the urban patterns resulting from unplanned settlement processes can now be analyzed and appreciated in terms of their underlying logic and rationality, ie, in terms of their hidden regularity and related performative power that result from the consistent constraining pressures that have been underlying their process of formation.

Le Corbusier realized that although 'nature presents itself to us as a chaos . . . the spirit which animates nature is a spirit of order'.[5] However, his understanding of nature's order was limited by the science of his day. He lacked the concepts and computational tools that can now reveal the complex order of those apparently chaotic patterns by means of simulating their lawful 'material computation'. Parametricist sensibility gives more credit to the 'pack-donkey's path' as a form of adaptive material computation than to the simplicity of clear geometries that can be imposed in one sweeping move . . . .

The organizing and articulating capacity of such relational fields is striking in comparison with the pure grid of the modern American city. This modern grid is undifferentiated and therefore non-adaptive. Its 'freedom' to receive any urban fabric and architectural morphology whatsoever is now limiting: it leads to indifference and arbitrary juxtapositions that soon result in impenetrable visual chaos . . .

. . . Modernism was founded on the concept of universal space. Parametricism differentiates fields. Space is empty. Fields are full, as if filled with a fluid medium. We might think of liquids in motion, structured by radiating waves, laminal flows and spiralling eddies. Swarms have also served as paradigmatic analogues for the field concept. We would like to think of swarms of buildings that drift across the landscape. There are no Platonic, discrete figures or zones with sharp outlines. Within fields, only the global and regional field qualities matter: biases, drifts, gradients, and perhaps conspicuous singularities like radiating centres. Deformation no longer spells the breakdown of order but the *lawful* inscription of information. Orientation in a complex, lawfully differentiated field affords navigation along vectors of transformation. The contemporary condition of arriving in a metropolis for the first time, without prior hotel arrangements, without a map, might instigate this kind of field navigation. Imagine there are no more landmarks to rely on, no axes to follow and no more boundaries to cross.

Parametricist urbanism aims to construct new field logics that operate via the mutually accentuating correlation of multiple urban systems: fabric modulation, street systems, system of open spaces etc. The agenda of deep relationality implies that the fabric modulation also extends to the tectonic articulation of the building mass . . .

. . .IMPLEMENTING PARAMETRICIST URBANISM. . .

. . . Current urban development patterns lack aesthetic coherence, even when the pragmatic logics of a vital urban life-process are secured via the rationality of market forces. The contemporary choice of typologies, construction options and styles is simply too large to expect pragmatic logics to become legible. The result is visual chaos, a cacophony of pure difference. Parametricism is able to further coordinate pragmatic concerns and articulate them with all their rich differentiations and relevant associations. The danger of overriding real-life richness is minimized because variety and adaptiveness are written into the heuristics of Parametricism.

The inherent advantages of Parametricism become most salient at the urban scale. The competition-winning urban design schemes of Zaha Hadid Architects indicate that Parametricism has the chance to be recognized as a rational approach that can deliver large-scale, high-performance projects. The initial societal success of Paramatric urbanism is important as context for the more radical design research that has been conducted under the title of 'Parametric Urbanism' at the AA Design Research Lab (AADRL). Parametric urbanism takes the tools of parametric design into the domain of urbanism. The power of parametric design systems is usually exploited to cope with the rapid succession of design changes, i.e. for the ability to produce variations of a single building, or for generating versions of building components for a complex building geometry that does not allow for the repetition of elements. Parametric Urbanism suggests that these techniques of versioning can be applied to an array of buildings, so that a new version does not replace an older version but comes to join and extend the field of simultaneous versions in the build up of a complex urban field. Whole buildings are treated as generative components that populate an urban site according to a rule of differentiation that is correlated with chosen aspects of the site's initial differentiations. Thus the build up of multiple urban layers is being initiated, each of its own logic of differentiations as well as within its own way of resonating with the other layers.

1 Le Corbusier, *The City of Tomorrow and its Planning*, Dover Publications (New York), 1987, translated from French original *Urbanisme*, Editions *Cres* & Cie (Paris), 1925 P 5.
2 Ibid, p 8.
3 Ibid, p 15.
4 The work of Frei Otto might be considered as the sole true precursor of Parametricism.
5 Le Corbusier, *The City of Tomorrow and its Planning*, p 18.

Patrik Schumacher, "Parametricist vs. Modernist Urbanism", *The Autopoiesis of Architecture: A New Agenda for Architecture*, vol. 2 (London: John Wiley and Sons, 2012); 680, 682–3, 685–6, 689–95.

Benjamin H. Bratton is a multidisciplinary theorist, weaving together varied academic fields such as philosophy, art, design, and computer science to explore the impacts of technology on society, culture, and politics. His seminal work, *The Stack: On Software and Sovereignty* (2015), provides a layered framework to understand the digital realm's complexities, highlighting the intersections of technology and geopolitics.[5] Bratton suggests that various computational forms—such as smart grids, online cloud platforms, mobile apps, the Internet of Things, and smart cities—should not be viewed as individual entities evolving independently. Instead, they collectively form a unified structure, which he terms "The Stack." This structure acts as both a computational apparatus and a framework for governance.

Backed by this larger view on technology and society, Bratton critically assesses parametricism. While parametricism emphasizes adaptability and flexibility, Bratton critiques its tendency to reduce complex problems to issues concerning aesthetics. He argues that this over-reliance on intricate forms can overlook deeper sociopolitical and environmental contexts. Moreover, Bratton challenges the notion that algorithms and computational solutions alone can address intricate architectural and urban challenges, cautioning against techno-solutionism.

Central to Bratton's critique is the call for a more profound political engagement in design. He argues that architectural and urban design's withdrawal from the political sphere is impossible and undesirable. In addition, he believes that the fluidity and continuity championed by parametricism can inadvertently obscure real-world discontinuities and sociopolitical boundaries. For Bratton, while technology offers potent tools for design, he warns that it should not eclipse the broader geopolitical and socioeconomic structures that architects and designers must grapple with.

FIGURE 8.3 The Soho Galaxy in Beijing, designed by Zaha Hadid Architects and completed in 2012, showcases a futuristic architectural design with fluid forms containing retail and offices, interconnected spaces, and a sunken urban square. Courtesy of Getty Images.

BENJAMIN H. BRATTON
"Parametricist Architecture Would Be a Good Idea"

... The initial emergence of planetary-scale computation as *urinfrastructure* and "information" as a historical category of economic and geographic substance are together the twin engines of the "new world" ...

... What does this really look like? The geopolitics of "the Cloud" is an involute geometry made real, but one realized by the overlapping of multiple claims and techniques of many platforms layered one on top of the other ...

... In the name of a speculative geopolitics, my remarks would argue for a universal model of parametric design, but one that is only partially recognizable in the one we have now. In short, Schumacher does not go nearly *far enough*. A universalist parametricism would be more radical than what we have seen to date, largely because it would not be, and already is not, limited to architecture per se. That universalist parametricism might be defined as the condition and method of material analysis and composition, endemic to the geologic and geopolitical era of planetary-scale computation, through which algorithmic operations, only partially controlled, can integrate and disintegrate fields of inter-faces into platforms, which in turn govern the further distribution of algorithmic events and opportunities ... This describes parametric architecture as within a larger field of parametric design, which is itself situated within a larger field of parametric geosystems ... the ultimate expression of parametricist design would not leave our politics intact or be subservient to it. To work, it would reform the political as such, not simply work on behalf of the political-as-is, and so my remarks also are at odds with some of the pointed critiques of Schumacher's positions and of Parametricism in general ...

... Interfaces ...

... Despite how Schumacher discusses interfaces as enabling maximal information flow, interfaces do not only grease the path of communication, they also retard it, and that is *good*; it is why you can actually design with them ... Interfaces not only accelerate communication, they also capture it, and so Deleuze's "society of control" is also a theory of urban interfaces ...

... Forms of spatial organization that society used to ask of architecture, we now ask of software, and so architecture becomes just one particular scale of cloud hardware. When parametricists talk about the possibility of two or three interpenetrating grids occupying the same space, transforming architecture's own performance as those grids change ratio, we should recognize that this is now the normal condition of urban space everywhere, not a novelty that expert designers might someday bring ...

... Platforms

With the regimes of planetary-scale computation, interfaces (in plural) congeal into a higher-order assemblage called *platforms* ... A strong universalist parametricism would work for and through platforms as an alternative institutional substrate, one that it would also help to realize ...

. . . Toward a universal parametricism? . . .

. . . We have parametric industrial design and interface design obviously. We have parametric logistics (Amazon's warehouses are far more sophisticated spatial expressions of algorithmic design and organization than anything that would work on building envelopes at the expense of the itinerant object). We have parametric politics of the algorithm (demonstrated at the least by State and non-State cyberwarfare, etc.). We have Parametric and algorithmic economics (seen most obviously in the berserker vagaries of high-speed algorithmic trading). We have parametric interfaces (such as Google's individuated maps, which redraw the urban space differently for different users, or better for their own driverless cars). Perhaps most importantly going forward, perhaps more important even than what we call today politics and economics, may be parametric synthetic intelligence, and what we today call robotics. Parametric architecture often already models the user as an automaton; why not go all the way? Why not an urbanism for all the nonhuman users of cities; of which there are always plenty and will be much more? . . .

. . . A schematic conclusion

As I have argued, Schumacher's limited version does not go far enough in its claim for how parametric and algorithmic logics of form, system, network, etc., can and do model alternative socio-political architectures. A radical parametricism would ultimately explode the legacy distinctions between art, architecture, the urban, politics and law that are held up as Aristotelian ideal realms, and introduce new realms of difference and distinction. The borders of these legacy realms are in fact as plastic and permeable as the membranes of fully parametric forms at architectural scales. For parametricism to make good on its claims, it has to be willing to actually think of itself as a real model for algorithmic geopolitical form in general and in all its guises. Let me say it as clearly as I can: to set the political to one side ("it is not the architect's problem or expertise to deal with the complexities of civil society") and at the same time to make grandiose claims for how architectural form can in fact "remake civilization" is a contradictory and self-defeating point of departure.

I am not arguing for the consolidation or holistic de-differentiation of art, architecture and politics as they exist . . .

. . . Put most schematically an alternative parametricist manifesto, as yet to be written, might include the following:

1 At this moment, the primary force for systemic formalization is algorithmic emergence, primarily as the transposition of mechanical systems into software systems, and then merging with generalized robotics, and so de-differentiating chemical and informational parametrics.

2 We see this across multiple domains simultaneously, from laboratory science, to warehouse supply chains, to agriculture, to architectural composition, and so on.

3 The formalization of the problems that define these domains into algorithmic logics is supported by the dissemination of media systems based on those logics. Among the most dramatic effects of this is the isomorphic convergence of effects across and between these different domains. Expertise slips and slides from one institution into the other in sometimes odd ways (i.e., the exact same big-data analysis tools and techniques might be applied to urban planning, cellular

biology or modeling financial derivatives, etc.). The isomorphic drift of technical-discursive forms is familiar to any reader of Foucault.

4 . . . At many scales new maps, new diagrams, new topologies are required, not just to imagine hypothetical possibilities, but first to make better sense of a reality that has overgrown those we innovated decades or centuries ago and still keep at our side.

5 In Architecture, parametricism has announced itself as the domain-specific paradigmatic formal language of the general phenomenon of algorithmic emergence. It does so through heterogeneous investigations of formal geometry, figuration, calculation and system, at multiple scales of site and temporality (we hope). We agree that it has important currency in other domains of design as well—urban design, industrial design, interaction design, etc.—but insist that the relative autonomy of these genres of design (as articulated in the early modern era by the differentiation of designer's tools is now reorganized by their shared suite of software tools, many of which are explicitly parametric, and which provide explicitly parametricist designs as their outcome) is less important than what links them together.

6 Architecture's disciplinary and methodological role in this parametric design economy may not be that of a "master discourse" because, as I put it, "all design is interface design" and, as Schumacher put it, "all design is communication design." In this, parametric architecture is only a specific application of the more algorithmic general design logos to architectural problems. As argued above, a universal parametricism is interested in design problems at multiple different registers and domains, especially those that are themselves remade in the image of algorithmic emergence (which is to say most everyone).

7 Nevertheless, architecture's expertise with form persists. But in practice, "form is always form *of* something." Except in mathematics—which is not at all the same thing as computation—form is also content. . ."

8 Its formal design interventions move into contemporary domains of the political (in the same examples above) that may be almost nothing like the political space of the "parliamentary legislatures, trade unions, and activist groups" that Schumacher suggests architects go to work with instead of trying to "do political architecture." . . .

9 Put another way, a disinterested artificial intelligence would observe that the most generally efficacious parametric space design software of our moment is Microsoft Excel. This has led globalization to a boring and unsustainable impasse. The impasse—equally aesthetic, political and ecological—demands a more radical response by progressive design. By radical, I mean "to the root," and by "root" we mean the universality of algorithmic logics themselves.

10 It is not that art, architecture, economics, politics, etc., can and should be consolidated into a "Total Plan" (no Lenin and no Le Corbusier). Total plans are antithetical to algorithmic emergence. Parametricism should be more at home with platforms, which are neither State nor Market. Instead, parametricist architecture should be attentive to the need for formal organization within and between nonarchitectural domains that have been disrupted by algorithmic logics both within themselves and between one another (politics and economics included). This is a connotation of Schumacher's definition of parametric architecture as "communication design" that I agree with.

11 The re-differentiations of these domains are not born of the philosophy seminar room but in the world itself, and specifically by algorithmic emergence let loose between them and across them. Philosophy has not caught up to this for the most part. Architectural theory has not either. Economics has led this, but has no idea what it is doing. Politics partially understands, but only on its *para*-margins (TOR, NSA, Google/China, etc.).

12 Parametric architecture is already political whether it wants to be or not, because its actual context as built form is inseparable from its actual context as social machine, and because its formal imaginary can be abstracted to intervene in design problems that organize the political domain directly. You think you are designing an art museum, but your form may be a new topology for contested air-space jurisdiction over international waters.

13 Yes, the fusion of art, architecture and politics into "one" was the method of mid-twentieth-century totalitarianism, but so was the "fission" of art from architecture from politics. It is the Leni Riefenstahl creative alibi: "Hitler may be the client, but I am just an artist and it is my job to make art and not politics," offering such grotesque cover, and this is still the method of early twenty-first-century totalitarianism ("now is not the time for politics: this is sports, art, entertainment, design, etc.").

14 A withdrawal of parametricism and especially parametricism of form (architecture's expertise) from the design problem of "the political" is both impossible and undesirable. A strong parametricism would not conflate architecture and politics; it would see both of them as algorithmic design problems.

Benjamin H. Bratton, "Parametricist Architecture Would Be a Good Idea", Matthew Poole and Manuel Schvatzberg (eds.), *The Politics of Parametricism in Architecture* (London: Bloomsbury Academic, 2015): 79–93.

In the final excerpt in this chapter, Michael Batty, in his book *Cities and Complexity: Understanding Cities with Cellular Automata, Agent-based Models, and Fractals* (2005), systematically studies the actions of individuals, understood and modelled as agents in a simulation space.[6] Batty introduces two primary modeling techniques: Cellular Automata (CA) and Agent-based Models (ABM). The behavior of CA involves grid-based cells that evolve using uniform rules based on neighbouring cell states, while Agent-Based Models (ABM) use individual agents with potentially heterogeneous rules, which can interact and move in diverse environments. CAs typically have simpler, local interactions, while ABMs allow for more complex behaviors and interactions among agents. These can simulate emergent behavior, or in the words of Batty, "the kinds of dynamics that characterize the growth of cities."[7]

In the introduction of this book, he also reflects on his understanding of Jane Jacobs' seminal work, *The Death and Life of Great American Cities* (1961).[8] Initially, Batty and his peers interpreted Jacobs's concerns as stemming from the threats to urban life due to unchecked suburban growth and the shift towards automobile usage over public transport. However, Batty now perceives a deeper message in Jacobs' writing, emphasizing the "organised complexity" inherent in cities. Jacobs portrayed cities as epitomes of organized complexity, entities where multiple variables interact in intricate, interconnected manners.

Through simulation computing, Batty has argued for the patterns of urban growth as having self-organized, self-similar fractal qualities. In cities, he sees a multi-scalar order, both large and small, coarse and fine. However, he limits the application of his work to "analogies as to how cities develop and evolve," rather than as tools intended for use in designing cities.[9]

MICHAEL BATTY
Cities and Complexity:
Understanding Cities with Cellular Automata, Agent-based Models, and Fractals

Cities happen to be problems in organized complexity, like the life sciences. They present situations in which half a dozen or several dozen quantities are all varying simultaneously and in subtly interconnected ways . . . The variables are many but they are not helter skelter; they are 'interelated into an organic whole.'

– **Jane Jacobs**, *The Death and Life of Great American Cities* (1961)

It is just short of forty years since I sat on a beach in southern Crete and read Jane Jacob's seminal work, *The Death and Life of Great American Cities*. But the message that I took from her book then was very different from what I read in her words now. Then, my main concern, and that of the generation of undergraduate students of architecture and planning of which I was a part, was her message that the quality of urban life – the "livability" of cities – was being split asunder by uncontrolled suburban growth, the rise of the automobile, and the demise of public transport. Cities were being slowly strangled by growth, a victim of their own success, and it was Jane Jacobs who was the foremost advocate of the need to do something about it, to act quickly. Her book provided, so we thought, broad support for the ideology of planning; but to my generation, this meant top-down, centralized planning, associated with the kinds of socialist societies that had emerged in the first half of the twentieth century, particularly in Europe.

This association was not entirely inconsistent with her thesis, but now we must read her message quite differently. Indeed, what she advocates in her Jane Jacobs was the first to propose that these "problems of organized complexity" included cities-indeed that the city was the example *par excellence* of organized complexity.

It did not take long for those involved in urban science to realize that theory without dynamics could do little more than provide a descriptive explanation of how various economic and social forces "could" work themselves out, given sufficient time. Such theory dealt with aggregate patterns and attempted an explanation using variables at an equivalent level. The level of abstraction in and of itself was a hindrance to progress, although the lack of data at anything but the aggregate tended to reinforce this paradigm. But since the mid-1960s, there has been a sea change in many of the factors that led to this conditioning. First and foremost, a little reflection shows that cities are far-from-equilibrium, as indeed are all human systems. Approximating a system as if it is in equilibrium might be acceptable if there is little or no change; but in the case of cities, this is very wide of the mark. Globalization, the ability to live anywhere given enough access to resources, and the increasingly footloose nature of economic activity have all conspired to impress on us that cities are always out of equilibrium. The challenge is to dig below the surface and detect the processes that generate what we see . . .

. . . The processing problem for urban systems models has changed out of all recognition in the last forty years. Until the mid-1980s, urban models were avid consumers of computer power, owing to their spatial extensiveness, which often extended to potential interactions between spatial units. Modern computing is now sufficiently powerful to deal with most models of this genre, and it has finally become possible to consider models that deal with a much larger number of units by disaggregating space, time, and the typology of activities and groups who locate in cities. In short, models based on individuals are now feasible both in terms of their computation and their representation using new programming languages. Data against which to calibrate these types of model are rapidly becoming available as more of society comes online and as much information is routinely recorded digitally, both directly and remotely. There is now the prospect that such models might be fitted against data and that the processes they embrace will genuinely capture the way spatial structures actually form, emerge, and develop . . .

The Essential Themes

. . . Our exposition here is as much about ideas based on models and systems as it is about applications to cities, and in this sense, it is a work in progress. In essence, the key theme that dominates all subsequent chapters is the notion that cities in particular and urban development in general emerge from the bottom up and that the spatial order we see in patterns at more aggregate scales can be explained only in this way. The way we simulate such emergence is by representing the basic elements or atoms of the city in two distinct but related ways: through *cells*, which represent the physical and spatial structure of the city, and through *agents*, which represent the human and social units that make the city work.

Our simplest models of the city compare locations containing activity, which are cells where change takes place based on actions that influence the cells' nearest neighbors. These make up cellular automata (CA) whose local action generates spatial order at more global scales. These structures are able to simulate the kinds of dynamics that characterize the growth of cities through spatial diffusion in the manner of epidemics, where activities influence only those next to or adjacent to them. Cells are fixed, and the simplest models, which we explore in the first chapters of this book, are based on simulating urban dynamics through the local actions of automata. Agents, however, are mobile and move between locations, and the models that these generate treat such locations as cells into which physical characteristics of the environment are encoded. In this sense, agents can be thought of as mobile cells. Here, however, we mainly characterize our agents as individuals, although in many treatments in the social sciences, such agents are used to represent agencies and institutions. In some contexts, however, they can be used to represent movable physical but nonhuman objects. We introduce such agent-based models or systems (ABS), sometimes referred to as multiagent models or systems (MAS), as developments of CA in the middle chapters of the book; applications of all these models to specific urban situations are developed in the later chapters. Ideas about how cells and agents represent cities, however, infuse all our discussion; urban examples and applications are presented in every chapter.

We begin our treatment dealing with basic ideas about urban change using cellular automata to illustrate how form and pattern emerge from relatively simple kinds of local dynamics. We map out the rudiments of CA in the first four chapters, showing how automata can be used to simulate urban growth and change that give rise to many kinds of real and ideal pattern. Ideas about agents are introduced in the middle four chapters of the book. We show how agents communicate with their environment and generate the sorts of feedback that represent the key to how growth occurs and patterns emerge, how novelty and surprise are built from the bottom up. Our models here relate to many scales – large and small, coarse and fine, where we begin by simulating movement at the scale of the street and conclude with models that show how individual behavior can be used to simulate patterns and structure at the scale of the urban region.

In fact, the development of cellular- and then agent-based models in the first eight chapters follows the historical evolution of these ideas in general. The last three chapters, however, apply these ideas specifically to cities, building mainly on cellular automata models-first reflecting ideas about diffusion and spatial epidemics, then ideas about dynamics. In this last part of the book, we return to the themes in the early chapters introducing concepts of criticality, threshold, surprise, novelty, and phase transition in the context of spatial development. These ideas are finally synthesized through order in urban morphology, which reflects notions of local action and global pattern through self-similarity and fractal geometry.

Four themes are woven throughout the models we develop. These indicate a concern for: dynamics that generate both continuous and discontinuous change; random processes that, when constrained by geometry, lead to explicit patterns and ordered forms; a range of spatial processes from one-off spatial events to recurring routine urban development across many spatial scales; and the effects of local repetitive actions that build up through feedback to create structures with global organization. Much of the dynamics we will articulate involve processes that generate surprise and novelty and are expressed in the language of phase transition, dependence on initial conditions, and far-from-equilibrium states. Diffusion and positive feedback are essential constituents of these processes, which give rise to both growing and declining structures. The baseline for change is often random, but when utility and human intention are added to such processes with geometry constraining the way they operate in space, highly ordered structures can emerge.

Generally these kinds of processes apply to aggregate urban development, but smaller-scale, one-off events occurring on diurnal rather than weekly or yearly cycles can also be handled using these ideas. Local action is central to all these notions in that the processes that underlie various models presented here operate from the bottom up, producing more aggregate spatial order as a result of such local operations. The focus of our concern will also vary with respect to different models. In the case of the CA models presented early in the book, local actions and diffusion are the key elements, whereas once we move to agent-based models, the focus shifts to more one-off events where geometry and randomness are central to the way we articulate movement in cities.

Michael Batty, "Introduction: Understanding Cities" *Cities and Complexity: Understanding Cities with Cellular Automata, Agent-based Models, and Fractals* (Cambridge, MA: MIT Press, 2005): 3–14.

This chapter explores how the introduction of computational methods and media has allowed architects and urban designers to engage with cities in new ways, reconceiving them as complex, evolutionary, and dynamic systems. Thinkers such as Gordon Pask developed core concepts from cybernetics regarding feedback loops and self-organization into the realm of planning and architecture. Pask and Batty argued that cities can be understood as adaptive, evolving entities which computational techniques can help simulate and understand. Building on these notions, Julia and John Frazer conceived of architecture and cities as artificial lifeforms with the capacity to evolve over time, proposing the use of genetic algorithms and code scripts to accelerate the generation and testing of design variations.

Tom Verebes highlighted how masterplans and static visions fail to embrace the inherent uncertainty and bottom-up change constantly shaping cities, urging planners to instead apply computational design towards the modeling of emergent behaviors found in nature and urban environments. Patrik Schumacher introduced the design theory of parametricism to describe the application of computational tools for producing organizational variation and differentiation in architectural and urban design systems. Proponents of parametricism argue that it represents a new modern style that can address the complexities and variegated demands of contemporary society. Critics, however, point out its potential over-reliance on technology, its pre-conceptions of spaces, and its tendency to emphasize form over function. Benjamin Bratton also critiqued parametric urbanism's apolitical nature and lack of engagement with planetary-scale systems, calling instead for a "universal parametricism" that situates architecture within larger technical, social, political, and ecological contexts. Overall, the chapter traces how concepts and techniques adapted from the computational realm have empowered designers to engage with cities using iterative, adaptive, and data-rich systems.

9

Virtuality, Extended Realities, and the Metaverse

Architecture and the visual arts have long histories with creating illusory spatial, visual and cognitive effects. In the Baroque era, artists created *trompe l'oeil* effects in two dimensions to deceive the eye into perceiving three-dimensional spaces. Drawing an arc through history reveals a transformation from illusory effects of images towards immersive experiences of increasingly virtual spaces, as summarized in Olivier Grau's book, *Virtual Art: From Illusion to Immersion* (2003).[1]

Over half a century ago, the urban designer Kevin Lynch, in his seminal book *The Image of the City* (1960),[2] emphasized the significance of understanding and enhancing a city's "image"—the collective mental representation of a physical place. Today, social media platforms, digital communication, and extended realities summon forth a plethora of competing images of cities, creating an increasingly saturated and immersive contemporary experience. From the hyper-stimulated landscapes of Tokyo's Shibuya and New York's Times Square, illuminated by structures entirely clad in ever-changing LED displays, to the augmented realities of games like Pokémon GO, which overlay virtual creatures via smartphones into our physical world, we are thrust into a realm where the line between the real and virtual has been blurred.

With continued technological progress, it becomes increasingly difficult to distinguish between classifications of the "digital" and "non-digital". Philosopher Jean Baudrillard recognizes a societal "hyperreality," where distinguishing between the "real" and the "virtual" becomes increasingly difficult. Key to understanding our present moment, he claims, in which we are inundated with a relentless stream of images, lies the notion of the simulacrum — a representation so hyper-realistic that it becomes preferable to reality itself. To elucidate this concept, Baudrillard, in his book *Simulacra and Simulation* (1984), draws upon a fable by Jorge Luis Borges, in which cartographers create a map so detailed that it covers the entire territory.[3] But where in Borges' story the map frays, Baudrillard inverts the story by suggesting the territory slowly rots away, as a metaphor for today's world, where the map is starting to precede the territory.

Furthermore, the emerging technological capacities of machine learning and the Internet of Things (IoT) have spawned "digital twins" or "mirror worlds"—virtual replicas of buildings and entire cities. These digital doppelgangers leverage real-time data from sensors embedded in urban and architectural spaces, monitoring variables like air quality and human activity. Artificial intelligence algorithms then conduct thousands of simulations in these virtual mirror worlds with the intent of optimizing real-world conditions. These technologies are primarily driven by the goals

FIGURE 9.1 After dusk, Shinjuku, a bustling entertainment hub, comes alive with its buildings featuring mesmerizing, immersive media displays, creating a futuristic urban landscape that defines modern Tokyo. Courtesy of Getty Images.

of safety, security and comfort, with the underlying assumption of greater efficiency, personalization, and profits. The abundance of large data sets, the by-products of data generation, and the rapid progress in internet bandwidth and computational processing capabilities collectively influence the image, form, and performance of our built environment. What are the consequences of these new disruptive technologies for cities in the twenty-first century? How can architects and urban designers navigate these fast-paced transformations?

This chapter investigates three texts spanning the past fifty years, all focused on the extension of reality through technological devices, showcasing how humans experience and interact in actual and virtual spaces. In his book, *Soft Architecture Machines* (1975), Nicholas Negroponte outlines a speculative projection of how computers can aid designed environments to be more responsive with respect to user requirements, needs and desires.[4] Along with other researchers in the 1950s and 1960s, Negroponte's work on the impact of artificial intelligence, automation, robotics, and screen-based user interfaces for architectural design experienced a lull in the 1970s. Yet, this research area has resurfaced in more recent years, once computational power had caught up to the conceptual advancements made decades earlier. Mario Carpo gives an account of these historical shifts in priorities in the leading university research units in these arenas, in his book, *Beyond Digital: Design and Automation at the End of Modernity* (2023).[5]

Meanwhile, urban theorists such as Paul Virilio coined the concept of "media buildings," architectural structures dedicated to communicating visual information rather than solely serving their human inhabitants. Sylvia Lavin, in her book, *Kissing Architecture* (2011), narrates the emerging associations of architecture with other fields of media-based art, creating powerful visual effects and atmospheres, alongside the more prosaic applications of media screens to facades of commercial buildings.[6] Several theorists call upon designers to act as bridges connecting the physical and digital realms. They urge designers to grapple with the emergence of these extended realities and harness them for constructive purposes. This can involve technologies such as Building Information Modeling (BIM) adapted to City Information Modeling (CIM), and digital twins, to explore opportunities for creating and managing a more sustainable world and crafting artistic augmented realities that enrich our urban experiences.

In 1964, science fiction writer, Arthur C. Clarke was interviewed on the BBC's Horizons programme, and he predicted our current world of mobile telephony and its virtual, distributed potential:

> We could be in instant contact with each other, wherever we may be, where we can contact our friends anywhere on earth, even if we don't know their actual physical location. It will be possible in that age, perhaps only 50 years from now, for a man to conduct his business from Tahiti or Bali just as well as he could from London.[1]
>
> Arthur C. Clarke (1964)
>
> **1** Arthur C. Clarke, Interview in BBC *Horizons* television programme, 1964.

Since Clarke's prediction, technology has made giant leaps beyond the telephone. In the 1960s, the pioneering computer scientist Ivan Sutherland introduced the foundational concept of Virtual Reality (VR) with the creation of the first head-mounted display, setting the stage for immersive digital experiences.[7] The 1980s saw the embryonic emergence of VR, primarily within arcade games, providing glimpses into the future potential of interactive and simulated worlds.

The 2010s marked a transformative era with the advent of personal headsets, which became accessible to the mass market and shattered the barriers that once constrained the adoption of extended realities. In 2013, Oculus Rift's release brought high-quality VR experiences to consumers, sparking revolutions in various design fields. Concurrently, smartphones played a significant role by making Augmented Reality (AR) accessible to the public, as was seen in apps like Layar and Wikitude, further obfuscating the classifications of the real and the virtual.

In 2019, Microsoft's HoloLens 2 propelled the Extended Reality (XR) landscape forward by seamlessly blending AR and VR, pushing the boundaries of Mixed Reality (MR). These innovations have enabled virtual objects to coexist harmoniously with the physical world, revolutionizing industries such as construction and surveying, where workers can don HoloLens devices to project digital representations of projects, bypassing traditional printed drawings. As MR technology continues to evolve, it furthers the integration of digital elements into our real-world surroundings, effectively erasing the boundaries between the physical and the virtual.

Theorists have drawn from the concept of the "cyborg" to illustrate the impact of this digital transformation. Coined in 1960 by researchers Manfred Clynes and Nathan S. Kline, inspired by the works of science fiction luminaries Philip K. Dick and Arthur C. Clarke, the term "cyborg" denotes a fusion of cybernetics and organisms. Theorists such as architect and MIT Professor

FIGURE 9.2 A man wearing goggles interacts with virtual computer graphics on a large screen interface within a mixed reality environment. Courtesy of Getty Images.

William J Mitchell have employed this concept to describe the contemporary state of humans and their handheld mobile devices used as interfaces with which to navigate.

In his work, *The Cyborg Self and the Networked City* (2003), Mitchell delves into the transformative power of digital technologies in reshaping our cities and the way we experience them.[8] Mitchell's ideas highlight the ways in which these emerging technologies can enhance our understanding of urban spaces and catalyse novel forms of human-computer interaction within the urban context. He explores how traditional boundaries that once defined spaces are evolving as digital networks reshape our urban experiences. These networks have become integral to our daily lives, transcending physical barriers and forging interconnected global communities. Mitchell's position resonates the concept of the disappearance of physical space as a result of technology and the media, articulated by Paul Virilio in his books, *The Aesthetics of Disappearance* (1980), and *Lost Dimension* (1983).[9]

This paradigm shift highlights the importance of considering the interplay between the physical and digital realms when assessing the impact of AR, MR, and VR on architecture and urbanism, as these technologies continue to integrate with human experience. Mitchell's work encourages architects and urban planners to embrace these technologies as tools for creating more responsive and adaptable urban environments, echoing and evolving Negroponte's notions in *Soft Architecture Machines* (1975).

For Mitchell, extended "constructed systems of boundaries and networks" surround our biological core, in which our own skin is "just layer zero of a nested boundary structure." These are electronic boundaries, such as radar curtains, or missile shields on a planetary scale. This shift from enclosures to networks captures the most common ideogram of the organization and behavior of cities. Mitchell sees the intricate diagrams of internet connectivity as "the most vivid icon of globalisation," akin to earlier diagrams, such as the underground network map of London, or the freeway map of Los Angeles. He asserts how "connectivity had become the defining characteristic of our twenty-first-century urban condition." As a consequence, Mitchell claims, "extension and entanglement trump enclosure and autonomy." Lastly, he argues how networks have reshaped all sectors, including "energy, transportation, finance and banking, telecommunications, public health, emergency services, water, chemical, defence industry base, food, agriculture, and postal and shipping."

WILLIAM J. MITCHELL
Me++: The Cyborg Self and the Networked City

BOUNDARIES/NETWORKS

Consider, if you will, Me++.

I consist of a biological core surrounded by extended, constructed systems of boundaries and networks. These boundary and network structures are topological and functional duals of each other.[1] The boundaries define a space of containers and places (the traditional domain of architecture), while the networks establish a space of links and flows. Walls, fences, and skins divide; paths, pipes, and wires connect.

BOUNDARIES

My natural skin is just layer zero of a nested boundary structure. When I shave, I coat my face with lather. When I'm nearly naked in the open air, I wear—at the very least—a second skin of spf 15 sunblock.

My clothing is a layer of soft architecture, shrinkwrapped around the contours of my body. Beds, rugs, and curtains are looser assemblages of surrounding fabric—somewhere between underwear and walls. My room is a sloughed-off carapace, cast into a more rigorous geometry, fixed in place, and enlarged in scale so that it encloses me at a comfortable distance. The building that contains it has a weatherproof exterior shell. Before modern mobile artillery, fortified city walls would have provided a final, hardened, outermost crust; these sorts of urban-scale skins remained reasonably effective at least until the 1871 siege of Paris, during the Franco-Prussian War.[2]

In the early years of the Cold War, outer defensive encasements reemerged, in extreme form, as domestic nuclear bunkers. The destruction of the Berlin Wall in 1989 marked the end of that edgy era. But still, if I end up in jail, an internment camp, or a walled retirement community, the distinction between intramural and extramural remains brutally literal. If I retire to a farm, a boundary fence stops my stock from straying. And if I locate myself within the homeland of a major military power, I take refuge behind a dubious high-tech bulwark that extends across thousands of kilometers; our extradermal armored layers have coevolved, with increasingly fearsome weapons systems, into invisible radar curtains and missile shields that create vast electronic enceintes. I surround myself with successive artificial skins that continually vary in number and character according to my changing needs and circumstances.[3]

All of my boundaries depend, for their effectiveness, upon combining sufficient capacity to attenuate flow with sufficient thickness. If I want to keep warm, for example, I can use a thin layer of highly insulating material or a thicker layer of a less effective insulator. If I want acoustic privacy, I can retreat behind a closed door, or I can simply rely on the attenuation of sound waves in air and move out of earshot. If I want to create a jail, I can construct escape-proof walls, or I can remove the prisoners to a sufficiently distant place—like the eighteenth-century British convicts transported to Australia. In sparsely populated territories, distance creates many natural barriers, while in buildings and cities, efficient artificial barriers subdivide closely packed spaces.

CONNECTIONS

But I am, as Georg Simmel observed, a "connecting creature who must always separate and who cannot connect without separating."[4] My enclosures are leaky. Crossing the various boundaries that surround me there are paths, pipes, wires, and other channels that spatially concentrate inflows and outflows of people, other living creatures, discrete goods, gases and fluids, energy, information, and money. I am inextricably entangled in the networks of my air, water, waste disposal, energy, transportation, and Internet service providers.

To create and maintain differences between the interiors and exteriors of enclosures—and there is no point to boundaries and enclosures if there are no differences—I seek to control these networked flows. So the crossing points are sites where I can survey what's coming and going, make access decisions, filter out what I don't want to admit or release, express desire, exercise power, and define otherness. Directly and indirectly, I employ doors, windows, bug screens, gates, cattle grids, adjustable apertures, valves, filters, prophylactics, diapers, face masks, receptionists, security checkpoints, customs and immigration checkpoints, traffic signals, routers and switches to determine who or what can go where, and when they can go there. So do you, of course, and so do others with the capacity to do so in particular contexts.

Through the interaction of our efforts to effect and control transfers among enclosures and our competition for network resources, we mutually construct and constrain one another's realms of daily action. Within the relatively stable framework of our interconnecting, overlapping, sometimes shared transfer networks, our intricately interwoven demands and responses create fluctuating conditions of freedom and constraint. And as networks become faster, more pervasive, and more essential, these dynamics become increasingly crucial to the conduct of our lives; we have all discovered that a traffic jam, a checkin line, a power outage, a server overwhelmed by a denial-of-service attack, or a market crash can create as effective a barrier as a locked door. The more we depend upon networks, the more tightly and dynamically interwoven our destinies become.

NETWORKS

The archetypal structure of the network, with its accumulation and habitation sites, links, dynamic flow patterns, interdependencies, and control points, is now repeated at every scale from that of neural networks (neurons, axons, synapses) and digital circuitry (registers, electron pathways, switches) to that of global transportation networks (warehouses, shipping and air routes, ports of entry).[5] And networks of different types and scales are integrated into larger network complexes serving multiple functions. Depending upon our relationships to the associated social and political structures, each of us can potentially play many different roles (some strong, some weak) at nodes within these complexes—owner, authorized user, operator, occupant, occupier, tenant, customer, guest, sojourner, tourist, immigrant, alien, interloper, infiltrator, trespasser, snooper, besieger, cracker, hijacker, invader, gatekeeper, jailer, or prisoner. Power and political identity have become inseparable from these roles.

With the proliferation of networks and our increasing dependence upon them, there has been a gradual inversion of the relationship between barriers and links. As the ancient use of a circle of walls to serve as the ideogram for a city illustrates, the enclosing, dividing, and sometimes-defended *boundary* was once the decisive mechanism of political geography. Joshua got access the old-fashioned way; when he blew his righteous trumpet, the walls of Jericho came tumbling down. By the mid-twentieth century, though, the most memorable ideogram of London was its underground network, and that of Los Angeles was its freeway map; riding the networks, not dwelling within walls, was what made you a Londoner or an Angeleno. And the story of recent urban growth has not been one of successive encircling walls, as it mostly would have been for ancient, medieval, and Renaissance cities, but of network-induced sprawl at the fringes.

More recently, the unbelievably intricate diagram of Internet interconnectivity has become the most vivid icon of globalization. Now you get access by typing in your password, and IT managers dissolve the perimeters between organizations by merging their network access authorization lists. Today the *network*, rather than the enclosure, is emerging as the desired and contested object: the dual now dominates.[6] Extension and entanglement trump enclosure and autonomy. Control of territory means little unless you also control the channel capacity and access points that service it.

A year after the September 11 attacks on New York and Washington, the implications of this were sinking in. The President's Critical Infrastructure Protection Board bluntly reported (to nobody's very great surprise),

Our economy and national security are fully dependent upon information technology and the information infrastructure. A network of networks directly supports the operation of all sectors of our economy—energy (electric power, oil and gas), transportation (rail, air, merchant marine), finance and banking, information and telecommunications, public health, emergency services, water, chemical, defense industrial base, food, agriculture, and postal and shipping. The reach of these computer networks exceeds the bounds of cyberspace. They also control physical objects such as electrical transformers, trains, pipeline pumps, chemical vats, radars, and stock markets.[7]

Connectivity had become the defining characteristic of our twenty-first-century urban condition.

. . .

. . . DISCONTINUITIES

In the fast-paced, digitally mediated world that we have constructed for ourselves, what exists between 0 and 1, a pixel and its neighbor, or a discrete time interval and the next? The answer, of course, is nothing—profoundly nothing; there's no there there. The digital world is logically, spatially, and temporally discontinuous.

Our networks are similarly discontinuous structures; they have well-defined access points, and between these points things are in a kind of limbo. If you drop a letter into a mailbox, it disappears into the mail network until it shows up at the recipient's box, and if you send an email, it's just packets in the Internet cloud until it is reassembled upon receipt. Obviously it is possible, in principle, to precisely track things through networks, but in practice we rarely care about this. We experience networks at their interfaces, and only worry about the plumbing behind the interfaces when something goes wrong.

If you transfer *yourself* through a network, you directly experience this limbo. It is, perhaps, most dramatic on intercontinental night flights. You have your headphones on, there is darkness all around, and there is no sensation of motion. The video monitor constructs a local reality, and occasionally interrupts it to display current times at origin and destination. It is best not to worry too much about how to set your watch right now, precisely where you are, or whose laws might apply to you.

The discontinuities produced by networks result from the drive for efficiency, safety, and security. Engineers want to limit the number of access points and provide fast, uninterrupted transfers among these points. So you can drink from a stream anywhere along its length, but you can only access piped water at a faucet. You can pause wherever you want when you're strolling along a dirt track, but you must use stations for trains, entry and exit ramps for freeways, and airports for airline networks—and your experience of the terrain between these points is very limited. You experience the architectural transitions between floors of a building when you climb the stairs, but you go into architectural limbo between the opening and closing of the doors when you use the elevator.

. . .

. . . COMMUNITIES

Sociologists would use more technical language to make much the same point as Moore's. They would say that I—like most urbanites today—get companionship, aid, support, and social control from a few strong social ties and many weak ones.[8] These ties, which might manifest themselves, for example, as the entries in my cellphone and email directories, establish social networks. In the past, such networks would mostly have been maintained by face-to-face contact within a contiguous locality—a compact, place-based community.[9] Today, they are maintained through a complex mix of local face-to-face interactions, travel, mail systems, synchronous electronic contact through telephones and video links, and asynchronous electronic contact through email and similar media.[10] They are far less dense, and they extend around the world, coming to earth at multiple, scattered, and unstable locations.[11] As Barry Wellman has crisply summarized, "People in networked societies live and work in multiple sets of overlapping relationships, cycling among different networks. Many of the people and the related social networks they deal with are sparsely knit, or physically dispersed and do not know one another."[12]

In the years since Moore wrote, our physical habitats have grown more fragmented and dispersed as transportation networks have extended further and operated faster. Simultaneously, the electronic glue has grown much stronger; it now includes voice, video, and data channels, broadcast and point-to-point links, place-to-place and person-to-person communication, the fixed infrastructure of the bank ATM system, the sleek portable equipment of the corporate road warrior jetting between global cities, and the cheap phone card of the migrant worker.

Wherever I currently happen to find myself, I can now discover many of the same channels on a nearby television, I can access the same bank account, and I can chat with the same people on my cellphone. I can download my email and send replies almost completely independently of location. And my online world, which once consisted of ephemeral and disconnected fragments, has become increasingly persistent, interconnected, and unified; it's there again, pretty much as I left it, whenever I log in again from a new location. The constants in my world are no longer provided by a contiguous home turf: increasingly, my sense of continuity and belonging derives from being electronically networked to the widely scattered people and places I care about.

1   The duality of enclosures and networks is more than just a metaphor; it is a basic fact of graph theory—the mathematical study of network structure. Consider a floor plan as a planar graph in which corners are nodes and walls are links. Construct the adjacency graph of the plan by locating a node within every enclosed room, plus the exterior zone, then representing room-to-room and room-to-exterior adjacencies by links. The adjacency graph is the dual of the floor plan graph, and vice versa. The circulation network, created by doorways through walls, is a subgraph of the adjacency graph. For more detailed, rigorous development of this point, see Lionel March and Christopher F. Earl, "Architectural Applications of Graph Theory," in Robin J. Wilson and Lowell W. Beineke, eds., *Applications of Graph Theory* (London: Academic Press, 1979), pp. 327–56.
2   The decline of the city wall is often dated from 1494, when Charles VIII of France first deployed horse-drawn artillery pieces in his invasion of northern Italy.
3   Gottfried Semper noticed that the German word for "garment" (*Gewand*) is very closely related to the word for "partition" (*Wand*). He developed an elaborate theory of the relationships among walls, textiles, and clothing in his two great theoretical works, *The Four Elements of Architecture* (1851) and *Style in the Technical and Tectonic Arts, or Practical Aesthetics* (1860–63). (See Harry Francis Mallgrave, *Gottfried Semper: Architect of the Nineteenth Century* [New Haven: Yale University Press, 1996.]) In his essay "Housing: New Look and New Outlook," in *Understanding Media: The Extensions of Man* (New York: McGraw-Hill, 1964), p. 123, Marshall McLuhan repackaged the point: "Clothing and housing, as extensions of the skin and heat-control mechanisms, are media of communication, first of all, in the sense that they shape and rearrange the patterns of human association and community." More recently, Vito Acconci has produced a series of provocative works exploring his contention that "First there is skin and bones, then clothing, then a chair and then hou*sing.*" See Sarah Boxer, "*Poet Turned Antic Architect Keeps Exploring Inner Space*," New York Times, 12 September 2002, pp. F1, F5. And the discourse continues with Claudia Benthien, *Skin* (New York: Columbia University Press, 2002), and Ellen Lupton, Jennifer Tobias, Alicia Imperiale, Grace Jeffers, and Randi Mates, Skin (New York: Princeton Architectural Press, 2002).
4   Georg Simmel, "Bridge and Door," trans. Mark Ritter, *Theory, Culture, and Society* 11 (1994): 5–10.
5   For discussions of the pervasiveness of networks, see Albert-László Barabási, *Linked: The New Science of Networks* (Cambridge, Mass.: Perseus, 2002), and Mark Buchanan, *Nexus: Small Worlds and the Groundbreaking Science of Networks* (New York: Norton, 2002).
6   In *The Production of Space* (1974; English trans., Cambridge, Mass.: Blackwell, 1991), p. 38, Henri Lefebvre argued, "The spatial practice of a society secretes that society's space; it propounds and presupposes it, in a dialectical interaction; it produces it slowly and surely as it masters and appropriates it." Lefebvre's analysis is extraordinarily suggestive, but it shows little curiosity about the specific technologies of spatial production and even less about the effects of changes in those technologies. In *The Informational City: Information Technology, Economic Restructuring, and the Urban-Regional Process* (Cambridge, Mass.: Blackwell, 1989), p. 6, Manuel Castells extended Lefebvre's argument by identifying "the emergence of a space of

flows which dominates the historically constructed space of places, as the logic of dominant organizations detaches itself from the social constraints of cultural identities and local societies through the powerful medium of information technologies." In *Empire* (Cambridge: Harvard University Press, 2000), Michael Hardt and Antonio Negri proposed that the "irresistible and irreversible globalization of economic and cultural exchanges" had produced "a decentered and deterritorializing apparatus of rule that progressively incorporates the entire global realm," and "manages hybrid identities, flexible hierarchies, and plural exchanges through modulating networks of command." In this volume I shall be particularly concerned with the technological infrastructure of the global space of flows, the secretion of spatial patterns by means of that infrastructure, and the specific changes that are resulting from the development of a pervasive, wireless computation and telecommunication infrastructure.

7 President's Critical Infrastructure Protection Board, *The National Strategy to Secure Cyberspace,* draft, September 2002, <www.whitehouse.gov/pcipb/cyberstrategy-draft.pdf> (accessed December 2002), p. 3.
8 Mark Granovetter, "The Strength of Weak Ties," *American Journal of Sociology* 78 (1973): 1360–80.
9 Traditional, place-based communities were described, in many cases idealized, and contrasted with life in the big city in some of the landmark works of sociology. See, in particular, Emile Durkheim, *The Division of Labor in Society* (1893; New York: Free Press, 1964), Ferdinand Tönnies, *Community and Society* (1887; East Lansing: Michigan State University Press, 1957), and Louis Wirth, "Urbanism as a Way of Life," *American Journal of Sociology* 44 (1938): 3–24.
10 Barry Wellman, *Networks in the Global Village* (Boulder Colo: Westview Press, 1999).
11 There is a growing empirical literature on the role of electronic interconnections in sustaining (or weakening) social networks. See, for example, Keith Hampton, "Living the Wired Life in the Wired Suburb" (Ph.D. diss., University of Toronto, 2001); Philip E. Howard, Lee Rainie, and Steve Jones, "Days and Nights on the Internet: The Impact of a Diffusing Technology," American Behavioral Scientist 45, no. 3 (2001): 383–404; Robert Kraut, Vicki Lundmark, Sara Kiesler, Tridas Mukopadhyay, and William Scherlis, "Internet Paradox: A Social Technology That Reduces Social Involvement and Psychological Well-Being," *American Psychologist* 53, no. 9 (1998): 1017–31; and Norman Nie, "Sociability, Interpersonal Relations, and the Internet: Reconciling Conflicting Findings," *American Behavioral Scientist* 45, no. 3 (2001): 420–35.
12 Barry Wellman, "Designing the Internet for a Networked Society," *Communications of the ACM* 45, no. 5 (May 2002): 91–96.

William J. Mitchell, "Boundaries / Networks", *Me++: The Cyborg Self and the Networked City* (Cambridge, MA: MIT Press, 2003): 7–15.

In today's world, the pervasive integration of sensors into the built environment can significantly augment human capabilities and awareness. The history of sensors in urban settings can be traced back to the early nineteenth century, when cities began installing gas lamps and water pumps equipped with rudimentary sensors. These sensors were deployed not only to monitor the functioning of utilities but also to ensure their safety and efficiency. Norbert Wiener, in his book, *Cybernetics: Or Control and Communication in the Animal and the Machine* (1948), was one of the first to articulate the theoretical and technical basis of the control of complex systems.[10] Subsequently, during the twentieth century, urban centers expanded their sensor usage to encompass more complex monitoring systems, including traffic lights and air quality monitoring stations. Second-order cybernetics, championed by Gilbert Simendon, emphasized the inclusion of the observer into the control systems, focusing on interactivity as a key element in managing dynamic systems' behavior.[11] More contemporaneously, Peter Trummer's book, *The City as a Technical Being: One the Mode of Existence of Architecture* (2023), rereads Gilbert Simendon's theories and applies them to the city.[12] Trummer's thesis on the city conceives of an urbanism with capacities to automatically generate its spaces and material order.

In the late twentieth and early twenty-first centuries, we have witnessed an explosive surge in augmenting sensor deployment within cities. Several factors have contributed to this phenomenon, including advancements in sensor technologies, a reduction in sensor costs, and the widespread availability of high-speed data networks. The advent of the Internet of Things (IoT) has ushered in a paradigm shift characterised by data-driven urbanization, enabling real-time data collection and analysis. This wealth of data has provided urban planners with the tools to make informed decisions, optimize transportation networks, manage resources efficiently, and even engage the public in the governance of urban spaces. However, this sensor-driven urban transformation also raises critical concerns regarding data privacy, security, and equity, prompting cities to strike a delicate balance between harnessing the benefits of sensor technology and safeguarding individual rights and freedoms.

Carlo Ratti, a visionary architect and the director of MIT's Senseable City Lab, has focused on improving our understanding of cities through sensors. Ratti is renowned for his research and innovative projects that explore the concept of the "Senseable City." Central to his work is the exploitation of data generated by cities to gain insights into urban dynamics and enhance the quality of urban life. His lab has been at the forefront of uncovering the potential of real-time data, sensors, and digital connectivity in creating smarter, more responsive, and more efficient urban environments.

One of Ratti's notable concepts is "urban data mining." For instance, his "Trash Track" project involved equipping discarded items with location-tracking devices, effectively tracing their journey from bins to landfills. The project aimed to illuminate inefficiencies in waste management and explore avenues for optimizing urban sanitation systems. This innovative approach to data collection and analysis not only enhances our understanding of urban processes but also provides practical solutions for building more sustainable and efficient cities. In this context, Augmented Reality (AR), Mixed Reality (MR), and Virtual Reality (VR) serve as interfaces for citizens to engage with and interpret the data-rich urban environments envisioned by Ratti's work.

In their book, *The City of Tomorrow: Sensors, Networks, Hackers, and the Future of Urban Life* (2016), Ratti and Claudel highlight the profound impact of data collection, aggregation, and dissemination on urban experiences. With the proliferation of digital technologies, ubiquitous smartphones, and an array of sensors, cities have evolved into data-rich environments where every action and interaction generates valuable information. The book emphasizes the transition from centralized data collection to bottom-up data aggregation, where individuals willingly contribute to a collective pool of knowledge via smartphones. This transformation not only empowers individuals to understand and enhance their lives within the city but also presents opportunities for urban planners and designers to create more responsive and efficient urban environments.

Similar to Mitchell's perspective, Ratti and Claudel allude to a "posthuman" condition, with people born "into a world of converged digital and material, where each individual's mental and social existence is enabled, sustained, and improved by technologies."[13] Facilitated by smartphones, individuals can "multiply the self to a conceivably infinite degree. The prosthetic smartphone has deeply permeated society along the backbone of wireless telecommunications, giving rise to a new networked humanism."

The following excerpt opens with a quote by the author, Italo Calvino, regarding an "archive of the human mind" containing virtually all of humanity's information. Ratti and Claudel liken Calvino's narrative to the current proliferation and accessibility of data, in which almost all of human activity is recorded and archived. Their focus is on "data by-products," data which is generated for a specific purpose, but then used in a different context, for another reason. They discuss various types of datasets, including data mined from consumer behaviors, telecommunications, transport, weather, shipping, and social media. This data, Ratti and Claudel claim, creates "a multidimensional portrait of cities and their patterns."[14] In this light, urban citizens leave behind "smart dust," ubiquitously generating vast data through their digital footprints. Individuals, according to Ratti and Claudel act as "agents of data collection" by unintentionally creating masses of data. At the scale of urban populations, this allows for a vast logging of valuable information. Ratti and Claudel observe a shift towards greater willingness of individuals to share information.

Nevertheless, it is crucial to acknowledge that these technological capacities are not universally considered beneficial. Researcher Stephen Graham raises concerns about stark "urban digital divides."[15] He highlights significant disparities in the adoption and access to information and communications technologies (ICT). In certain urban areas, highly connected clusters contrast starkly with large populations lacking even basic ICT access. These trends exacerbate social and geographic inequalities within and between cities, spanning both developed and developing regions globally.

Furthermore, researcher Shannon Mattern warns that while computational models of urbanism offer the promise of heightened efficiencies and conveniences, they also carry the risk

FIGURE 9.3 The CityScope Project by MIT Media Lab's City Science Group leverages a data-driven platform, visual projections and LEGO components to model the impacts of large-scale urban planning decisions in a highly interactive and innovative way, 2016. Courtesy of MIT Media Lab City Science Group.

of promoting a technocratic and utilitarian perspective in urban management. In her book, *A City is Not a Computer: Other Urban Intelligences* (2021),[16] Mattern asserts that cities are more than data grids; they are repositories of local and indigenous knowledge and biodiversity. The data-driven, computational reasoning championed by many municipalities and "smart city" advocates is restrictive in nature. This approach often aligns itself with the interests of capital and the elite, neglecting under-represented communities and the rich diversity of urban life. Mattern advocates for a more holistic and sustainable approach to urban planning and design that embraces these diverse dimensions of urban existence. See Chapter 10 for a more in-depth presentation and critique of the issues related to the Smart City.

CARLO RATTI AND MATTHEW CLAUDEL
The City of Tomorrow: Sensors, Networks, Hackers, and the Future of Urban Life

Not only have we already put the contents of the most important libraries of the world, and likewise the archives and museums and newspaper annals of every nation, on our punch cards, but also a great deal of documentation gathered ad hoc, person by person, place by place . . . What we are planning to build is a centralized archive of human kind."

Italo Calvino, 1968

Big (Urban) Data

In a short story, the Italian writer Italo Calvino imagined a society—a gently terminal dystopia—in which every detail and every moment is recorded for posterity.[1] All information would be compiled into the greatest document ever conceived, blending details of every individual life. The short story is problematized by intrigue and paradox surrounding information access, control, and deletion, and a final shocking twist puts an uncanny spotlight on the precipitous condition of absolute archiving. How will humanity remember itself? And how will it act when it knows that it is being recorded? These are prescient questions for a society that, today, is confronted with a similar situation of total recall.[2] Data are turning Calvino's fictional world into reality.

Consider every phone call, retail purchase, mile driven, mile run, Tweet, text, load of laundry that took place in the past twenty-four hours. Humans leave these kinds of virtual traces every second of every day, particularly in cities, and each is stored in a digital database. We are creating, archiving, and recalling digital copies of our world, forging a collective memory. "What would happen," Bill Gates once asked, "if we could instantly access all the information we were exposed to throughout our lives?"[3] It seems that, now, we can.

As digital technologies become increasingly pervasive (and networked online, as with the Internet of Things), every individual is generating a staggering amount of data, all of which are compounded across the entire population. Eric Schmidt, arguably one of the key individuals behind the big data revolution through his tenure at Google, noted that every two days humans create as much information as we did from the dawn of civilization up until 2003, approaching five exabytes of data (an exabyte is a quintillion— 10^{18} bytes).[4] As digital information is captured and stored, the virtual copy of our world becomes increasingly high-resolution.

Any dataset collected for a specific purpose has an array of potential data by-products. Working with this deluge of urban information is what researchers often call opportunistic sensing: using data that have been generated for a specific reason and analyzing them in a different context to arrive at new conclusions. Datasets are often enriched with many dimensions, and whether or not every one of those dimensions is intended to have an explicit use when it is created, every aspect of the data can subsequently be instrumentalized in unexpected and creative ways. Credit card transaction data, for example, include unique IDs for the vendor and the consumer. These tags allow researchers to filter the data by location and type of purchase (food, gas, clothing) to understand patterns of economic behavior in cities.[5] Analyses of telecommunications data and social media have proven them both to be powerful tools for understanding human networks and dynamics.

Datasets can be considered individually, but far greater insights lie at their intersection and superposition. Geographic space is a common denominator that allows them to be linked. Particularly now that different streams of information can be interwoven and connected, urban data may offer an ever-clearer view of the human condition. As early as 2006, researchers began compounding telecommunications with transportation data.[6] The aggregate urban portrait that emerged—specifically during such extraordinary events as the final match of the 2006 soccer World Cup in Rome—revealed collective behavior tied directly to the event. Before the game, movement and communication were frenzied, activity slowed almost to a stop during the match, spiked sharply at halftime, fell almost to zero during the tense final minutes, and exploded when the match was called. Communication traces during the following hours revealed mass movement into the downtown area to celebrate the national team's victory. Subsequent projects in cities with more readily accessible data, such as Singapore, have compounded even more datasets. Data from weather, shipping, social media, public transit, cell networks, and more flow together to create a multidimensional portrait of cities and their patterns.[7]

In addition to opportunistic sensing, data can also be generated by deploying an array of sensors with a specific intent. Embedding technology into the urban environment can yield robust and fine-grained data, whether to map an existing system, to reveal dynamics that have never been brought to light, or to gain a new understanding of humanity's fingerprint. On a macro scale, the Google Street View car, for example, has driven across the world photographing 360-degree panoramas. After its first five years of operation, the Street View team announced that the car had captured five million miles of road in thirty-nine countries, generating a staggering twenty petabytes of data—quadrillions of images.

As more and more of these digital elements are embedded in physical space, many other aspects of the urban environment can be revealed—for example, the waste disposal system . . . The Senseable City Lab began a project, TrashTrack, that addressed the scenario of ubiquitous tracking. Researchers created geolocating tags and worked with residents of Seattle to attach them to thousands of ordinary pieces of garbage—effectively creating an "Internet of trash"—to map the waste removal chain across the United States.[8] Over the following months, the devices revealed a surprising network that had been completely unknown before. In the future, an accelerating diffusion of technology into urban space may offer an unprecedented understanding of systems like waste management dynamics and may create data that can be used to optimize the entire system, even in real time . . .

. . . The trend points toward a phenomenon that has been termed "smart dust." Physical space could be laced ubiquitously with nanosensors—scattered micro devices that are smaller than grains of rice. "Large-scale networks of wireless sensors are becoming an active topic of research. Advances in hardware technology and engineering design have led to dramatic reductions in size, power consumption and cost . . . This has enabled very compact, autonomous and mobile nodes, each containing one or more sensors, computation and communication capabilities, and a power supply."[9]

A rich array of data will be available in a future scenario of ubiquitous smart dust. In the meanwhile, a pervasive network already exists in our cities today: citizens themselves. In some cases, collecting personal data is fully intentional. The computer scientist Gordon Bell was one of the first to explore the idea of individual data in a practical way—in 1998 he began a project called Your Life, Uploaded, making himself the subject of the first full-resolution experiment in so-called life-logging. Bell created the hardware and software to capture every moment and every action of his life through photos, computer activity, biometrics, and more. The technology was primitive, and in many ways disruptive, but the project was successful in cataloguing his existence for more than a decade. "The result?" he wrote. "An amazing enhancement of human experience from health and education to productivity and just reminiscing about good times. And then, when you are gone, your memories, your life will still be accessible for your grandchildren."[10] . . .

. . . What Bell initially set out to do as a full-scale scientific and sociological study is now the unconscious norm—the default condition—of an Internet generation. Our spatial and social activity is tracked and logged (in many cases, it requires more effort and determination to opt out of documentation than to engage in it). Tweets, Uber calls, text messaging, Yelp reviews, and check-ins are becoming the natural activities of daily living. A trove of information is flowing out of and through the population, and people are more and more interconnected. The bulk of the extraordinary (and growing) amount of data being created today is user-generated content, an almost constant stream of personal data.

There are many platforms for users to upload and share photos, for example, and underneath their straightforward functionality lies an enormous and rich dataset, including the GPS location, keywords, time, social networks, and popularity associated with each image. This trove can provide a deep understanding of how people interact with and in physical space as digital traces are mapped and overlaid—revealing, for example, the movement and activity of tourists. Using Flickr data, Senseable City Lab researchers mapped a crowd-generated cartography of Spain, showing how visitors and residents see and use their environment, identifying, among other things, hotspots, or "visual magnets."[11] Researchers could effectively borrow the eyes of the population in a continuing analysis, applying computer vision image-processing and color-matching to landscape photos. The user-generated photographic data began to reveal natural ecological conditions like drought and urban green spaces. This futurecraft scenario extrapolates from the perpetually expanding global knowledge base, the fabric of a digital blanket that covers and suffuses the cities we live in.

Anyone and everyone can put tiny chunks of data online—and we do, almost constantly, whether intentionally or unintentionally. Some incentive-based platforms give individuals a small monetary compensation for completing a single task that contributes to a greater collective effort, while other systems enable deliberate civic action through a more altruistic motivation. Numerous community-based smartphone applications automatically upload detailed information about road damage, traffic, and gas prices for the benefit of all drivers. Citizen contributors to the collaborative OpenStreetMap (particularly relevant in areas not yet graced by Google) draw roads and make the information publicly available. Many 311 apps allow city dwellers to report nonemergencies, including potholes, fallen trees, and damaged street signs, and either alert city government or organize the community to fix the problem. Another category of data is unintentionally created, encompassing the broad (and expanding) array of social media platforms, such as Twitter, Facebook, and Flickr. Users may hardly realize that their actions online are a rich source of data—a fact that was exploited for a research collaboration between Facebook and Cornell University, to much controversy.[12] . . .

. . . The three categories of data collection in cities—opportunistic sensing, ad hoc sensor deployment, and crowdsensing—can be hybridized to a various extent. On the backbone of telecommunications networks, a new universe of urban apps has appeared, allowing people to broadcast and exchange geolocated information and reveal the city from their personal perspective. Air quality, for example, is poorly understood because data are collected in static and sparse ground-based stations. In a possible future, citizens themselves could carry a distributed network of sensors that create a dynamic real-time atmospheric map. Using smartphone-integrated sensing devices, pedestrian commuters could generate data at the human scale, as though a tracer were running through the veins of the cities, showing the urban environment that the commuters live in and move through.[13] This concept may inspire manufacturers of consumer electronics to include environmental sensors and to publicly release the resulting data for analysis.

Individuals are becoming agents of data collection, and at the scale of an urban population, we all constitute a vast trove of crowdsourced information. As Gordon Bell's experiment recedes into the past, society is moving from "life-logging" to "city-logging." We are all enmeshed in a distributed sensing ecosystem.

Calvino imagined a situation of total recall, where every detail was recorded. What he did not imagine was that individuals would share that information willingly. This is a radical shift from a top-down vision of data collection to a bottom-up vision of data aggregation and dissemination—it is a shift from "Big Brother" to "little sisters." A (re)distribution of control over information may empower individuals, providing insight into the kind and quantity of data that they create and a choice of what and when to share—even, perhaps, prompting claims to some of the information's value. Today, for example, Gmail users let Google read their e-mail and send them targeted advertisements in exchange for using the service free of charge.[14] Researchers have proposed that, in the future, a personal data management tool—a "data box"—could explicitly give individuals the choice to keep data private or to upload it freely and receive benefits in return. This idea is effectively a "mutation" of our present system and might emerge from an active discussion among all involved parties. The most desirable future might be one in which people have the opportunity to directly benefit from the inherent value of their daily actions.

Broad trends point toward an increasing number of apps and technologies that create urban data, wider adoption across demographics, and faster response from city governments. Entirely new positions are being created at the city level—urban CTOs (chief technology officers), for example, will nimbly manage the urban implications of digital systems on the macro scale, while personal data management tools will govern on the micro scale. People are quantifying themselves to better understand who they are and how they can improve their lives. Together, we compose a mosaic portrait of the city. People are becoming more and more aware of the digital shadows they cast and will be empowered to take a more active role in inhabiting—and contributing to—the places where they live. We are moving from the quantified *self* to the quantified *city*.

1. Epigraph: Italo Calvino, "World Memory," in *Numbers in the Dark*, trans. Tim Parks (New York: Vintage, 1995), 135.
2. The term "total recall" was coined by Gordon Bell: see Gordon Bell and Jim Gemmell, *Your Life, Uploaded: The Digital Way to Better Memory, Health, and Productivity* (New York: PLUME, 2009).
3. Bill Gates, foreword to *Your Life, Uploaded: The Digital Way to Better Memory, Health, and Productivity*, by Gordon Bell and Jim Gemmell (New York: PLUME, 2009), x–xi.
4. Eric Schmidt, "Google," Techonomy Conference, Lake Tahoe, CA, August 4, 2010, presentation at a panel discussion with Debby Hopkins, Kevin Kelly, and Lisa Randall, moderated by David Kirkpatrick.
5. S. Sobolevsky, I. Sitko, R. Tachet des Combes, B. Hawelka, J. M. Arias, and C. Ratti, "Money on the Move: Big Data of Bank Card Transactions as the New Proxy for Human Mobility Patterns and Regional Delineation—The Case of Residents and Foreign Visitors in Spain," *2014 IEEE International Congress on Big Data*, 136–143, http://www.ieee.org/conferences_events/.
6. F. Calabrese and C. Ratti, "Real Time Rome," *Networks and Communications Studies* 20 (2006): 247–258.
7. C. Kang, S. Sobolevsky, Y. Liu, and C. Ratti, "Exploring Human Movements in Singapore: A Comparative Analysis Based on Mobile Phone and Taxicab Usages," *UrbComp '13: Proceedings of the 2nd ACM SIGKDD International Workshop on Urban Computing* (New York: ACM, 2013), article 1, http://dl.acm.org/citation.cfm?id=2505826; C. Ratti and K. Kloeckl, "Enacting the Real Time City, *Proceedings of Futur en Seine 2009*, Cap Digital, 2010, 72–84.
8. Carlo Ratti et al., "Investigation of the Waste-Removal Chain through Pervasive Computing," *IEEE Xplore: IBM Journal of Research and Development* 55.1.2 (2011): 1–11.
9. Kristofer Pister, "Emerging Challenges: Mobile Networking for 'Smart Dust.'" *Journal of Communications and Networks* 2.3 (2000): 188–196.
10. Bell and Gemmell, *Your Life, Uploaded*.
11. F. Girardin, F. Calabrese, F. Dal Fiore, C. Ratti, and J. Blat, "Digital Footprinting: Uncovering Tourists with User-Generated Content," *IEEE Pervasive Computing* 7.4 (2008): 36–43; F. Girardin, F. Dal Fiore, C. Ratti, and J. Blat, "Leveraging Explicitly Disclosed Location Information to Understand Tourist Dynamics: A Case Study," *Journal of Location-Based Services* 2.1 (2008): 41–54.
12. Adam D. I. Kramer, Jamie E. Guillory, and Jeffrey T. Hancock, "Experimental Evidence of Massive-Scale Emotional Contagion through Social Networks," *Proceedings of the National Academy of Sciences* 111.24 (2014): 8788–8790.
13. Carlo Ratti and Otto Ng, "One Country, Two Lungs," MIT Senseable City Lab with LAAB, exhibition, presented at the Hong Kong and Shenzhen Bi-City Biennale of Urbanism and Architecture, 2013.
14. Hamed Haddadi, Heidi Howard, Amir Chaudhry, Jon Crow-croft, Anil Madhavapeddy, and Richard Mortier, "Personal Data: Thinking Inside the Box," arXiv.org [cs.CY], 2015, http://arxiv.org/abs/1501.04737.

Carlo Ratti and Matthew Claudel, *The City of Tomorrow: Sensors, Networks, Hackers, and the Future of Urban Life* (New Haven, CT: Yale University Press, 2016): 43–6, 48, 50–2, 54–6.

In 1965, Ivan Sutherland, a pioneer in the field of computer graphics, envisioned what he called the "ultimate display." He contemplated a future where virtual reality (VR) could seamlessly substitute for reality itself. He mused, "The ultimate display would, of course, be a room within which the computer can control the existence of matter. A chair displayed in such a room would be sufficient to sit on. Handcuffs displayed in such a room would be confining, and a bullet displayed in such a room would be fatal. With appropriate programming such a display could literally be the Wonderland into which Alice walked."[17]

Though we have not quite achieved Sutherland's "ultimate display," we have witnessed the emergence of unique innovations in the realm of the built environment. One such innovation is the Cave Automatic Virtual Environment, or CAVE—a comprehensive VR system consisting of a room-sized enclosure enveloping users with high-resolution display screens on all sides, including the floor and ceiling. Users wear stereoscopic glasses or use 3D visualization technology to engage with computer-generated 3D environments, while motion sensors and tracking systems monitor their movements, enabling real-time adjustments to the virtual world. CAVEs have found applications across diverse fields, including scientific research, architectural design, medical simulations, engineering, and immersive training, providing an interactive and realistic platform for data analysis, prototype testing, and simulating real-world scenarios.

Moreover, in addition to rooms becoming displays, we have witnessed the integration of LED displays into architectural structures. Virilio introduced the concept of a "media building" to describe buildings in which LED screens are integrated onto the facade, reminiscent of those found in iconic locations such as Times Square in New York City.[18] These are architectural structures primarily intended for the storage and dissemination of media and information, rather than habitation. In his book, *The Lost Dimension* (1983), Virilio contends that the proliferation of computers and monitors has led to the "loss" and "disappearance" of traditional architectural dimensions. Traditional urban spaces such as the agora and the forum have been supplanted by screens. "The man / machine interface replaces the facades of buildings as the surfaces of property allotments," he writes.[19] Consequently, "with the interfacing of computer terminals and video monitors, distinctions of *here* and *there* no longer mean anything."

This evolution is closely tied to the notion of cyberspace—coined by William Gibson in his dystopian novel *Neuromancer* (1984) —a virtual realm accessible through computer networks.[20] The protagonist, Case, connects his consciousness to the digital realm, blurring the lines between physical and virtual experiences. In 1991, Marcos Novak theorized the concept of dematerialized, fluid, and transitory architecture spatialized within computational environments in his chapter, "Liquid Architectures in Cyberspace."[21] He later expanded on these ideas by a guest-editing an issue of *AD* (*Architectural Design*), titled "Architects in Cyberspace" (1995).[22]

However, today, the term "metaverse" holds greater prominence. Neal Stephenson introduced this term in his novel *Snow Crash* (1992), envisioning a parallel virtual universe where individuals escape the challenges of a real-world economic collapse.[23] The metaverse, designed to be more immersive and interactive than the earlier concept of cyberspace, allows people to use avatars to interact realistically with each other and their surroundings in a virtual environment. Furthermore, this environment persists even when users are offline, fostering the creation of virtual spaces and relationships. Known as the "collective virtual shared space," the metaverse is envisioned as the foundational framework for the forthcoming iteration of the Internet, offering a more interactive world encompassing the physical and the virtual.

Platforms like Roblox and Minecraft serve as proto-metaverse environments, empowering users to craft their own 3D-rendered virtual realms. But how should designers create for the metaverse? Philosopher David Chalmers, in his work *Reality+: Virtual Worlds and the Problems of Philosophy* (2022), delves into the ethics of VR world creation. In single-user virtual worlds, ethical concerns revolve around the content's impact, as evidenced by criticism of video games like Grand Theft Auto for allegedly glorifying violence and sexism. VR's potential to influence behavior and empathy is substantial, with experiments demonstrating the impact of virtual experiences on subsequent real-world actions. Furthermore, in multi-user virtual worlds, complex ethical issues merge with social and political concerns, raising questions about their creation, organization, governance, and the establishment of laws within these realms. He asks, "Who should have ultimate authority about what happens in a virtual world? Should there be laws in a virtual world, and if so, what should they be? How can a virtual world be a truly fair and just place for its inhabitants?"[24]

Chalmers sees promise in the metaverse concept for its potential for "virtual abundance," where space and construction are limitless, offering the potential for a utopian "post-scarcity society." Nevertheless, he recognizes that at present, most virtual worlds are essentially "corporatocracies," a situation exemplified by Second Life, leading to internal conflicts when certain groups took over areas, with vigilantes rising in response. Users even started their own online newspaper to protest how the world was run.

The Metaverse, representing the consolidation of Web 3.0 along with AR, VR, MR technologies is still in its pioneering phase at the time of writing. However, advances are progressing at a rapid rate. Speculations for real-life cities involve blockchain's applications for data exchange and monitoring for urban management. Ultimately, the commercial implications of the metaverse involve the inseparable relationship between spatial production and capitalism. Wendy W. Fok, in her book, *Digital Structures: Data and Urban Strategies of the Civic Future* (2023), critically assesses notions of ownership, intellectual property, authorship, and the environmental impacts of energy use in blockchain and cryptocurrency mining and exchange in virtual space.[25]

Futurist Greg Lindsay sees more reasons for concern in what he calls the "Metaverse Metropolis."[26] For over a decade, cities have grappled with the unintended consequences of disruptive business models aimed at extracting value from urban spaces. Whether it's ride-hailing, short-term rentals, or the broad "sharing economy," these innovations have led to increased congestion, reduced housing availability, and exacerbated economic disparities, primarily benefiting a privileged minority. It has taken considerable effort for public officials to begin to learn how to regulate and collaborate with these start-ups to distribute both the advantages and challenges posed by their technologies. With technology giants such as Meta and Apple launching new XR headsets, it becomes imperative for cities to proactively prepare for the ramifications of a widely adopted metaverse.

Furthermore, according to the academic Ted Striphas, in our contemporary society, algorithms wield considerable influence over cultural decision-making, effectively moulding and at times redefining our perception of culture. In his book, *Algorithmic Culture Before the Internet* (2023), he demonstrates how automated computational processes gained the authority to undertake this role and examines the historic factors that gave rise to the phenomenon of algorithmic culture, where culture and computation intertwine.[27]

In their book, *Disruptive Technologies: The Convergence of New Paradigms in Architecture* (2023), co-editors Philippe Morel and Henriette Bier have compiled a comprehensive collection of essays at the intersection of design, automation, and the metaverse. Their introduction and various chapters focus on the integration of virtual space and the city, and the ways in which new business models involve the metaverse as a commercial space for economic transactions.[28] Morel and Bier see possibilities of new social, cultural, educational and business exchanges in the metaverse. Questions arise concerning which design field bears the responsibility for designing the spaces of the Metaverse and its implications for real cities. In his chapter, "Cyber-Urban Integration" (2023), Patrik Schumacher predicts the expansion of the architect's "core competencies" to include the design and experience of architectural and urban spaces represented in cyberspace.[29]

Finally, researcher Andrea Moneta critiques typical virtual worlds, especially those created for computer games, for lacking architectural depth and a profound understanding of space and time due to the absence of architects and architectural principles in their design.[30] He argues that these spaces tend to mimic real-world architecture without fully embracing the creative and artistic potential of the digital realm. Instead of merely replicating built architecture, he argues, virtual environments should explore architectural concepts and theories to create imaginative and utopian designs, harnessing the unique potential of the digital medium.

Moneta critiques the superficial replication of real-world architecture in the virtual world.[31] He claims that virtual worlds "are never isolated from the real world," calling for a "constructive dialogue" between architecture and gaming.[32] Moneta concludes by declaring our current time as a "postdigital era," in which "it is difficult to draw a line between the digital and the non-digital." Consequently, designers need to better comprehend "the oneness of the digital and the nondigital."[33]

In sum, the virtual realm has become an integral part of our personal and collective space, and should be designed with a deep understanding of its potential impact on our lives and society. At its best, it has the potential to be a force for positive change and create a better society. At its worst, it runs the risk of devolving into yet another medium for advertising, marketing, and data harvesting.

ANDREA MONETA
"Architecture, Heritage, and the Metaverse"

GAMING AND VIRTUAL WORLDS

A virtual world can be considered a brand-new digital built environment, an extension of the real world that includes not just a physical appearance, but also cultural and social interaction, aesthetic appreciation, and philosophical engagement. Awareness of the importance of these concerns in the built environment is part of design training in architecture, but it is generally not included in the education of those who design and build virtual worlds – i.e., game designers, programmers, and (sometimes) users. As a consequence, the design of a typical virtual world, such as that produced as the background for computer games, may be broadly described as similar to a film set, characterized by a fairy-tale naivety, yet generally aimed at reproducing a real-world environment.[1]

Thirty years since they first exploded into the entertainment industry, one result of this limited development is that these games are starting to look and play the same. Despite the recent massive increase in Internet speed and the improvement of IT devices, the novelty factor of games developed in the last fifteen years has thus reached a low point.[2] In response, developers nowadays are spending a great amount of resources trying to turn games into movies, to improve their look and "appeal." One could argue this condition is the direct consequence of the lack of architects in the virtual world. Without architects, the virtual world has come to be filled only with scenography that seeks to imitate real architecture. Absurdly, in the virtual world, where everything is unlimited, architecture is limited.

Virtual environments need to go beyond the limitations of such purely mimetic realism. A bold new attitude is needed to create a basis for the full development of the virtual world's creative and artistic potential. Put simply, to realize a digital spatial revolution, games and other virtual worlds need to abandon the depiction of reality. Instead, they need to develop an understanding of architectural concepts and theories to give life to truly utopian designs – to make the impossible possible.

To realize such a future, however, it is fundamentally important to consider the main difference between buildings in the real and virtual worlds. In the first realm, buildings are fixed and not generally transformable. But in the digital realm, they can change and quickly reconfigure themselves as "performances" in a dynamic interactive process with the user.[3] The virtual world is also a place for action and functionality, where gamers may use architecture with specific purpose, as might a *parkour* athlete.

Applying architectural principles to the virtual world should also involve understanding history and context. Bringing history into a virtual world may seem to be nonsense because virtual worlds are commonly considered to be timeless, without a tie to chronology. In fact, however, they typically "borrow" themes and characteristics from a specific real past – as games may be set, for example, in the Middle Ages or during World War II. But the use of the past as a process by which historical architectural archetypes form the "elements" of a language can also open up new territories for architecture, at the same time as it may enhance the quality of the digital built environment in game design and other reaches of the metaverse.

Since the 1980s, when virtual worlds first started to appear in gaming, digital built environments have typically been created from scratch by software developers, conceptual artists, 3D modelers, and game designers. On specific platforms and in certain conditions, users (game players), may also be given the chance to modify and/or create content in a virtual world. Game designers are currently trained to be proficient with IT skills, but also to create 2D and 3D art. Depending on their role and skill level (junior, senior) they are then authorized to design and realize characters, objects and environments; to create textures; and to visualize other virtual elements through digital and nondigital sketches and animations.

A game designer's skill set, however, does not include specialized training in architectural, landscape, or urban design. As a consequence, virtual worlds are currently being created by a legion of nonarchitects (I will call them designers of architectures), who assume the role played in the real world by architects, landscape designers, urban planners, and interior designers. But designing architecture in the metaverse is a challenging task even for experienced architects, let alone for those without their cultural background and technical training. Freed from spatial, economic and technical limitations, without a natural environment to fit into or an anthropic history to respect, designers of architectures may easily become lost in a digital magic domain, where everything is possible and potentially huge.

A further complication is that virtual worlds are never isolated from the real world; indeed, the two realms extend into and influence each other.[4] *Minecraft* (2009), the most popular computer game in history, which offers a form of "digital LEGO" to its users, has thus been successfully utilized to facilitate engagement and participation in real architectural and urban-planning processes. The real world can also influence the virtual world on an imaginary level, for example, through the influence of the imaginary worlds of books, movies, television, role-playing games, and religion.

Such "real world" imaginaries may provide a powerful background for the design of characters, narratives and spaces in the virtual world. It is why so many computer games are related to old myths, famous novels, and fantasy books, and why their architectures reflect a sort of fairy-tale expressionism.

However, the real world can also influence the virtual world on a more factual, *objective* level. Thus it is that past events and recent history often lie behind many of the landscapes users experience in virtual worlds and games. History is not tangible, but it does live within individual memories, which reproduce over time to produce cultural memory. This is why individuals can maintain a sense of personal identity by linking to a shared culture, based on collective memory of the past.

The virtual world can also record and display shared cultural memory through physical appearances, with the aim of linking the past to the present, enhancing the user's connection with a specific environment and architecture.[5] But this will require that designers of virtual architectures evolve the skills and knowledge to include a more solid array of competences that only architectural training can offer. At the same time, the role of the architect needs to be extended into the virtual world to understand the functional aspects of gaming and storytelling. What is really needed is a constructive dialogue between the disciplines of architecture and gaming.

Such a dialogue can be seen to be even more necessary when the design of a virtual world involves the reproduction of historical environments and their architectures. Most of the time, this reproduction follows controversial philological approaches and methods. Take, for example, the development of the video game *Assassin's Creed II*, where, as a background for the actions of players, industry giant Ubisoft created a detailed virtual replica of Florence during the Renaissance. To help ensure historical accuracy, the company even employed a young professor of architectural history and theory, Maria Elisa Navarro, as a consultant. The result was a movie-like, impressively detailed reproduction of period costumes and architectures – but with major "adjustments." Among these were the increased total height of buildings to improve climbing movements, and the introduction of curved streets to a totally reinvented map of Florence to enhance the potential for surprise encounters among players.[6]

Context is another important aspect to consider in the design of real-world architectures. Thus, architects are trained to analyze and understand the environments in which they design, including both tangible and intangible elements inherited from the past. These elements include the anthropic history, the landscape and natural environment, the past use of the place, and the memory of inhabitants. Good architects thus usually start their design efforts by recognizing the value of preexisting elements, which they then reinterpret through their own cultural background and cognitive and professional experiences.

None of these processes exist in the virtual world. Direct emotional exchanges are mediated through a user interface and/or an avatar. Gamers are alone, but at the same time share the experience of a virtual space with other people. They likewise occupy a meta-space in which there is no sense of gravity, there are no smells, nothing may be physically touched, and there is no evidence of history other than that which has been (re)created specifically to provide a sense of time in the metaverse.[7]

. . .

TOWARD A POSTDIGITAL SPATIAL REVOLUTION

After decades of experimentation, as Nicholas Negroponte declared in his 1998 book *Beyond Digital*, it is now evident that the digital revolution is over. We currently live in the postdigital era, where it is difficult to draw a line between the digital and the nondigital. As an acknowledgement of the hegemony of computational processes, life in the postdigital era is thus focused on enhancing the application of the computer age to life and society.[8] While the digital revolution enhanced architecture with CAD and virtual reality, the postdigital paradigm will allow architects and designers of architectures to better understand the oneness of the digital and the nondigital. Paraphrasing Mel Alexenberg, we need to consider postdigital architecture as works that

> *". . . address the humanization of digital technologies through interplay between digital, biological, cultural, and spiritual systems, between cyberspace and real space, between embodied media and mixed reality in social and physical communication, between visual, haptic, auditory, and kinaesthetic media experiences, between virtual and augmented reality."*[9]

As predicted by Guy Debord in his 1967 *The Society of the Spectacle*, contemporary cultures are replacing authentic social life with its representation. As an aspect of social life, the built environment is constantly shaped by social interactions, and, at the same time, it shapes them.[10] Consequently, we need to acknowledge that the virtual world is becoming a wider expression of our personal and collective space, an interactive spatial dimension where at the very same moment we shape it, it shapes us.

This revolutionary ongoing process has had major consequences on architecture, specifically with regard to the loss of permanence, one of its principal former characteristics. No longer an expression of immortality, for the first time the millennial discipline is shifting its essence from the creation of tangible artifacts to the realization of ephemeral places. Architecture of the virtual world, in fact, evades permanency as a function of time, by integrating space and time. This new architecture is thus an expression of the fluid, instable, ever-changing digital environment that is the virtual world.[11]

1. M. Gerosa, *Second Life* (Rome: Meltemi Editore, 2007), p.223.
2. This topic is discussed on gamestop. com, retrieved July 4, 2020, from https://www.gamespot.com/forums/games- discussion-1000000/do-a-lot-of-modern- games-look-the-same-32846070/.
3. S. Boyd Davis, *The Design of Virtual Environments with Particular Reference to VRML* (Centre for Electronic Arts, Middlesex University, 1996).
4. R.A. Bartle, *Designing Virtual Worlds* (Indianapolis: New Riders Pub., 2004), p.65.
5. M. Veltman, "Remembering the Old World: An Analysis of the Interaction between Virtual Heritage and Cultural Memory," *Junctions, Graduate Journal of the Humanities*, Vol.2 (2017), p.42, retrieved January 12, 2020, from http://junctionsjournal.org/.
6. M. Saga, "What It's Like to Be an Architectural Consultant for Assassin's Creed II," *ArchDaily*, May 7, 2015, retrieved March 28, 2020, from https://www.archdaily.com/774210/maria-elisa-navarro-the-architectural-consultant-for-assassins-creed-ii/.
7. M. Crocco, L. Nappi, and A. Moneta, *Progettare su Second Life: l'Architettura del Metaverso* (Rome: Weretomato, 2008), retrieved February 5, 2020, from https://www.andreamoneta.it/Architecture/ portfolio.html.
8. D. M. Berry, "Post-Digital Humanities: Computation and Cultural Critique in the Arts and Humanities," *Educause Review*, May 19, 2014, retrieved September 20, 2020, from https://er.educause.edu/articles/2014/5/postdigital-humanities-computation-and-cultural-critique-in-the- arts-and-humanities.
9. M. Alexenberg, *The Future of Art in a Post-Digital Age* (Bristol: Intellect Books Ltd., 2011).

10 J. White, *Virtual Reality and the Built Environment* (Oxford: Architectural Press, 2002), p.73.
11 *Designing Digital Space: An Architect's Guide to Virtual Reality*, pp.289, 312.

Andrea Moneta, "Architecture, Heritage, and the Metaverse" *Traditional Dwellings and Settlements Review* 32, no. 1 (2020): 37–49, 37, 39, 40, 48.

This chapter explores the expanding role of urban design and architecture in the era of extended reality technologies. As the boundaries between the physical and virtual worlds continue to blur, urban designers and architects are called upon to navigate the complex implications of these technologies and the metaverse. The proliferation of sensors and data-driven design offers opportunities for enhanced decision-making and public engagement. However, it also raises concerns about privacy, equity, and bias.

Urban designers and architects need to critically examine the social, cultural, and ethical implications of creating virtual spaces while harnessing the potential of AR, MR, and VR to enhance urban living experiences. Addressing these challenges effectively requires engaging in constructive dialogue across disciplines, drawing upon architectural theory and practice while collaborating with experts in gaming, computer science, data science, and the social sciences. Embracing AR, VR, and MR technologies encourages designers to create visually engaging and socially enriching environments. By thoughtfully addressing the ethical and social implications of these technologies, urban designers and architects can shape a more connected and responsive urban future, redefining the relationship between the built and virtual worlds to enhance human experience and foster meaningful interactions.

Embracing AR, VR, and MR technologies encourages designers to create visually engaging and socially enriching environments. By thoughtfully addressing the ethical and social implications of these technologies, urban designers and architects can shape a more connected and responsive urban future, redefining the relationship between the built environment and the virtual world to enhance human experience and foster meaningful interactions.

10

Artificial Intelligence, the Internet of Things, and Technological Determinism

In the novel by Arthur C. Clarke, *2001: A Space Odyssey* (1968) and its immediate film adaptation (Stanley Kubrick, 1968), the sentient computer HAL 9000 symbolizes AI's potential for autonomy and malevolence, challenging human decision-making aboard a spacecraft and leading to existential confrontations. The film *Blade Runner* (Ridley Scott, 1982), drawing from Philip K. Dick's novel *Do Androids Dream of Electric Sheep?* (1968), envisions a future where lifelike androids, known as "replicants," blur the lines between human and machine, raising questions about what it means to be human and the ethics of creating sentient life.

These narrative works offer a lens through which urban futures were imagined in their time, having been reshaped by the more recent rise of Artificial Intelligence (AI). Throughout history, from literature, to film, to design, human culture has speculated about the consequences of technological evolution, especially in the context of urban transformation. Urban design stands currently at the crossroads of AI, the field of computer science aiming to simulate human intelligence, encompassing tasks focusing on decision-making and language understanding. As part of this field, Machine Learning (ML), a branch of AI, enables large language model algorithms to learn and make predictions or decisions autonomously. Many of these systems are already embedded in our everyday lives, such as automated recommendations of movies based on someone's movie viewing history. These intelligent interfaces and systems are expanding the designer's toolbox with new and accelerated capacities to harness complexity.

At the time of writing, disruptive AI technologies such as ChatGPT, and generative text-based and image-based AI tools have taken root with a vast number of users increasing worldwide. We are witnessing a proliferation of open source, easily-available platforms that enable the generation, simulation, modeling, and design through processes that apply and develop artificial forms of intelligence. Designers are increasingly able to automate the mechanics of traditionally manual design approaches, leading some people to question what status and role designers will have in the future in the design of cities.

AI is fundamentally reshaping architectural and urban design workflows, dramatically altering the human agency of traditional design processes. What once progressed from sketching, to 3D modeling, to rendering, can now leap directly from initial sketches to advanced renderings. Enhanced by AI-driven tools, design optimization enables architects to swiftly explore and evaluate a myriad of design variations based on specific constraints. Predictive analysis provides real-time feedback on architectural choices, and generative design tools offer multiple design solutions immediately after inputting parameters, streamlining the conceptual phase of designing. Moreover, AI's ability to optimize material usage can minimize waste and reduce construction costs. While these advancements in automation can be argued to make design processes more efficient, questions arise as to how architects and urban designers can maintain a balance, ensuring that designs outcomes retain the human subjectivity and cultural considerations inherent in traditional methods.

This chapter investigates the consequences of AI for urban design and management, particularly through the increasing presence of sensors in cities.[1] AI combined with these sensors create the capacity for urban systems to process information and learn independently. In his book, *Architecture in the Age of Artificial Intelligence: An Introduction to AI for Architects* (2021), Neil Leach, rhetorically questions what future cities designed with AI will look like and advocates for enhancing the intelligence of existing cities. He calls for retrofitting these cities with sensors, signals, and control systems.[2] This view is also supported by Shannon Mattern, who writes that "data driven planning" and "algorithmic administration" are the basis of intelligent cities, optimistically pointing towards citizen participation in governance. Mattern supports Leach's view of how "twenty-first century 'smartness'" is continuously grafted onto "the existing urban scaffolds and substrates" of cities.[3] Other contributions come from architects Areti Markopoulou and Matias del Campo, co-directors of the practice SPAN with Sandra Manninger, who focus on the design consequences of the rapidly evolving and available AI tools. Concluding this final chapter is an excerpt from Kate Crawford's book, *Atlas of AI: Power, Politics and the Planetary Costs of Artificial Intelligence* (2021), which discusses the various ethical concerns and considerations of AI.[4]

Cities are undergoing an intelligence revolution, not driven by humans but by the pervasive sensing and actuating systems embedded within them. Antoine Picon, in his book *Smart Cities: A Spatialised Intelligence* (2015), states: "Our cities are on the verge of a radical transformation, a revolution in intelligence comparable in scale to the one that, in its time, brought about industrialisation."[5] However, the dark side of this new technological apparatus lies in its application collecting, collating, and monitoring the behavior and actions of large populations.

Proponents of "smart cities" champion the promise of enhanced comfort, security, and efficiency achieved through advanced management of city functions such as traffic and waste disposal, climatic and weather events, crime, and other urban occurrences. They envision a future of seamless urban living facilitated by heightened security measures. Conversely, sceptics voice concerns over the potential erosion of democracy and individual autonomy, citing the rise of surveillance and increased control over citizens. These dynamics present a spectrum of possibilities for urban design and governance to navigate. On one extreme, there is a scenario reminiscent of George Orwell's "Big Brother," characterized by ubiquitous and pervasive surveillance.[6] On the other, there are hopes for a cityscape that embodies greater democracy, transparency, equity, and justice.

Picon's work delves deeper into this dichotomy. He envisions cities that balance efficient digital control with fostering knowledge exchange and enhancing overall quality of life. However, he also questions whether the pursuit of "smart cities" represents "the ultimate set up for surveillance"?[7] While the driving principles of smart city advocates are efficiency, security, resilience, and comfort, the very concept of a "smart city" remains contested. At its heart lies a tug-of-war: centralized control and surveillance versus distributed empowerment, democratization, with a focus on enhancing urban efficiencies, from infrastructure to air quality and public safety.[8]

Redefining cities in the digital age means understanding them as entities shaped by a myriad of interactions, both human and non-human. In addition to Picon, other key contributors to this discourse include Mark Shepard's *Sentient City: Ubiquitous Computing, Architecture, and the Future of Urban Space* (2011), and Anthony Townsend's *Smart Cities: Big Data, Civic Hackers, and the Quest for a New Utopia* (2013). Townsend, in the context of AI, asserts: "Every city contains the DNA of its own destruction—some existing fissure that, under pressure, can erupt into conflict or cascade into collapse."[9]

Benjamin Bratton critiques the mobilization of AI for "smart city" applications at an urban scale as prematurely fixing solutions limited to urban efficiency and service optimization. He rather outlines how AI integration as "a distributed, discontinuous, landscape-scale technology" can have broader ecological and spatial implications on urban settings.[10]

In addition, AI systems can only function as well as the training data which feeds them. Pablo Lorenzo-Eiroa, in his book, *Digital Signifiers in an Architecture of Information: From Big Data and Simulation to Artificial Intelligence* (2023), articulates this tension between the instrumentalization of big data and architectural representations, in what he refers to as, "an architecture of information."[11]

In her introduction to *Learning Cities: Collective Intelligence in Urban Design* (2023), Areti Markopoulou explores urban intelligence in the context of the modern technological landscape. She begins with a quote by Warren Brody of the various progressive stages of how we teach our environments first to be complex, then self-organizing, and ultimately evolutionary.[12] Markopoulou examines the incorporation of AI, machine learning, and algorithmic models in urban planning and design. The text highlights the increasing reliance on data from interconnected objects, such as the Internet of Things (IoT), and the mining of vast web-based image databases. This data, collected from user patterns in housing or urban transportation, promises a more optimized urban future, aiding in predicting traffic and refining mobility planning. However, she advocates for a shift in understanding, urging us to move beyond the traditional "smart city" idea to embrace optimization as co-creative patterns that integrate both human and non-human perspectives. Markopoulou, along with Neil Leach later in this chapter, presents a new paradigm—the metaphor of the "City as Brain." This vision conseives the city as self-regulating and life-like, striving to achieve dynamic equilibrium.

The extensive integration of AI, rooted in the cybernetic framework first established in the 1950s, opens a myriad of new possibilities and challenges in the fields of architecture and urban design. Markopoulou contemplates the differences and connections between AI and earlier cybernetics, focusing on the broader implications of AI on future visions of urban development. Digital intelligence, which is increasingly infiltrating every aspect of previously analog systems, can herald both utopian and dystopian futures. AI presents opportunities for empowerment in urban planning, such as "the potential of recognising the diverse (microbial, animal, vegetable, machine, human) intelligences in cities and reorchestrating them for better planning."[13] However, Markopoulou also raises alarms over the risks of intelligent machines, such as surveillance and behaviour manipulation.

This dual nature of AI is evident in the design and management of urban spaces, which encompass aspects like real-time digital twins to improve environmental sustainability and the possible misuse of monitoring as surveillance. While her text is enthusiastic about new technological and social possibilities for urbanism, Markopoulou remains cautious about the "hesitations and risks" associated with the cultural, ethical, and aesthetic consequences of embedded intelligence.[14]

Markopoulou emphasizes the significance of human conditions in shaping the urban environment, underlining the potential pitfalls of viewing urban problems purely through a technological lens. Her introduction considers the systemic fusion of bottom-up and top-down approaches, facilitating bi-directional feedback loops. Aided by simple video gaming interfaces, such as in the Superbarrio project by IAAC, Markopoulou speculates on the development of more participatory and intuitive urban design processes. Such tools fostering dialogue between urban developers and citizens can improve urban planning, allowing for a design paradigm of "collective creation." Markopoulou proposes a post-anthropocentric design paradigm, underscoring the intertwined roles of humans, technology, and other living entities in the creation of future cities.

Markopoulou argues for the empowerment of crowds through the democratization of data, and a unique intersection of "crowd and machine wisdom." The idea of a "collective intelligence" harkens back to Marshall McLuhan's earlier notion of the "Global Village" introduced in the 1960s, which suggests that the rapid spread of communication technologies effectively shrinks the world into a village-like community.[15] The term "collective intelligence" also refers to Pierre Levy's book, *Collective Intelligence: Mankind's Emerging World in Cyberspace* (1997).[16] Christopher Hight and Chris Perry's guest-edited issue of *AD, Collective Intelligence* (2006) focused on the emerging "new social organisations based on principles of decentralisation and collectivity" and "hyper communicative networks."[17] The intent to form community from discrete locations continues to have implications on the scale of design practice, design products, and of society, and by implication, urbanism. Big data-based design and participatory planning models could blend top-down and bottom-up processes.

Finally, Markopoulou's concerns about AI resonate with Keller Easterling's 2011 chapter, "Action is the Form,"[18] in the book, *Sentient City: Ubiquitous Computing, Architecture and the Future of Urban Space* (2011), in which she emphasizes the often overlooked yet omnipresent nature of digital infrastructure. Easterling observes that "Digital infrastructure is just one of the things that, in its ubiquity, often becomes more obscure." She describes infrastructural space as a hidden substrate, "the binding medium or current between objects of positive consequence, shape, and law." However, Easterling also brings to the fore the idea that infrastructure is not just a backdrop; it is crucial and shapes power relations. It stands as "the point of contact and access, the spatial outcropping of underlying laws and logistics."[19]

ARETI MARKOPOULOU
Learning Cities: Collective Intelligence in Urban Design

. . . we teach our environments first complex, then self-organizing, intelligence that could eventually become evolutionary.

Warren Brodey (1967)

The application of artificial intelligence, machine learning or statistical models and algorithms for the creation of predictive models in architectural design and urban planning is based on relational and evolutionary logics that promise a more (multi-objective) "optimized" design or a "smarter" city, where "smart" is usually defined based on notions of improvement at infrastructural scales.

Most of the discussions around the idea of urban "intelligence" focus on the use of sensory technology in billions of interconnected objects (Internet of Things) or on the processing of billions of images that can be mined from web services to collect vast amounts of data produced by human behaviour and other sources, such as the environment or the material world of our built space. Data from user occupation patterns in housing, for instance, can generate economically viable interior distributions in building development. Similarly, data on how people move in cities can be inserted into computers and generative algorithms with the goal of helping predict traffic and optimizing mobility planning.

In a highly human-centric technocratic world, such notions of optimization might be the gold standard for urban policies and national strategies.

But moving beyond an understanding of optimization as selecting the best result from a variety of computed and quantified data-based possibilities (a reading which carries the heavy burden of the last two decade's mainstream idea of the "smart city"), we need to explore optimization as patterns of co-creation and as a continuous changing state incorporating both human and non-human perspectives. Within a multiverse inhabited by different human, technological and cultural others, purely quantified data sets may be significant, but they fall short, if they are only observed by a cognitive, and always biased, perspective.[1]

Machine Intelligence

While the idea of intelligent machines that simulate "cognitive functions" such as "learning" or "problem solving" has its roots back in the cybernetics of the 1950s, its extensive use, in recent years, in the architectural and urban design disciplines opens up a series of new possibilities – as well as plenty of cultural, ethical or even aesthetic hesitations and risks.

Although it seems to be common thinking that AI is an evolution of cybernetics, one could argue that cybernetics deals with a much more holistic view of intelligence, especially because it focuses on how systems can self-regulate and act in constant feedback with the environment, which contains far more diverse factors (biological, social, mechanical, economic) than the AI computational stored representations of the world.[2] [3] Beyond the technical and systemic differences between cybernetics and AI, however, there is a common connotation to AI related to the question of the future, which is of major social (rather than computational) significance. As Steenson highlights in her contribution to this issue, "AI is not only about using the computer, but about having a vision of it. If we talk about AI, we want to talk about a vision of what computation does today and could do in the future."

The digital intelligence that is inevitably starting to penetrate every aspect of our previously analogue systems of living, working or interacting socially becomes the central core of a variety of utopic or dystopic futures. That is the case because such intelligence can be an empowering tool as well as a disempowering one for both the people who inhabit the built environment and those who design and manage it. The potential of recognizing the diverse (microbial, animal, vegetable, machine, human) intelligences in cities and reorchestrating them for better planning (Bratton pp. 15), the ability to create real time digital twins for multi-stakeholder decision making (Chronis pp. 87), or the novel modes of machinic perception generated (Del Campo & Manninger pp.97), which can enrich the field of urban design (Vivaldi pp. 37) are some aspects of one of the sides of the AI reality that has been embedded in our everyday life and habits, usually without us even noticing it. Other issues such as the anonymous, faceless city designed from the top down, based on statistical simplifications (vardouli pp. 49), digital exclusion, planning processes with no democratic ends, and mass surveillance followed by the rise of new forms of behavior manipulation (Sollazzo pp. 109), are critical risks that can be found on the other side of the exact same reality, fully powered by the applications of AI in the design and management of urban environments.

Within this context, how do we define "intelligence" in built space? How can we structure the vast data powered by geocoded web services or by millions of interconnected objects (IoT) and turn it into valuable input for informed decision (and design) making? The first two sections of "Learning Cities" promote a number of established and emerging innovators who are tackling these questions through critical thinking, research and practice.

Crowd & Collective Intelligence

No doubt in order to plan more infrastructurally optimized cities, the significance of IoT, sensors or actuators is fundamental. The data collected from the billions of devices and digital footprints of our era is the most precious fuel for sustainable planning engines to operate and for informed decision-making processes to be applied. This current scenario, though, fully embedded in techno-centric governance approaches propelled by the smart city movements, tends to equate urban problems with technological ones, while excluding actual people and their problems that are beyond the reach of technologies.[4] Aligned with both the possibilities and limitations of such a context, the third section of "Learning Cities" calls into question how human conditions are viewed as a key factor in comprehending and shaping the urban environment.

Human-generated data sets may be substantial, but they fall short when they are observed externally and statistically analysed as the total of individual values that could be inserted into computational algorithms. Big-data-based design and planning calls for novel models that systemically blend bottom-up and top-down processes while operating in bidirectional and circular feedback loops. That is, the models allow designers to learn about the wishes and needs of users and citizens, but citizens can also learn about the impact of their desires so that behavioural change can occur. The Superbarrio project developed by IAAC is a video game interface for participatory urban design that collects citizens' qualitative data and desires while they play and uses machine learning to leverage data, inform players on the impact of their actions, and provide more informed decisions for planning the Superblock in Barcelona. Similarly, the gaming platform Common'hood by Jose Sanchez uses data structures that group and store a series of player actions (blueprints) and is therefore able to store and analyze human decisions in space instead of geometries, establishing a peer-to-peer protocol for knowledge transfer.

Access to and collection of data needs to be democratized for communities and individuals in need, who do not always have access to technology. At the same time, between the data collection and urban action there is a huge unresolved abyss that needs to be addressed by both urban developers and citizens to create tools that facilitate conversation and inform participatory city-making (Rodrigo Delso & Javier Argota, pp. 173). Different techniques, including crowd sensing, as Sarah Williams explains..., can contribute not only to harvesting crowd-intelligence but also to empowering the crowd itself in different communities to gather the evidence to both fight for and understand their rights.

Can we, then, learn from the intelligence embedded in the bottom-up and disorganized decisions of users in our built environment? Is it possible to quantify qualitative data on communities' desires and perceptions to understand our current cities and help us plan future ones?

And how can we merge AI with an inter-species (post Anthropocene) approach that boosts knowledge and facilitates participatory city-making?

From real-time digital twins to emerging processes of cognitive and machinic co-creation, "Learning Cities" explores novel creative and design processes in which designers, communities, machines, and digital codes all play a fundamental role, with a unique resonance among them. Beyond the traditional human-driven multi-stakeholder approach, these novel technologically enhanced design processes represent a new collective intelligence (and maybe inter-species) design paradigm. The cities emerging have no predefined and closed form, while designers, citizens and their environment become participants in unique exchanges and dialogues facilitated by diverse living and non-living intelligences.

Who designs and who decides in such complex urban systems of cognitive behaviour and computational operation become crucial questions opening new pathways for our discipline. "Learning Cities" promotes an emerging collective intelligence design paradigm that empowers the applications of collective creation, following both cognitive and machine generative processes. This post-anthropocentric approach highlights a unique combination of crowd and machine wisdom that, together with other forms of intelligence (including animal, vegetable, or microbial), marks a significant milestone in the creation of our future cities.

1 Gausa, M., Markopoulou, A. and Vivaldi, J., 2020. *Black Ecologies*. Institute for Advanced Architecture of Catalonia and Actar Publishers.
2 Weiner, N. *Cybernetics or Control and Communication in the Animal and the Machine*. Vol. 25. MIT Press, 1961.
3 Martelaro, N., J. Wendy, *Cybernetics and the Design of the user experience of AI systems, Association for Computing Machinery*, 2018.
4 Biloria N., *From smart to empathic cities,* Frontiers of Architectural Research, Volume 10, Issue 1, 2021, pg 3-16

Areti Markopoulou, *Learning Cities: Collective Intelligence in Urban Design* (Barcelona: IAAC, 2023); 9–13.

In his chapter, "AI and the City of the Future," in *Architecture in the Age of Artificial Intelligence: An Introduction to AI for Architects* (2022), Neil Leach asks, "What will the city of the future look like?" Will cities designed with AI echo space age imagery of past images and impressions of the city of the future, or will they resemble contemporary cities today, retrofitted with embedded AI technologies?[20]

On one hand, Leach questions whether AI can genuinely create new architectural forms, in his critique of Patrik Schumacher's formulation of Parametricism, and Parametric Urbanism[21] and whether the future of cities will be shaped by novel architectural forms. Conversely, he highlights how devices like the iPhone allow us to navigate and understand existing cities in new ways. He cites the rise of Uber and other GPS-based apps as examples of how the true marvel of computation lies not in beguiling aesthetics but in new operational methods. This challenge is based on Benjamin Bratton's article, "iPhone City" (2009) in the AD issue, "Digital Cities,"[22] which calls for architects to pivot from the traditional role of designers to become "information architects," focused on reimagining existing infrastructures through software.

Leach brings to the fore Manuel Castells' exploration of the "Information City" in *The Informational City: Economic Restructuring and Urban Development* (1989). Castells contends that while cities in the information age will not mirror Silicon Valley, just as the industrial city was not a "worldwide replica of Manchester", they will undeniably be shaped by the digital revolution.

FIGURE 10.1 Aerial view of Agriport, The Netherlands, a business park hosting state-of-the-art greenhouses and data centers. Courtesy of Getty Images.

Mario Carpo asserts in this light, how "big data does not change the forms we design, . . . but the way we design."[23] Cities are becoming the site of various information interfaces, with AI and AI-driven applications taking on a more prominent role.

Drawing inspiration from Jane Jacobs, Leach underscores the significance of understanding cities from the grassroots level, observing "behaviors at street level." His fascination lies in ambient intelligence, where individual agents traverse intelligent environments that evolve through association and communication, recalling discussions on "swarm intelligence." Leach introduces the notion of 'City Brain,' highlighting corporate tech initiatives such as like Alibaba's 'City Brain' that use AI to create a 'digital twin' of the city, This initiative aims to enhance urban operations through real-time data processing and machine learning, akin to the interconnectedness and collective intelligence found in neural networks. He advocates for the decentralized self-regulated capacities of cities, emphasizing how their balance is maintained through homeostasis.

Leach concludes by stressing the emergence of urban intelligence, facilitated by the Internet-of-Things, where devices are smartly interconnected. His chapter sidesteps the alarm raised by other authors referred to in this chapter concerning any potential use, or mis-use, of AI technologies for surveillance by corporate entities or governments. With AI employed to enhance and regulate urban performance, Leach posits that a city's inherent intelligence, and its optimum performance, can indeed be augmented by AI.

NEIL LEACH
Architecture in the Age of Artificial Intelligence: An Introduction to AI for Architects

What will the city of the future look like? Will it look strikingly different to cities of today? Will it look like something out of The Jetsons, complete with flying cars and space age buildings? Or will it look much like our contemporary cities, with a few new buildings, but with much of the existing building stock retained and simply retrofitted with the latest AI technologies? In other words, will the primary driver of change be a language of novel architectural forms? Or will it be the introduction of ever more sophisticated AI-based technologies?

For Patrik Schumacher the city of the future will consist of novel architectural forms designed using the latest computational tools. In his article in 'Digital Cities', an issue of Architectural Design (AD) published in 2009, 'Parametricism: A New Global Style for Architecture and Urban Design', Schumacher outlines the design logic of Parametricism, which, he maintains, has now superseded modernism and other contemporary styles as the new global style of architecture . . .

. . . It (Parametricism) is a style, moreover, with its own quite recognisable characteristics: "Aesthetically, it is the elegance of ordered complexity and the sense of seamless fluidity, akin to natural systems that constitute the hallmark of parametricism".[1] And it is a style that, although it can be expressed at any scale from interior design to urban design, is most effective in large-scale urban developments: "So pervasive is the application of its techniques that parametricism is now evidenced at all scales from architecture to interior design to large urban design . . ." . . .

. . . iPhone City

In his own contribution to the same issue of AD, 'iPhone City', Benjamin Bratton takes a completely different approach.[2] Forget futuristic architectural forms. Think informational processes.[3] Bratton observes that there is an advanced computational device that is already changing our experience of cities: the simple iPhone. Although the iPhone has had little impact as yet on the design of new cities, it has already had a profound impact on how we operate in our existing cities. The development of smart navigation apps, for example, has allowed us to navigate and understand cities in new ways . . .

. . . as the success of Uber has shown us, is to harness the capacity of informational interfaces to generate new kinds of employment. In other words, computation has not given us new seductive forms, but rather new ways of operating . . .

. . . The information architect

In his essay, (Benjamin) Bratton includes a provocation, calling tor half of all architects to abandon the traditional model of the architect form-maker to effectively become what we might call 'information architects', drawing upon their design skills and computational abilities to develop not new designs, but new software that could be used to rework existing structures and systems . . .

. . . The future city, for Bratton, cannot be based on innovative forms alone. It also needs to embrace new informational systems. And we need to rethink the logic of architectural practice, shifting away from the all but exclusive model of the architect form-maker of the past, and opening up to also embrace a new model of the 'information architect'. . .

. . . The informational city

The idea of the informational city is not new. Manuel Castells published the book *The Informational City: Information Technology, Economic Restructuring and the Urban-Regional Process* back in 1989.[4] Castells followed this up with a trilogy of books on 'the information age', where he celebrates the 'network society', which operates not through integrated hierarchies but through organisational networks, and which depends upon the "constant flow of information through technology."

More recently, we have seen the development of the 'smart city', equipped, as Michael Batty comments, with 'constellations of instruments across many scales that are connected through multiple networks which provide continuous data regarding the movements of people and materials and the status of various structures and system'?[5]

. . . Whether we refer to the 'informational city', the 'smart city' or the 'city layer' of the stack, however, it is clear that cities of today are becoming the sites of informational interfaces, where AI and AI-based apps are playing an increasing role.

Ambient intelligence

The impact of AI on the city does not need to be viewed at the scale of the overall city. Indeed, the secret to understanding the city, as Jane Jacobs reminds us, is to perceive it in terms not of top-down major changes, such as master planning, but of incremental behaviours at a street level? The city could therefore be understood as constituted by a multiplicity of users, no less than flocks of birds or schools of fish are constituted by individual agents. The city might be significantly larger in scale than individual agents, but the city is constituted precisely by individual agents. In this way, we can understand that the city is already populated with AI-informed devices . . .

. . . Swarm intelligence

. . . Emergence can be observed wherever two or more agents interact in a bottom-up manner.[6] But it is most evident in a multiagent system whose interaction leads to a global behaviour. As the subtitle of the book suggests, Johnson makes an explicit connection between the emergent behaviours of a range of multiagent systems – such as ants, brains, cities and software – no matter how incommensurable their constituent elements.[7] We can therefore make direct comparisons between the operations of a city and the behaviour of a brain.[8]

Emergence has become a highly popular term in recent architectural discourse, but it is worth recalling that the term itself does not necessarily refer to contemporary design issues.[9] On the contrary, it could be argued that emergence can be viewed most clearly in traditional urban formations . . . . . . These forms of urbanism constitute a relatively homogeneous field of operations, where individual components do not stand out but conform to the pervasive logic of their surrounding environment.

Another way to think about emergence is through the logic of swarm intelligence. This is expressed in the decentralised, self-organising behaviour of multi-agent systems.[10] As Roland Snooks observes, 'Swarm Intelligence operates through the local interaction of autonomous agents that gives rise to emergent collective behavior within decentralised self-organising systems.'[11] . . ."

. . . The self-regulating city

John Holland describes how the city somehow manages to maintain a form of dynamic equilibrium, despite the constant changes that it experiences. He likens it to a 'standing wave' in a stream. A city can be seen as a 'pattern in time' . . .

. . . But how does a city manage to maintain this equilibrium?[12] Could the model of the 'city as brain' help us to understand this mechanism? . . .

. . . While the brain itself is highly adaptive, it can also serve as a mechanism of adaptation.

The self-organisation of cities can therefore be compared to the dynamic equilibrium of the brain. After all, cities are governed by both positive and negative feedback, much like the brain itself. At a very basic level, then, we can see parallels between Damasio's understanding of the homeostasis of the brain and the principles of self-organisation that underpin a city which could be reflected potentially in the behaviour of any multi-agent system, such as a neural network.

> 'Brains and cities, it would seem, have much in common.'

Could the city be understood literally *as* a brain? In strict neuroscientific terms, it obviously could not be. One is a human-mineral hybrid system, and one a biological organism.[13] Nonetheless a city could be described as a *kind* of brain, albeit perhaps not a human brain. Brains and cities, it would seem, have much in common.[14] Both are multi-agent systems. The same could be said of certain software systems. A neural network, after all, is composed of individual neurons which contribute to an emergent collective behaviour . . .

. . . 'City Brain'

Perhaps the most extensive exploration of the application of AI to the city has been the 'City Brain' initiative developed by Alibaba, a leading Chinese ecommerce company at the forefront of machine-learning development.[15] City Brain is effectively a 'digital twin' of the city itself. The idea behind the City Brain project is to develop a cloud-based system that stores information about the city in real time and uses machine learning to process that information in order to control the operations of the city and improve its performance . . ."

. . . Internet-city-brain

The concept of the 'Internet of Things' (IoT) refers to the idea that devices can be interconnected wirelessly. But what would happen if our AI-informed devices were not just connected through the IoT, but *intelligently* connected, like the neurons in the brain? . . ."

. . . How, then, are we to understand the intelligence of the AI assisted city? As Wang Jiang comments, "With the evolution of the city, the city has its own intelligence. It's not artificial intelligence. So, you can't put human intelligence into a city. The city is going to have its own intelligence ... The city is going to start its own thinking."[16] It could be argued, however, that the city already has a form of intelligence – although possibly not the capacity to actually 'think' through the logic of swarm intelligence. As such, AI can be seen to operate as a form of auxiliary intelligence to an intelligent system constituted by the city itself. The role of AI can therefore be seen as a supplementary one, to regulate and improve the performance of the city, much as a pacemaker serves to regulate and improve the performance of the heart. From this perspective, we can perhaps compare the role of AI-based technology in augmenting the operations of a city to the role of AI in augmenting human intelligence. Seen in this light, the city of AI can be understood as a city whose performance is *augmented* by AI.

Brain City – the city of the future – is the city of augmented intelligence . . . .

1. Schumacher, 'Parametricism', p. 16.
2. Ben Bratton, "iPhone City", in Leach, 'Digital Cities'.
3. Against the primacy of material form, we might therefore posit an alternative logic, and make a distinction between form – as in 'form for the sake of form' – and information. If, over the past few decades, we have seen a shift away from an obsession with pure form towards a set of more performative considerations, such as structural or environmental factors, whereby *form* is informed by *performative* constraints, should we not be recognizing a further shift towards pure information?
4. Manuel Castells, *The Informational City: Information Technology, Economic Restructuring and the Urban-Regional Process*, Oxford: Blackwell, 1989.
5. M. Batty, K. Axhausen, G. Fosca, A. Pozdoukhov, A. Bazzani, M. Wachowicz, G. Ouzounis and Y. Portugali, 'Smart Cities of the Future', *European Physics Journal*, Special Topics 214 (2012): 481–518. Anthony Townsend stresses a similar point: 'Information technology needs to be part of the solution, but it does not solve any problems by itself, no matter how powerful it is.' Townsend defines smart cities as 'places where information technology is combined with architecture, infrastructure, everyday objects, and even our bodies to address social, economic and environmental problems.' Anthony Townsend, *Smart Cities: Big Data, Civic Hackers, and the Quest for a New Utopia*, New York: Norton, 2014, p. 15.
6. Steve Johnson, Emergence: The Connected Lives of Ants, Brains, Cities and Software. New York: Schribner, 2002.
7. Within the field of architecture, multi-agent systems have become an important field of research. Neil Leach, and Roland Snooks (eds), *Swarm Intelligence: Architectures of Multi-Agent Systems*, Shanghai: Tongji University Press, 2017. The interest in a distributed model of design is forecast by Stan Allen when he cites Craig Reynold's work and suggests that swarm logic offers an insight int emergent methodologies: 'Crowds and swarms operate at the edge of control. Aside from the suggestive formal possibilities. I wish to suggest with these two examples that architecture could profitably shift its attention from its traditional top-down forms of control and begin to investigate the possibilities of a more fluid, bottom-up approach.' Stan Allen, 'From Object to Field', Architectural Design 67, no. 5/6 (May–June 1997): 24–31.
8. German neurophysiologist Wolf Singer has also made comparisons between the city and the brain. Wolf Singer, 'Die Architektur des Gehirns als Model l fur komplexe Stadtstrukturen ?', in C. Maar and F. Retzer (eds), Virtual Cities, Basel: Birkhauser, 1997, pp. 153–61. This comparison inspired Coop Himmelb(l)au to develop a research group, Brain City Lab, which exhibited a model of a city at the Venice Biennale 2008. The model used computational methods to projection-map the behaviour of neurons on to a landscape model of the city. Coop Himmelb(l)au, 'Future Revisited', http://www.coop-himmelblau.at/architecture/projects/coop-himmelblau-futurerevisited/.
9. See, for example, Michal Hensel, Achim Menges and Michael Weinstock, 'Emergence: Morphogenetic Design Strategies', AD (July-August 2004); Michael Weinstock, *The Architecture of Emergence: The Evolution of Form in Nature and Civilisation*, London: Wiley, 2010.
10. This is also sometimes referred to as populational behaviour. As Manuel De Landa observes, 'The dynamics of populations of dislocations are very closely related to the population dynamics of very different entities, such as molecules in a rhythmic chemical reaction, termites in a nest-building colony, and perhaps even human agents in a market. In other words, despite the great difference in the nature and behavior of the components, a given population of interacting entities will tend to display similar collective behavior.' Manuel De Landa, 'Deleuze and the Use of the Genetic Algorithm in Architecture', in Leach, *Designing for a Digital World*.
11. Leach and Snooks, Swarm Intelligence, p. 108.

12 This model of the city maintaining a form of dynamic equilibrium echoes the larger model of the Earth as a self-regulating complex system, as postulated by James Lovelock. James Lovelock, *Gaia: A New Look at Life on Earth*, Oxford: Oxford University Press, 1979.

13 For sure, Damasio himself would never equate a city to the brain. Nor would he compare AI to the brain. In fact Damasio actually has a background in AI, and counts the renowned AI pioneer Warren McCulloch as his first American mentor. Indeed at the time, Damasio shared some of the early excitement in neurobiology, computation and AI. And yet now he is aware of the shortcomings of this view, in that it overlooks the importance of the body. 'In retrospect, however, it had little to offer by way of a realistic view of what human minds look and feel like. How could it, given that the respective theory disengaged the dried up mathematical description of the activity of neurons from the thermodynamics of life processes? Boolean algebra has its limits when it comes to making minds.' Damasio, The Strange Order of Things, p. 240.

14 Previously I have also explored the possibility of the house operating as a form of brain: Neil Leach, 'Emergent Interactivities: From the primitive hut to the cerebral hut', Proceedings of the 34th Annual Conference of the Association for Computer Aided Design in Architecture, 23–25 October 2014, n.p.p.: n.p., pp. 145–52.

15 Alibaba is a Chinese multinational conglomerate holding company

16 Wang Jiang, 'City Brain: Rethinking the Relationship Between Technology and the City', ULI Asia Pacific, 2 July 2019, https://www.youtube.com/watcvh?v=RTpjzeQKg2w.

Neil Leach "AI and the City of the Future", *Architecture in the Age of Artificial Intelligence: An Introduction to AI for Architects* (London: Bloomsbury, 2022); 137–45, 151–8.

Investigating the consequences of AI for urban design and architecture, the practice, SPAN, led by partners Matias del Campo and Sandra Manninger, is taking a leading role, along with many others, including Immanuel Koh, Daniel Bolojan, and Kory Bieg. They express the design potentials of AI not only as scholars, but as designers promiscuously experimenting at the frontiers of their disciplines. Immanuel Koh, an early adopter of deep learning algorithms in architecture, co-authored a chapter with Jeffrey Huang, "Citizen Visual Search Engine: Detection and Curation of Urban Objects" (2017), in which a newly found agency for citizen science is proposed as an urban design method with which to generate novel outcomes from existing databases.[24]

Shifting to the use of AI as design tools, Matias del Campo, in his chapter, "How Machines Learn to Plan: A Critical Interrogation of Machine Vision Techniques in Architecture," in *Neural Architecture: Design and Artificial Intelligence* (2022), delves into the philosophical depths of the potential cognitive capacities of machines. He explores the ability of machines to think, grounding his contemplation in notions of creativity, sensibility, and the nature of non-human agency. Here, creativity is defined not only as novelty but also as the recognition of value. On the other hand, he argues that "sensibility" is the intricate designer's touch, the artistry that machines find challenging to emulate.

His work with deep neural networks showcases them as sophisticated algorithms that can learn, mirroring human neural processes. Paraphrasing Alan Turing, del Campo asks "can machines form plans"? In other words, can they configure "symbolic and abstract tasks," extending this to creating urban and architectural plans. In this light, thinking is defined by the capacity of neural networks to process exemplary information and "to generate a well-informed decision." Having experimented with the exploration of planimetric order at various scales, he notes how AI incorporates various styles, eras, and expressions, "influenced by the aesthetic choices of humans."[25] Again, parallels of these AI based machinic interfaces to the human brain arise, in mimicking the processes of human neural function to augment, assist, and possibly even to replace the human mind of the designer.

FIGURE 10.2 Image of an intensely landscaped public urban space, created with the platform Midjourney through generative artificial intelligence, by Carlos Bañon in 2023. Courtesy of Carlos Bañon.

Planning or designing involves the abstraction and materialisation of space and matter, representing "a vast collection of possible solutions to design problems." Del Campo argues that the judgment of plans on utilitarian grounds is "almost impossible." He explains that plans speak "simultaneously" of "planning processes, economic environments, material preferences, political conditions, and stylistic fashions when the urban design was created."[26]

Using style transfer to generate imagery, through a content image and a style image, Del Campo acknowledges the inherent bias of human training datasets of images. However, these AI tools—including del Campo's application of GANs, but also the more readily usable MidJourney, Dall-E, Ostagram, Runway ML, and others proliferating in design studios worldwide—possess capacities akin to neural networks, enabling them to morphologically alter images "completely independent and divorced from human agency."[27] He notes how these tools can hallucinate "alien features into conventional maps" with neurons that process and organize spatial information and communicate with other nodes in the network.[28]

Image classification is based on visual features such as a street or plaza. Varying weights enable multivariate differentiation, calculating predictions for neural networks that learn to represent objects without being affected by images outside their training data. When used for generating urban plans, the semantic content captured in images—such as "color, texture, and geometric structure"—creates unexpectedly rich mash-ups and hybrids through 2D neural style transfer.[29] Del Campo refers to these urban design processes and outcomes as the defamiliarization of the city proposing an alternative utopia. The notion of authorship is challenged by the ambiguity of human and non-human agency, amplified by the advent of AI.

Del Campo believes that whilst ". . . machines can certainly model and/or recognise styles . . . a planning process needs far more semantic information in order to successfully fulfil the task."[30] How then can AI be used in urban design on deeper levels of information than that of the 2D plan? He suggests further datamining and refinement of the dataset, which could potentially evaluate whether plans comply with building codes or functional requirements. This process requires training the model, "relying heavily on human judgment."[31] In this rapidly changing technological space, significant advances are expected in automating databases to use AI design tools more effectively into mainstream design practice.

In his book, *Artificial Intelligence and Architecture From Research to Practice* (2022), Stanislas Chaillou focuses on "The Urban Fiction Project" by SPAN (Matias del Campo and Sandra Manninger), and the technical ways in which style transfer algorithms of Generative Adversarial Networks (GANs) and Neural Turtle Graphics (NTG) models are used to generate urban mashups of diverse urban planimetric patterns and textures. SPAN's work, and del Campo's writing builds upon "the ever increasing amount of data documenting cities' multiple information layers," such as GPS and GIS maps, topographic information, infrastructure, and more.[32]

MATIAS DEL CAMPO
Neural Architecture: Design and Artificial Intelligence

Can machines think? This profound question was asked by computer science pioneer Alan Turing in his seminal paper Computing Machinery and Intelligence.[1] Considering this question leads immediately to specific stumbling blocks, as the terms "machine" and "thinking" are inherently difficult to define in a generally satisfying way. Turing, aware of this problem, suggested in the same paper to:

> "replace the question with another, which is closely related to it and is expressed in relatively unambiguous words."

Steven Harnad, a cognitive scientist, and Alan Turing scholar, reframed Turing's question closer to the research presented in this chapter by paraphrasing Turing:

> "Can machines do what we (as thinking entities) can do?"[2]

Both cases, Turing's as well as Harnard's, provoke the same seminal questions-questions that delve deeply into aspects of creativity, sensibility, and agency . . .

. . . In the frame of the presented conversation, creativity is the ability to find novel, surprising, or valuable solutions based on existing data and knowledge. These creations can be intangible (theories, political ideas, philosophical concepts, and jokes) and tangible (sculptures, buildings, paintings, instruments, and doodles). Sometimes these creations even exist in combination, considering that a computer is an actual object that can produce intangible products through an agent's input. I define agency[3] in this context as both unconscious, involuntary behavior and goal-driven, deliberate action with specific intentions . . . Sensibility is probably the most challenging category to be described objectively . . . I define sensibility as the ability of creative minds to conceive unique aesthetic expressions that are unique to them and inherently difficult to replicate. Unfortunately, this area of interrogation is difficult to corroborate as most of the inquiry into the term sensibility is closer to ideas of the consumption of art rather than the process of artistic production.[4] . . .

. . . Deep neural networks, which are robust, high performance algorithms that comprise a branch of the research on artificial intelligence and machine learning, are designed to learn from visual input in a fashion similar to humans. They are designed to mimic how the human brain processes incoming information. To train a neural network to understand and distinguish specific visual features of any kind of architecture, it needs to be trained to both identify and extract those features with thousands or millions of images. Paraphrasing Turing once more, I ask the question, "Can machines form plans?" My argument is that if machines can be trained to perceive their environment and use these perceptions to perform symbolic and abstract tasks. why should machines not form plans? . . .

. . . First of all, the machines used in the presented cases consist of code. Second, thinking in itself is a highly elusive term, lacking any generalized description. For clarity, I would like to rely on the following definition: Thinking, in this frame of interrogation, is defined as the ability of a neural network to process large amounts of exemplary information (plan images) to generate a well-informed decision.

At their most basic level. neural networks are mathematical functions that are structured and trained to extract features from their input that will maximize task performance. Nonetheless, because neural network structures are based upon our current understanding of how the human brain functions . . . in this case, the goal is to demonstrate and explore a plan design technique based on the style and spatial features learned by neural networks influenced by the aesthetic choices of humans . . .

. . . A Posthuman Trajectory for Plan Formation

The plan is undoubtedly an icon of architecture design that goes far beyond its mere meaning as an abstraction that allows it to execute the materialization of matter and space in a controlled manner. Architecture plans represent a vast collection of possible solutions to design problems . . .

. . . It is almost impossible to judge plans[5] on a purely utilitarian level. They always simultaneously talk about planning processes, economic environments, material preferences, political conditions, and stylistic fashions when the urban design was created . . .

. . . How can this rather difficult to grasp concept of "the plan" be realized through a neural network? This is where the aspects of the neural network's learned features take effect. The feature representations extracted by trained neural networks can be utilized to quantify and define textures within images . . . In the context of architecture designs, we can create a "plan or section texture" and hallucinate[6] its specific features in other images of plans or sections. This texture hallucination is referred to as style transfer, as it preserves the content of an image but modifies its appearance and style . . .

. . . Estranged-but in a Good Way

In my research investigating the implementation of AI-based style algorithms in planning processes, I made a crucial discovery . . . Neural networks rely on initial human training to do anything; humans design and collect the training dataset, which constrains the information the network has access to . . .

. . . During the research presented here, which focused on using 2D neural style transfer[7] for plan formation, it became apparent how much the behavior of a neural network depends on the training and parameter tuning conducted by a human being. My most exciting discovery in applying this style transfer technique is manipulating the influence and impact of style and spatial imagery, producing unexpected, atmospheric, and profoundly other, defamiliarized, and estranged results. They are estranged in a good way.[8]

If we turn the focus back on its consequences for architecture design, I would claim that when this style transfer technique is applied to design, it can blend a chronology of styles to create a dynamic style that captures and reflects a variety of design techniques over some time, including social and cultural evolution. Style artifacts can be exaggerated to a point of hyperbole, transforming the natural balance and harmony of human style and design into a pareidolic and compositionally unstable but novel form rooted in posthuman (in the sense that they were not primarily authored by human ingenuity), but humanly accessible, architectural features . . .

. . . The Defamiliarization of the City, or An Alternative Utopia

In architecture discourse, the line, the plan, and the abstract representation of materiality have played a major role, and they have always been interpreted as the result of human cognition . . . What position does the discipline take when it comes to understanding the potentialities of applications, such as neural networks, that are able to produce results that question the sole authorship of human ingenuity? . . . In a materialist tradition, though, thinking is just the result of material processes in our brain, neurochemical reactions able to form thought. If this position is taken, then the conclusion is that AIs can think as much, and form original language or shape as humans can, the only difference being that their neural processes are not based on neurochemical processes, but computational processes within another material paradigm. In this book, we present the possibility of utilizing AI applications for the generation of planning processes. In particular the application of style transfers with neural networks. This approach, on the one hand, critically interrogates the unique position of the human mind when it comes to creative processes and in addition questions aspects of creativity in planning processes . . . .

. . . this is only a first attempt in the area of the critical interrogation of planning in architecture in the age of AI. In fact, there is still much to be done. The first alien results achieved in this paper can only be seen as a first tapping into the potentialities of this approach, from a novel design direction that rather talks about how machines see our world—with all its wonderfully strange results in terms of morphologies, chromatics, and possible theories—to profoundly pragmatic approaches.

Going back to the initial question of whether machines can learn to plan, we can state that machines can certainly model and/or recognize styles, but a planning process needs far more semantic information in order to successfully fulfill the task. This means that the recognition of a style alone is not sufficient to label it as a successful planning process. For this to be synthesized in any form of neural network, a deeper level of information is necessary. Theoretically speaking, it is possible to create an entire series of databases instead of just one containing more semantic details on plans, such as doors, windows, living rooms, sleeping rooms, toilets, and baths, etc. . . .

. . . It is feasible to speculate about the pragmatic applications, such as the possibility of creating an application as a corrective tool in the planning process. Through data mining and dataset design, it would be possible to train a neural network that could analyze plans to see, for example, whether they comply with local building codes. Or the plans could be analyzed in regards to their functionality. All of these abilities need to be trained, heavily relying on human judgment at the beginning, but increasing their abilities after a period of training . . .

1 Alan M. Turing, "Computing Machinery and Intelligence," *Mind LIX*, No. 236, (Oxford: 1950), 433–60.
2 Stevan Harnad, "The Annotation Game: On Turing (1950) on Computing, Machinery, and Intelligence," in Robert Epstein, Gary Roberts and Grace Beber (eds), *Parsing the Turing Test: Philosophical and Methodological Issues in the Quest for the Thinking Computer* (New York: Springer, 2007), pp. 23–66.
3 George Wilson and Samuel Shpall, "Action," Stanford Encyclopedia of Philosophy, accessed June 15, 2021. https://plato.stanford.edu/entries/action/
4 Suzanne K. Langer, "On Artistic Sensibility," Daedalus 89, *No. 1, The Visual Arts Today* (Winter, 1960), The MIT Press, Cambridge, (Massachusetts, USA, 1960): pp. 242–244.
5 Of course, the same is true for sections. Plans are just a stand-in for every kind of construction document.
6 Leon A. Gatys, Alexander S. Ecker and Matthias Bethge. "A Neural Algorithm of Artistic Style." arXiv preprintarXiv"1508.06576 (2015).
7 ibid.
8 Graham Harman, *Weird Realism: Lovecraft and Philosophy* (Hants, UK: Zero Books, 2012), p. 93.

Matias del Campo, "How Machines Learn to Plan: A Critical Interrogation of Machine Vision Techniques in Architecture", *Neural Architecture: Design and Artificial Intelligence* (Hong Kong, Shenzhen: ORO, 2022); 133, 135, 138–9, 142–5, 147, 149, 152.

In the final text in this chapter, Kate Crawford's "Conclusion," in *Atlas of AI: Power, Politics and the Planetary Costs of Artificial Intelligence* (2021), raises alarms over the applications of AI, highlighting their racial biases and the questionable sources for materials and parts. Other texts that address emerging ethical issues and concerns include Ruha Benjamin's *Race After Technology: Abolitionist Tools for the New Jim Code* (2019) and Safiya Umoja Noble's *Algorithms of Oppression* (2018), amongst many others.

Delving into the ethical minefield of AI, Kate Crawford argues that AI should not be viewed as a neutral or purely objective computational tool that functions without human influence and direction. Instead, she emphasizes that AI is deeply intertwined with societal, cultural, and economic contexts, and is moulded by human hands, much like our societal institutions. She contends that AI systems inherently possess the capacity to discriminate and reinforce societal hierarchies by amplifying existing structural inequalities. Crawford provocatively asks: whose interests does this system really serve? Is it the corporate sector, established institutions, or governments? And what are the broader planetary consequences?

Crawford describes AI systems as manifestations of power, created to bolster profits and consolidate control for those in power. She challenges the prevalent notion of "algorithmic exceptionalism"—the idea that AI, being computational, surpasses human fallibility. Echoing Karl Marx's concept of the "commodity fetish," which describes the obscuring of social relations underlying commodities, she introduces the term "enchanted determinism" to describe this perspective. Crawford warns against an oversimplification of complexities and placing an unwavering faith in AI's predictive accuracy.[33]

Crawford identifies two polar viewpoints on AI: "Tech utopianism," which champions AI as a panacea, and "Tech dystopianism," which portrays AI as a looming threat while distancing it from its human creators. In essence, one perspective views AI as an omnipotent solution, while the other perceives it as an imminent danger. In either of these polarities, Crawford cautions against "technological determinism," which views AI as "fundamentally abstract" and overlooks the crucial sociopolitical and economic contexts that foster social inequality and environmental issues such as climate change. While these extreme dialectics may be useful – viewing AI as either an "all-purpose tool" or an "all-powerful overlord" – she insists on prioritizing discussions on power dynamics. Crawford also critiques the paradigm, or metaphor, of the "disembodied brain," which suggests that AI produces knowledge independently of its human creators.[34]

Crawford aims to expose the "interrelatedness of capitalism, computation, and control," and "the deep entanglement of technology, capital, and power, of which AI is the latest manifestation."[35] She warns of the potential "surveillance armory" that such tools can create, noting the risks of misuse by military forces, governmental agencies, and corporations. She highlights Google Street View as a case in point, evaluating its aggressive accumulation and categorization of data as a distinctly political act.

Crawford also juxtaposes the vast scope of automation against the looming climate crisis. Her research reveals that AI is an extremely energy-intensive technology, relying on raw resources from salt lakes and mines, inseparable from the logistics of planetary-scaled associations of flows and energy consumption. AI depends on data centers that consume significant electricity, often sourced from non-renewable energies, further increasing society's carbon footprint.

Finally, Crawford prompts us to contemplate: How can technology align with visions of a more equitable and just society? She advocates for the democratisation of AI, aiming for its use in promoting greater labour, climatic, environmental, racial and data justice, rather than merely serving as a tool for industrial data extraction and the reinforcement of societal biases.

KATE CRAWFORD
Atlas of AI: Power, Politics and the Planetary Costs of Artificial Intelligence

"Artificial intelligence is not an objective, universal, or neutral computational technique that makes determinations without human direction. Its systems are embedded in social, political, cultural, and economic worlds, shaped by humans, institutions, and imperatives that determine what they do and how they do it. They are designed to discriminate, to amplify hierarchies, and to encode narrow classifications. When applied in social contexts such as policing, the court system, health care, and education, they can reproduce, optimize, and amplify existing structural inequalities. This is no accident: AI systems are built to see and intervene in the world in ways that primarily benefit the states, institutions, and corporations that they serve. In this sense, AI systems are expressions of power that emerge from wider economic and political forces, created to increase profits and centralize control for those who wield them. But this is not how the story of artificial intelligence is typically told."

The standard accounts of AI often center on a kind of algorithmic exceptionalism—the idea that because AI systems can perform uncanny feats of computation, they must be smarter and more objective than their flawed human creators. . ."

Games without Frontiers

. . . A strong emphasis on rationalization and prediction emerged, along with a faith that mathematical formalisms would help us understand humans and society.[1] The belief that accurate prediction is fundamentally about reducing the complexity of the world gave rise to an implicit theory of the social: find the signal in the noise and make order from disorder.

This epistemological flattening of complexity into clean signal for the purposes of prediction is now a central logic of machine learning. The historian of technology Alex Campolo and I call this *enchanted determinism*: AI systems are seen as enchanted, beyond the known world, yet deterministic in that they discover patterns that can be applied with predictive certainty to everyday life.[2] . . . Above all, enchanted determinism obscures power and closes off informed public discussion, critical scrutiny, or outright rejection.

Enchanted determinism has two dominant strands, each a mirror image of the other. One is a form of tech utopianism that offers computational interventions as universal solutions applicable to any problem. The other is a tech dystopian perspective that blames algorithms for their negative outcomes as though they are independent agents, without contending with the contexts that shape them and in which they operate . . .

. . . These dystopian and utopian discourses are metaphysical twins: one places its faith in AI as a solution to every problem, while the other fears AI as the greatest peril. Each offers a profoundly ahistorical view that locates power solely within technology itself. Whether AI is abstracted as an all-purpose tool or an all-powerful overlord, the result is technological determinism. AI takes the central position in society's redemption or ruin, permitting us to ignore the systemic forces of unfettered neoliberalism, austerity politics, racial inequality, and widespread labor exploitation. Both the tech utopians and dystopians frame the problem with technology always at the center, inevitably expanding into every part of life, decoupled from the forms of power that it magnifies and serves . . .

. . . the tales of preternatural machine intelligence persist.[3] Over and over, we see the ideology of Cartesian dualism in AI: the fantasy that AI systems are disembodied brains that absorb and produce knowledge independently from their creators, infrastructures, and the world at large. These illusions distract from the far more relevant questions: Whom do these systems serve? What are the political economies of their construction? And what are the wider planetary consequences? . . .

. . . The Pipelines of AI

. . . AI began as a major public project of the twentieth century and was relentlessly privatized to produce enormous financial gains for the tiny minority at the top of the extraction pyramid . . .

. . . The description of AI as fundamentally abstract distances it from the energy, labor, and capital needed to produce it and the many different kinds of mining that enable it.

This book has explored the planetary infrastructure of AI as an extractive industry: from its material genesis to the political economy of its operations to the discourses that support its aura of immateriality and inevitability. We have seen the politics inherent in how AI systems are trained to recognize the world. And we've observed the systemic forms of inequity that make AI what it is today. The core issue is the deep entanglement of technology, capital, and power, of which AI is the latest manifestation. Rather than being inscrutable and alien, these systems are products of larger social and economic structures with profound material consequences.

The Map Is Not the Territory

How do we see the full life cycle of artificial intelligence and the dynamics of power that drive it? We have to go beyond the conventional maps of AI to locate it in a wider landscape. Atlases can provoke a shift in scale, to see how spaces are joined in relation to one another. This book proposes that the real stakes of AI are the global interconnected systems of extraction and power, not the technocratic imaginaries of artificiality, abstraction, and automation. To understand AI for what it is, we need to see the structures of power it serves.

AI is born from salt lakes in Bolivia and mines in Congo, constructed from crowd-worker-labeled datasets that seek to classify human actions, emotions, and identities . . .

. . . This book began below the ground, where the extractive politics of artificial intelligence can be seen at their most literal. Rare earth minerals, water, coal, and oil: the tech sector carves out the earth to fuel its highly energy-intensive infrastructures. AI's carbon footprint is never fully admitted or accounted for by the tech sector, which is simultaneously expanding the networks of data centers while helping the oil and gas industry locate and strip remaining reserves of fossil fuels. The opacity of the larger supply chain for computation in general, and AI in particular, is part of a long-established business model of extracting value from the commons and avoiding restitution for the lasting damage . . .

... At the data layer, we can see a different geography of extraction. "We are building a mirror of the real world," a Google Street View engineer said in 2012. "Anything that you see in the real world needs to be in our databases."[4] Since then, the harvesting of the real world has only intensified to reach into spaces that were previously hard to capture. . . . The collect-it-all mentality, once the remit of intelligence agencies, is not only normalized but moralized—it is seen as wasteful not to collect data wherever possible.[5]

Once data is extracted and ordered into training sets, it becomes the epistemic foundation by which AI systems classify the world . . .

. . . The result is a profound and rapid expansion of surveillance and a blurring between private contractors, law enforcement, and the tech sector, fueled by kickbacks and secret deals. It is a radical redrawing of civic life, where the centers of power are strengthened by tools that see with the logics of capital, policing, and militarization.

Toward Connected Movements for Justice

If AI currently serves the existing structures of power, an obvious question might be: Should we not seek to democratize it? Could there not be an AI for the people that is reoriented toward justice and equality rather than industrial extraction and discrimination? . . .

. . . To understand what is at stake, we must focus less on ethics and more on power. AI is invariably designed to amplify and reproduce the forms of power it has been deployed to optimize. When someone says, "AI ethics," we should assess the labor conditions for miners, contractors, and crowdworkers. When we hear "optimization," we should ask if these are tools for the inhumane treatment of immigrants. When there is applause for "large-scale automation," we should remember the resulting carbon footprint at a time when the planet is already under extreme stress. What would it mean to work toward justice across all these systems? . . . When AI's rapid expansion is seen as unstoppable, it is possible only to patch together legal and technical restraints on systems after the fact: to clean up datasets, strengthen privacy laws, or create ethics boards. But these will always be partial and incomplete responses in which technology is assumed and everything else must adapt. But what happens if we reverse this polarity and egin with the commitment to a more just and sustainable world? How can we intervene to address interdependent issues of social, economic, and climate injustice? Where does technology serve that vision? And are there places where AI should not be used, where it undermines justice? . . .

. . . The calls for labor, climate, and data justice are at their most powerful when they are united. Above all, I see the greatest hope in the growing justice movements that address the interrelatedness of capitalism, computation, and control: bringing together issues of climate justice, labor rights, racial justice, data protection, and the overreach of police and military power. By rejecting systems that further inequity and violence, we challenge the structures of power that AI currently reinforces and create the foundations for a different society.[6] As Ruha Benjamin notes, "Derrick Bell said it like this: 'To see things as they really are, you must imagine them for what they might be.' We are pattern makers and we must change the content of our existing patterns."[7] To do so will require shaking off the enchantments of tech solutionism and embracing alternative solidarities—what Mbembé calls "a different politics of inhabiting the Earth, of repairing and sharing the planet."[8] There are sustainable collective politics beyond value extraction; there are commons worth keeping, worlds beyond the market, and ways to live beyond discrimination and brutal modes of optimization. Our task is to chart a course there.

1   Galison, "Ontology of the Enemy."
2   Campalo and Crawford, "Enchanted Determinism."
3   Bostrom, Superintelligence.
4   Quoted in McNeil, "Two Eyes See More Than Nine," 23.
5   On the idea of data and capital, see Sadowski, "When Data Is Capital."
6   Mohamed, Phg, and Isaac, "Decolonial AI," 405.
7   Ruha Benjamin, "Race After Technology."
8   Bangstad et al., "Thoughts on the Planetary."

Kate Crawford, *Atlas of AI: Power, Politics and the Planetary Costs of Artificial Intelligence* (New Haven, CT: Yale University Press, 2021); 211, 215, 218-9, 220–7.

This final chapter draws tentative conclusions about the implications of emerging technologies for twenty-first-century cities. Addressing the rapidly evolving topics of AI and automation is a challenging task in this book, as chronicling such dynamic subjects as historical events is always fraught with uncertainty. While predicting the future of cities carries a certain allure, the inherent unpredictability of technological advancements makes it a precarious endeavour. The 2020s have been particularly pivotal, with disruptive AI technologies like ChatGPT, MidJourney, Stable Diffusion, Dall-E, and Runway ML reaching broader audiences. The proliferation and open-source availability of these tools has triggered architects and urban designers to reflect on their potential urban impacts.

This chapter unpacked the fractured narratives surrounding smart cities. It highlighted the aspirations of its champions who advocate for enhanced safety, security, comfort, and notably, efficiency. On the flip side, critics caution against the unchecked integration of AI in urban systems, fearing the erosion of democratic values in the face of technological surveillance. Yet, amidst these debates, there is no unanimous definition of a smart city. Does "smart" encompass sustainability, adaptability, safety, or inclusivity? Or does it lean towards control, automation, and surveillance? This debate places the smart city as the battleground between regimes of technocratic surveillance and those who promote civic empowerment and democratisation.[36]

While the integration of AI systems and the Internet of Things (IoT) into existing urban fabrics does not radically alter city structures, it imbues them with newfound intelligent capabilities, transforming urban spaces, experiences, and interfaces. Moreover, it compels urbanists to consider the ethical ramifications of AI and the pressing need to ensure digital, environmental, and social justice in an increasingly interconnected urban landscape. Navigating the post-COVID-19 world, urbanists bear a profound duty to operate ethically and champion greater equity, health and inclusivity in the design of our urban spaces.

In addition, the evolving dynamics between human and machine agency in design challenge traditional notions of authorship. If machines can design and innovate, what does this mean for human designers?

Similarly, what would it imply if cities could self-regulate, with humans no longer at the helm? Michael Weinstock delineates the evolution of urban intelligence paradigms into four progressive stages, each reflecting a deeper integration of intelligence and interactivity within city frameworks. These stages commence with the "Situated City," advance to the "Reactive/Responsive City," progress to the "Adaptive/Attentional City," and culminate in the "Self-Aware City."[37] In this

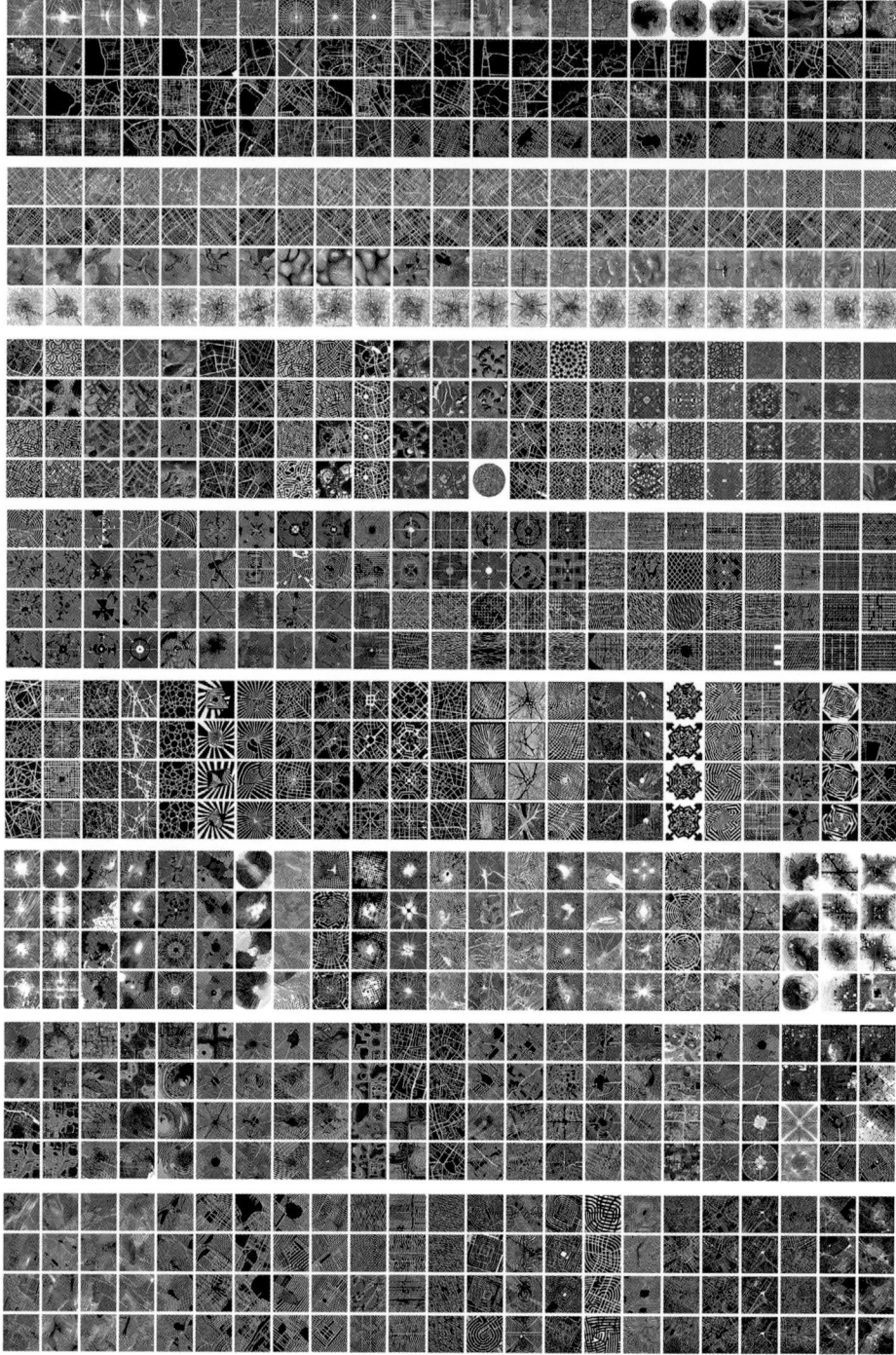

FIGURE 10.3 Arrays of urban plan diagrams, swiftly generated and visualized using Midjourney's generative artificial intelligence, during the Generative Urbanism workshop led by Tom Verebes and assisted by Gong Lei at DigitalFUTURES, hosted at Tongji University in 2023. Courtesy of Tom Verebes.

ultimate paradigm, the city reaches full intelligence, possessing self-awareness, an understanding of the behavior of its inhabitants, and the capability to harmonize its urban systems with climatic and ecological phenomena.

Discussions about the future of cities in our rapidly evolving technological age frequently arrive at conclusions that information technologies will dissolve traditional urban spaces. Despite predictions of the decline of cities—especially during events like the Covid-19 pandemic when remote work surged and urban dwellers sought suburban refuge—urban populations worldwide continue to grow. Past innovations, from the telegraph and telephone to the internet, similarly prompted declarations of the city's obsolescence and eventual irrelevance. Yet, in the post-Covid-19 era, cities persist as the locus of social, cultural and economic interchange.

With the advent of geolocation technology, there is a renewed emphasis on the importance of space in this century. As we find ourselves at the intersection of technology, urban design, and culture, we are presented with both thrilling design possibilities for urban environments and urgent challenges concerning the well-being and equity of urbanites.

Notes

Introduction

1 United Nations Department of Economic and Social Affairs, "2018 Revision of world urbanization prospects," May 16, 2018, https://www.un.org.

1 Spatial Heterogeneity, Diversity, and Difference after Modernist Planning

1 Jane Jacobs, *Downtown is for the People* (New York: Fortune Magazine, 1958): 87
2 Jane Jacobs, The Death and Life of Great American Cities (New York: Random House, 1961).
3 Katharine G. Bristol, "The Pruitt-Igoe Myth," *Journal of Architectural Education* 44, no. 3 (1991): 163–71.
4 Manfredo Tafuri, *Architecture and Utopia* (Cambridge, MA: MIT Press, 1973).
5 Aldo Rossi, *Architecture and the City* (Padova: Marsilio, 1966).
6 Andres Duany and Elizabeth Plater-Zyberk, *Charter of the New Urbanism* (New York: McGraw Hill, 2000).
7 Robert Venturi, Denise Scott Brown, and Steven Izenour, *Learning from Las Vegas: The Forgotten Symbolism of Architectural Form* (Cambridge, MA: MIT Press, 1972).
8 Colin Rowe and Fred Koetter, *Collage City* (Cambridge, MA: MIT Press, 1978).
9 Kenneth Frampton, "Towards a Critical Regionalism: Six Points for an Architecture of Resistance," in Hal Foster (ed.), *The Anti-Aesthetic: Essays on Postmodern Culture* (Seattle, WA: Bay Press, 1983).
10 Bernard Rudofsky, *Architecture without Architects: A Short Introduction to Non-pedigreed Architecture* (Albuquerque, NM: University of New Mexico Press, 1987).
11 Venturi, Scott Brown, and Izenour, *Learning from Las Vegas*.
12 Robert Venturi and Denise Scott Brown, and Steven Izenour, "Preface" and "Part 1: A Significance for A&P Parking Lots, or Learning from Las Vegas," in Learning from Las Vegas: The Forgotten Symbolism of Architectural Form (Cambridge: MIT Press, (1972), xi.
13 Robert Venturi, *Complexity and Contradiction in Architecture* (New York: MOMA, 1966).
14 Ibid, xii.
15 Ibid., 20.
16 Ibid., 3.
17 Ibid., 3.
18 Stefan Al, *The Strip: Las Vegas and the Architecture of the American Dream* (Cambridge, MA, and London: MIT Press, 2017).

19. Reyner Banham, "In the Rear-view Mirror," in *Los Angeles: The Architecture of Four Ecologies* (New York: Harper and Row. 1971), 23.
20. Reyner Banham, *Megastructure: Urban Futures of the Recent Past* (New York: Monacelli Press, 1976).
21. Fredric Jameson, "Postmodernism and Consumer Culture," Hal Foster (ed.), *Postmodern Culture* (London: Pluto Press, 1983).
22. Mike Davis, "*Fortress LA*" in *City of quartz: Excavating the future in Los Angeles* (Verso Books, 2006). (New York: Vintage Books, 1992), 154.
23. Colin Rowe and Fred Koetter, "Collision City and the Politics of 'Bricolage,'" in *Collage City* (Cambridge, MA: MIT Press, 1978), 86.
24. Ibid., 91.
25. Ibid., 90.
26. Ibid., 102.
27. Reinhold Martin, Utopias Ghost: Architecture and Postmodernism, Again (Minneapolis: University of Minnesota, xxvii).
28. "Postmodernism," 112.
29. Michael Sorkin, "See You in Disneyland," in Michael Sorkin (ed.), *Variations on a Theme Park* (New York: Hill and Wang, 1992), 205.
30. Ibid, 208.
31. Marc Augé, "Prologue" and "From Places to Non-Places," *Non-Places: Introduction to an Anthropology of Supermodernity*, translated by John Howe (London and New York: Verso, 1995), 1–6 and 75–115.
32. Rem Koolhaas, "The Generic City," in OMA, Rem Koolhaas, and Bruce Mau (eds.), *S,M,L,XL* (Rotterdam: 010).
33. Frampton, "Towards a Critical Regionalism," 25.
34. Ibid, 24.
35. Ibid., 19.
36. Ibid., 21.
37. Frampton, "Towards a Critical Regionalism," 17.
38. Ibid. 18–20.
39. Ibid., 26.
40. Ibid., 18.
41. Bernard Tschumi, "De-, Dis-, Ex-," in *Architecture and Disjunction* (Cambridge, MA: MIT Press, 1987), 215.
42. Ibid.,.216.
43. Ibid., 216.
44. Ibid., 218–20.
45. Ibid., 217.

2 Urbanism and Models of Design Complexity

1. Jane Jacobs, *The Death and Life of Great American Cities* (New York: Random House, 1961).
2. Ian McHarg, *Design with Nature* (New York: American Museum of Natural History, 1969).

3. Christopher Alexander, "The City is Not a Tree," Part 1, *Architectural Forum* 122, no. 1 (April 1965): 58–2; and Part 2, *Architectural Forum* 122, no. 2 (May 1965): 58–61.
4. Ibid., 61.
5. Manuel De Landa, *A Thousand Years of Nonlinear History* (Cambridge, MA: MIT Press, 1997).
6. Sanford Kwinter, "Soft Systems," in Brian Boigon (ed.), *Culture Lab* (New York: Princeton Architectural Press, 1993), 207–8.
7. Charles Jencks, *Architecture and the Jumping Universe* (London: Academy Editions, 1995), 167.
8. Steven Johnson, *Emergence: The Connected Lives of Ants, Brains, Cities and Software* (London: Penguin, 2001), 113.
9. Kevin Kelly, *Out of Control: The New Biology of Machines, Social Systems, & the Economic World* (New York: Basic Books, 1992), 87.
10. Peter Eisenman, "Strong Form, Weak Form," in *Architecture in Transition: between Deconstruction and New Modernism* (Munich: Pretsel, 1991), 33–45.
11. Ibid., 33, 44, 45.
12. Stan Allen, "From Object to Field," in Donald Bates and Peter Davidson (eds.), Architecture after Geometry. *AD (Architectural Design)* 127 (May–June, 1997): 24–31.
13. Roberto Magabeira Unger, "The Better Futures of Architecture," in Cynthia C. Davidson (ed.), *Anyone* (New York: Rizzoli, 1991).
14. Ibid., 29–30.
15. Ibid.
16. Ibid., 31.
17. Ibid., 29–30.
18. Ibid., 28.
19. Ibid.
20. Peter Eisenman, "Diagram: An Original Scene of Writing," *Any (Architecture: New York)* 23 (1998): 28.
21. Ibid.
22. Gilles Deleuze, *The Fold: Leibnitz and the Baroque*, translated by Tom Conley (Paris: Éditions de Minuit, 1988).
23. Greg Lynn, *Animate Form* (New York: Princeton Architectural Press, 1999).
24. Sanford Kwinter, "Who's Afraid of Formalism?," *Any (Architecture: New York)* 7/8 (1994).
25. Sanford Kwinter, "Wildness: Prolegomena to a New Urbanism," in *Far from Equilibrium: Essays on Technology and Design Culture* (Barcelona: Actar, 2007), 187.
26. Ibid., 189.

3 Intensities, Flows, Connectivity, and Network Urbanism

1. Keller Easterling, *Extrastatecraft: The Power of Infrastructure Space* (New York: Verso Books, 2014).
2. Frei Otto, *Occupying and Connecting: Thoughts on Territories and Spheres of Influence with Particular Reference to Human Settlement*, edited by Berthold Burkhardt (Stuttgart: Edition Axel Menges, 2009).

3 Michael Weinstock, *The Architecture of Emergence: The Evolution of Form in Nature and Civilisation* (London: John Wiley and Sons Inc., 2010).
4 Ibid., "City Forms," in ibid., 178.
5 Ibid.
6 Saskia Sassen. T*he Global City: New York, London, Tokyo* (Princeton, NJ: Princeton University Press, 1991).
7 Charles Waldheim and Alan Berger, "Logistic Landscape," *Landscape Journal* 27, no. 2 (2008): 219–46.
8 Jesse LeCavalier, *The Rule of Logistics: Walmart and the Architecture of Fulfilment* (Minneapolis, MN: University of Minnesota Press, 2016).
9 Reinhold Martin, *The Urban Apparatus: Mediapolitics and the City* (Minneapolis, MN: University of Minnesota Press, 2016).
10 Manuel Castells, *The Rise of the Network Society* (Oxford: Blackwell, 1996).
11 Manuel Castells, "Advanced Services, Information Flows, and the Global City," in *The Rise of the Network Society: The Information Age: Economy, Society, and Culture*. John Wiley & Sons, 2011), 429.
12 Manuel Castells (2011). "Advanced Services, Information Flows, and the Global City" in *The Rise of the Network Society: The Information Age: Economy, Society, and Culture*. John Wiley & Sons, 2011. p. 436.
13 Manuel Castells (2011). "Advanced Services, Information Flows, and the Global City" in *The Rise of the Network Society: The Information Age: Economy, Society, and Culture*. John Wiley & Sons, 2011. p. 429.
14 Adam Frampton, Jonathan Solomon, and Clara Wong, *Cities without Ground* (Novatao, CA: ORO Publishers, 2011).
15 Barrie Shelton, Justyna Karakiewicz and Thomas Kvan, *The Making of Hong Kong: From Vertical to Volumetric* (New York: Routledge, 2011).
16 Stefan Al, Mall City: Hong Kong's Dreamworlds of Consumption (Hong Kong: University of Hong Kong Press, 2016).
17 Jonathan Solomon, "Hong Kong – Aformal Urbanism," in Rodolphe El-Khoury and Edward Robbins (eds.), *Shaping The City* (New York: Routledge, 2013), 110.
18 Reyner Banham, *Megastructure: Urban Futures of the Recent Past* (New York: Harper and Collins, 1976).
19 Claude Parent and Paul Virilio, *The Function of the Oblique 1963–1969* (London: AA Publications, 2004).
20 Michael Kubo, Farshid Moussavi, and Alejandro Zaera Polo, *The Yokohama Project* (Barcelona: Actar, 2002), 11.

4 Density, the Compact City, and Metropolitan Culture

1 Jean Gottmann, "Megalopolis or the Urbanization of the Northeastern Seaboard," *Economic Geography* 33, no. 3 (1957): 189–200.
2 Frank Lloyd Wright (1928). *The Living City* (1928).

3   Terry G. McGee, "The Emergence of Desakota Regions in Asia: Expanding a Hypothesis," in Norton Ginsburg, Bruce Koppel, and T. G. McGee (eds.), *The Extended Metropolis: Settlement Transition in Asia* (Honolulu, HI: University of Hawaii Press, 1991).

4   Peter G. Newman and Jeffrey R. Kenworthy, *Cities and Automobile Dependence: An International Sourcebook* (Farnham: Gower Publishing Company, 1989).

5   Cervero, Robert, Erick Guerra, and Stefan Al, *Beyond Mobility: Planning Cities for People and Places* (Washington, DC: Island Press, 2017).

6   Architecture 2030, "Why the Building Sector?" accessed February 27, 2021, https://architecture2030.org/.

7   Jane Jacobs, *The Death and Life of Great American Cities* (New York: Random House, 1961).

8   [*Brundtland Report*] World Commission on Environment and Development, *Our Common Future: The World Commission on Environment and Development* (Oxford: Oxford University Press, 1987).

9   Richard Rogers, *Cities for a Small Planet* (London: Basic Books, 2008), 32.

10 Ibid., 34.

11 Ibid., 38.

12 Ibid., 40.

13 Ibid, 32.

14 Lewis Mumford, *The City in History: Its Origins, Its Transformations, and Its Prospects* (Boston, MA: Houghton Mifflin Harcourt, 1961), 34.

15 Alan Berube, *MetroNation: How US Metropolitan Areas Fuel American Prosperity*, Metropolitan Policy Program at Brookings (Washigton, DC: Brookings Institution, 2007).

16 Enrico Berkes and Ruben Gaetani, "The Geography of Unconventional Innovation," *Rotman School of Management Working Paper* 3423143 (July 19, 2019).

17 Bettencourt, Luís MA, José Lobo, Deborah Strumsky, and Geoffrey B. West. "Urban scaling and its deviations: Revealing the structure of wealth, innovation and crime across cities." *PloS one* 5, no. 11 (2010): e13541.

18 Steven Johnson, "Blueprint for a Better City," in *Wired*, December 1, 2001.

19 Rem Koolhaas, *Delirious New York: A Retroactive Manifesto for Manhattan* (New York: Monacelli Press, 2014).

20 Ibid., 155.

21 Ibid., 157.

22 Ibid., 125.

23 Rem Koolhaas, "Bigness, or the Problem of the Large," in OMA, Rem Koolhaas, and Bruce Mau (eds.), *S,M,L,XL* (Rotterdam: 010, 1994).

24 Ibid., 515

25 Winy Maas, Jacob van Rijs, and Richard Koek, *Farmax: Excursions on Density* (Rotterdam: 010 Publishers, 1998).

26 MVRDV, *KM3: Excursions on Capacities* (Barcelona: ACTAR, 2005).

27 Winy Maas, "Datascape: The Final Extravaganza," *Daidalos*, 69/70 (1998/1999), 48–54.

28 Hugh Ferriss, *The Metropolis of Tomorrow* (New York: Ives Washburn, 1929).

29 Winy Maas and MDRDV, *Metacity / Datatown* (Rotterdam: 010 Publishers, 1999).

30 Ibid., 59

5 Ecology, Resilience, and Green Infrastructure

1 Jared Diamond, *Collapse: How Societies Choose to Fail or Succeed*, revded. (London: Penguin, 2011).
2 Victor Olgyay, *Design with Climate: Bioclimatic Approach to Architectural Regionalism* (Princeton, NJ: Princeton University Press, 1963).
3 Rachel Carson, *Silent Spring* (Boston, MA: Houghton Mifflin, 1962).
4 R. Buckminster Fuller, *Operating Manual for Spaceship Earth* (Zurich: Lars Müller Publishers, Estate of R. Buckminster Fuller, 2008).
5 Donella H. Meadows, Dennis L. Meadows, Jørgen Randers, and William W. Behrens III, *The Limits to Growth: A Report for the Club of Rome's Project on the Predicament of Mankind*. Commissioned by the Club of Rome. (New York: Potomac Associates, Universe Books, 1972).
6 Ian L. McHarg, *Design With Nature* (New York: American Museum of Natural History, 1969), 16.
7 Mohsen Mostafavi, edited with Gareth Doherty, *Ecological Urbanism* (Cambridge, MA: Harvard University Graduate School of Design, co-published by Baden: Lars Müller Publishers, 2010).
8 Mohsen Mostafavi and Ciro Najle, "Landscapes of Urbanism," in Mohsen Mostafavi and Ciro Najle (eds.), *Landscape Urbanism: A Manual for Machinic Landscape*. (London: AA Publications, 2003), 6.
9 James Corner, "Landscape Urbanism" in in *Landscape Urbanism: A Manual for Machinic Landscape*. London: AA Publications, 2003), .58.
10 Charles Waldheim, "Landscape as Urbanism," in Charles Waldheim (ed.), *The Landscape Urbanism Reader* (Princeton, NJ: Princeton Architectural Press, 2006), 37.
11 Mark A. Benedict and Edward T. McMahon, *Green I nfrastructure: Linking Landscapes and Communities* (Washington, DC: Island Press, 2012).
12 Nate Berg, "Green Infrastructure Could Save Cities Billions," *City Lab*, April 24, 2012, available online: https://www.bloomberg.com/ (accessed February 27, 2021).
13 Mathew P. White et al., "Spending at Least 120 Minutes a Week in Nature is Associated with Good Health and Wellbeing," *Scientific Reports* 9, no. 1 (2019): 1–11.
14 Roger S. Ulrich, "View through a Window May Influence Recovery from Surgery," *Science* 224, no. 4647 (1984): 420–1.
15 Edward O. Wilson, *Biophilia* (Cambridge, MA: Harvard University Press, 1986).
16 William Saunders (ed.), *Designed Ecologies: The Landscape Architecture of Kongjian Yu* (Basel: Birkhäuser Architecture, 2012).
17 Bernard Rudofsky, *Architecture without Architects: A Short Introduction to Non-pedigreed Architecture* (Albuquerque, NM: University of New Mexico Press, 1987).
18 Julia Watson, *Lo-TEK: Design by Radical Indigenism* (Taschen, 2019).
19 Kenneth Frampton, ""Towards a Critical Regionalism," in *The Anti-Aesthetic*, Hal Foster, Ed. (Seattle: Bay Press, 21).

6 Health, Equity, and Livable Cities

1 Emily Anthes, *The Great Indoors: The Surprising Science of How Buildings Shape Our Behavior, Health, and Happiness* (New York: Scientific American / Farrar, Straus and Giroux, 2020).
2 Hilary Sample, "Emergency Urbanism and Preventive Architecture," in Giovanna Borasi and Mirko Zardini (eds.), *Imperfect Health: The Medicalization of Architecture* (Canadian Centre for Architecture, Montreal & Lars Müller, Canada, 2012).

3 Friedrich Engels, *The Condition of the Working Class in England* (Oxford: Oxford University Press, 1993), 65.
4 James Thomson, "The City of Dreadful Night," *National Reformer,* March 22, 1874.
5 Le Corbusier, *The City of To-morrow and Its Planning*, 131.
6 Jane Jacobs, *The Death and Life of Great American Cities* (New York: Vintage Press, 1961).
7 Jane Jacobs, "Downtown is for People," in William H. Whyte, Jr. (ed.), *The Exploding Metropolis* (Berkeley, Los Angeles, CA, and London: University of California Press, 1958), 168.
8 Ria S. Hutabarat Lo, "Walkability Planning in Jakarta," *University of California Transportation Center* (2011).
9 Annette Miae Kim, *Sidewalk City: Remapping Public Space in Ho Chi Minh City* (Chicago, IL: University of Chicago Press, 2015).
10 Michael Southworth and Eran Ben-Joseph, *Streets and the Shaping of Towns and Cities* (Washington, DC: Island Press, 2013).
11 Eran Ben-Joseph, *ReThinking a Lot: The Design and Culture of Parking* (Cambridge, MA: MIT Press, 2012).
12 Peter Newman and Jeff Kenworthy, "Peak Car Use: Understanding the Demise of Automobile Dependence," *World Transport Policy and Practice* 17, no. 2 (2011): 35–6; UN Habitat, *Planning and Design for Sustainable Urban Mobility: Global Report on Human Settlements 2013* (Nairobi: UN Habitat, 2013).
13 International Energy Agency (IEA), "CO_2 Emissions from Fuel Combustion by Sector in 2014, in CO_2 Emissions from Fuel Combustion," *CO_2 Highlights 2016* (Paris: IEA, 2016).
14 Lawrence D. Frank, Martin A. Andresen, and Thomas L. Schmid, "Obesity Relationships with Community Design, Physical Activity, and Time Spent in Cars," *American Journal of Preventive Medicine* 27, no. 2 (2004): 87–96.
15 World Health Organization (WHO), *Global Status Report on Road Safety* (Geneva: WHO, 2009).
16 A. Huzayyin, "Urban Transport and the Environment in Developing Countries: Complexities and Simplifications," in W. Rothengatter, Y. Hayashi, and W. Shade (eds.), *Moving to Climate Change Intelligence* (New York: Springer, 2011), 95–109.
17 Robert D. Putnam, "Bowling Alone: America's Declining Social Capital," *Journal of Democracy* 6, no. 1 (1995): 65–78.
18 Robert D. Putnam, *Bowling Alone: The Collapse and Revival of American Community* (New York: Simon & Schuster, 2000).
19 Don Appleyard, *Liveable Streets* (London: Elsevier, 1981); Jan Gehl, *Life between Buildings: Using Public Space* (Washington, DC: Island Press, 2011); and Jeff Speck, *Walkable City: How Downtown Can Save America, One Step at a Time* (New York: Macmillan, 2013).
20 Jan Gehl, *Life Between Buildings: Using Public Space* (Washington, DC: Island Press, 2011).
21 Chris Rissel, Nada Curac, and Mark Greenaway, "Physical Activity Associated with Public Transport Use—A Review and Modelling of Potential Benefits," *International Journal of Environmental Research and Public Health* 9, no. 7 (2012): 2454–78.
22 Allan Jacobs and Donald Appleyard, "Toward an Urban Design Manifesto," *Journal of the American Planning Association* 53, no. 1 (1987): 112–20.
23 Herbert J. Gans, "Planning and Social Life: Friendship and Neighbor Relations in Suburban Communities," *Journal of the American Institute of Planners* 27, no. 2 (1961): 134–40.
24 Marshall, Alex. *How cities work: Suburbs, sprawl, and the roads not taken.* University of Texas Press, 2001.

25 William H. Whyte, *City: Rediscovering the Center* (New York: Doubleday, 1988), 233.
26 William Hollingsworth Whyte, *The Social Life of Small Urban Spaces* (New York: The Conservation Foundation, 1980), 15.
27 "New York City's Privately Owned Public Plazas," New York City Department of City Planning, NYC.gov, available online: https://www.nyc.gov/site/planning/plans/pops/pops-plaza-standards.page. (accessed January 10, 2024).
28 Louise Plouffe and Alexandre Kalache, "Towards Global Age-Friendly Cities: Determining Urban Features that Promote Active Aging," *Journal of Urban Health* 87, no. 5 (2010): 733–9.
29 Dolores Hayden, "What Would a Non-sexist City Be Like? Speculations on Housing, Urban Design, and Human Work," in Susan S. Fainstein and Lisa J. Servon (eds.), *Gender and Planning: A Reader* (New Brunswick, NJ: Rutgers University Press, 2005).
30 Elizabeth Wilson, *The Sphinx in the City: Urban Life, the Control of Disorder, and Women* (Berkeley, CA: University of California Press, 1991), 9.
31 Aaron Betsky, *Queer Space: Architecture and Same Sex Drive* (London: HarperCollins, 1997).
32 Richard Rothstein, *The Color of Law: A Forgotten History of How Our Government Segregated America* (New York: Liveright Publishing, 2017).
33 Matthew Desmond, *Evicted: Poverty and Profit in the American City* (New York: Crown, 2017).
34 Robert D. Bullard, *Dumping in Dixie: Race, Class, and Environmental Quality* (Boulder, CO: Westview Press, 1990).
35 Paul Stanton Kibel, "Access to Parkland: Environmental Justice at East Bay Parks," *Environmental Law and Justice Clinic* 2 (2007).
36 Walter Hood, "Afterword," in Walter Hood and Grace Mitchell Tada (eds.), *Black Landscapes Matter* (Charlottesville, VA: University of Virginia Press, 2020).
37 Walter Hood, "Introduction," in Walter Hood and Grace Mitchell Tada (eds.), *Black Landscapes Matter* (Charlottesville, VA: University of Virginia Press, 2020).

7 Emergent, Tactical, and Informal Urbanism

1 Jason Ur, "Households and the Emergence of Cities in Ancient Mesopotamia," *Cambridge Archaeological Journal* 24, no. 2 (2014): 249–68.
2 See, for instance, E. J. Malecki and R. Ramanath (eds.), *Illegal Cities: Law and Urban Change in Developing Countries* (London and New York: Zed Books, 2002); and Felipe H. Hernández, Peter W. Kellett, and Lea K. Allen (eds.), *Rethinking the Informal City: Critical Perspectives from Latin America* (New York and Oxford: Berghahn Books, 2010.
3 Peter M. Ward, *Colonias and Public Policy in Texas and Mexico: Urbanization by Stealth* (Austin, TX: University of Texas Press, 1999).
4 Mike Davis, *Planet of Slums* (London and New York: Verso Books, 2006).
5 UN-Habitat, *Informal Settlements* (Habitat III Issue Papers 22) (Nairobi: UN-Habitat, 2015).
6 Ananya Roy and Nezar AlSayyad (eds.), *Urban Informality: Transnational Perspectives from the Middle East, Latin America, and South Asia* (Lanham, MD: Lexington Books, 2003).
7 Janice E. Perlman, *The Myth of Marginality: Urban Poverty and Politics in Rio de Janeiro* (Los Angeles, CA: University of California Press, 1976).
8 Asher Ghertner, *Rule by Aesthetics: World-Class City Making in Delhi* (Oxford: Oxford University Press, 2015).

9 Asef Bayat, "From 'Dangerous Classes' to 'Quiet Rebels': Politics of the Urban Subaltern in the Global South," *International Sociology* 15, no. 3 (2000): 533–57.

10 Thomas J. Campanella, *The Concrete Dragon: China's Urban Revolution and What It Means for the World* (New York: Princeton Architectural Press, 2008).

11 Stefan Al (ed.), *Villages in the City: A Guide to Southern China's Informal Settlement* (Honolulu, HI: University of Hawaii, 2014).

12 Juan Du, *The Shenzhen Experiment: The Story of China's Instant City* (Cambridge, MA: Harvard University Press, 2020).

13 World Bank, *Better Infrastructure for 7.5 Million Urban Residents in Vietnam*. December 19, 2014, available online: https://www.worldbank.org/en/news/feature/2014/12/19/better-infrastructure-for-75-million-urban-residents-in-vietnam. (accessed January 11, 2024).

14 Gita Dewan Verma, "Indore's Habitat Improvement Project: Success or Failure?," *Habitat International: A Journal for the Study of Human Settlements* 24 (2000): 91–117.

15 Gita Dewan Verma, *Slumming India: A Chronicle of Slums and Their Saviors* (London: Penguin Books, 2002).

16 Roy, "Urban Informality," 147.

17 Hernández, Kellett, and Knudsen Allen (eds.), *Rethinking the Informal City*, 15.

18 Alfredo Brillembourg and Hubert Klumpner, "Rules of Engagement: Caracas and the Informal City," in Hernándéz, Kellett, and Allen (eds.), *Rethinking the Informal City*, 119.

19 Alfredo Brillembourg and Hubert Klumpner (eds.), *Torre David: Informal Vertical Communities* (Baden: Lars Müller Publishers, 2013).

20 Justin McGuirk, *Radical Cities: Across Latin America in Search of a New Architecture* (London and New York: Verso Trade, 2014).

21 John Turner and Robert Fichter (eds.), *Freedom to Build: Dweller Control of the Housing Process* (London: Macmillan, 1972).

22 Alejandro Aravena, "Elemental: A Do Tank," *AD* (*Architectural Design*) 81, no. 3 (2011): 32–7.

23 Michel de Certeau, *The Practice of Everyday Life*, translated by Steven Rendall (Berkeley, CA: University of California Press, 1984).

24 Margaret Crawford, *Everyday Urbanism* (New York: Monacelli Press, 2008).

25 Mike Lydon and Anthony Garcia, "A Tactical Urbanism How-to," in *Tactical Urbanism: Short-Term Action for Long-Term Change* (Washington, DC: Island Press, 2015), ___page___.

26 Ibid., ___page___.

8 Evolutionary, Computational, and Parametric Urbanism

1 Jane and Mark Burry, *The New Mathematics of Architecture* (London: Thames and Hudson, 2010), 54.

2 Neil Spiller, "The Architectural Relevance of Cybernetics," in Neil Spiller (ed.), *Cyber Reader* (London: Phaidon, 2002), 68.

3 Gordon Pask, "Foreword," in John Frazer, *An Evolutionary Architecture* (London: AA Publications, 1995).

4 Nicholas Negroponte, Soft Architecture Machines (Cambridge, MA: MIT Press, 1970).

5 Benjamin H. Bratton, *The Stack: On Software and Sovereignty* (Cambridge, MA: MIT Press, 2015).

6 Michael Batty, *Cities and Complexity: Understanding Cities with Cellular Automata, Agent-based Models, and Fractals* (Cambridge, MA: MIT Press, 2005).

7 Michael Batty (2005). "Introduction: Understanding Cities" in *Cities and Complexity: Understanding Cities with Cellular Automata, Agent-based Models, and Fractals*. MIT Press, Cambridge. p.6.
8 Jane Jacobs, *The Death and Life of Great American Cities* (New York: Random House, 1961).
9 Michael Batty (2005). "Introduction: Understanding Cities" in *Cities and Complexity: Understanding Cities with Cellular Automata, Agent-based Models, and Fractals*. MIT Press, Cambridge. p.9.

9 Virtuality, Extended Realities, and the Metaverse

1 Olivier Grau, *Virtual Art: From Illusion to Immersion* (Cambridge, MA: MIT Press, 2003).
2 Kevin Lynch, *The Image of the City* (Cambridge, MA: MIT Press, 1964).
3 Jean Baudrillard, Simulacra and S imulation (Ann Arbor, MI: University of Michigan Press, 1994).
4 Nicholas Negroponte, "Introduction," in *Soft Architecture Machines* (Cambridge, MA: MIT Press, 1970).
5 Mario Carpo (2023). *Beyond Digital: Design and Automation at the End of Modernity*. Cambridge: MIT Press. p. 61-63.
6 Sylvia Lavin, *Kissing Architecture* (Princeton, NJ: Princeton University Press, 2011).
7 Ivan Edward Sutherland, *Sketchpad: A Man- Machine Graphical Communication System*. Technical Report – Massachusetts Institute of Technology, Lincoln Laboratory (Cambridge: MIT Press, 1963).
8 William J. Mitchell, "Boundaries / Networks," In *Me++: The Cyborg Self and the Networked City* (Cambridge, MA: MIT Press, 2003).
9 Paul Virilio, *The Aesthetics of Disappearance* (Cambridge, MA: MIT Press, 1980); and ibid., *The Lost Dimension* (New York: Semiotext(e), 1991).
10 Norbert Wiener, *Cybernetics: Or Control and Communication in the Animal and the Machine* (Paris: Hermann & Cie; and Cambridge, MA: MIT Press, 1948).
11 Gilbert Simondon, On the Mode of Existence of Technical Objects (Paris: Aubier, Editions Montaigne, 1958).
12 Peter Trummer, (2023). The City as a Technical Being: One the Mode of Existence of Architecture. (New York: ORO Publications).
13 Carlo Ratti and Matthew Claudel, *The City of Tomorrow: Sensors, Networks, Hackers, and the Future of Urban Life* (New Haven, CT: Yale University Press, 2016),62.
14 Ibid., 73.
15 Stephen Graham, "Bridging Urban Digital Divides? Urban Polarisation and Information and Communications Technologies (ICTs)," *Urban Studies* 39, no. 1 (2002): 33–56.
16 Shannon Mattern, *A City is Not a Computer: Other U rban I ntelligences*, vol. 2 (Princeton, NJ: Princeton University Press, 2021).
17 Ivan E. Sutherland, "The Ultimate Display," in Wayne A. Kalenich (ed.), *Information Processing 1965: Proceedings of the IFIP Congress 65*, vol. 2, no. 506–8 (London: Macmillan & Co., 1965).
18 John Armitage, "Virilio Live: Selected Interviews," *Virilio Live* (2001): 1–240.
19 Virilio, *The Lost Dimension*.
20 William Gibson, *Neuromancer* (New York: Ace Books, 1984).
21 Marcos Novak, "Liquid Architectures in Cyberspace," in Michael Benedikt (ed.), *Cyberspace: First Steps* (Cambridge, MA: MIT Press, 1991).

22 Marcos Novak, "Transmitting Architecture," Architects in Cyberspace, *AD (Architectural Design)* 118 (1995): 42–7.
23 Neal Stephenson, *Snow Crash: A Novel* (New York: Spectra, [1992] 2003).
24 David J. Chalmers, *Reality+: Virtual Worlds and the Problems of Philosophy* (London: Penguin, 2022).
25 Wendy W. Fok, *Digital Structures: Data and Urban Strategies of the Civic Future* (New York: ORO Publications, 2023).
26 Greg Lindsay, "What is the Metaverse Metropolis?," Greglindsay.org. December 10, 2022, available online: https://www.greglindsay.org/blog/2022/12/what-is-the-metaverse-metropolis/.
27 Ted Striphas, *Algorithmic Culture Before the Internet* (New York: Columbia University Press, 2023).
28 Philippe Morel, (2023). *Disruptive Technologies: The Convergence of New Paradigms in Architecture*, Henriette Bier and Philippe Morel, eds. (London: Springer, 2023).
29 Patrik Schumacher, (2023). "Cyber-Urban Integration," in Bier and Morel (eds.), *Disruptive Technologies* (2023)*: The Convergence of New Paradigms in Architecture*, Henriette Bier and Philippe Morel, eds. London : Springer.
30 Andrea Moneta, "Architecture, Heritage, and the Metaverse," *Traditional Dwellings and Settlements Review* 32, no. 1 (2020): 37– 49.
31 Ibid., 37.
32 Ibid., 39.
33 Ibid., 48.

10 Artificial Intelligence, the Internet of Things, and Technological Determinism

1 Benjamin Bratton, "AI Urbanism: A Design Framework for Governance, Program, and Platform Cognition," *AI & Society*, 36 (2021): 1307–12.
2 Neil Leach, *Architecture in the Age of Artificial Intelligence: An Introduction to AI for Architects* (London: Bloomsbury, 2022).
3 Shannon Mattern, *A City is Not a Computer: Other Urban Intelligences* (New York: Princeton Architectural Press, 2021), 5.
4 Kate Crawford, *Atlas of AI: Power, Politics and the Planetary Costs of Artificial Intelligence* (New Haven, CT: Yale University Press), 213.
5 Antoine Picon, "Introduction: A New Urban Ideal," in *Smart Cities: A Spatialised Intelligence* (London: Wiley, 2015), 14.
6 George Orwell, Nineteen Eighty-Four. (London: Penguin Classics, 2021).
7 Ibid., 17.
8 Tom Verebes, "UrbanISMS: Paradigmatic Practices and their Multifarious Platforms," PhD diss. (RMIT University, Melbourne, 2018), 334.
9 Mark Shepard (ed.), *Sentient City: Ubiquitous Computing, Architecture, and the Future of Urban Space* (Cambridge, MA: MIT Press, 2011); Anthony M. Townsend, "Introduction: Urbanisation and Ubiquity," in *Smart Cities: Big Data, Civic Hackers, and the Quest for a New Utopia* (New York: W. W. Norton, 2013), 11.
10 Bratton, "AI Urbanism."
11 Pablo Lorenzo-Eiroa, *Digital Signifiers in an Architecture of Information: From Big Data and Simulation to Artificial Intelligence* (New York: Routledge, 2023).

NOTES

12 Areti Markopoulou, *Learning Cities: Collective Intelligence in Urban Design* (Barcelona: IAAC, 2023), 9. Reference to Warren Brody (1967).

13 Markopoulou, *Learning Cities*, 11.

14 Ibid., 10.

15 Marshall McLuhan, *Understanding Media* (Toronto: McGraw Hill, 1964).

16 Pierre Levy, *Collective Intelligence: Mankind's Emerging World in Cyberspace* (Cambridge, MA: Perseus, 1997).

17 Christopher Hight and Chris Perry (guest eds.), Collective Intelligence. AD (*Architectural Design*) Profile No. 183, vol. 76, no. 5 (2006): 5–6.

18 Keller Easterling, "The Action is the Form," in Mark Shepard (ed.), *Sentient City: Ubiquitous Computing, Architecture and the Future of Urban Space* (New York and Cambridge, MA: Architectural League and MIT Press, 2011).

19 Keller Easterling, "Action is the Form", Mark Shepherd Ed. Sentient City: ubiquitous computing, architecture, and the future of urban space (New York and Cambridge: Architecture League and MIT Press, 2011).

20 Neil Leach (2022). *Architecture in the Age of Artificial Intelligence: An Introduction to AI for Architects*. London: Bloomsbury. p.137.

21 "Parametric Urbanism" was initially formulated as a research agenda in the post-professional Master of Architecture and Urbanism programme, the AA Design Research Lab (AADRL) at the AA School of Architecture in London, 2005-2009, conceived, taught, and co-directed by Yusuke Obuchi, Patrik Schumacher, Theo Spyropoulos, and Tom Verebes.

22 Benjamin Bratton, "iPhone City." Digital Cities. AD (*Architectural Design*) 79, no. 4 (July/August 2009): 90–9.

23 Neil Leach (2022). *Architecture in the Age of Artificial Intelligence: An Introduction to AI for Architects*. London: Bloomsbury. p. 141.

24 Jeffrey Huang and Immanuel Koh, "Citizen Visual Search Engine: Detection and Curation of Urban Objects," in J.-H. Lee (ed.), *Computer-Aided Architectural Design* (Singapore: Springer, 2019), 168–82.

25 Matias del Campo, "Introduction," in *Neural Architecture: Design and Artificial Intelligence* (Hong Kong, Shenzhen: ORO, 2022), 133.

26 Ibid., 149.

27 Ibid., 142.

28 Ibid., 138.

29 Ibid., 147.

30 Ibid., 149.

31 Ibid., 152.

32 Stanislas Chaillou, Artificial Intelligence and Architecture: From Research to Practice, 1st ed. (Basel: Verlag GmbHBirkhäuser, 2022), 85.

33 Crawford, *Atlas of AI*, 213.

34 Ibid., 214–15.

35 Ibid., 217.

36 Verebes, "UrbanISMS," 301.

37 Michael Weinstock, "System City: Infrastructure and the Space of Flows," in M. Weinstock (guest ed.), System City. AD (*Architectural Design*) 224 (2013): 14–23.

Bibliography

Chapter 1

Al, Stefan. *The Strip: Las Vegas and the Architecture of the American Dream*. Cambridge, MA, and London: MIT Press, 2017.

Augé, Marc. "Prologue" and "From Places to Non-places." In *Non-Places: Introduction to an Anthropology of Supermodernity*. Translated by John Howe. London and New York: Verso, 1995.

Banham, Reyner. "In the Rear-view Mirror." In *Los Angeles: The Architecture of Four Ecologies*. New York: Harper and Row, 1971.

Banham, Reyner. *Megastructure: Urban Futures of the Recent Past*. Los Angeles, CA: Harper and Row, 1976.

Bristol, Katharine G. "The Pruitt-Igoe Myth." *Journal of Architectural Education* 44, no. 3 (1991): 163–71.

Davis, Mike. "Fortress Los Angeles: The Militarization of Urban Space." In Michael Sorkin (ed.), *Variations on a Theme Park: The New American City and the End of Public Space*. New York: Hill and Wang, 1992.

Duany, Andres, and Elizabeth Plater-Zyberk. *The Charter of New Urbanism*. New York: McGraw Hill, 2000.

Frampton, Kenneth. "Towards a Critical Regionalism: Six Points for an Architecture of Resistance." In Hal Foster (ed.), *The Anti-Aesthetic: Essays on Postmodern Culture*. Seattle, WA: Bay Press, 1983.

Jacobs, Jane. *The Death and Life of Great American Cities*. New York: Random House, 1961.

Jameson, Fredric. *Postmodernism, or, The Cultural Logic of Late Capitalism*. Durham, NC: Duke University Press, 1991.

Jameson, Fredric. "Postmodernism and Consumer Culture." In Hal Foster (ed.), *Postmodern Culture*. London: Pluto Press, 1983.

Koolhaas, Rem. "The Generic City." In OMA, Rem Koolhaas, and Bruce Mau (eds.), *S,M,L,XL*. Rotterdam: 010, 1995.

Rossi, Aldo. *Architecture and the City*. Padova: Marsilio, 1966.

Rowe, Colin, and Fred Koetter. "Collision City and the Politics of Bricolage." In *Collage City*. Cambridge, MA: MIT Press, 1978.

Rudofsky, Bernard. *Architecture without Architects: A Short Introduction to Non-pedigreed Architecture*. Albuquerque, NM: University of New Mexico Press, 1987.

Sorkin, Michael. "See You in Disneyland." In Michael Sorkin (ed.), *Variations on a Theme Park*. New York: Hill and Wang, 1992.

Tafuri, Manfredo. *Architecture and Utopia*. Cambridge, MA: MIT Press, 1973.

Tschumi, Bernard. "De-, Dis-, Ex-." In *Architecture and Disjunction*. Cambridge, MA: MIT Press, 1987.

Tschumi, Bernard. "Manhattan Transcripts." In *Architecture and Disjunction*. Cambridge, MA: MIT Press, 1976–81.

Venturi, Robert. *Complexity and Contradiction in Architecture*. New York: MOMA, 1966.

Venturi, Robert, Denise Scott Brown, and Steven Izenour. *Learning from Las Vegas: The Forgotten Symbolism of Architectural Form*. Cambridge, MA: MIT Press, 1972.

Venturi, Robert, Denise Scott Brown, and Steven Izenour. "Preface" and "Part 1: A Significance for A&P Parking Lots, or Learning from Las Vegas." In *Learning from Las Vegas: The Forgotten Symbolism of Architectural Form*. Cambridge, MA: MIT Press, 1972.

Verebes, Tom. "Cities and Their Specificities." In Tom Verebes (guest ed.), Mass Customised Cities. *AD* (*Architectural Design*), Profile No. 238 (2015).

Chapter 2

Alexander, Christopher. "The City is Not a Tree." Part 1, *Architectural Forum* 122, no. 1 (April 1965): 58–2; and Part 2, *Architectural Forum* 122, no. 2 (May 1965): 58–61.
Allen, Stan. "From Object to Field." In Donald Bates and Peter Davidson (eds.), Architecture after Geometry. *AD* (*Architectural Design*) 127 (May–June, 1997): 24–31.
De Landa, Manuel. "Introduction." In *A Thousand Years of Nonlinear History*. Cambridge, MA: MIT Press, 1997.
Deleuze, Gilles. *The Fold: Liebnitz and the Baroque*. Translated by Tom Conley. Paris: Éditions de Minuit, 1988.
Eisenman, Peter. "Diagram: An Original Scene of Writing." *Any* (*Architecture: New York*) 23 (1998).
Eisenman, Peter. "Diagrams of Exteriority." In *Diagram Diaries*. London: Thames and Hudson, 1999.
Eisenman, Peter. "Strong Form, Weak Form." In *Architecture in Transition: Between Deconstruction and New Modernism*. Munich: Pretsel, 1991.
Jacobs, Jane. *The Death and Life of Great American Cities*. New York: Random House, 1961.
Jencks, Charles. "Polemical Introduction: The Trap and the Butterfly." In *Architecture and the Jumping Universe*. London: Academy Editions, 1995.
Kelly, Kevin. *Out of Control: The New Biology of Machines, Social Systems, & the Economic World*. New York: basic Books, 1992.
Kipnis, Jeffrey. "Towards a New Architecture." In Greg Lynn (ed.), Folding in Architecture. *AD* (*Architectural Design*) Profile No. 102 (1993): 40–9.
Kwinter, Sanford. "Soft Systems." In Brian Boigon (ed.), *Culture Lab*. New York: Princeton Architectural Press, 1992.
Kwinter, Sanford. "Wildness: Prolegomena to a New Urbanism." In *Far from Equilibrium: Essays on Technology and Design Culture*. Barcelona: Actar, 2007.
Kwinter, Sanford. "Who's Afraid of Formalism?." *Any* (*Architecture: New York*) 7/8 (1994).
Lynn, Greg. *Animate Form*. New York: Princeton Architectural Press, 1999.
McHarg, Ian. *Design with Nature*. New York: American Museum of Natural History, 1969.
"Queen of the Curve: An Interview with Zaha Hadid," available online: https://www.lumens.com/the-edit/the-makers/interview-with-zaha-hadid/.
Rowe, Colin. "Chicago Frame." In *The Mathematics of the Ideal Villa and Other Essays*. Cambridge, MA: MIT Press, 1995.
Shane, David Grahame. "Conclusion: Heterotopias, the Net City, and Recombinant Urbanism." In *Recombinant Urbanism*. London: Wiley, 2005.
Unger, Roberto Magabeira. "The Better Futures of Architecture." In Cynthia C. Davidson (ed.), *Anyone*. New York: Rizzoli, 1991.

Chapter 3

Alexander, Christopher. "The City is Not a Tree." Part 1. *Architectural Forum* 122, no. 1 (April 1965): 58–62; and Part 2. *Architectural Forum* 122, no. 2 (May 1965): 58–61.
Banham, Reyner. *Megastructure: Urban Futures of the Recent Past*. New York: Harper and Collins, 1976.
Boyer, Christine M. "On Modelling Complexity and Urban Form." In Tom Verebes (guest ed.), Mass Customised Cities. *AD* (*Architectural Design*) Profile No. 138 (November 2015): 54-59.

Castells, Manuel. "Advanced Services, Information Flows, and the Global City." In *The Rise of the Network Society: The Information Age: Economy, Society, and Culture*. Oxford: John Wiley & Sons, 2011.

Castells, Manuel. "Conclusion: The Network Society." In *The Rise of the Network Society*. Oxford: Blackwell, 1996.

Easterling, Keller. *Extrastatecraft: The Power of Infrastructure Space*. New York: Verso Books, 2014.

Easterling, Keller. *Organization Space: Landscapes, Highways, and Houses in America*. Cambridge: MIT Press, 1999.

Frampton, Adam, Jonathan Solomon, and Clara Wong. *Cities without Ground*. Novato, CA: ORO Publishers, 2011.

Graham, Stephen, and Simon Marvin. "Social Landscapes of Splintering Urbanism." In *Splintering Urbanism: Networked Infrastructures, Technological Mobilities, and the Urban Condition*. London: Routledge, 2001.

Koolhaas, Rem. "Ignored Realm." In *Countryside: A Report*. Berlin: Taschen, 2020.

Koolhaas, Rem. "Junkspace." *October* N100 (Spring 2002): 175–90.

Kubo, Michael, Farshid Moussavi, and Alejandro Zaera Polo. *The Yokohama Project*. Barcelona: Actar, 2002.

LeCavalier, Jesse. *The Rule of Logistics: Walmart and the Architecture of Fulfilment*. Minneapolis, MN: University of Minnesota Press, 2016.

Martin, Reinhold. *The Urban Apparatus: Mediapolitics and the City*. Minneapolis, MN: University of Minnesota Press, 2016.

Otto, Frei. *Occupying and Connecting: Thoughts on Territories and Spheres of Influence with Particular Reference to Human Settlement*. Edited by Berthold Burkhardt. Stuttgart: Edition Axel Menges, 2009.

Parent, Claude, and Paul Virilio. *The Function of the Oblique 1963–1969*. London: AA Publications, 2004.

Sassen, Saskia. *The Global City: New York, London, Tokyo*. Princeton, NJ: Princeton University Press, 1991.

Solomon, Jonathan D. "Hong Kong – Aformal Urbanism." In Rodolphe El-Khoury and Edwards Robbins (eds.), *Shaping the City: Studies in History, Theory and Urban Design*. New York: Routledge, 2013.

Waldheim, Charles, and Alan Berger. "Logistic Landscape." *Landscape Journal* 27, no. 2 (2008): 219–46.

Weinstock, Michael. "City Forms." In *The Architecture of Emergence: The Evolution of Form in Nature and Civilisation*. London: John Wiley and Sons Inc., 2010.

Weinstock, Michael (ed.). System City. *AD (Architectural Design)* 224 (2013).

Wigley, Mark. "Resisting the City." In *TransUrbanism*. Rotterdam: V2 and NAi Publishers, 2002.

Chapter 4

Al, Stefan. "Hong Kong's Transit-Oriented Podium-Tower Development." In Zhongjie Lin and Jose Gamez (ed.), *Vertical Urbanism: Designing Compact Cities in China*. New York: Routledge, 2018.

Bay, Joo Hwa Philip, and Steffen Lehmann. "Compact Urban Form, Density and Sustainability: Correlations and Holistic Approaches." In Joo Hwa Philip Bay and Steffen Lehmann (eds.), *Growing Compact: Urban Form, Density and Sustainability*. London and New York: Routledge, 2017.

Berkes, Enrico, and Ruben Gaetani. "The Geography of Unconventional Innovation." *Rotman School of Management Working Paper* 3423143 (July 19, 2019).

Berube, Alan. *MetroNation: How US Metropolitan Areas Fuel American Prosperity*, Metropolitan Policy Program at Brookings. Washigton, DC: Brookings Institution, 2007.

Boyarsky, Alvin. "Chicago *à la Carte*: The City as an Energy System." *AD (Architectural Design)* (December 1970). 1968: 595-618.

[*Brundtland Report*]. World Commission on Environment and Development. *Our Common Future: The World Commission on Environment and Development.* Oxford: Oxford University Press, 1987.

Campanella, Thomas J. *The Concrete Dragon: China's Urban Revolution and What It Means for the World.* New York: Princeton Architectural Press, 2008.

Cervero, Robert, Erick Guerra, and Stefan Al. *Beyond Mobility: Planning Cities for People and Places.* Washington, DC: Island Press, 2017.

Chung, Chihua Judy, Jeffrey Inaba, Rem Koolhaas, and Sze Tsung Leong (eds.). *The Great Leap Forward.* Köln: Taschen, 2001.

Ferriss, Hugh. *The Metropolis of Tomorrow.* New York: Ives Washburn, 1929.

Gartman, David. "Introduction." In *Autos to Architecture: Fordism and Architectural Aesthetics in the Twentieth Century.* New York: Princeton University Press, 2009.

Gottmann, Jean. "Megalopolis or the Urbanization of the Northeastern Seaboard." *Economic Geography* 33, no. 3 (1957): 189–200.

Jacobs, Jane. *The Death and Life of Great American Cities.* New York: Random House, 1961.

Johnson, Jeffrey, Cressica Brazier, and Tat Lam (eds.). *China Lab Guide to Megablock Urbanism.* Barcelona: Actar, 2020.

Johnson, Steven. "Blueprint for a Better City." *Wired*, December 1, 2001.

Koolhaas, Rem. "Bigness, or the Problem of the Large." In OMA, Rem Koolhaas, and Bruce Mau (eds.), *S,M,L,XL.* Rotterdam: 010, 1994.

Koolhaas, Rem. "Definitive Instability: The Downtown Athletic Club" and "The Skyscraper Theorists." In *Delirious New York: A Retroactive Manifesto for Manhattan.* Rotterdam: 010 Publishers, 1978.

Koolhaas, Rem. "The Future's Past." *Wilson Quarterly* (1976–) 3, no. 1 (Winter, 1979): 135–40.

Maas, Winy. "Datascape: The Final Extravaganza." *Daidalos* 69/70 (1998/1999): 48–53.

Maas, Winy, and MDRDV. *Metacity / Datatown.* Rotterdam: 010 Publishers, 1999.

Maas, Winy, Jacob van Rijs, and Richard Koek, *Farmax: Excursions on Density.* Rotterdam: 010 Publishers, 1998.

Mars, Neville, and Adrian Hornsby (eds.). *The Chinese Dream: A Society Under Construction.* Rotterdam: 010 Publishers, 2008.

McGee, Terry G. "The Emergence of Desakota Regions in Asia: Expanding a Hypothesis." In Norton Ginsburg, Bruce Koppel, and T. G. McGee (eds.), *The Extended Metropolis: Settlement Transition in Asia.* Honolulu, HI: University of Hawaii Press, 1991.

Mumford, Lewis. *The City in History: Its Origins, Its Transformations, and Its Prospects.* Boston, MA: Houghton Mifflin Harcourt, 1961.

MVRDV. *KM3: Excursions on Capacities.* Barcelona: ACTAR, 2005.

Newman, Peter G., and Jeffrey R. Kenworthy. *Cities and Automobile Dependence: An International Sourcebook.* Farnham: Gower Publishing Company, 1989.

Rogers, Richard. *Cities for a Small Planet.* London: Basic Books, 2008.

Verebes, Tom. "Hong Kong: Appearing Dense but Growing Smarter." In Philip Joo Hwa Bay and Steffen Lehmann (eds.), *Growing Compact: Urban Form, Density, Sustainability.* New York: Routledge, 2017.

Wright, Frank Lloyd. *The Living City.* 1928.

Chapter 5

Al, Stefan. *Adapting Cities to Sea Level Rise: Green and Gray Strategies.* Washington, DC: Island Press, 2018.

Al, Stefan. "The Vertical Garden City: Singapore." In *Supertall: How the World's Tallest Buildings are Reshaping Our Cities and Our Lives.* New York: W.W. Norton, 2022.

BIBLIOGRAPHY

Allen, Stan. "Mat Urbanism: The Thick 2-D." In Hashim Sarkis (ed.), *CASE: Le Corbusier's Venice Hospital*. Munich: Prestel, 2001.

Allen, Stan, and Marc McQuade. *Landform Building: Architecture's New Terrain and Groundwork: Between Landscape and Architecture*. Zurich: Lars Müller Publications, 2013.

Benedict, Mark A., and Edward T. McMahon. *Green Infrastructure: Linking Landscapes and Communities*. Washington, DC: Island Press, 2012.

Berg, Nate. "Green Infrastructure Could Save Cities Billions." *City Lab*, April 24, 2012. Available online: https://www.bloomberg.com/ (accessed February 27, 2021).

Carson, Rachel. *Silent Spring*. Boston, MA: Houghton Mifflin, 1962.

Cervero, Robert, Erick Guerra, and Stefan Al. *Beyond Mobility: Planning Cities for People and Places*. Washington, DC: Island Press, 2017.

Corner, James. "Landscape Urbanism." In Mohsen Mostafavi and Ciro Najle (eds.), *Landscape Urbanism: A Manual for the Machinic Landscape*. London: Architectural Association, 2003.

Diamond, Jared. *Collapse: How Societies Choose to Fail or Succeed*, rev. ed. London: Penguin, 2011.

Dwyre, Cathryn, Chris Perry, David Salomon, and Kathy Velikov. "Weird Worlds and Peculiar Practices: Imagining a Tentative Future." In Cathryn Dwyre, Chris Perry, David Salomon, and Kathy Velikov (eds.), *Ambiguous Territory: Architecture, Landscape and the Postnatural*. Barcelona: Actar, 2022.

Fuller, R. Buckminster. *Operating Manual for Spaceship Earth*. Zurich: Lars Müller Publishers, Estate of R. Buckminster Fuller, 2008.

McHarg, Ian. "Introduction" and "Nature in the Metropolis." In *Design with Nature*. New York: American Museum of Natural History, 1969.

Meadows, Donella H., Dennis L. Meadows, Jørgen Randers, and William W. Behrens III, *The Limits to Growth: A Report for the Club of Rome's Project on the Predicament of Mankind*. Commissioned by the Club of Rome. (New York: Potomac Associates, Universe Books, 1972).

Mostafavi, Mohsen, edited with Gareth Doherty. *Ecological Urbanism*. Cambridge, MA: Harvard University Graduate School of Design, co-published by Baden: Lars Müller Publishers, 2010.

Mostafavi, Mohsen. "Landscapes of Urbanism." In Mohsen Mostafavi and Ciro Najle (eds.), *Landscape Urbanism: A Manual for the Machinic Landscape*. London: Architectural Association, 2003.

Olgyay, Victor. *Design with Climate: Bioclimatic Approach to Architectural Regionalism*. Princeton, NJ: Princeton University Press, 1963.

Rudofsky, Bernard. *Architecture without Architects: A Short Introduction to Non-pedigreed Architecture*. Albuquerque, NM: University of New Mexico Press, 1987.

Saunders, William (ed.). *Designed Ecologies: The Landscape Architecture of Kongjian Yu*. Basel: Birkhäuser Architecture, 2012.

Spirn, Anne Whiston. "Ecological Urbanism." In Tridib Banerjee and Anastasia Loukaitou-Sideris (eds.), *Companion to Urban Design*. New York: Routledge, 2011.

Spirn, Anne Whiston. *The Granite Garden*. New York: Basic Books, 1984.

Ulrich, Roger S., "View through a Window May Influence Recovery from Surgery," *Science* 224, no. 4647 (1984): 420–1.

Waldheim, Charles. "Landscape as Urbanism." In Charles Waldheim (ed.), *The Landscape Urbanism Reader*. Princeton, NJ: Princeton Architectural Press, 2006.

Watson, Julia. *Lo-TEK: Design by Radical Indigenism*. Taschen, 2019.

Watson, Julia, Avery Robertson, and Félix de Rosen. "Designing by Radical Indigenism." *Landscape Architecture Frontiers* 8, no. 3 (2020): 148–55.

White, Mathew P., Ian Alcock, James Gellner, and Benedict W. Wheeler, "Spending at Least 120 Minutes a Week in Nature is Associated with Good Health and Wellbeing." *Scientific Reports* 9, no. 1 (2019): 1–11.

Wilson, Edward O. *Biophilia*. Cambridge, MA: Harvard University Press, 1986.

Yu, Kongjian. "Beautiful Big Feet: Toward a New Landscape Aesthetic." *Harvard Design Magazine* (Fall/Winter 2009): 4–59.

Yu, Kongjian. *Letters to the Leaders of China: Kongjian Yu and the Future of the Chinese City*. New York: Terraform, 2018.

Chapter 6

Anthes, Emily. *The Great Indoors: The Surprising Science of How Buildings Shape Our Behavior, Health, and Happiness*. New York: Scientific American / Farrar, Straus and Giroux, 2020.
Appleyard, Don. *Liveable Streets*. London: Elsevier, 1981.
Armborst, Tobias, Daniel D'Oca, and Georgeen Theodore. *The Arsenal of Exclusion & Inclusion*. Barcelona: Actar, 2014.
Ben-Joseph, Eran. *ReThinking a Lot: The Design and Culture of Parking*. Cambridge, MA: MIT Press, 2012.
Betsky, Aaron. *Queer Space: Architecture and Same Sex Drive*. London: HarperCollins, 1997.
Bullard, Robert D. *Dumping in Dixie: Race, Class, and Environmental Quality*. Boulder, CO: Westview Press, 1990.
Crawford, Margaret, and Michael Speaks. *Everyday Urbanism: Michigan Debates on Urbanism*. Edited by Rahul Mehrotra. Ann Arbor, MI: University of Michigan, 2005.
Desmond, Matthew. *Evicted: Poverty and Profit in the American City*. New York: Crown, 2017.
Engels, Friedrich. *The Condition of the Working Class in England*. Oxford: Oxford University Press, 1993.
Ferguson, Russell, Martha Gever, Trinh T. Minh-ha, and Cornel West (eds.). *Out There: Marginalization and Contemporary Culture*. Cambridge, MA: MIT Press, 1992.
Frank, Lawrence D., Martin A. Andresen, and Thomas L. Schmid. "Obesity Relationships with Community Design, Physical Activity, and Time Spent in Cars." *American Journal of Preventive Medicine* 27, no. 2 (2004): 87–96.
Gans, Herbert J. "Planning and Social Life: Friendship and Neighbor Relations in Suburban Communities." *Journal of the American Institute of Planners* 27, no. 2 (1961): 134–40.
Gehl, Jan. *Life between Buildings: Using Public Space*. Washington, DC: Island Press, 2011.
Gehl, Jan, and Birgitte Svarre. *How to Study Public Life*. Washington, DC: Island Press, 2013.
Goh, Kian, Anastasia Loukaitou-Sideris, and Vinit Mukhija (eds.). *Just Urban Design: The Struggle for a Public City*. Cambridge, MA: MIT Press, 2022.
Hayden, Dolores. "What Would a Non-Sexist City Be Like? Speculations on Housing, Urban Design, and Human Work." *Signs* 5, no. 53 (1980): S170–87.
Hayden, Dolores. "What Would a Non-sexist City Be Like? Speculations on Housing, Urban Design, and Human Work." In Susan S. Fainstein and Lisa J. Servon (eds.), *Gender and Planning: A Reader*. New Brunswick, NJ: Rutgers University Press, 2005.
Hood, Walter, and Grace Mitchell Tada (eds.). *Black Landscapes Matter*. Charlottesville, VA: University of Virginia Press, 2020.
Huzayyin, A. "Urban Transport and the Environment in Developing Countries: Complexities and Simplifications." In W. Rothengatter, Y. Hayashi, and W. Shade (eds.), *Moving to Climate Change Intelligence*. New York: Springer, 2011.
International Energy Agency (IEA). "CO2 Emissions from Fuel Combustion by Sector in 2014, in CO2 Emissions from Fuel Combustion." *CO2 Highlights 2016*. Paris: IEA, 2016.
Jacobs, Allan B. *Great Streets*. Berkeley, CA: University of California Transportation Center, 1993.
Jacobs, Allan, and Donald Appleyard. "Toward an Urban Design Manifesto." *Journal of the American Planning Association* 53, no. 1 (1987): 112–20.
Jacobs, Jane. "Downtown is for People." *The Exploding Metropolis*. Berkeley, Los Angeles, CA, and London: University of California Press, 1958.
Jacobs, Jane M. *Edge of Empire: Postcolonialism and the City*. London: Routledge, 2002.
Jacobs, Jane. *The Death and Life of Great American Cities*. New York: Random House, 1961.

Kallipoliti, L. *The Architecture of Closed Worlds: Or, What is the Power of Shit?* Zurich: Lars Müller Publications, 2018.

Kern, Leslie. *Feminist City: Claiming Space in a Man-Made World*. London and New York: Verso Trade, 2020.

Kibel, Paul Stanton. "Access to Parkland: Environmental Justice at East Bay Parks." *Environmental Law and Justice Clinic* 2 (2007).

Kim, Annette. *Sidewalk City: Remapping Public Space in Ho Chi Minh City*. Chicago, IL: University of Chicago Press, 2015.

Le Corbusier, *The City of To-morrow and Its Planning*, 131.

Lo, Ria S. Hutabarat. "Walkability Planning in Jakarta." University of California Transportation Center (2011).

Marshall, Alex. *How Cities Work: Suburbs, Sprawl, and the Roads Not Taken*. Austin, TX: University of Texas Press, 2001.

Mehrotra, Rahul. *Ephemeral Urbanism: Does Permanence Matter?* Cambridge, MA: Harvard University Press, 2017.

Montgomery, Charles. *Happy City: Transforming Our Lives through Urban Design*. London: Macmillan, 2013.

"New York City's Privately Owned Public Plazas." New York City Department of City Planning, NYC.gov. Available online: https://www.nyc.gov/site/planning/plans/pops/pops-plaza-standards.page.

Newman, Peter and Jeff Kenworthy. "Peak Car Use: Understanding the Demise of Automobile Dependence." *World Transport Policy and Practice* 17, no. 2 (2011): 31–42.

Plouffe, Louise and Alexandre Kalache. "Towards Global Age-Friendly Cities: Determining Urban Features that Promote Active Aging." *Journal of Urban Health* 87, no. 5 (2010): 733–9.

Putnam, Robert D. "Bowling Alone: America's Declining Social Capital," *Journal of Democracy* 6, no. 1 (1995): 65–78.

Putnam, Robert D. *Bowling Alone: The Collapse and Revival of American Community* (New York: Simon & Schuster, 2000).

Rissel, Chris, Nada Curac, and Mark Greenaway, "Physical Activity Associated with Public Transport Use—A Review and Modelling of Potential Benefits," *International Journal of Environmental Research and Public Health* 9, no. 7 (2012): 2454–78.

Rothstein, Richard. *The Color of Law: A Forgotten History of How Our Government Segregated America*. New York: Liveright Publishing, 2017

Sample, Hilary. "Emergency Urbanism and Preventive Architecture." In Giovanna Borasi and Mirko Zardini (eds.), *Imperfect Health: The Medicalization of Architecture*. Canadian Centre for Architecture, Montreal & Lars Müller, Canada, 2012.

Southworth, Michael, and Eran Ben-Joseph. *Streets and the Shaping of Towns and Cities*. Washington, DC: Island Press, 2013.

Speck, Jeff. *Walkable City: How Downtown Can Save America, One Step at a Time*. New York: Macmillan, 2013.

Thomson, James. "The City of Dreadful Night." *National Reformer,* March 22, 1874.

UN Habitat. *Planning and Design for Sustainable Urban Mobility: Global Report on Human Settlements 2013*. Nairobi: UN Habitat, 2013.

Vitruvius Pollio. "The Site of a City." Edited by Morris Hicky Morgan, *The Ten Books on Architecture*. New York: Dover, 1960.

Whyte, William H. *City: Rediscovering the* Center. New York: Doubleday, 1988.

Whyte, William Hollingsworth. *The Social Life of Small Urban Spaces*. New York: The Conservation Foundation, 1980.

Wilson, Elizabeth. *The Sphinx in the City: Urban Life, the Control of Disorder, and Women*. Berkeley, CA: University of California Press, 1991.

World Health Organization (WHO). *Global Status Report on Road Safety*. Geneva: WHO, 2009.

Chapter 7

Al, Stefan (ed.). *Villages in the City: A Guide to Southern China's Informal Settlements*. Honolulu, HI: University of Hawaii, 2014.
Aravena, Alejandro. "Elemental: A Do Tank." *AD (Architectural Design)* 81, no. 3 (2011): 32–7.
Aravena, Alejandro. *Reporting from the Front: Venice Architecture Biennale*. Padova: Marsillio, 2016.
Arefi, M., and C. Kickert (eds.). *The Palgrave Handbook of Bottom-up Urbanism*. Cham: Palgrave Macmillan, 2019.
Bayat, Asef. "From 'Dangerous Classes' to 'Quiet Rebels': Politics of the Urban Subaltern in the Global South." *International Sociology* 15, no. 3 (2000): 533–57.
Bertaud, Alain. *Order without Design: How Markets Shape Cities*. Cambridge, MA: MIT Press, 2018.
Brillembourg, Alfredo, and Hubert Klumpner. *Beyond Shelter: Architecture and Human Dignity*. New York: Metropolis Books, 2011.
Brillembourg, Alfredo, and Hubert Klumpner. "Rules of engagement: Caracas and the Informal City." In Felipe Hernandéz, Peter Kellett, and Lea K. Allen (eds.), *Rethinking the Informal City: Critical Perspectives from Latin America*. New York and Oxford: Berghahn Books, 2010.
Brillemboug, Alfredo, and Hubert Klumpner (eds.). *Torre David: Informal Vertical Communities*. Baden: Lars Müller Publishers, 2013.
Campanella, Thomas J. *The Concrete Dragon: China's Urban Revolution and What it Means for the World*. New York: Princeton Architectural Press.
Crawford, Margaret, "Preface: The Current State of Everyday Urbanism" and "Blurring the Boundaries: Public Space and Private Life." In Michael Larice and Elizabeth Macdonald (eds.), *The Urban Design Reader*. Abingdon: Routledge, 2013.
Crawford, Margaret, Leighton Chase, and John Kaliski (ed.). *Everyday Urbanism: Expanded*. New York: Monacelli Press, 2008.
Cruz, Teddy, and Fonna Forman. *Socializing Architecture: Top Down / Bottom Up*. Cambridge, MA: MIT Press, 2023.
Davis, Mike. "Planet of Slums: Urban Involution and the Informal Proletariat." *New Left Review* 26 (2004): 5–34.
Davis, Mike. "Urban Climacteric" & "Haussmann in the Tropics." In *Planet of Slums*. London and New York: Verso Books, 2006.
de Certeau, Michel. *The Practice of Everyday Life*, translated by Steven Rendall. Berkeley, CA: University of California Press, 1984.
Dewan Verma, Giita. "Indore's Habitat Improvement Project: Success or Failure?." *Habitat International: A Journal for the Study of Human Settlements* 24 (2000): 91–117.
Dewan Verma, Gita. *Slumming India: A Chronicle of Slums and Their Saviors*. London: Penguin Books, 2002.
Du, Juan. *The Shenzhen Experiment: The Story of China's Instant City*. Cambridge, MA: Harvard University Press, 2020.
Ghertner, Asher. *Rule by Aesthetics: World-Class City Making in Delhi*. Oxford: Oxford University Press, 2015.
Hernandéz, Felipe H., Peter W. Kellett, and Lea K. Allen (eds.). *Rethinking the Informal City: Critical Perspectives from Latin America*. New York and Oxford: Berghahn Books, 2010.
Lydon, Mike and Anthony Garcia. "A Tactical Urbanism How-to." In *Tactical Urbanism: Short-Term Action for Long-Term Change*. Washington, DC: Island Press, 2015.
Malecki, E. J. and R. Ramanath (eds.). *Illegal Cities: Law and Urban Change in Developing Countries*. London and New York: Zed Books, 2002.
Mars, Neville. *Mumbai Planning Study*. 2017.
Marshall, Stephen. *Cities, Design, Evolution*. New York: Routledge, 2009.
McGuirk, Justin. *Radical Cities: Across Latin America in Search of a New Architecture*. London and New York: Verso Trade, 2014.

Perlman, Janice E. *The Myth of Marginality: Urban Poverty and Politics in Rio de Janeiro*. Los Angeles, CA: University of California Press, 1976.
Roy, Ananya. "Urban Informality: Toward an Epistemology of Planning." *Journal of the American Planning Association* 71, no. 2 (2005): 147–58.
Roy, Ananya, and Nezar AlSayyad (eds.). *Urban Informality: Transnational Perspectives from the Middle East, Latin America, and South Asia*. Lanham, MD: Lexington Books, 2003.
Sadler, Simon. "Open Ends: The Social Visions of 1960s Non-Planning." In *Non-Plan: Essays on Freedom, Participation and Change in Modern Architecture and Urbanism*. Oxford: Architectural Press, 2000.
Turner, John F. C., and Robert Fichter (eds.). *Freedom to Build: Dweller Control of the Housing Process*. London: Macmillan, 1972.
UN-Habitat, *Informal Settlements* (Habitat III Issue Papers 22). Nairobi: UN-Habitat, 2015.
Ur, Jason. "Households and the Emergence of Cities in Ancient Mesopotamia." *Cambridge Archaeological Journal* 24, no. 2 (2014): 249–68.
Ward, Peter M. *Colonias and Public Policy in Texas and Mexico: Urbanization by Stealth*. Austin, TX: University of Texas Press, 1999.
Whyte, William H. *City: Rediscovering the Center*. New York: Doubleday, 1989.
World Bank, *Better Infrastructure for 7.5 Million Urban Residents in Vietna*, December 19, 2014. Available online: https://www.worldbank.org/en/news/feature/2014/12/19/better-infrastructure-for-75-million-urban-residents-in-vietnam.

Chapter 8

Alexander, Christopher. "Systems Generating Systems." In *Systemat*. Berkeley, CA: Inland Steel Products Company, 1968.
Batty, Michael. "Introduction: Understanding Cities." In *Cities and Complexity: Understanding Cities with Cellular Automata, Agent-based Models, and Fractals*. Cambridge, MA: MIT Press, 2005.
Batty, Michael. *The New Science of Cities*. Cambridge, MA: MIT Press, 2013.
Bratton, Benjamin H. "Parametricist Architecture Would Be a Good Idea." In Matthew Poole and Manuel Schvatzberg (eds.), *The Politics of Parametricism in Architecture*. London: Bloomsbury Academic, 2015.
Bratton, Benjamin H. *The Stack: On Software and Sovereignty*. Cambridge, MA: MIT Press, 2015.
Burry, Jane and Mark Burry. *The New Mathematics of Architecture*. London: Thames and Hudson, 2010.
De Landa, M. "The Limits of Urban Simulation." *AD (Architectural Design)* 53 (2009): 50-55.
Easterling, Keller. "The Action is the Form." In Mark Shepard (ed.), *Sentient City: Ubiquitous Computing, Architecture and the Future of Urban Space*. New York and Cambridge, MA: Architectural League and MIT Press, 2011.
Frazer, John. "Introduction: A Natural Model for Architecture." In *An Evolutionary Architecture*. London: AA Publications, 1995.
Halpern, Orit. *Beautiful Data: A History of Vision and Reason since 1945*. Durham, NC: Duke University Press, 2014.
Jacobs, Jane. *The Death and Life of Great American Cities*. New York: Random House, 1961.
Johnson, Steven. *Emergence: The Connected Lives of Ants, Brains, Cities and Software*. London: Penguin, 2001.
Pask, Gordon. "Foreword." In John Frazer, *An Evolutionary Architecture*. London: AA Publications, 1995.
Pask, Gordon. "The Architectural Relevance of Cybernetics." *AD (Architectural Design)* 7/6 (1969): 949–6.
Pask, Gordon. "The Architectural Relevance of Cybernetics." In Neil Spiller (ed.), *Cyber Reader: Critical Writings for the Digital Era*. London: Phaidon, 2002.

Schumacher, Patrik. "Parametricism – A New Global Style for Architecture and Urban Design." In Neil Leach (guest ed.), Digital Cities. *AD (Architectural Design)* 79, no. 4 (July/August 2009): 14–23.

Schumacher, Patrik. "Parametricist vs. Modernist Urbanism." In *The Autopoiesis of Architecture: A New Agenda for Architecture*, vol. 2. London: John Wiley and Sons, 2012.

Spiller, Neil. "The Architectural Relevance of Cybernetics." In Neil Spiller (ed.), *Cyber Reader*. London: Phaidon, 2002.

Verebes, Tom. "The Death of Masterplanning in the Age of Indeterminacy." In *Masterplanning the Adaptive City: Computational Urbanism in the Twenty-first Century*. New York: Routledge, 2013.

Chapter 9

Armitage, John "Virilio Live: Selected Interviews." *Virilio Live* (2001): 1–240.

Baudrillard, Jean. *Simulacra and Simulation*. Ann Arbor, MI: University of Michigan Press, 1994.

Carpo, Mario. *Beyond Digital: Design and Automation at the End of Modernity*. Cambridge: MIT Press, 2023.

Chalmers, David J. *Reality+: Virtual Worlds and the Problems of Philosophy*. London: Penguin, 2022.

Clarke, Arthur C. Interview in BBC *Horizons* television programme, 1964.

Fok, Wendy W. *Digital Structures: Data and Urban Strategies of the Civic Future*. New York: ORO Publications, 2023.

Gibson, William. *Neuromancer*. New York: Ace Books, 1984.

Graham, Stephen. "Bridging Urban Digital Divides? Urban Polarisation and Information and Communications Technologies (ICTs)," *Urban Studies* 39, no. 1 (2002): 33–56.

Grau, Olivier. *Virtual Art: From Illusion to Immersion*. Cambridge, MA: MIT Press, 2003.

Hopkins, Owen (ed.). "Multispace: Architecture at the Dawn of the Metaverse." *AD (Architectural Design)* January (2024).

Lavin, Sylvia. *Kissing Architecture*. Princeton, NJ: Princeton University Press, 2011.

Leach, Neil (ed.). Digital Cities. *AD (Architectural Design)* (2009).

Lindsay, Greg. "What is the Metaverse Metropolis?." Greglindsay.org. December 10, 2022. Available online: https://www.greglindsay.org/blog/2022/12/what-is-the-metaverse-metropolis/.

Lynch, Kevin. *The Image of the City*. Cambridge, MA: MIT Press, 1964.

Mattern, Shannon. *A City is Not a Computer: Other Urban Intelligences*. Vol. 2. Princeton, NJ: Princeton University Press, 2021.

Mitchell, William J. "Boundaries / Networks." In *Me++: The Cyborg Self and the Networked City*. Cambridge, MA: MIT Press, 2003.

Moneta, Andrea. "Architecture, Heritage, and the Metaverse." *Traditional Dwellings and Settlements Review* 32, no. 1 (2020): 37–49.

Morel, Philippe. "Why Disruptive Business Models are Inseparable from Disruptive Technologies." In Henriette Bier and Philippe Morel (eds.), *Disruptive Technologies: The Convergence of New Paradigms in Architecture*. London: Springer, 2023.

Negroponte, Nicholas. "Introduction." In *Soft Architecture Machines*. Cambridge, MA: MIT Press, 1970.

Novak, Marcos. "Liquid Architectures in Cyberspace." In Michael Benedikt (ed.), *Cyberspace: First Steps*. Cambridge, MA: MIT Press, 1991.

Novak, Marcos. "Transmitting Architecture." Architects in Cyberspace. *AD (Architectural Design)* Profile No. 118 (1995): 42–7.

Park, Giyoung, and Gary W. Evans. "Lynch's Elements of the City in the Digital Era." *Journal of the American Planning Association* 84, nos 3–4 (2018).

Ratti, Carlo, and Matthew Claudel. *The City of Tomorrow: Sensors, Networks, Hackers, and the Future of Urban Life*. New Haven, CT: Yale University Press, 2016.

Simendon, Gilbert. *On the Mode of Existence of Technical Objects.* Paris: Aubier, Editions Montaigne, 1958.
Schumacher, Patrik. "Cyber-Urban Integration." In Henriette Bier and Philippe Morel (eds.), *Disruptive Technologies: The Convergence of New Paradigms in Architecture.* London: Springer, 2023.
Schumacher, Patrik. "The Metaverse as Opportunity for Architecture and Society: Design Drivers and Core." *Architectural Intelligence* 1, no. 11 (2022).
Stephenson, Neal. *Snow Crash: A Novel.* New York: Spectra, [1992] 2003.
Striphas, Ted. *Algorithmic Culture before the Internet.* New York: Columbia University Press, 2023.
Sutherland, Ivan Edward. *Sketchpad: A Man-Machine Graphical Communication System.* Technical Report – Massachusetts Institute of Technology, Lincoln Laboratory. Cambridge, MA: MIT Press, 1963.
Sutherland, Ivan E. "The Ultimate Display." In Wayne A. Kalenich (ed.), *Information Processing 1965: Proceedings of the IFIP Congress 65*, vol. 2, no. 506–8. London: Macmillan & Co., 1965.
Trummer, Peter. *The City as a Technical Being: On the Mode of Existence of Architecture.* New York: ORO Publications, 2023.
Virilio, Paul. *The Aesthetics of Disappearance.* Cambridge, MA: MIT Press, 1980.
Virilio, Paul. *The Lost Dimension.* New York: Semiotext(e), 1991.
Virilio, Paul. "The Overexposed City." In *The Lost Dimension*, translated by Daniel Moshenberg. New York: Semiotext(e), 1991.
Wark, McKenzie. *Virtual Geography: Living with Global Media Events.* Bloomington, IN: Indiana University Press, 1994.
White, J. *Virtual Reality and the Built Environment.* Oxford: Architectural Press, 2002. (Note: The author initials are assumed based on the citation style, as no specific author initials were provided in the original reference.)
Wiener, Norbert. *Cybernetics: Or Control and Communication in the Animal and the Machine.* Paris: Hermann & Cie; and Cambridge, MA: MIT Press, 1948.

Chapter 10

Benjamin, Ruha. *Race after Technology: Abolitionist Tools for the New Jim Code.* Cambridge: Polity, 2019.
Bratton, Benjamin. "AI Urbanism: A Design Framework for Governance, Program, and Platform Cognition." *AI & Society* 36 (2021): 1307–12.
Bratton, Benjamin. "iPhone City." Digital Cities. *AD (Architectural Design)* 79, no. 4 (July/August 2009): 90–9.
Chaillou, Stanislas. *Artificial Intelligence and Architecture: From Research to Practice*, 1st ed. Basel: Verlag GmbH Birkhäuser, 2022.
Crawford, Kate. "Conclusion." In *Atlas of AI: Power, Politics and the Planetary Costs of Artificial Intelligence.* New Haven, CT: Yale University Press, 2021.
del Campo, Matias. *Neural Architecture: Design and Artificial Intelligence.* Hong Kong, Shenzhen: ORO, 2022.
del Campo, Matias. "How Machines Learn to Plan: A Critical Interrogation of Machine Vision Techniques in Architecture." In *Neural Architecture: Design and Artificial Intelligence.* Novato, VA: ORO Editions, 2022.
del Campo, Matias, and Neil Leach (eds.). Machine Hallucinations: Architecture and Artificial Intelligence. *AD (Architectural Design)* 92, no. 3 (May–June 2022).
Easterling, Keller. "The Action is the Form." In Mark Shepard (ed.), *Sentient City: Ubiquitous Computing, Architecture and the Future of Urban Space.* New York and Cambridge, MA: Architectural League and MIT Press, 2011.

Galle, Nadinè, Sophie Nitoslawski, and Francesco Pilla. "The Internet of Nature: How Taking Nature Online Can Shape Urban Ecosystems." *Anthropocene Review* 6, no. 3 (2019).

Halpern, Orit, Robert Mitchell, and Bernard Dionysius. "The Smartness Mandate: Notes Toward a Critique." *Gray Room* 68 (2017): 106–29.

Harman, Graham. *Weird Realism: Lovecraft and Philosophy*. Hants, UK: Zero Books, 2012.

Hight, Christopher, and Chris Perry (guest eds.). Collective Intelligence. *AD (Architectural Design)* Profile No. 183, vol. 76, no. 5 (2006).

Huang, Jeffrey, and Immanuel Koh. "Citizen Visual Search Engine: Detection and Curation of Urban Objects." In J.-H. Lee (ed.), *Computer-Aided Architectural Design*. Singapore: Springer, 2019.

Koh, Immanuel. "AI-Urban-Sketching: Deep Learning and Automating Design Perception for Creativity." In B. Romic and B. Reimer (eds.), Artificial Creativity. *Transformations: Journal of Media, Culture and Technology* 36 (2022): 131–45.

Koh, Immanuel. *Artificial and Architectural Intelligence in Design*. Singapore: SUTD, 2020.

Leach, Neil. "AI and the City of the Future." In *Architecture in the Age of Artificial Intelligence: An Introduction to AI for Architects*. London: Bloomsbury, 2022.

Leach, Neil. *Architecture in the Age of Artificial Intelligence: An Introduction to AI for Architects*. London: Bloomsbury, 2022.

Levy, Pierre. *Collective Intelligence: Mankind's Emerging World in Cyberspace*. Cambridge, MA: Perseus, 1997.

Lorenzo-Eiroa, Pablo. *Digital Signifiers in an Architecture of Information: From Big Data and Simulation to Artificial Intelligence*. New York: Routledge, 2023.

Markopoulou, Areti. *Learning Cities: Collective Intelligence in Urban Design*. Barcelona: IAAC, 2023.

Mattern, Shannon. *A City is Not a Computer: Other Urban Intelligences*. New York: Princeton Architectural Press, 2021.

McLuhan, Marshall. *Understanding Media*. Toronto: McGraw Hill, 1964.

Noble, Safiya Umoja. *Algorithms of Oppression*. New York: New York University Press, 2018.

Picon, Antoine. *Smart Cities: A Spatialised Intelligence*. London: Wiley, 2015.

Shepherd, Mark (ed.), *Sentient City: Ubiquitous Computing, Architecture, and the Future of Urban Space*. Cambridge, MA: MIT Press, 2011.

Townsend, Anthony M. "Introduction: Urbanisation and Ubiquity." In *Smart Cities: Big Data, Civic Hackers, and the Quest for a New Utopia*. New York: W. W. Norton, 2013.

Verebes, Tom, "UrbanISMS: Paradigmatic Practices and their Multifarious Platforms." PhD diss. RMIT University, Melbourne, 2018.

Weinstock, Michael. "System City: Infrastructure and the Space of Flows." In M. Weinstock (guest ed.), System City. *AD (Architectural Design)* 224 (2013): 14–23.

Wiener, Norbert. *Cybernetics or Control and Communication in the Animal and the Machine*. Vol. 25. Cambridge, MA: MIT Press, 1961.

Williams, Sara. Data Action: Using Data for Public Good. MIT Press, 2020.

Index

active aging 129
addressing Racial Equity 136–139
affordability 154–158
"aformal" urbanism 70–75
age-friendly cities 129
AI (artificial intelligence) 163, 165, 170, 183, 189–191, 213–237
    ethical concerns 4, 8, 213–215, 219, 231–237
    machine learning 189, 213, 215–218, 220, 223, 225, 228, 232, 234
    for urban design 214–220, 225–230
Alexander, Christopher 34–37, 170
Alibaba City Brain 220, 223, 225
Allen, Stan 43–49, 106–107
Allen Curve 87
Appadurai, Arjun 147
Appleyard, Donald 14, 123, 125
Aravena, Alejandro 155–158
Archigram 9, 57
architecture without architects 10, 115
Archizoom 9
artificial life 168–169, 187
Augé, Marc 21
augmented reality (AR) 191, 199, 215
Auyero, Javier 146

barrio 138, 150–154
Bauhaus 129, 165
Ben-Joseph, Eran 122
Betsky, Aaron 130
biophilia 110
Black landscapes 136–139
Bonaventure Hotel 16, 72
Bratton, Benjamin H. 163, 179–184, 188, 215, 217, 219, 221–225
Brillembourg, Alfredo 148–155
Broadacre City 12, 14, 81
Bullard, Robert 135

Calthorpe, Peter 125
Campanella, Thomas J. 144

car-centric urbanism 122–125
Castells, Manuel 69–74, 219–224
cellular automata 184–187
Central Park 54, 104–105
Cheonggyecheon stream 109
CIAM (Congrès Internationaux d'Architecture Moderne) 9–11, 15, 84
City in History, The (Mumford) 87
City of To-morrow and Its Planning (Le Corbusier) 122
collage 6, 10–11, 16–20, 28, 42–43, 48, 50, 52
colonias 142
Color of Law, The (Rothstein) 135
compact city 81, 83–87
Complexity and Contradiction in Architecture (Venturi) 10
computational urbanism 163–165, 173–175
Corner, James 104, 106–108
Crawford, Kate 230–235
Crawford, Margaret 158–159
Critical Regionalism 21–26
cybernetics 4, 163–167, 215, 217
cyberspace 195, 206

datascape 92–97
Davis, Mike 16, 73, 142
Death and Life of Great American Cities, The (Jacobs) 9, 34, 83, 122, 184–185
de Certeau, Michel 158
del Campo, Matias 214, 217, 225–230
density 1, 7, 37, 47, 59, 70, 72, 74, 81–88, 92–98, 106, 125, 130, 152, 157
Design with Nature (McHarg) 100–101
Desmond, Matthew 135
Diamond, Jared 99
digital twins 8, 189–190, 215–219, 223
Downsview Park 106–107
Downtown Athletic Club 89–90
Du, Juan 144
Duany, Andres 10, 125
Dumping in Dixie (Bullard) 135

INDEX

Easterling, Keller 58, 216
Eisenman, Peter 10, 26, 43, 49–53
Elemental 154–158
emergency urbanism 120–121
Engels, Friedrich 122
equity 120–140
Evicted (Desmond) 135
evolutionary architecture 167–171

favela-bairro program 144–146
favelas 2, 142–149
Ferriss, Hugh 94
Fichter, Robert 153–154
Field Operations 104, 108–109
Frampton, Kenneth 21–26, 39–40
Frankfurt kitchen 129
Frazer, John 163, 167–171
Freedom to Build (Turner and Fichter) 153–154
Fresh Kills 106–107

Geddes, Patrick 14, 106
Gehl, Jan 123–128
Gehl Architects 124
generative urbanism 163–171, 225–230, 236
Geuze, Adriaan 104
Ghertner, Asher 144
globalization 9, 21, 57, 67–70, 115, 183, 185, 195
green infrastructure 99–119
Greenway, Rose Kennedy 159–160
guerrilla urbanism 159–161

"Half a House" concept 155–156
Hayden, Dolores 129
health 120–140
High Line 104–105
Hong Kong 67, 69–75, 80, 82, 97, 145
Hood, Walter 135–139
Houtan Park 110
Howard, Ebenezer 9, 14, 84

informal settlements 141–153
informality 71, 142–148, 150–151
Internet of Things (IoT) 179, 189–190, 198–199, 215–216, 223–224
Iquique housing project 154–155

Jackson, Kenneth T. 123
Jacobs, Allan 125
Jacobs, Jane 9, 34, 83, 122, 139, 147, 184–185, 220, 222

Kalms, Nicole 130–134
Kelly, Kevin 41
Kipnis, Jeffrey 41–43, 49
Klumpner, Hubert 148–153
KM3: Excursions on Capacities (MVRDV) 92
Koolhaas, Rem 3, 21, 88–92, 98
Kwinter, Sanford 41, 49, 53–55, 100

landscape urbanism 2, 5, 99, 103–108, 111
Leach, Neil 214–215, 219–224
Learning from Las Vegas (Venturi, Scott Brown and Izenour) 10–16, 28
Lerner, Jaime 159
livability 123–128
Lo-TEK: Design by Radical Indigenism (Watson) 115
Lynch, Kevin 14, 189

Maas, Winy 92–97
MacKaye, Benton 106
Make It Right Foundation-New Orleans 156
Markopoulou, Areti 215–219
McGuirk, Justin 149
McHarg, Ian 100–101
Medellín Metrocable 149
metabolic urbanism 62–66
Metacity / Datatown (MVRDV) 94
metaverse 189–192, 206–212
Mitchell, William J. 191–198
Modulor (Le Corbusier) 129
Moneta, Andrea 208–212
Mumford, Lewis 87, 106
MVRDV 92–97
Myth of Marginality, The (Perlman) 144

Negroponte, Nicholas 167, 169–170, 190, 211
network urbanism 57–80
New Urbanism 10, 125
non-places 21, 25

Olgyay, Victor and Aladar 100
Operating Manual for Spaceship Earth (Fuller) 100
Otto, Frei 58–62

parametricism 8, 175–179, 181–184, 188, 219–221
Parc de la Villette 27–28, 92
participatory design 132–134
Pask, Gordon 163–167, 171, 187,
Perlman, Janice E. 144–145
Pig City 94

Planet of Slums (Davis) 142
Plater-Zyberk, Elizabeth 10, 125
postmodernism 9–13, 16, 20, 72, 176
Practice of Everyday Life, The (de Certeau) 158
PRES (Plan de Reconstrucción Sustentable) 157–158
Pruitt-Igoe 9
Putnam, Robert D. 123

Queer Space (Betsky) 130
Quinta Monroy housing 154

Radical Cities (McGuirk) 149
Ratti, Carlo 199–205
Rogers, Richard 83–87, 98
Rothstein, Richard 135
Rowe, Colin 10, 16–20, 46
Roy, Ananya 144–148
Rudofsky, Bernard 10, 115
Rule by Aesthetics (Ghertner) 144

Sadik-Khan, Janette 159
Sample, Hilary 121
Schumacher, Patrik 163, 175–183, 188, 207, 219–220
Scott Brown, Denise 10–15
sensors in cities 189, 198–206, 212
Sert, Josep Lluís 2, 9
Sheffield, Carole 131–132
Shenzhen Experiment, The (Du) 144
Silent Spring (Carson) 100
sites and services 154, 162
slum upgrading 144–146, 162
smart cities 8, 179, 214–215, 220–224, 235
Smart Growth 125
Snøhetta 159
Social Life of Small Urban Spaces, The (Whyte) 128
Solomon, Jonathan D. 70–75
Sorkin, Michael 20, 24
Space of Flows 66–67, 198
spatial heterogeneity 9–32
Speck, Jeff 123
Sphinx in the City, The (Wilson) 130
Spirn, Anne Whiston 101–103

Sponge City model 110–111
Strip, The (AI) 12
Superstudio 9

tactical urbanism 141, 158–161
Tafuri, Manfredo 10
Team X 10
Times Square pedestrianization 159
Torre David 149
Toyota Way 161
transit-oriented development (TOD) 84, 124
Tschumi, Bernard 16, 27–32
Turenscape 110
Turner, John 153–154

Urban Apparatus, The (Martin) 66
Urban Informality (Roy and AlSayyad) 142
Urban Think Tank 148–153

Variations on a Theme Park (Sorkin) 20
Venturi, Robert 10–15
Verebes, Tom 163, 171–175, 187, 236
Vertical Village, The 94
Villa El Salvador 154
Virilio, Paul 3031, 75, 190–192, 206
virtual reality (VR) 189–192, 199, 205–207, 211–212
Vitruvius 121

Waldheim, Charles 66, 105–108
Ward, Peter 142
Watson, Julia 115–119
Weinstock, Michael 62–66, 235
West 8 104
"What Would a Non-sexist City Be Like?" (Hayden) 129
Whyte, William H. 128–129, 139, 161
Wilson, Elizabeth 130
World Bank 144

Yokohama Ferry Port Terminal 75–80
Yu Kongjian 110–115

Zeilenbau concept 1